UML for Visual Basic 6.0 Developers

➤ ➤ ➤ ➤ ➤ ➤ ➤ ➤ ➤ ➤ ➤ ➤ ➤ ➤ ➤ ➤ ➤ ➤ ➤

Using Visual Modeler and Rational Rose 98

UML for Visual Basic 6.0 Developers

Using Visual Modeler and Rational Rose 98

Paul Harmon
Brian Sawyer

Morgan Kaufmann Publishers, Inc.
San Francisco, California

Senior Editor	Diane Cerra
Director of Production & Manufacturing	Yonie Overton
Assistant Production Manager	Julie Pabst
Production Editor	Edward Wade
Editorial Assistant	Belinda Breyer
Cover Design	Ross Carron Design
Text Design, Illustration, and Composition	Helios Productions
Copyeditor	Donna King/Progressive Publishing Alternatives
Proofreader	Ken DellaPenta
Indexer	Steve Rath
Cover Photograph	Tom Till/Tony Stone Images
Printer	Courier Corporation

Morgan Kaufmann Publishers, Inc.
Editorial and Sales Office
340 Pine Street, Sixth Floor
San Francisco, CA 94104-3205
USA
Telephone 415/392-2665
Facsimile 415/982-2665
Email *mkp@mkp.com*
WWW *http://www.mkp.com*

Order toll free 800/745-7323

03 02 01 00 99 5 4 3 2 1

Library of Congress Cataloging-in-Publication Data

Harmon, Paul, date.
UML for Visual Basic 6.0 developers : using Visual Modeler and Rational Rose 98 / Paul Harmon, Brian Sawyer.
p. cm.
Includes bibliographical references and index.
ISBN 1-55860-545-2 (pbk.)
1. Microsoft Visual Basic. 2. UML (Computer science)
3. Application software--Development. I. Sawyer, Brian.
II. Title.
QA76.76.B3H3575 1999
005.1'2--dc21 98-46046
CIP

To Ivar Jacobson, the most consistent innovator:
Use cases, OOSE, OOBRR, Reuse, UML, and
component-based development

Contents

Acknowledgments

This book is actually the third book on an OO methodology that the lead author has written. As he has worked on each book, he has learned from the people he's worked with. In 1996 Myrna Kasser, manager of Research and Technical Communications at Popkin Software, convinced the lead author that he should write a book providing an overview of OMT. In working with customers, she noticed that Popkin Software's customers complained about the traditional methodology books and wanted a simpler overview that could get them started on their first OO development effort. Ms. Kasser first encouraged Mr. Harmon to write a book on OMT, then, later, encouraged him to write a book on UML for Java developers.

To develop the book for Java developers, *Understanding UML: The Developer's Guide,* Mr. Harmon worked with Mark Watson, who made a significant contribution. In addition, many people at Popkin Software, including Lou Varveris, Ron Scherma, and Mark McGreggor, all contributed to the second effort.

This third effort presents UML for Visual Basic developers. In the course of developing this book, the authors had help from people at both Microsoft and Rational Software.

Throughout this process, Diane Cerra, senior editor at Morgan Kaufmann, has once again provided support and encouragement. We would like to thank Jim Odell, cochair of the Object Management Group's Analysis and Design Task Force, and one of the leading OO methodologists who kept us up on the OMG standardization effort, read our second book, and offered lots of good advice. We want to thank Jon Hopkins of Blueprint Technologies, who helped me understand some confusing points of UML notation. We especially want to thank Shoshanna Budzianowski and Phil Bernstein of Microsoft, and Matthew Drahzal, from Rational Software for their assistance in obtaining software and correcting errors.

Others who read various versions of this book and made good suggestions include Curt Hall, Bob Harmon, Bill Morrissey, Pooks Rutherford, and two anonymous readers. We would also like to thank Eden Zoll for her valuable comments and suggestions. Finally, we also want to thank Edward Wade, production editor at Morgan Kaufmann, and Donna King at Progressive Publishing Alternatives, who handled the copyediting of the manuscript.

We want to thank all the people who helped make this book possible although they are, of course, innocent of its imperfections, which derive solely from its authors.

1

Introduction

This book is for Visual Basic developers who want to learn about objects and component-based application development. Reading this book should give you a good overview of how to use an OO notation to analyze and design object- and component-based applications. It provides an introduction to the newest object notation, the Object Management Group's Unified Modeling Language (UML), which is used in Microsoft's Visual Modeler—a modeling tool that comes with Enterprise Editions of Visual Basic 6.0 and Visual Studio 6.0. In addition, since our example involves a Visual Basic application designed for the Internet, this book can be used by those who know Visual Basic and want to learn how to use an OO approach to analyzing and designing new Visual Basic applications for the Internet.

The Unified Modeling Language was specifically designed to supersede earlier OO notational conventions.

We'll use the UML notation to develop a simple application that will be written in Visual Basic 6.0 and designed to be accessed over the Internet. This type of application will become increasingly common in the next few years. As Internet applications become more complex, developers will need to analyze their applications before they begin to develop them. Equally important, Visual Basic 6.0 is designed to support a whole new approach to application development, generally termed *component-based development.*

Most companies hope that the use of component-based development will allow developers to reuse more code in their applications. Component-based development requires the kind of analysis that UML supports. The fact that Visual Basic 6.0 is an OO language and that there will increasingly be class and component libraries and tools to support Visual Basic/Internet development means that there will also be a growing need for Visual Basic developers to understand OO analysis and design techniques.

An introductory book like this can't take the place of larger, more detailed books on the Object Management Group's UML that will be published later. Nor can it take the place of books that explore Visual Basic 6.0 in great detail. It can, however, do a better job of explaining the basics, showing how all the pieces fit together, and helping you walk through an example of a simple Visual Basic/Internet application development effort.

1.1 Development of UML

In the process of developing UML, two things happened. First, the methodologies that were an integral part of earlier OO systems created by authors such as Booch, Rumbaugh, and Jacobson were separated from the notation. UML does not specify a methodology (a series of steps to follow to develop an application). Instead, UML provides a set of notational conventions that a developer can use to describe or model an application. When you actually start to develop an application, however, you need some kind of sequence to follow, just to understand why you might want to use one diagram rather than another at any point in the development process. Hence, we provide a generic methodology that is used to develop a simple distributed Internet application. We have tried to keep our methodology separate from the UML notation so that you'll understand what the Object Management Group (OMG) standardized and what we are adding.

The second thing that occurred along the way to standardization was the addition of metamodeling elements. In general, when you are developing an application, you only use a subset of the notational elements. If you are developing a more complex application, you might require more specialized notational elements. If you are going to create a visual modeling tool that supports the UML notation, or store components in the Microsoft Repository, however, you need to be sure that elements in one diagram are always kept consistent with elements in other diagrams. In other words, you need a very precise, abstract specification of the relationships between all of the elements. This high-level specification is called a *metamodel.* The distinctions, for example, between class and type or between class and the stereotype of a class aren't important for most developers who are writing mid-sized Visual Basic applications. They are very important, however, if you are designing a repository and need to keep track of the kinds of elements that any user might want to store in the repository. UML is a very detailed notation that is accompanied by a precise metamodel.

In fact, UML is more precisely specified than any previous OO notation. Thus, UML will perform better when implemented on OO modeling tools or stored in a repository. UML is also the product of several committees and includes lots of things that are only used under rather special circumstances. Indeed, at first glance, the UML specification appears to be quite a bit more complex and intimidating than the earlier Booch, Rumbaugh, or Jacobson notations. In fact, however, if you ignore all the metanotational elements and the many features included for more specialized applications and focus only on those elements needed for basic OO analysis and design diagrams, the new notation is more elegant and much simpler than the earlier notations. In this book we'll focus only on the basic UML notational elements that you will need to develop beginning applications. As you become more skilled in using UML, you will probably want to study a more comprehensive book and learn some of the more complex notational conventions. In the meantime, however, you can use what you learn in this introduction to create all the basic diagrams you will need for most of the projects you will undertake while you are first learning UML.

1.2 Using UML to Develop Applications

Anyone who has been programming for any length of time has either been involved in, or has at least heard about, a project that was overanalyzed: The development team worked with a consultant or a modeling tool for months and created a very detailed design. Then, when they switched to the programming phase, they quickly found that the design could not be implemented. So a group of hackers had to start from scratch and put something together at the last moment to save the project.

Similarly, most experienced programmers have either been involved in or heard of a project that was launched after only a cursory analysis phase and soon ran into so much trouble that the project had to be abandoned.

There has to be a middle road—something between overanalysis and underanalysis—that will make it easier and more efficient to develop good applications. We aren't prepared to say that we know exactly what that middle road is, but in writing this book, we've tried to aim for a balance.

We think it's especially important to try to lay out a middle path for programmers who are just beginning to develop Visual Basic 6.0 applications. Most Visual Basic programmers are new to objects and distributed programming and are going to find that it takes more analysis than they may have used for programs they have written in the past. Even if you don't like to do a lot of analysis, if you are going to use Visual Basic 6.0 for the first time, you owe it to yourself to spend a little time considering what a good object- or component-based design might look like. And if you are a more experienced developer who is working on a more complex application, you will definitely want to spend the time to consider how an OO application should be designed to work well on the Internet.

In an earlier book on OMT, which has been well received, the lead author used an example that involved an automated teller machine (ATM). The ATM example was used because several OO methodologists had used it. In the end, it proved less than satisfactory, however, because real ATM systems are quite different from the simpler models that were used to illustrate OO notations. Moreover, the design problems were very complex.

To assure that we played fair this time, we first analyzed a problem and then designed and implemented a Visual Basic application, both by writing Visual Basic 6.0 code and by creating diagrams in two OO modeling tools. We carried the application all the way through to code that will run on the Internet to be sure that our analysis and design models would lead to an application that could really be implemented. We'll explain the analysis effort that resulted in the initial object model. Then we'll consider the kinds of issues we focused on during the design phase and explain how this led us to modify our application. Finally, we'll provide you with the code generated both by hand and by means of the modeling tool so you can examine the resulting application in detail.

In other words, this book is designed to be a realistic introduction to UML and to analysis and design. We created it to help guide real developers as they tackle OO Internet applications.

1.3 How This Book Is Organized

In Chapter 2 we'll briefly consider the basic concepts of object and component technology, just to assure that we all have a common vocabulary for what follows. If you are already familiar with OO concepts, you can probably skip this chapter.

In Chapter 3 we'll provide an overview of a simple, generic OO development methodology. We won't present a formal methodology. Instead, we'll simply describe an informal, iterative approach to OO development that underlies most of the formal OO methodologies. We'll use this informal overview as a way of explaining how the diagrams and the various notations we'll be discussing in later chapters all fit together.

We'll provide a broad overview of UML in Chapter 4. We'll describe all of the diagrams you can develop using UML and how each of those diagrams works with each of the others.

Next, in Chapter 5, we'll briefly discuss some of the features of the Visual Basic 6.0 language, the Component Object Model (COM), and Microsoft's approach to component-based development.

In Chapter 6 we'll consider what OO modeling tools are and how they are useful for object- or component-based analysis and design efforts. Then we'll introduce Microsoft's Visual Modeler 2.0 and Rational Software's Rose 98, which we will use to illustrate how modeling tools can be used to develop our application.

For a simple application like the example we'll be discussing in this book, frankly, it's faster to code the application by hand, using Visual Basic 6.0 controls where appropriate. As you approach more complex applications, however, using an OO modeling tool can simplify the application development effort. In this book we'll illustrate both approaches.

In Chapter 7 we will introduce a specific problem and then show how the problem could be modeled with use cases. Then we will extend that analysis by using one of the UML stereotypes—ideal object models. Use case analysis is a popular way of analyzing the overall requirements for a system. It also provides a good way of generating the scenarios you will need to use throughout the rest of the development process. Ideal object modeling is a good way to develop an initial analysis of the objects that will be needed for an OO application.

In Chapter 8, we'll take a break from considering UML notation and consider an informal way of developing an object model. Specifically, we'll discuss CRC cards and use them to analyze our simple sales application. CRC stands for Classes, Responsibilities, and Collaborators. You can use this method on your own, or with a group of end users, to identify the main business classes you will need to create for your application.

In Chapter 9 we'll introduce the basic concepts and the notation used with UML class and object diagrams. Then we'll use that notation to diagram our sales example. We'll show how it could be done if you were drawing the diagrams by hand and how it would be done if you were using an OO modeling tool.

Chapters 10 and 11 follow up with descriptions of the concepts and the notation of UML sequence, collaboration, state, and activity diagrams. We'll see how our sales application could be modeled using these diagrams. We'll also consider how we could develop the four types of diagrams in an OO modeling tool.

Chapter 12 moves on to design. We'll consider some of the things that you should think about during the design phase of a development cycle. In Chapter 13, we'll consider the issues involved in determining the architecture of a system. We'll introduce the UML documentation, package, and component diagrams and then use them to model the design for our Sales-Web application. Finally, we'll see how these implementation diagrams can be used in an OO modeling tool.

In Chapter 14 we'll expand the object model we developed during the analysis phase of our effort. We'll see how to add infrastructure classes to our various UML diagrams. We'll also discuss how to create user screens or Web pages, how to access data, and other more specialized concerns. We'll also discuss whether we should stick with the classes we've developed or convert some of them into ActiveX components that can be reused in other applications. We'll also touch on coding and testing and then consider how all these things could be done in an OO modeling tool.

Appendix A provides the Visual Basic 6.0 code for the example and provides information about how to acquire the Visual Basic code discussed in this book. Appendix B provides a UML Job Aid that summarizes all the basic UML symbols. Appendix C contains a table that shows how UML notation compares with equivalent notation in Booch and OMT. Appendix D lists organizations and products mentioned throughout the book.

Finally, a bibliography lists some books and Web sites that can help you explore the topics we discuss in detail. Unfortunately, since this is one of the first UML books, we can't provide lots of pointers to advanced books on UML, but most leading OO methodologists will be publishing advanced books in the near future.

2

The Vocabulary of Object Technology

In this chapter we'll review the basic vocabulary that developers use when they talk about object-oriented languages and applications. We'll also discuss how components differ from objects. If you already have a good grasp of object and component basics, you may want to skip this chapter. For others, however, it should provide a very brief overview of the essential elements of object technology.

Visual Basic has evolved into an OO language. Similarly, Microsoft's approach to component development has evolved from VBXs to OLE Controls to ActiveX components and its component object model (COM). As Microsoft's technology has evolved, so has the vocabulary used to describe various aspects of objects and components. Thus, when talking about a Visual Basic 6.0 class, you can use a variety of different names to refer to what most OO developers would call a method or an operation. Specifically, a method can be a sub, a function, an event, or a property. To keep things simple, in this overview we will describe objects and components in very general terms, as they are usually described in books on object-oriented programming and as they are described in the OMG's UML specification. Later, in Chapter 5, when we discuss how you use Visual Basic 6.0 to develop an OO application, we'll relate the generic OO and UML terms to the specific terms used in Visual Basic 6.0 and in Microsoft's COM.

2.1 What Are Objects?

An object is a complex data type that contains other data types, usually called attributes or variables, and modules of code, usually called operations or methods. (UML uses attributes and operations; most OO developers call them attributes and methods.)

The attributes and associated values are "hidden" inside the object. Any other object that wants to obtain or change a value associated with the first object must do so by sending a message to one of the first object's operations. (A message is object-speak for a function call.) Each object's operations manage their own attributes. This is called *encapsulation*. Encapsulation means that objects don't know or care how other objects store or process data. One object sends a message to an operation associated with a second object. One of the second object's operations, in turn, replies or takes action. We often say that the first object requests that the second object perform some task or service for it.

Figure 2.1 provides an overview of objects and message passing. We've used a special way of diagramming objects that shows the attributes in the middle of a circle surrounded by cells that represent operations. This way of diagramming objects dramatizes encapsulation and stresses that attributes can only be accessed by the object's own methods.

To appreciate an OO approach, you should contrast it to conventional programming. A conventional software system is basically composed of (1) a block of procedural code, the program, and (2) data, which is independent of the procedural code and is stored in files or tables. In a conventional

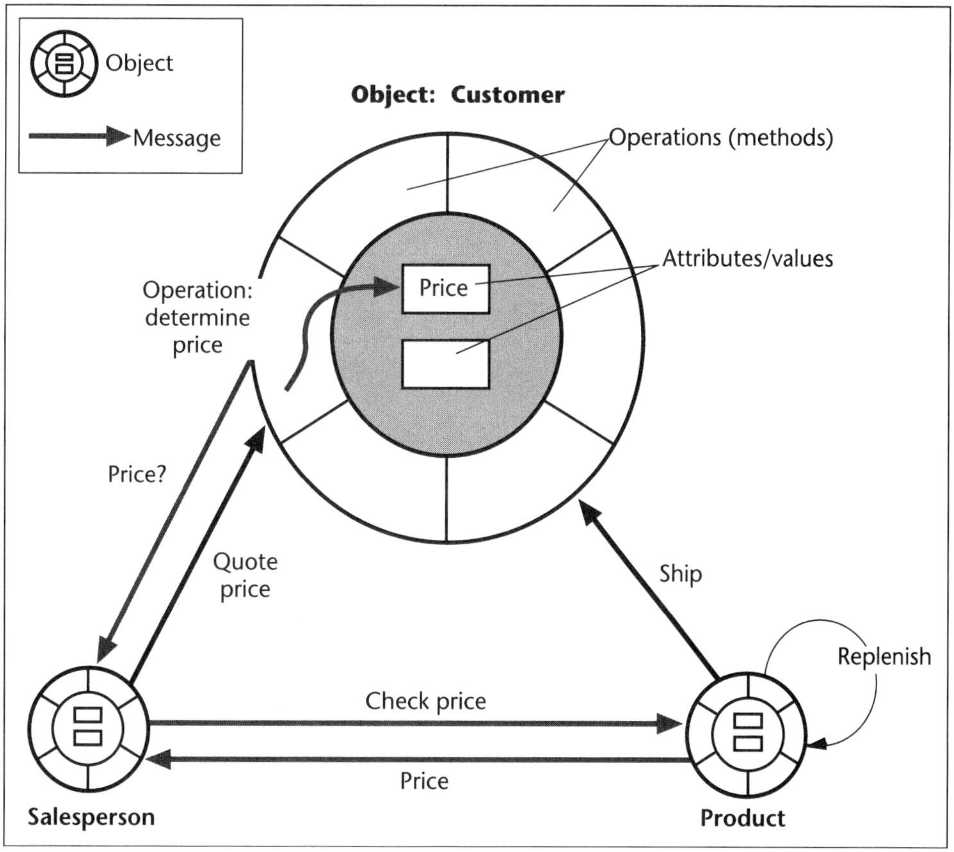

Figure 2.1 *Objects and message passing.*

application all of the procedural code is stored as a single block, and any changes in the program must be carefully made to assure that changes at one point in the code don't have unwanted side effects elsewhere. Similarly, since the procedural code calls the data, any changes must be carefully made to assure that one procedure doesn't change the data in inappropriate ways before another procedure can use the data. It's possible to modularize a conventional program—that's exactly what the structured methodologies of the late seventies and early eighties tried to do—but the very nature of the

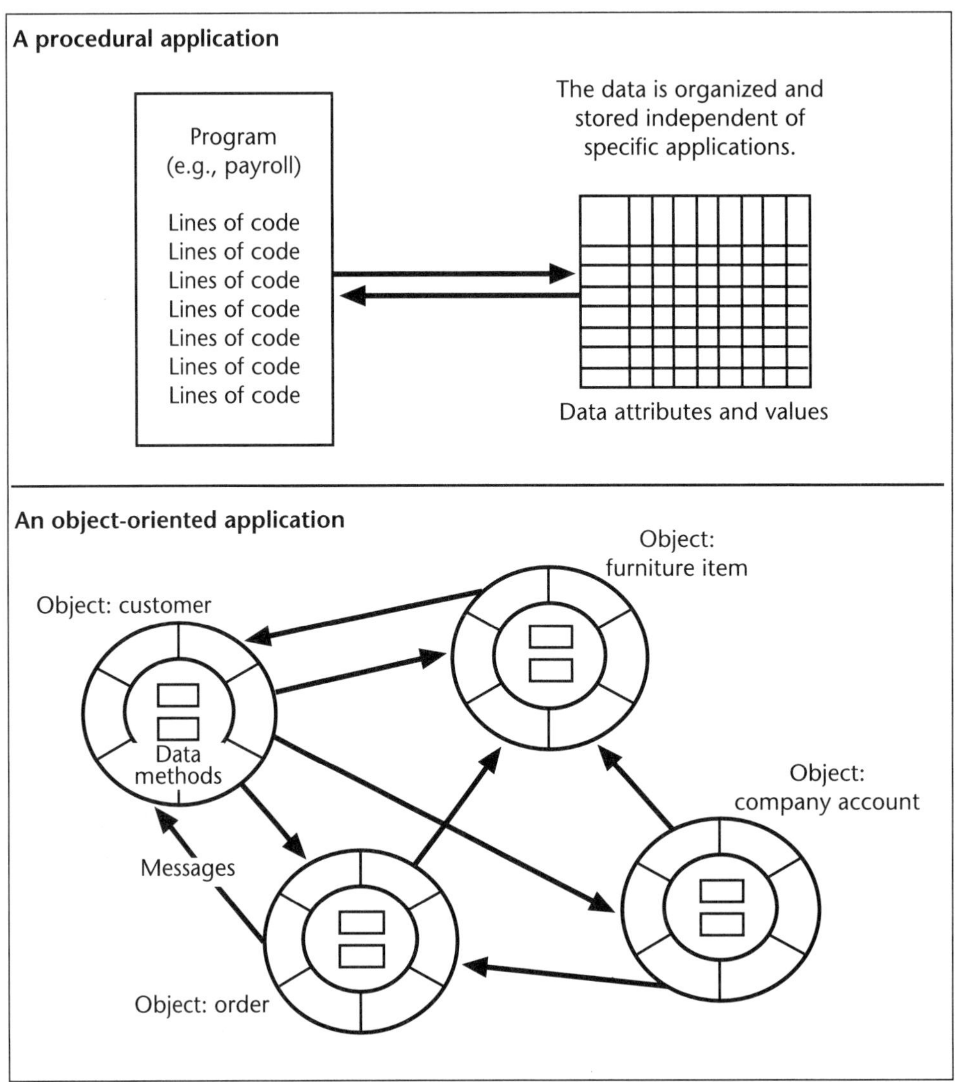

Figure 2.2 *A procedural application versus an OO application.*

procedural approach guarantees that modularization will usually be limited and that subsequent modifications will be difficult.

Figure 2.2 contrasts a conventional application and an OO application. Unlike a monolithic procedural application, an

OO application is modularized in the sense that each object is independent of every other object. Moreover, the procedural code contained in each object is modularized into several independent operations. A message usually only triggers a single operation. If a change needs to be made, the developer often only needs to change one operation. If changes are made to the internal data structures associated with one object, a developer can be confident that all the procedural code changes that will need to be made will only involve operations associated with that same object.

The basic idea of an object can be used in a number of ways. In some situations, the object becomes the fundamental unit of the system. In this case, all of the basic concepts used in an application, including bags, strings, numbers, and addition, are all represented as objects. This occurs in a language such as Smalltalk. (In Visual Basic 6.0, object structures are available, but the basic structures of the language, such as char, booleans, int, long, float, and other computational elements, are primitives.)

Objects may also encapsulate more complex groups of attributes and methods or even other objects. Thus, we can use objects to capture the various elements of a graphical user interface (GUI). Thus, icons, windows, scroll bars, and tools all become objects.

At a still higher level, an object can encapsulate all of the attributes and methods that make up business concepts. These business objects include things like employee, machine, product, plan, customer, and so on. Using objects of this kind, models of the company and its activities can be developed. At this level, the OO metaphor comes very close to reality, and we speak of employees sending messages to customers, or sending requests to update corporate plans, or causing machines to generate products. Each of these higher-level objects, often called composite objects, are, of course, made up of more basic objects.

Objects can also be used to encapsulate existing programs. Thus, if a company needs to continue to use a large legacy system—say, the application that handles the company's payroll—the entire application can be placed "inside" an object, and access to the system can henceforth be managed by operations associated with the "legacy object." In fact, although we speak of the application as being "placed inside" an object, normally an object simply serves as an interface to the legacy application, taking messages directed at the legacy application, causing the application to run, and then sending the results back to other objects. In a similar way we can "encapsulate" databases with objects that stand between other objects and the database. The database object receives messages requesting information from a database, converts them into SQL, and sends the SQL to the database. Later, the database object formats any information it receives from the database into a message format and sends it back to the objects that originated the request.

The variety of different ways that object concepts can be used might make them confusing, at first. Once the basic concepts are understood, however, object technology becomes a powerful aid in thinking about computing. The same basic concepts can be used at many different levels of abstraction and in many different situations. In fact, objects are gradually becoming the great unifying concept underlying all software systems.

2.2 Objects, Classes, and Instances

When we get ready to develop an OO application, we need to talk more precisely about how we use the term *object*. Indeed, one of the common sources of confusion for those new to OO development comes from the fact that the various OO languages and methodologists use this and other terms in different ways. As most developers start using UML, we hope they will begin to standardize their use of two important terms: *classes* and *objects*.

Classes are templates that have methods and attribute names and type information, but no actual values. Objects are generated by the classes and actually contain values. Some classes are very abstract and are simply used to provide structure for other classes. Most classes, however, are templates that are used to generate the objects that actually do the work when an application runs. When you compile an OO application, you save information about classes. Classes later generate objects when the application is run. An object has values associated with its attributes.

Some developers use the term *instance* as a synonym for object. Most developers use the term *instantiation* to refer to the process whereby an object (instance) is generated by a class. UML specifies that there can be instances of classes that are other classes (i.e., subclasses) or instances of classes that are called objects. Thus, in UML, objects and instances are not synonyms. We will try to avoid using the term *instance* altogether and use class, object, and occasionally, instantiation. We won't talk of instances.

When we initially create an OO system, we focus primarily on the classes that will be needed by the application. In effect, we design the application at the class level. When the system is actually run, objects are generated by classes as they are needed to contain the state information (i.e., attribute values) that is processed by the system. A single class, like Employee, can have hundreds of objects in existence at the same time, one for each specific employee in the company, for example.

When an object receives a message, it accesses the methods defined in its parent class to find the operation it needs to use to process the message. Specific values derived from message passing are stored within objects. When objects are no longer needed by an application, they are eliminated. Figure 2.3 illustrates the relationship among three objects and their parent class.

In Figure 2.3 the class Furniture describes the set of all possible furniture items. It specifies that they have names and item numbers and operations to create a new item or to change an item's number. An object of the furniture class would have values for the name attribute and for the item number, as shown.

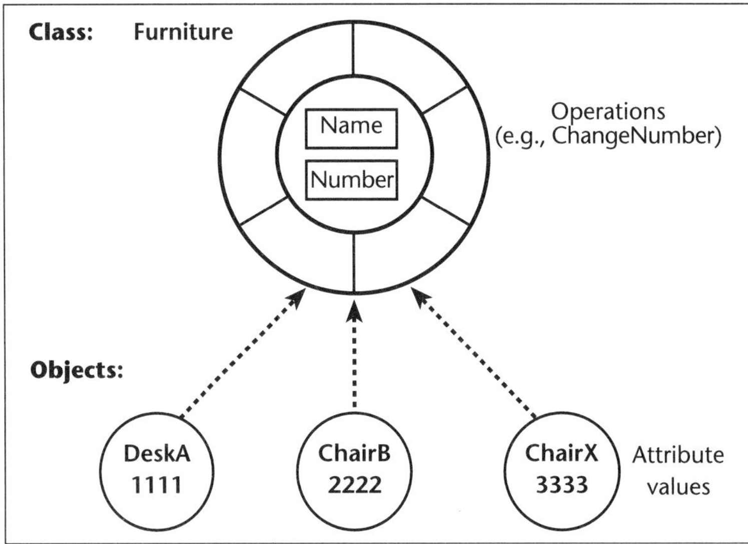

Figure 2.3 *Classes and objects.*

2.3 Message Passing and Associations

As a generalization, operations are associated with classes. Classes, however, don't normally send messages to each other; objects send messages to each other when the system is actually running. Thus, a static diagram that pictures classes only shows the logical associations between classes. It doesn't show the movement of messages. An association between two classes usually means that the objects of the two classes can send messages to one another.

Some authors discriminate between class operations (also called static methods) and object operations. In most OO languages, when one object wants to send a message to another, it begins by sending a message that is received by a class, which then uses a class operation to generate an object to deal with the message. Later, when the object is no longer needed, the class uses another operation to eliminate the object. Similarly, a developer will sometimes place operations and even store data in classes to keep track of certain things—the number of objects that have been generated by the class, for example. In modeling OO applications we normally only focus on the attributes and operations that are inherited by the objects and ignore the class operations that handle the creation and destruction of objects or that track the existence of the number of objects. Throughout the remainder of this book, a reference to an operation will always be a reference to an object operation.

Objects can "contain" other objects. These objects are often called *composite objects*. In some cases, this means that a message is sent to one object that acts as the coordinator for several objects, but it may mean that one object is actually contained within another. These part-whole relationships are also called aggregations. We might have a car object that was made up of a motor, drive train, interior compartment, wheels, and so forth. These objects might themselves be made up of still smaller part-objects. Thus, if I sent a message to a car object asking about its oil level, it would, in turn, send a message to the engine object, which would probably pass another message to the oil subsystem. Eventually an object would be found that contained the value needed, and it would then be passed back up the chain.

2.4 Generalization

UML refers to any relationships where one class shares its properties, methods, relationships, and constraints with another class as a *generalization*. There are two common varieties of generalization: *class (or implementation) inheritance* and *interface inheritance*. Some OO languages only support class inheritance, some only support interface inheritance, and some support both.

2.5 Class Hierarchies and Class Inheritance

In class or implementation inheritance, when a developer indicates that one class, B, is the child of another class, A, the child class automatically acquires all of the attributes and operations that are implemented in the parent class, A. Similarly, if a developer creates still another class, C, and indicates that class C is the child of class B, class C acquires all of the attributes and operations of both classes A and B. (See Figure 2.4.)

Using class inheritance, most OO language classes can be arranged in hierarchies so that more concrete classes inherit attributes and operations from more abstract classes. In class hierarchy diagrams, the arrows always point from the class or

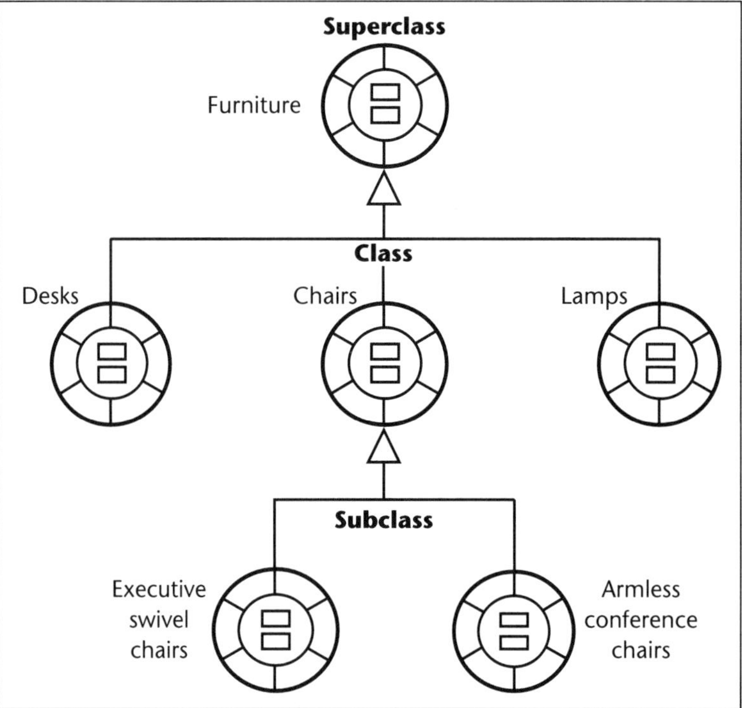

Figure 2.4 *Class or implementation inheritance.*

object inheriting to the higher-level class from which the attributes and operations are derived.

By adding new attributes and methods or changing the code associated with inherited methods, more concrete classes can be created. Thus, we might begin with a class that describes employees and then create two subclasses that are each specialized so that one represents hourly employees and the other represents full-time (or exempt) employees. Because we reuse most of the code that is associated with the employee class and only need to add a few refinements to the subclasses for hourly and full-time employees, OO development tends to go faster than conventional programming, once a developer has accumulated a library of commonly used classes. When an OO developer begins a new application, he or she usually begins by looking for previously developed classes that contain most of the general code needed for the new application.

Relative to any specific class in a hierarchy, classes that are above the class in the hierarchy—classes the specific class inherits from—are called parent or superclasses, and classes below the specific class are called children or subclasses.

Some OO languages, such as C++, allow a class to inherit from more than one superclass. If this occurs, it's called multiple inheritance. Java and Smalltalk only support class inheritance from single classes. Java also supports interface inheritance, which we'll consider a little later in this chapter. Visual Basic doesn't support class inheritance, but does support interface inheritance.

Figure 2.5 illustrates an example of single class inheritance and specialization. Until now we've been drawing classes as circles with the operations around the outside and the attributes in the center. This model of a class always reminds us of some kind of simple biological organism, and it works well as a way of illustrating how attributes can be encapsulated inside a wall of operations. These diagrams (which we always think of as Taylor diagrams because David Taylor has done so much to popularize them) are good for introducing objects, but they aren't very efficient to draw and they don't scale up to classes with lots of attributes. Thus, in Figure 2.5, we've switched to UML class notation. The large box represents the class and is

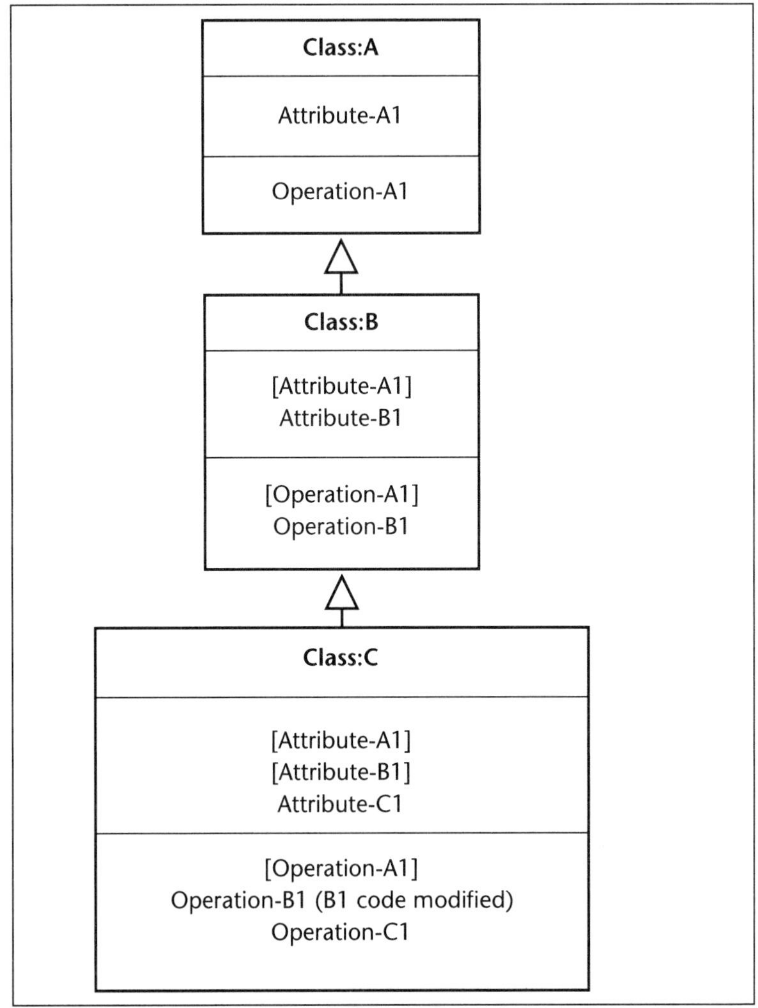

Figure 2.5 *Class inheritance and specialization.*

subdivided into three sections. In the top section we indicate the class name. In the next section we list the class attributes, and in the lower section we list the names of the operations supported by the class.

Consider Figure 2.5. In this case, the A class has one attribute and one operation. The B class is a subclass of A, and therefore it inherits both the attribute (A1) and the operation

(A1). (We've put the inherited attributes and operations in brackets to remind you that in a real UML diagram they wouldn't be shown. When you look at a real UML diagram, you just assume that anything shown in a superclass is also available in any subclasses.) The B class also has a unique attribute and operation of its own. The C class inherits from B and thus gets all the attributes and operations from both the A and the B classes. Classes lower in a hierarchy always inherit all the attributes of all the classes above them in the hierarchy. The UML model only shows the operation names, but in a real application, once the code is written to implement a specific operation, both the name and the code are inherited down through the class hierarchy.

Assume that when a developer created the C class, he or she wanted it to perform just like its parent classes, except that C would (1) need to keep track of one additional attribute, (2) need one additional operation, and (3) have to perform operation-B1 in a slightly more specific manner. Thus, the developer created the C class and then added a new attribute and a new operation. The developer also created a new operation-B1, using the same name but changing the code associated with operation-B1 so that it performed in a slightly different way than it did in the B class. This illustrates the use of inheritance—the creation of a new class that inherits attributes and operations from parent classes. It also illustrates operation specialization, where an operation's code is modified so the operation will perform in a more specialized way as a subclass. The developer specialized operation-B1 because he or she knew that instances of the C class would receive messages addressed to operation-B1 and didn't want the instances to perform in the manner specified by the operation code linked to the name, operation-B1, that was associated with the B class. By specializing operation-B1, the developer assured that any instance of the C class would use the new version of operation-B1, while any other instance of the B class would use the old version.

When we actually begin to create UML class diagrams, we won't repeat the attributes and operations that are inherited as we did in Figure 2.5. Normally, to determine all of the attributes and operations of a specific class, you'll need to check both the attributes and operations particular to that class and then also check all of the attributes and operations of any superclasses that that class inherits from. Under those circumstances, if you see an operation name repeated in a subclass, you can be sure that that operation will be a specialized operation.

2.6 Public, Private, and Protected

Now let's qualify what we just said a little more. In most OO languages, including Visual Basic, the developer can specify whether an attribute can be accessed by other objects or can only be accessed by the methods or operations associated with the specific class (and its subclasses and objects). An attribute that can only be accessed by its own methods is called a *private attribute*. This is the normal situation and the one we have been assuming in everything we have said previously. The alternative is a *public attribute*. A public attribute would be an attribute that could be modified by operations associated with any class. This would violate encapsulation and should not normally be used in Visual Basic 6.0 programming. So, unless otherwise specified, all attributes referred to in this text are private attributes.

In UML, operations can come in three flavors: public, private, and protected. A *public operation* is one whose name is exposed to other objects. Thus, a public operation is a method that can receive messages from other objects.

A *private operation* is a method that can't be accessed by other objects. In effect, it's an operation that is only used by other operations associated with the same object for some internal purpose. Imagine you have an object that provides some complex calculation. There is a public operation or method called *ReturnCalculationResult*. Whenever I send a message to that operation from an external object, the method is fired, and eventually the result is returned to the object that sent the query. Now consider that I may not want to write the calculation as a single block of code, and

I may need to use several attributes (or even some complex data formats) to keep track of intermediate results. Thus, I create several private operations, termed *CalculateStep1, CalculateStep2,* and so on. These operations are private; no outside object knows of their existence.

If I were to decide to change the way I performed the calculation, I would leave the public operation name, ReturnCalculationResult, as it is since other objects in my system would depend on it to obtain results they needed. Public operations are promises that my object will perform certain activities when asked. Once established, you should avoid changing them, since other objects in the system have operations that expect to be able to send messages to them. On the other hand, since no one knows of the private operations, I can change them as needed, without needing to change anything else in my system.

Protected operations are a special case. Only subclasses directly descended from the class that contains a protected operation know of its existence and can use it.

When we speak of operations throughout the remainder of this text, we will be referring to public operations, unless otherwise specified. In creating our example, we may very well use private operations, but if we do, we'll make a point of referring to them as private operations.

One more detail: An *operation signature* refers to both the operation or method name and the parameters that must be passed with the message in order for the operation to function. I might send a message to evoke the Add operation to an object that carries out arithmetic functions for my system. I would need to send, along with the operation name, the numbers to be added; thus, *Add (2, 3).* The two numbers, in this case, are parameters. In describing my Add operation, I would need to specify the types and number of integers I could send along with the name, *Add.*

An *interface* is made up of the signatures of all the public operations associated with a class. When we build interfaces, we specify the public operation names and their parameters. The parameters are important because they assure that the operation will function properly. In addition, they occasionally allow the compiler or interpreter to discriminate between two operation names that are otherwise the same. In fact, if you consider our example in Figure 2.5, you will see that we changed the code associated with operation-B1 in *Class-C.* If an interpreter were trying to decide if a message being sent to operation-B1 were to be sent to *Class-B* or to *Class-C,* it would check the parameters associated with each name to help it decide. In other words, it would check their signatures.

2.7 Interface Inheritance

The second type of generalization is termed *interface inheritance.* Interface inheritance is also represented by an open-headed arrow pointing from the subclass to the interface class from which it inherits. Whenever you see a UML generalization arrow, keep in mind that the generalization can be implemented with either a class inheritance approach or with a design that relies on interface inheritance.

Interface inheritance isn't as simple or as powerful as class inheritance, but it offers some advantages by avoiding design problems that can occur when programmers use class inheritance. Visual Basic and ActiveX don't support class inheritance at all, but they both support multiple interface inheritance.

An interface class defines a set of attributes and methods that another class might want to use. If a developer creates a new class and wants it to inherit an interface, she must create an attribute that references the interface class (i.e., delegation). She must also create operation names that point to the operations of the interface class. Once this is done, the new class has access to the attributes and operations of the interface class. One class can inherit from any number of interface classes. (See Figure 2.6.)

Interfaces inherited by one class do not automatically pass to the children of that class. Thus, in a language like Visual Basic that only supports interface inheritance, you need to add pointers to the interface class in each class that is to inherit the interface.

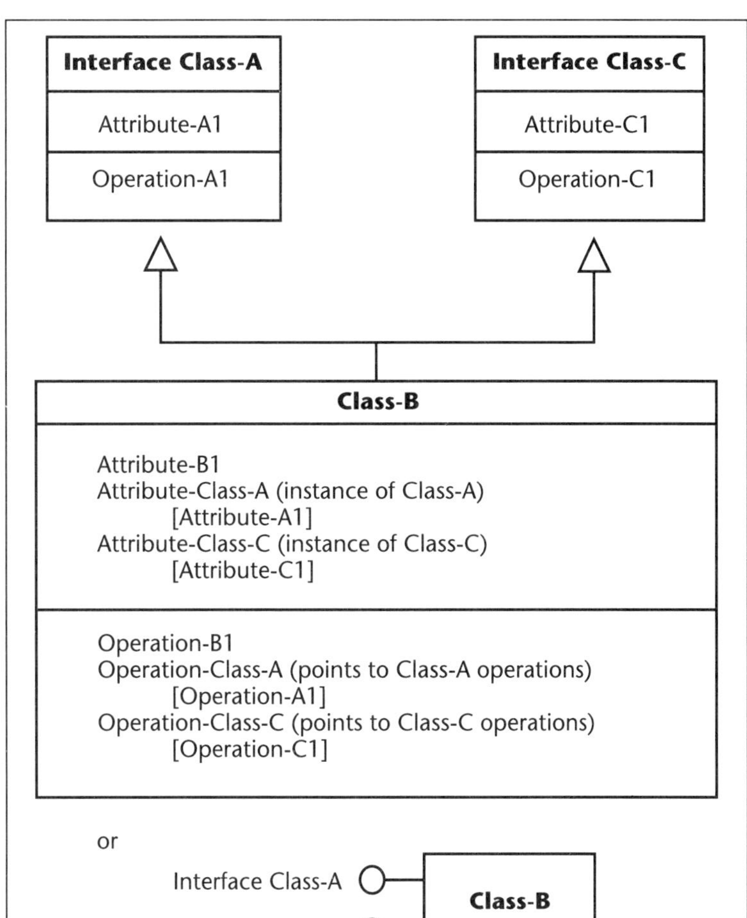

Figure 2.6 *Inheritance of interface classes.*

An efficient shorthand for complex diagrams is to note when standard interface classes are supported by using a "lollipop" symbol to indicate which interface is supported. UML's lollipop notation is borrowed from Microsoft diagrams where it was originally used to show that an OLE component was included within a compound document.

As a general rule, interface classes are predesigned to solve specific problems. By incorporating an interface, you guarantee that your class will have the functionality provided by the interface class. We'll consider interface inheritance in more detail when we talk about Microsoft's COM model.

2.8 Polymorphism

Polymorphism means that the same operation will behave differently when it is applied to the objects of different classes. It also means that different operations associated with different classes can interpret the same message in different ways. Thus, for example, an object can send a PRINT message to several objects, and each object will use its own PRINT operation to execute the message.

In most OO languages, polymorphism is associated with class inheritance. In Visual Basic, polymorphism occurs when a class supports more than one interface class. In other words, a class responds differently depending on the interface implementation to which the class refers messages.

Languages vary in the degree to which they support polymorphism. Languages that support many forms of polymorphism are more flexible. Typed languages, for example, are less flexible than untyped languages. Say you specify that a *Customer* class will have an attribute called *name*. You might simply specify the attribute name, and leave it at that. Or, you might go ahead and specify that the *name* attribute could only take a value that was a string. If some method tried to associate an integer data type with the attribute name, it would be rejected by the compiler. Similarly, you might want to specify that when an operation passed a message to another object, asking for a person's name, that you would only want the target object to return a string. If developers have to spell out all the data type constraints for all of their classes before the system will compile (or can be interpreted), then the system can't handle certain situations and is therefore less flexible. On the other hand, certain kinds of errors won't occur if the developer has predetermined the data type of each attribute and operation.

C++ is a strongly typed language. It requires that the programmer indicate the data type of each attribute and operation in advance. Visual Basic is strongly typed, like C++. Smalltalk, on the other hand, is weakly typed. You can omit specifying the data types of attributes if you wish. Thus, in Smalltalk, you could easily write a handwriting recognition application that allowed a user to enter a sales price either by spelling out the number or by entering numerals. If there were no data type associated with the *SalesPrice* attribute, it would accept either value. Smalltalk is more flexible and supports a greater degree of polymorphism than either C++ or Visual Basic.

2.9 Components

People use the word *component* in a number of different ways. Some OO developers would say that a component is just a synonym for a composite object. Others argue that a component is something quite different. Since this book is for Visual Basic developers, we'll lean toward the Microsoft view and argue that objects and components are different.

An object is a language-oriented concept. In general, the object is written in the source code of a specific language and inherits from a class hierarchy that comes with the language. Objects communicate by means of messages written in the same language, and the language environment provides a context in which the objects are executed.

Components, on the other hand, are a higher-order concept. A component can be composed of one or more classes, or a component may incorporate a legacy application written in procedural code. The classes or the procedural code contained within components can be written in different languages. A component is defined by one or more interfaces written in a component interface language, not by the code inside the component. Components send messages to each other via a language-neutral message-passing environment or container. Figure 2.7 compares these two concepts.

We'll discuss components in more detail in Chapter 5 when we consider COM.

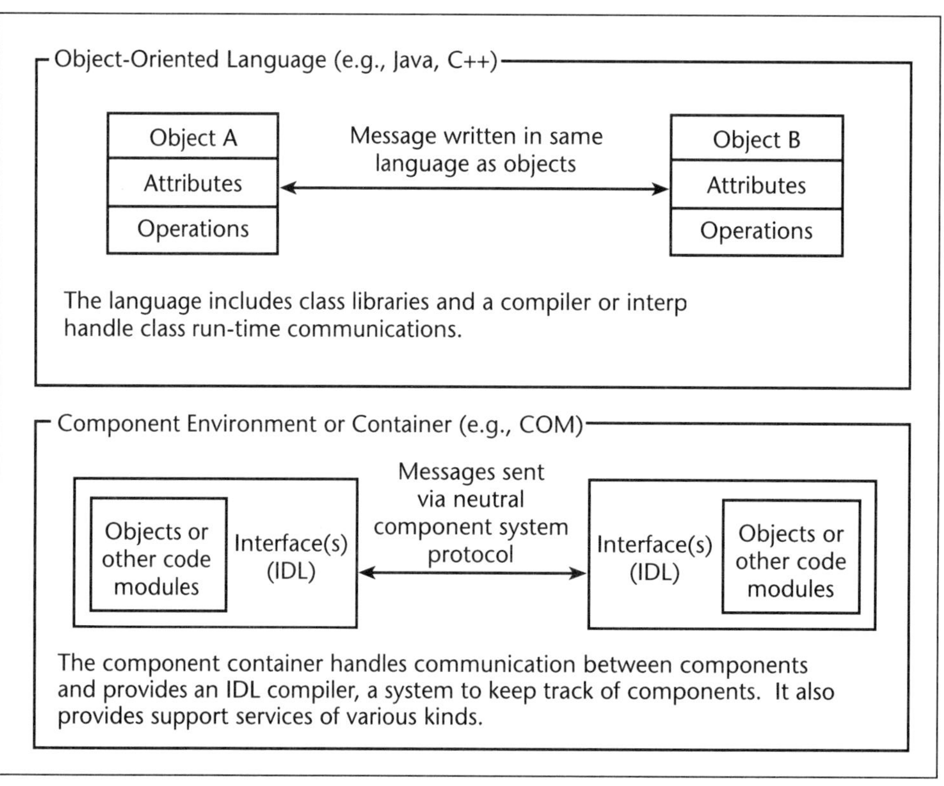

Figure 2.7 *An OO language versus a component system.*

2.10 Beyond the Basics

Object technology is much more complex than we have suggested here. Moreover, each language and each notation supports several variations on the general themes we have discussed. We don't want to go into any more detail at this point, however. We've given you enough to make sense of what we'll be saying in subsequent chapters. If you would like a more detailed discussion of any aspect of object technology, we recommend that you read one of the introductory texts listed in the Bibliography at the end of this book.

3

A Simple Object-Oriented Methodology

There are many different kinds of object-oriented and component-based applications being developed. Some are developed in OO languages. Others are being developed with OO modeling tools, like Microsoft's Visual Modeler and Rational Software's Rational Rose 98. Some applications rely heavily on preexisting components, while other applications are developed from scratch. Some applications are designed to handle report generation. Others are designed to be distributed on the Internet, like the example we will consider in this book. Some are designed to handle high-speed transaction processing situations, while still others are designed to control oil refineries in real time. Each of these different types of applications suggests a different developmental approach. The object models used in each type of application, however, can be recorded using the same notation. Different types of applications may require special extensions of the basic UML notation to denote unique features of the application, but the basic notation is the same for all.

When Grady Booch, James Rumbaugh, and Ivar Jacobson of Rational Software Corporation began to work on a common OO notation, they made a decision to separate notation from methodology. A notation allows an analyst to describe the problem. In effect, a notational system is a modeling language. A methodology, on the other hand, prescribes a series of steps and actions to take in order to develop an application. A methodology tells a developer what to do, how to do it, and in what order it should be done.

Someone following a methodology will use a notation system when he or she wants to describe a problem, but there is no necessary connection between a specific methodology and a notational system. The three methodologists at Rational Software felt that the time had come to create a common notational system. They did not feel that it was time to create a common object- or component-based development methodology.

When the OMG decided to try to standardize some elements of OO analysis and design, they also decided to call for the standardization of OO notation and to avoid trying to standardize the steps by which an OO application should be developed.

In this chapter we will describe a generic approach to OO development. Our approach is not a complete OO methodology. We are simply describing a generic approach that highlights the main features that most OO methodologies have in common. Our overall OO development model provides a very general set of developmental phases and allows us to discuss when different diagrams might be used during a generic application development effort.

In addition to describing a simple, generic approach to development, we will consider two alternative ways of actually developing an application. In one case we will discuss writing a program in Visual Basic code. In the second, we'll discuss developing the application diagrams with an OO modeling tool and then we'll use that tool to generate Visual Basic code.

As we've stated earlier, this book is designed to introduce you to the new UML notation. It is not designed to teach you a specific OO methodology. Once you have completed this book, you will need to turn to other books if you want to learn a detailed, step-by-step approach to creating a real OO application. Having said that, we'll now describe a very informal approach to creating an OO application.

3.1 An Iterative Approach to Object-Oriented Development

Figure 3.1 provides an overview of what we'll simply call an iterative approach to OO development. Others might call it a cyclical or spiral model, and still others might describe it as a Rapid Application Development (RAD) model. Rational refers to it as a Round-Trip Engineering model. The essence of this approach is that you develop an application by successive approximations. First you develop a core application—an initial prototype. Then you refine the prototype, improving and extending it. Depending on the complexity of the application, you may go through many cycles or iterations.

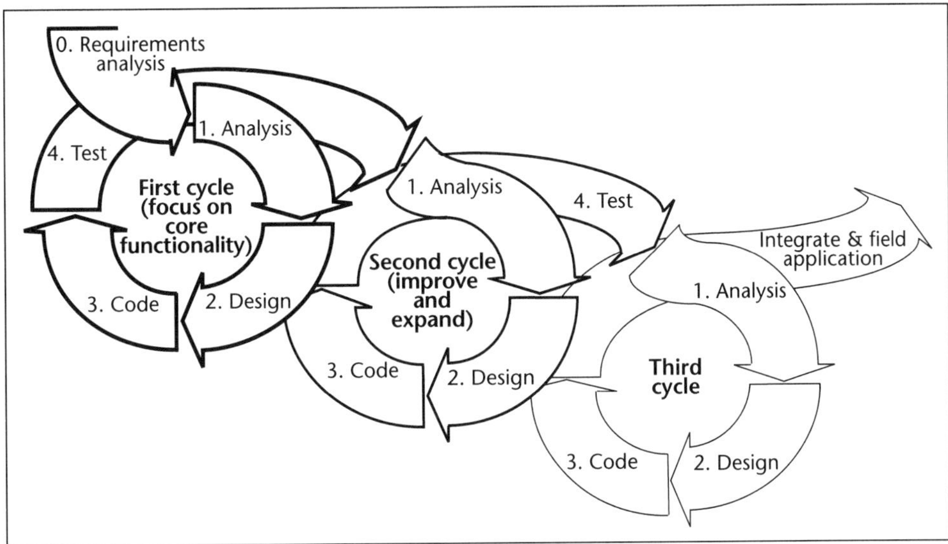

Figure 3.1 *An iterative approach to OO development.*

Some methodologists use the term *prototype* to refer to a single application that is developed prior to developing a complete application. Others use prototype to refer to any of several approximations that are developed in order to gradually expand and enhance an initial approximation into a full-blown application. We'll use prototype in this second sense. Thus, we would say that each cycle results in a prototype and that you keep developing approximations or prototypes until you finally get an application that you regard as complete.

You begin by defining the scope and requirements for the entire project and creating a high-level description of the entire application. You document what the system will do, who will use it, and what constraints or performance criteria it will need to meet to be judged a success. The requirement statement serves as a "contract" between the users who request the system and the developers who agree to build it. Next, you will probably lay out a high-level object model of all the business objects that will be required for your application.

Following this, once you have a good idea of the entire scope of your application, you select a portion of the entire application to develop first. Some people suggest you should begin by developing the hardest part of the application first. If there is any uncertainty about whether the application can be developed or not and you tackle the trickiest part and succeed, then you will be confident you can do the remainder. For example, many large system development efforts fail because developers design systems without adequately considering all the infrastructure issues involved in actually deploying the system. Thus, developers of large OO systems often develop an initial prototype system that doesn't do much, but demonstrates that it can interface with all the infrastructure elements it will need to deal with in order to assure that the overall infrastructure design is adequate.

In other cases, the portion of the system that supports some of the functionality that the end users are most interested in is developed first to assure that the system will satisfy the end users. However you approach it, there should be some overall plan that determines what part of the application you will develop during the first prototyping cycle, the second cycle, and so on. Obviously, this can change. As you develop your first approximation, you may identify problems that require you to revise your overall design. Still, when you begin, you should have some idea of the cycles you plan to go through as you successively approximate your final product.

3.2 Phases of a Development Cycle

To repeat: During your initial requirements effort you develop an overview of the entire system. Then, in your initial analysis phase, you subdivide the system and select a portion of it to develop during the first cycle.

During analysis you focus on designing an ideal or logical system that satisfies the requirements statement without being overly concerned with implementation considerations. During design you modify your work to take real-world constraints into account. During the design phase you design a concrete, physical system. During the coding phase you write code. Then you test the initial prototype. In some cases you will be testing to see if the prototype satisfies user needs, and in other cases you will be testing to see how it will work in the environment in which you expect to field the system. In some cases you will be able to field the first prototype of the application and solve at least a portion of the problem.

After you are satisfied with the first prototype, you proceed to the second analysis phase. In this round, you begin by reexamining your overall analysis in light of what you learned as you developed the initial prototype. Usually, you will want to make at least some modifications. In other cases, you will decide, as a result of testing the prototype, that you should completely redesign the basic class model or even switch to a completely different application architecture before you continue. This may sound discouraging, but it's far better to throw away a prototype and start over than to develop a complete application and then discover it won't do what it's expected to do.

Once you have settled on the overall application architecture you will use during the second cycle, you're ready to expand your first prototype or to begin to prototype another portion of the application. This is how iteration works: you build a prototype, test it, modify and extend it, test it some more, and keep going around until you have completed your entire application and are ready to field it.

Figure 3.2 provides a more detailed look at the first iteration cycle. In this illustration we've focused on a single cycle, and we've added some details.

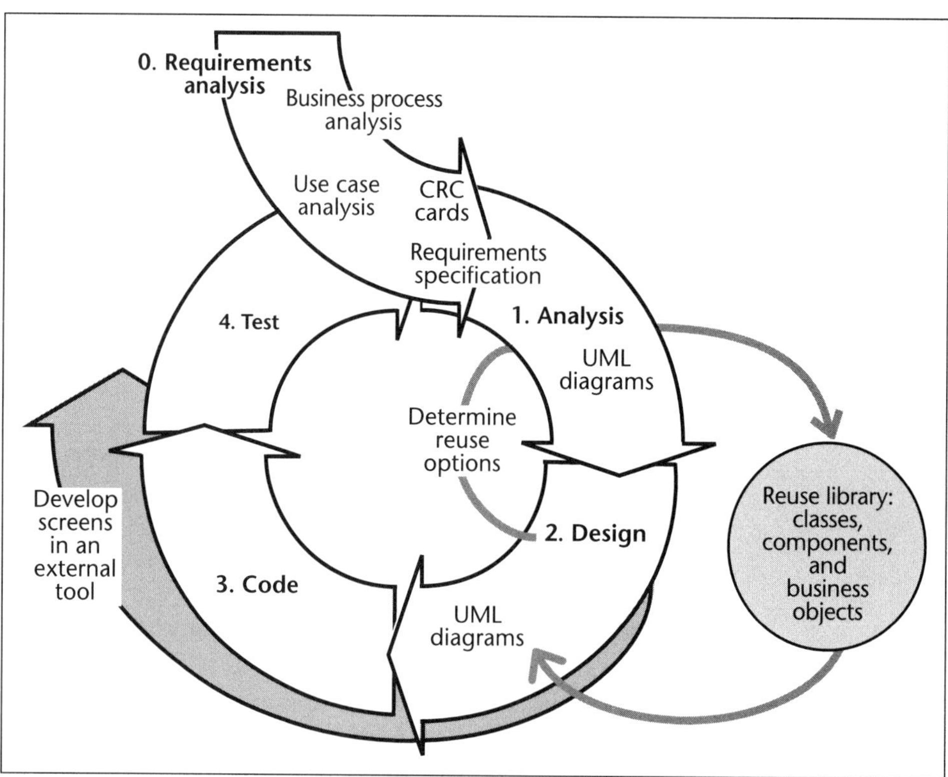

Figure 3.2 *A detailed look at one cycle of the iterative approach to OO development.*

3.2.1 Requirements Analysis

Our first cycle is unique because it begins with a requirements phase that precedes the analysis phase. In effect, the requirements phase is a kind of frontend analysis. Different things can occur during this preliminary phase. Some companies begin with a formal Business Process Reengineering (BPR) study. Others create scenarios, use cases, or CRC cards to help get an overview of the problem. In any case, this initial state ends with some kind of requirements specification—a document that provides an overall description of the application to be developed.

If you undertake a BPR effort and identify software that needs to be developed, or if you are simply assigned a software project, once you begin to focus on defining the scope of a specific software development effort, you will probably want to undertake a *use case analysis*. Almost all formal OO development efforts begin with at least an informal, high-level use case analysis. And, if you wish, you can extend this initial use case analysis by breaking the application up and doing finer-grained use case diagrams of the various subsections of the application. In addition, you can use ideal object models to convert use cases into rudimentary class diagrams.

Whether you begin with a BPR analysis or explore the problem by creating use case diagrams and descriptions, sooner or later you will want to write a formal *requirements statement*. The requirements statement can be a one-page overview, or it can be a very complex document. Its overall purpose is to say what the new software system will do. Requirements statements are often accompanied or supplemented by scenarios describing specific sequences that follow users from when they make inputs until they obtain outputs from the system. Many developers undertake use case analysis simply because they consider it a particularly effective way to generate scenarios.

Another way of developing an overview of your system and determining the classes you will need in your system at the same time is to use an informal approach referred to as *CRC cards*. In this case a group works together to construct scenarios and to simultaneously identify the classes that will be needed to implement the scenarios.

A good requirements statement should provide a sufficiently complete description of the application to be developed to enable the developers to consider how the application can be modularized. This isn't important for small applications, but if the application is large at all, then it's best to develop it by means of successive approximations. To do this, the complete application is subdivided, and the first effort focuses on developing a prototype of only a portion of the complete system. This approach would not work very well if you were using a conventional procedural language, but it works well when you undertake an OO approach because it's much easier to modify and expand an OO application.

3.2.2 The Analysis Phase

Once you begin the OO analysis phase, there are five groups of UML diagrams that you can use. These diagrams constitute the UML notational system. In addition, each of the basic diagrams can be modified or extended in various ways to handle special problems. Some diagrams (e.g., the class diagram and the sequence diagram) are used over and over throughout the development effort and are continually expanded and refined. Others (e.g., the collaboration diagram and the state diagram) are only used when you encounter particular problems and need to define a specific object or interaction in more detail. We'll provide an overview of all the UML diagrams in Chapter 4 and then consider each in more detail in later chapters.

You will notice that we have not laid out a specific series of steps. We have mentioned several different approaches to frontend analysis, including BPR, CRC cards, and others, that are not formally included in the UML system. We'll consider various techniques, but we don't expect that you'll use them all. In effect, we're presenting you with several alternatives. There's no one right way to do OO analysis. We'll simply show you how the various methods and diagrams work and leave it to you to decide what combination works best for you.

Analysis versus Design

In traditionally structured "waterfall" methodologies, gurus used to insist that developers maintain a rigid distinction between analysis and design. Analysis was when you figured out what the application should do. Design was when you decided how to do it. By keeping analysis and design separate, you kept your options open. And you avoided situations in which you created systems hampered by the constraints imposed by some unspoken, but assumed, system design. In reality, things were never as neat as the gurus would have liked. It's hard to undertake an analysis in the abstract. The real business situation always does, in fact, impose some constraints, and only fools ignore constraints that they know they will have to live with when they start writing code. So a sharp distinction between analysis and design has always been more a goal than a reality.

In OO systems development, the split between analysis and design becomes even harder to maintain. If you undertake a BPR project, you often end up agreeing to an architecture for the new software system before you've even begun to analyze the nature of the specific application. More important, if you develop an overview of your system and then break it into modules so you can prototype one module at a time, you are already assuming some kind of design. And, of course, when you do iterative or cyclical development, as we recommend in this book, you will be constantly shifting between analysis and design. Moreover, it will get even more complex as companies begin to rely on class libraries and reuse software components that already incorporate design assumptions.

Having said all that, we still recommend that when you are in the analysis phase of a project—and especially during the first analysis phase, when you are conceptualizing your first general object model—that you think of the classes in your model as abstractly as you can. There are many different ways to do the same thing. Design always imposes efficiency considerations that require you to modify good class models in ways an OO purist wouldn't recommend. Still, in the early phase of each cycle, when you are focused on the class diagram, try to create the cleanest, most logical model possible.

Clean models make it easy to see whether you've considered everything that needs to be included. Later, during design, you can always figure out how to rearrange your model to make it more efficient.

One way we will discriminate between analysis and design in this book is with our vocabulary. During the analysis phases of this book we will use terms like attributes, methods, and inheritance—generic OO modeling terms. When we switch to design, we will switch to the specific vocabulary of Visual Basic 6.0 and talk about properties, functions, and delegation and containment.

One of the advantages of a cyclical approach that moves from analysis to design and then, when you begin the next cycle, returns to analysis, is the opportunity that it affords developers to reconsider what they have done during the design phase and clean it up. In large system-development efforts there is a natural tendency for things to get complex. Complex applications, however, are harder to maintain. Thus, something you should do during each analysis phase is review what you have done to date and see if you can simplify your application. Sometimes this only involves cleaning up the names being used. In other cases it involves remodularizing the system or revising a group of class associations to provide a cleaner way of handling a problem. (Smalltalk developers call this "refactoring"—a process during which they step back and reconsider the overall structure of an application and then modify it to make it easier to understand.)

UML offers a number of ways of modeling system architectures. In some cases you will use UML package diagrams just after you complete the use case analysis. In other cases, you won't consider packaging until you get to design or development. In this book we'll try to avoid talking about architectural issues until we get to design, even though it will prove impossible in some situations. In those cases we'll simply admit that we are making assumptions and hope we can make them without committing ourselves to too much before we understand the full scope of the application.

Business Objects versus Infrastructure Objects

In analyzing and designing an OO application, you'll avoid a lot of confusion if you make a distinction between classes or components that refer to real things in the company environment—which we'll call business objects—and classes or components that are used to facilitate GUI development and other software processes, which we'll call infrastructure objects.

Business objects (or business components) are the kinds of things that end users talk about, and they are the classes that you will want to identify during your initial analysis effort. Business objects include things like employees, sales orders, accounts, machines, rejection slips, and company sites.

Infrastructure objects are classes or components that the developer creates to assure that the software works. Business analysts don't usually know or care about these classes. Infrastructure classes do things like put windows on the screen, manage the sequencing of other classes, transfer data between a server application and a database, and provide a time stamp for orders. When you use Visual Basic, ActiveX components are often used to handle infrastructure concerns. You can usually identify a few infrastructure classes during the initial analysis phase, but most infrastructure classes are ignored during analysis and are identified instead when you reach the design phase and begin to consider where different parts of the application will reside.

Different developers use different terms, but the important thing to keep in mind is that the initial analysis models should focus primarily on objects that represent real things in the corporate environment. Classes that handle GUI, data transfers, and bookkeeping tasks should largely be ignored during the initial analysis phase and then considered in detail during the design phase.

One of the misleading things about some analysis books is that they focus almost entirely on analysis and therefore on business objects. This might seem to suggest that OO applications have a relatively small number of very high-level classes. In fact, most OO applications have a few high-level business classes and many infrastructure classes that actually handle all the behind-the-scenes work.

In this book we'll begin by focusing on the business objects that are developed during the analysis phase of any development effort. Then, when we turn to the design phase, we'll consider what additional classes will be needed to actually implement the application we are building and offer some advice on how to identify and model infrastructure classes.

3.2.3 The Design Phase

Design begins when you shift your focus from the logical relationships between objects to the physical layout of your systems. Unlike earlier software development methodologies, which usually required the developer to shift to an entirely new notation to record design decisions, an OO notation is unchanged when you move from analysis to design. Indeed, that's one of the reasons it's so easy to slip back and forth between the two phases.

In design, you simply extend the diagrams you used in analysis and add information. Specifically, you add infrastructure objects to the business objects you developed during analysis. You also get much more specific about how operations will accomplish specific tasks. And you make concrete decisions about the physical layout of your system, what hardware you will use, how your software will get modularized, and which modules will be placed on which machines.

In addition to extending the system in the ways we've mentioned, you'll want to develop users' screens, Web pages, and any other interfaces required by your system. In OO systems, you also need to face some serious "buy versus build" decisions. Can you incorporate existing classes into your software? Can you reuse components? All these practical issues need to get sorted out during the design phase.

Screen and Other Interface Development

In some application development efforts, the code for the application interface is developed right along with the rest of the application. The windows are objects of classes created specifically to provide an interface to the application. In other cases, special tools are used to develop interfaces. Thus, if you were to use Visual Modeler or Rational's Rose 98 tool, you would still develop the user interfaces in the Visual Basic 6.0 programming environment, using forms and ActiveX controls. If you were to create an Internet application, you might use an HTML interface tool, like Microsoft's Visual InterDev. In effect, the screen development effort is often done in parallel with the basic development effort. If the application is to be produced in several iterations, screens are typically developed for each prototype as it is designed and coded. We've indicated this in Figure 3.2 by showing a secondary arrow that begins during the design phase and continues past the coding phase.

Reuse and Components

In addition to other considerations, in all OO development efforts there is the question of reuse. Most companies that have been involved in OO development efforts have at least some components that they use for interface development. Visual Basic developers, of course, have an extensive set of ActiveX controls that they can use for GUI development. In addition, we predict that companies will rapidly develop other COM components (DLLs and EXEs) to support specific business functions.

In your first OO projects, we recommend that you ignore the possibility of creating classes for reuse. Concentrate, instead, on developing an object model that works for your specific project. Use existing ActiveX or COM components, as appropriate, but don't create any new ones with the idea that you will reuse them later. After you have used and modified classes a bit, you will begin to understand how to generalize a design and create components for reuse. It's not easy, however, and if you try developing classes or components for reuse while you are still trying to understand how to create classes and reuse existing component libraries, you will probably find yourself overwhelmed.

While you shouldn't worry about creating components for reuse too early, you should begin to use any existing classes and components as soon as possible. The reuse of existing classes will significantly reduce the time it takes you to develop an application.

When OO developers start talking about the reuse of class libraries, environments, components, or frameworks, the conversation is usually rather imprecise. No one has a very clear idea of how to classify the different types of objects developers commonly reuse. Similarly, no two people seem to use the word *component* in the same way.

Figure 3.3 illustrates some of the ways that the terms *objects* and *components* are used. Keep in mind that the word *component* is used in a wide variety of ways, but we will be using it in the more narrow sense that it is used when people talk of JavaBeans or COM objects like ActiveX controls or ActiveX EXEs.

If you are using an object-oriented language like C++ or Java, then the language will have class libraries—collections of C++ or Java classes that you can use when you develop an application. Similarly, you can use ActiveX controls to create interfaces in Visual C++, Visual J++, or Visual Basic. Some C++ developers would develop larger composite objects to represent business entities like employees, machines, or orders. As a Visual Basic developer, you will probably develop COM components (e.g., an ActiveX EXE) to represent business entities. Either would work and each has its advantages and disadvantages.

In Figure 3.3 we have divided all the objects and components into two broad groups: those involved in developing interfaces and handling various communication and utility functions, which we term either *infrastructure objects* or *infrastructure components,* and those that represent business entities, which we term either *business objects* or *business components.*

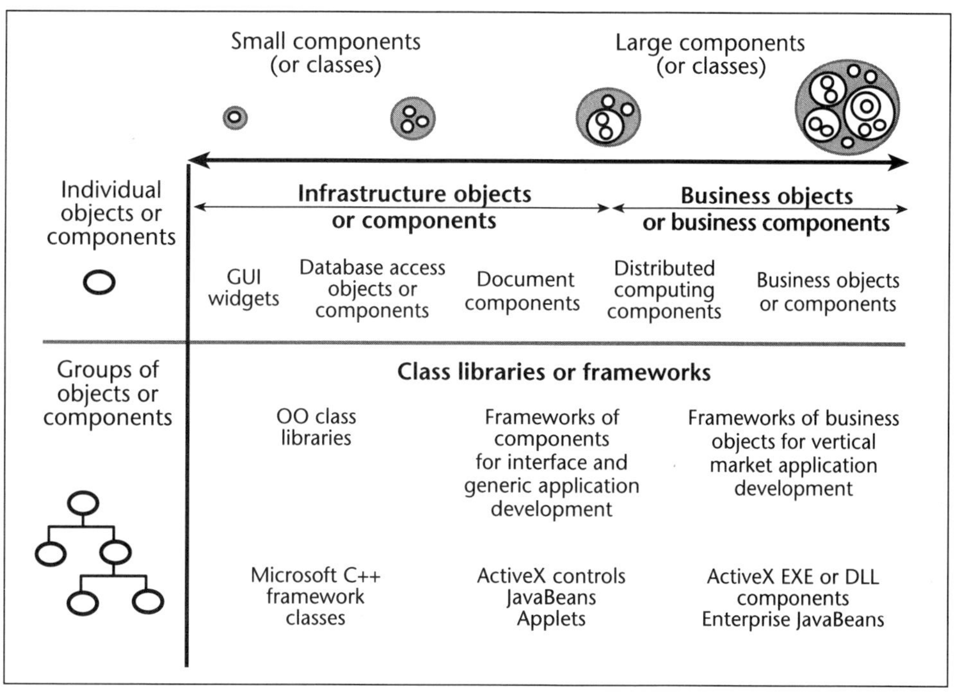

Figure 3.3 *Some of the ways the words* object *and* component *are used.*

Libraries are used to store collections of objects. The Java Development Kit (JDK) and the Microsoft Foundation Classes are examples of class libraries. The term *framework* is generally used to refer to a set of objects or components that are closely related and used for some specific task. Thus, a bank developer might use a framework of objects or components to handle changing currency from one denomination to another, or to handle payroll bookkeeping.

Some companies have also begun to develop frameworks of business objects or components that can be reused. If you have class or component libraries available, you will need to determine whether you can use any components or business objects that already exist. If components are to be used, the design effort changes from designing new objects to identifying and modifying preexisting objects. At the moment, most companies practice a combination of both.

Just as we can distinguish business objects that describe actual entities and processes in the company environment from infrastructure objects that are simply used to handle the details of programming, we can also distinguish between components that function as business objects and components that provide infrastructure services. Most components currently available are designed to handle infrastructure details. In the future, however, companies are likely to develop components that capture the functionality of an Employee class or a Machine class. These high-level components will make it possible to snap together high-level analysis models without having to write code and should significantly reduce the time it takes to create new applications. At the moment, however, developers usually need to create the business objects for the initial analysis model and can then use components to reduce the effort during the design phase.

IBM has developed a complex, layered set of Java components to aid companies in large-scale application development. The initial release of the overall collection of components, referred to as the San Francisco Project, is pictured in Figure 3.4. In effect, IBM has completed the foundation and utilities layer and the common business object layer, as well as a set of application program interfaces (APIs) that lie between these two layers. IBM has also completed one of the business process frameworks: the general ledger framework. Source code is available for the general ledger framework. The initial delivery consists of some 3100 Java classes, including some 23,700 methods and 275,000 lines of source code. Full installation requires 250MB of disk space. Binary code is available for the foundation and common business object layers.

IBM expects that companies using the foundations and a business process component such as general ledger will have 40% of the application complete. Moreover, since all the IBM components have been extensively tested, IBM hopes this approach will allow companies to avoid lots of the infrastructure problems that typically plague new developers when they attempt distributed applications. Microsoft also is working

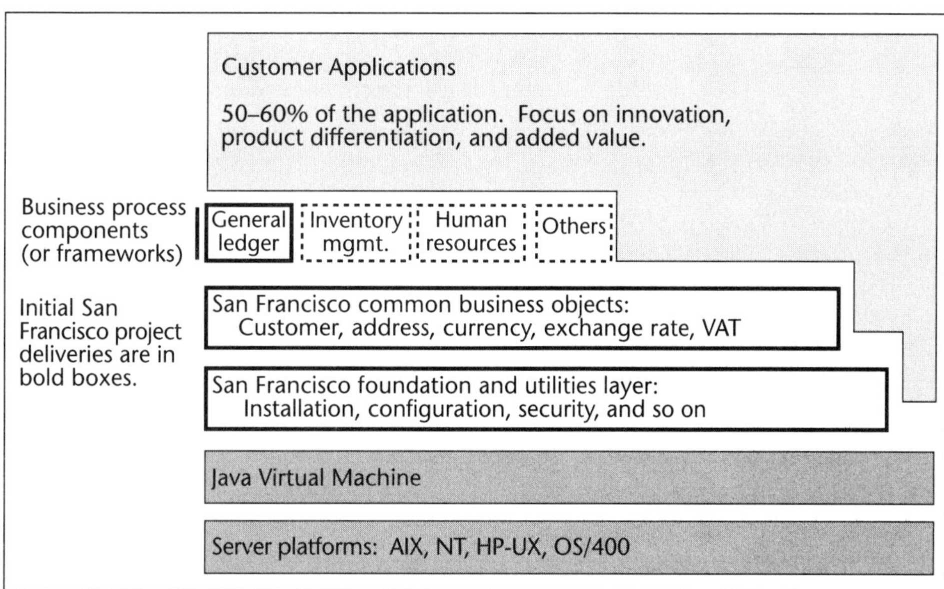

Figure 3.4 *The components in IBM's San Francisco Project.*

with several groups of companies to develop similar frameworks using COM components.

If companies are interested in developing business objects or business-level components for reuse in subsequent projects, they must be especially careful in developing their initial classes to assure they will have the generality required for extensive reuse. Most companies find that if this type of effort is to be undertaken, a separate individual should be appointed to take responsibility for identifying, refining, and storing classes for reuse. Moreover, most developers who try to develop classes for reuse find that they must do two or three different application development efforts before they understand what kind of general classes they need. Suffice it to say that this task is beyond the scope of this book.

We have indicated the use of components in Figure 3.2 by adding a circle for a reuse library to the right of our development cycle. An arrow begins in the design phase, leads to the reuse library, then back to the design process to suggest that developers should look for classes, components, and business objects during design. We'll consider many of these issues in more detail in Chapter 12 when we return to design issues.

3.2.4 The Coding Phase

The next phase in the development cycle begins when you start writing code. During the design phase you will have specified all the objects in the system, and you probably will have identified most of the attributes and operations. You may even have written pseudocode to specify what each operation will do.

In OO development, the class structures and names that you have created during the analysis and design phase become code elements during the coding phase. Thus, once again, there is no sharp break between design and coding. It's simply a matter of getting more specific about how each operation is going to be carried out and finally expressing the operations in an OO language.

If you are doing your development in an OO modeling tool, like Microsoft's Visual Modeler, at this point you could generate code and it would include all your class structures and the names, data types, and other information you have specified about the attributes and operations. During the coding phase you need to complete the actual code required to implement each operation and write any specific code needed for interfaces or linkages.

We won't consider coding in any detail in this book, although we will provide the annotated code for the sample application that we will discuss throughout the book so that you can see how we carried that specific application from design to code.

3.2.5 The Testing Phase

The final phase in the cycle involves testing the code you have developed to see if it functions properly. Depending on the nature of the first prototype, testing may be a formal affair or it may involve fielding your prototype application and determining how users react to it.

Once again, we won't spend much time on testing, since it is well described by others and has little to do with UML notation. The important thing for our purposes is to remind you that, in an iterative development cycle, testing leads right back to analysis and design. You test your prototype, and then, according to what you find, you change your original model, or you begin to expand and enhance it, and the cycle begins again. Of course, each subsequent cycle is a little more confused, from a traditional perspective, than the last because some analysis, design, and coding has already been done. On each subsequent cycle you examine all the analysis and design work you did in previous cycles and then extend it. In many cases you will find yourself working, once again, with the same diagrams you used in the previous phase and simply modifying objects to provide more functionality.

The Unified Modeling Language

In this chapter we'll provide a very general overview of the UML notation. We'll describe each UML diagram in a superficial way and consider how you might use each diagram during an application development effort.

4.1 UML Symbols

Before looking at UML diagrams, it might help to consider the nature of the symbols used in the diagrams. UML symbols are of three basic types: *core* (or *first-class*) *symbols;* common extensions to the core symbols, called *adornments;* and very specialized symbols, which are termed *stereotypes.* All of the symbols are broadly divided into two groups: *modeling symbols* and *relationship symbols.*

We've illustrated the relationships between some of the common UML symbols in Figure 4.1. Notice that class, state,

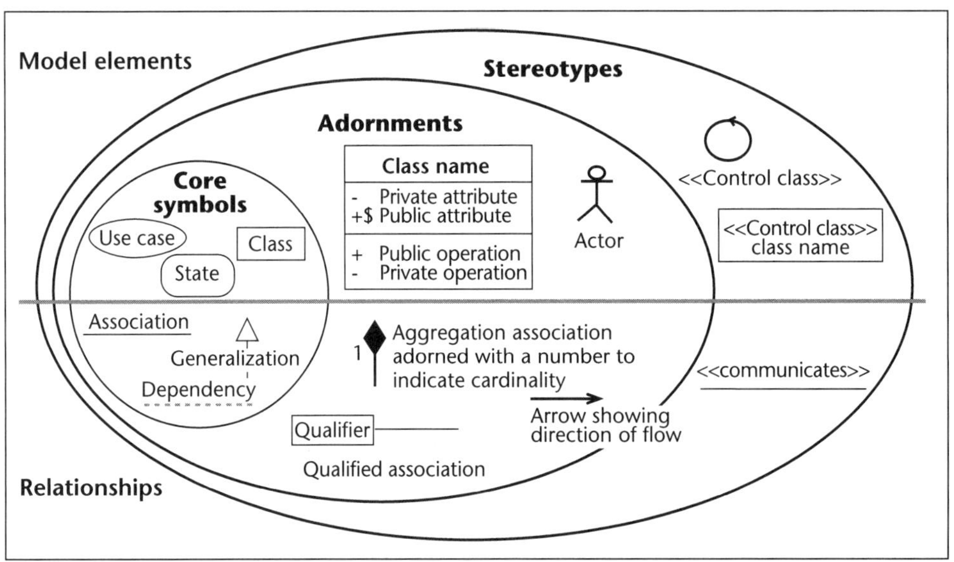

Figure 4.1 *UML notational symbols.*

and use case are core modeling symbols. Similarly, association, dependency, and generalization are core relationship symbols. You can adorn a class by adding information about its attributes and operations. If you want to use really specialized versions of classes, you are into the range of stereotypes, as, for example, OOSE's control and entity classes. In a similar way, a straight line is an association. Placing a diamond on the line—an adornment—indicates that the association is an aggregation. Using a generalization arrow between two classes indicates a class inheritance relationship. Adorning the line with numbers indicates how many instances are involved in the relationship.

Since this book is an informal approach to UML, we won't discuss all the UML symbols in detail. Nor will we draw sharp lines between core elements and adornments. As a rule of thumb, symbols used in different diagrams tend to be core symbols. We will introduce most of the UML core symbols. We won't begin to introduce all of the adornments or the stereotypes. We will always note when symbols are stereotypes. That said, let's consider the different sets of UML diagrams.

4.2 UML Diagrams

Five different groups of UML diagrams offer five different ways of looking at the same problem. By creating the diagrams in each group, you can analyze a problem from different perspectives. The UML diagrams are grouped as follows:

- Use Case Diagrams
  - Use case diagrams
  - Use case descriptions
  - (OOSE) Ideal object models
- Static Structure Diagrams
  - Class diagrams
  - Object diagrams
- Interaction Diagrams
  - Sequence diagrams
  - Collaboration diagrams
- State Diagrams
  - State diagrams
  - Activity diagrams
- Implementation Diagrams
  - Package diagrams
  - Component diagrams
  - Deployment diagrams

A complete UML analysis and design documentation set consists of all of the UML diagrams you have developed. We'll consider each group of diagrams, in turn.

4.2.1 *Use Case Diagrams*

The UML use case diagram can be used to describe the main processes in a system and the interactions between the processes (use cases) and external systems or individuals, called *actors*. Once the use case overview is developed it can be expanded to show more detail, including subprocesses and processes that are sometimes added to other processes.

To define an interaction between a use case and an actor, you write a generic scenario, called a *use case description*. The use case description is a series of sentences describing each step in the interaction. The use case description is subsequently used to generate specific scenarios and interaction diagrams.

Although not an official part of the UML notation, there are extensions for the UML notation that allow developers to define *ideal object models,* which were originally defined in Jacobson's OOSE methodology. In effect, an ideal object model suggests some of the high-level classes that will be needed to implement a use case. When using ideal object models, you usually develop one for each use case. Ideal object models provide a nice intermediate step to make the transition from use cases to class diagrams easier.

4.2.2 Static Structure Diagrams

The UML *class diagram* is one of the two central diagrams in UML development. The class diagram shows the classes that will be included in your application and the relationships between classes. You create other diagrams primarily to refine your understanding of what is going on in the class diagram. Moreover, there are several class diagrams—a high-level class diagram that identifies a few classes and the basic relationships between them and then a whole series of more complex class diagrams that incorporate more and more information. Indeed, if you are creating a very large system, you will probably divide your system into modules, called packages in UML, and do one class diagram for each package.

UML does not define a specific object diagram. Technically, UML says that a collaboration diagram is the way to represent objects. In fact, however, many developers use a simpler version of a collaboration diagram, which we include here and term an *object diagram*. In some cases you create object diagrams to show the interaction of a set of objects. In other cases, objects are added to class diagrams to show how specific objects will be used within the context of the overall class model.

You only do object diagrams when you encounter special problems and need to analyze how a specific set of objects will function. In many cases, it's easier to develop a prototype and test your assumptions than to worry about diagramming object interactions.

4.2.3 Interaction Diagrams

The *sequence diagram* (or event trace diagram or interaction diagram) shows the relationships between specific objects. The sequence diagram represents objects as vertical lines and shows how messages are sent between the various objects. (The messages are sometimes called events. Technically, the line shows a message passing between two objects. An event occurs at the instant when the target object responds to the message.) A sequence diagram allows you to study how a set of objects interact in time. You do not need to do sequence diagrams for every set of objects that interact, but most OO developers rely on sequence diagrams second only to class diagrams. When in doubt about how some set of objects will interact, prepare a sequence diagram.

A sequence diagram should correspond to a specific scenario. Sometimes developers prepare sequence diagrams from scenarios and then compare them to the class diagram to see how they correspond. At other times, developers prepare sequence diagrams right after preparing use cases and scenarios and then use them to prepare a class diagram. There is no correct order in which to do this, except that you need to know the classes in your system before you can prepare a sequence diagram, so most developers begin by preparing at least a very informal class diagram before starting on a sequence diagram.

A *collaboration diagram* is a cross between a simple object diagram and a sequence diagram. Some or all of the objects from a scenario are shown as they would be in an object diagram. Then, instead of showing lines that merely link the objects, arrows are inserted and numbered to illustrate a specific sequence of events. By following the numbered arrows, you can follow the movement of messages during the course of a scenario. Thus, like a sequence diagram, a collaboration diagram describes a specific scenario.

4.2.4 State Diagrams

A *state diagram* (or Harel diagram) provides a very detailed picture of how a specific object changes states. (A state refers to the value that is associated with a specific attribute of an object and to any actions or side effects that occur when the attribute's value changes.) Imagine an object with an attribute called color. Each time you flicked a switch, the value of the attribute would change, always going from red to blue to white and then back to red. If you wanted to document this specific activity, you would use a state diagram. Many systems are developed without the use of state diagrams. On the other hand, they are indispensable if you are working on real-time process control applications or systems that involve concurrent processing.

According to Rational's UML specification, an *activity diagram* is a special type of state diagram. We've included it within the general state diagram group, just as the UML documentation does. But we have to tell you that this only makes sense in a narrow, logical way. A real state diagram describes a detailed picture of how a specific object changes state. An activity diagram, on the other hand, describes activities and flows of data or decisions between activities. In effect, activity diagrams are the diagrams used in most workflow analysis tools. Activity diagrams provide very broad views of business processes. Or they can be used to break out the activities that occur within a use case. Activity diagrams commonly show many different activities that will be handled by lots of different objects.

4.2.5 Implementation Diagrams

Implementation diagrams capture design information. Once again, we've grouped three diagrams in this category, just as Rational's UML documentation does. First, *package diagrams* are used to show how classes can be divided into modules and to indicate high-level relationships between packages. Packages are used strictly for logical modularization. If we had our choice, we'd include package diagrams with class and object diagrams.

Component diagrams are used to show how code is actually divided into modules. In many applications there is a one-to-one relationship between package diagrams and component diagrams. The package diagram shows the logical divisions, and the component diagram shows that you actually went ahead and implemented it as you had proposed via the package diagram. Of course, you might have changed your mind during design and moved some classes to a different module when you actually compiled the code, and in that case, the component diagram would be different. Component diagrams are not normally used to represent the smaller components, such as ActiveX or JavaBean components, that are used in user interface design.

The third type of implementation diagrams, *deployment diagrams,* are used to describe the physical architecture of the application. Nodes in a deployment diagram usually represent hardware platforms. It is common to place component diagrams on top of deployment diagrams to indicate which modules of code will go on which hardware platforms.

4.2.6 The Diagramming Process

In all cases, if you are working on a large system, you will need to prepare many different versions of all of these various UML diagrams to capture all of the information you need for a full understanding of your system. The important thing is that you don't have to develop all of the possible diagrams before you can begin to develop code and test your assumptions by running a prototype version of your system. You begin by limiting the system you want to develop during your first iteration and then only develop the diagrams you need to understand your first prototype system. After testing the prototype, you revise your diagrams to capture what you have learned, and then you expand existing diagrams and prepare new diagrams to analyze your second prototype, and so on.

4.3 Additional Diagrams and Notations

In addition to the UML diagrams we have just described, we use and explain two other types of diagramming notations in this book: CRC cards and ideal object diagrams.

CRC cards are literally 3-inch × 5-inch cards that some analysts use to help them work with users to identify the initial classes in an application. This technique, though informal, is popular because it is so simple and because it usually gets good results. It's an especially useful way to get a group of people thinking in an OO way. We've included a chapter on CRC cards primarily to provide some additional help for those new to OO development.

We have already mentioned that ideal object models are a special kind of diagram used in Jacobson's OOSE methodology. They weren't directly incorporated into the UML notation. Ideal object diagrams are a stereotype that falls between use case diagrams and UML class diagrams. They provide one more good way for new developers to quickly see what classes might be needed for a specific application.

4.4 A Generic Approach to Object-Oriented Development

Figure 4.2 illustrates one way of looking at the relationships between the various diagrams. The figure assumes that you will begin by using BPR, use cases, or CRC cards to identify the overall structure of your problem and to develop some scenarios. It also assumes that you will develop a requirements statement that states what your finished system will do.

Once you have created your requirements statement, Figure 4.2 suggests which UML diagrams you will use to analyze, design, and develop your application. The bold arrows suggest major paths. Most developers create at least one use case diagram and several scenarios. They also create several sequence and class diagrams. The sequence and especially the class diagrams are at the heart of your analysis and design effort. They just keep getting more elaborate as you understand your application better. The other diagrams are used less frequently. Each has special functions and tends to get used according to the specific type of application you are developing. Again, there is no set order in which you use any specific diagram. Large system-development efforts often generate hundreds of diagrams and use all of the various diagramming types. Small systems often get by with two or three class diagrams, two or three sequence diagrams, and nothing else. Most application development efforts, of course, fall in between these extremes.

Neither the OMG nor Rational Software advocates a specific development methodology. Booch, Rumbaugh, and Jacobson have each recommended different methodologies in the past. And many other OO methodologists recommend still other developmental sequences.

Figure 4.2 *Relationships between various UML diagrams.*

BPR workflow diagrams

Workflow diagrams are a kind of activity diagram used to define an entire process.

The UML use case diagrams

Use cases define generic processes the system must be able to handle. Descriptions define generic scenarios.

Use case descriptions

Use case diagram

Ideal object model

Jacobson's ideal object model defines three types of classes according to their overall function.

CRC cards

CRC cards provide users and developers with an informal way to identify classes, attributes, and messages by working through scenarios.

Requirements specification

Scenarios

Scenarios describe specific step-by-step examples of system use. The nouns used in scenario descriptions often define classes.

The UML state diagrams

Activity diagrams show all the activities that occur as the values of an object change. Activity diagrams are used to capture workflows or decision sequences.

Activity diagram

A state diagram shows all of the values (states) that the attribute of an object can take as messages (events) are processed. State diagrams are only prepared for classes whose instances are very dynamic.

State diagram

The UML static structure diagrams

The class diagram describes classes, their associations with other classes (responsibilities), and inheritance relationships. More complex class diagrams describe class attributes and operation names.

Class diagram

Class diagram

Object diagrams are used to explore specific problems with specific classes.

Object diagram

The UML interaction diagrams

Sequence diagrams show the flow of messages (events) between objects. In effect they provide a formal way to specify a scenario.

Sequence diagram

Collaboration diagram

1 2 3

Collaboration diagrams are a combination of object and sequence diagrams. They show the flow of events between objects.

The UML implementation diagrams

Implementation diagrams show design and architectural decisions.

Package diagram

Package diagrams show the logical division of classes into modules.

Component diagram

Component diagrams show the actual software modules in the final system. These are often the same as the package diagrams.

Deployment diagram

Deployment diagrams show the actual platforms (nodes) and network links used by the application.

4.5 A UML Notation Job Aid

Throughout the chapters in which we talk about UML diagrams, we'll introduce lots of names and diagramming conventions. To make it easier to remember the conventions while you prepare your initial diagrams, we've prepared a job aid with the basic symbols on it and included it in this book as Appendix B. If you are going to prepare diagrams by hand, you can photocopy it and use it as a job aid when you begin preparing UML diagrams. If you use an OO modeling tool, the tool will probably provide palettes of UML notational elements that will serve as a job aid when you go to draw the diagrams within the tool environment.

5

Developing Applications in Visual Basic 6.0

At this point we want to provide you with an overview of Visual Basic 6.0, Microsoft's Component Object Model (COM), some of Microsoft's component standards (e.g., OLE and ActiveX), and various support software packages, including things like Microsoft's Component Manager and the Microsoft Repository.

Our goal here is not to teach you how to be a Visual Basic or COM programmer. We assume most readers already know about Visual Basic. In any case, our discussion of UML and the example we develop in this book do not depend on a deep knowledge of Visual Basic. Our concern here is simply to place Visual Basic and Microsoft's supporting technologies within the object-oriented context we have developed in the early chapters of this book, and to assure that readers know which terms in Visual Basic and COM match those in UML.

We initially created the example in this book in Visual Basic 5.0 and then revised it in Visual Basic 6.0 when that version became available. The move from Visual Basic 5.0 to 6.0 didn't require many changes in either the design or the code of our application. The key OO and COM features that were introduced in Visual Basic 5.0 are just the same in Visual Basic 6.0.

The improvements in Visual Basic 6.0 occur primarily in two areas: better database integration and better Internet development and deployment. If we were, in fact, to continue to develop the example we began in this book, we would probably take advantage of some of Visual Basic 6.0's database integration features to improve our database connections. (Specifically, we could use either ActiveX data objects or OLE DB to handle links to databases.) In addition, Visual Basic 6.0 has incorporated screens that help a developer create databases. We assumed that our application would be using existing mainframe databases. OLE DB would certainly have helped with database access. (In fact, we used FoxPro to create a file that contains the data you will need if you download the code from the Morgan Kaufmann Web site.)

Similarly, if we were to continue to develop our application, we might take advantage of Visual Basic's ability to support dynamic HTML to spiff up the GUI components. Moreover, we might use some of Microsoft's new server-side component technology to allow our system to handle each sales order as a transaction. Visual Basic 6.0 supports a new COM component, WebClasses, used to create server components that are tailored for Internet applications. (We'll discuss these features when we consider how Microsoft enhanced COM and the Microsoft Transaction Server.)

But those are all things that we would do to enhance the application, after we had developed the initial prototype. As far as the prototype we describe in this book, you could just as well develop it in Visual Basic 5.0 or 6.0.

The important thing about Visual Basic 6.0 is that it isn't really an OO language in the sense of Java or C++. Instead, it is an application development environment that allows developers to create applications that combine Visual Basic code with COM components and HTML code to create a new application. This isn't to say that you couldn't create an entire application in Visual Basic without using anything else, but few developers would do it. Instead, most developers use

Visual Basic in combination with COM components and HTML elements to create a mixed application. Other languages are moving in the same direction and combining Internet and component elements in their designs, but Visual Basic is ahead of the curve.

It was easier to discuss Visual Basic as a stand-alone language when Visual Basic 4.0 developers used COM components like OCXs that were developed in C++. In this case there was a clean distinction between Visual Basic code and COM components. Since Visual Basic 5.0, however, most Visual Basic developers create COM components with Visual Basic and then mix Visual Basic and COM code so casually that its hard to know where one begins and the other ends. We say this simply to illustrate that trying to provide a quick overview of Visual Basic can be confusing.

You can create COM components in any language, including C++ or Visual Basic. It's easier, however, to create COM components in an OO language, and most COM components are written in either C++ or Visual Basic. Thus, you could use Visual Basic to create COM components that are later used in the development of another Visual Basic application. To try to keep this distinction clear, Microsoft literature sometimes refers to people who develop COM components, no matter what language they use, as *authors,* and saves the term *developers* for individuals who create applications that incorporate COM components. Thus, if you create an ActiveX control, you are an author, but if you create a Visual Basic application and use the ActiveX controls provided with the language to create a GUI, then you are a developer. Obviously the same individual could do both, but it's less confusing if you think of these two efforts as separate programming tasks.

It gets even more complex. Languages like C++ and Java are completely independent of COM and each evolved independently of COM. For example, C++ and Java both support class inheritance, while COM only supports interface inheritance. Visual Basic 6.0, on the other hand, was co-evolved with COM. In effect, Microsoft used some of its COM technology to add OO features to Visual Basic to turn it into an OO language. Moreover, from early on, Microsoft designers clearly intended Visual Basic to rely heavily on COM components. At the same time, Visual Basic is often used as a scripting language for COM. If this sounds a bit circular, it is. (It's very much the same as the relationship between Java objects and the JavaBeans component model.) If you aren't careful, you can find yourself confused about what is a Visual Basic feature and what is a COM feature. If we were talking about C++ and COM, we could draw sharp distinctions. When we talk about Visual Basic and COM, however, the distinctions are often blurred. With that warning in mind, let's consider how each works.

5.1 Visual Basic 6.0 As an Object-Based Language

Basic originated as a teaching language at Dartmouth College in the sixties. It was designed to be an easy-to-learn language that could be used to give students a clear idea of how programs worked. Basic, like most early languages, was a procedural language. That is, one developed a series of statements that told the computer what to do, and then ran the program.

When Microsoft shipped DOS in 1981, they included a version of DOS Basic with the operating system, to provide developers with an easy way to develop simple applications for DOS platforms. Later, when Microsoft introduced Windows, they upgraded Basic and turned it into Visual Basic, a language that developers could use to create good GUIs for Windows environments. In effect, Microsoft used Visual Basic as a scripting language that developers could use to tie together GUI elements. One might describe the early Visual Basic language as an event-driven language. It was tuned to run subroutines in response to external events, like mouse clicks.

In the late eighties, Microsoft began to develop its Object Linking and Embedding (OLE) technology to facilitate the creation of compound documents. Simultaneously, and initially independently, Microsoft began to develop a component model for Visual Basic. The components were called Visual Basic extensions (VBXs). By the early nineties, these technologies had evolved and merged into what Microsoft now calls COM, a core technology for component-oriented application development. As the COM model and Microsoft's component standards developed from OLE and VBXs to OCX to ActiveX, Microsoft evolved Visual Basic so that it could continue to support Windows development.

Version 4.0 of Visual Basic began the transition from a procedural language to an object-based language. It supported OCXs but didn't provide tools for their development. (OCXs were developed in C++.) Visual Basic 5.0 completed that transition and provided an object-oriented programming environment. It also provided full support for ActiveX development. Visual Basic 6.0, as we noted, includes several refinements to Visual Basic 5.0, but is otherwise the same.

Visual Basic 6.0 is a hybrid language, in the sense that it can support either procedural or object-oriented programming. In effect, Visual Basic 6.0 has the same relationship to Visual Basic 1.0 as C++ has to C. You can ignore the OO features in Visual Basic 6.0 and use it to develop purely procedural applications. Or you can take advantage of the OO features and create OO applications. Mixing procedural and object-oriented techniques is also easy, but very dangerous, since once you mix the two styles, it is particularly hard to modify or maintain the resulting programs. Each Visual Basic developer should decide which style of programming he or she wants to use for a specific application, and then stick to either a procedural or an OO style within the specific application.

We'll review the object-oriented features of Visual Basic 5.0 and 6.0 in more or less the same order that we looked at object technology in Chapter 2, then turn to Microsoft's COM.

5.1.1 Objects, Classes, and Instances

Visual Basic 5.0 added a new data type, the *class module,* which functions as a class for OO development. (Forms for GUI development also serve as a special type of class in Visual Basic.) Class modules are like other Visual Basic modules. They have a declaration section followed by a series of Sub, Function, and Property subroutines. The important difference, however, is that a class module can only be used (at run time) as a template to generate instances of the class module.

Class modules contain *attributes,* which Visual Basic calls *properties* (or *instance variables*). (It's unfortunate that Visual Basic, Visual Modeler, and Rose 98 refer to attributes as properties, and then use the term "property" to refer to a method that can be used to set and change the values associated with different properties. It can lead to some confusion.) Visual Basic properties are stored as module-level variables inside a class module. Each property can be declared to be either public or private.

Class modules also contain *operations* or *methods.* Visual Basic methods take four forms: properties, sub and function routines, and events. A pure OO language would have a single, more generic method. Because Visual Basic has evolved from a procedural language, however, Microsoft has retained four different ways of providing objects with behavioral functionality.

Property "methods" (as opposed to the attribute names of the variables themselves) are used to obtain or assign values associated with property attributes. Visual Basic supports three types of property methods (routines): *Property Get, Property Let,* and *Property Set.*

Most method calls are handled by sub and function routines that perform very much like traditional OO language methods. Visual Basic has always been good at responding to events. The new event "method" provides Visual Basic developers with a way to initiate events that will stimulate other actions. Thus, for example, you might set an event method to fire whenever an attribute took a certain value; that, in turn, would cause other objects in the application to take various actions. Thus, an application could be developed that would notify a number of users whenever daily sales fell below some specified number.

UML and tools that support UML use more abstract concepts than Visual Basic. Thus, UML supports a generic approach to methods, while Visual Basic subdivides methods into four subcategories. In many cases, Visual Modeler or Rational Rose 98 will be able to determine which of the four specific types of methods you intend and will be able to generate Visual Basic code without being told which method type is intended. In other cases, the developer will have to specify, during the design phase, what kind of Visual Basic code should be generated from a specific UML method.

5.1.2 Encapsulation

Pure OO languages like Smalltalk and Java rely only on methods to communicate between objects. Moreover, these languages make it impossible or difficult for one class to know how another class is structured. Visual Basic, like C++, supports both public and private attributes. It also supports routines that are not encapsulated within object modules. Thus, if you want, you can create a routine that stands outside of any object and that changes public attributes within various objects. In other words, Visual Basic makes it possible to encapsulate everything within objects, but it also makes it possible to bypass OO techniques.

If you are familiar with older versions of Visual Basic, the temptation to mix styles and fall back on procedural techniques when you are in a hurry will be very strong. Lots of experience gained by watching C programmers do exactly that in C++ leads us to urge readers not to do it. Mixing the techniques results in really bad software designs. Better to do one or the other, but don't mix them. Thus, if you set out to do an OO application, respect encapsulation! Using UML and tools like Visual Modeler and Rose 98 is one good way to help assure that you program in a good OO style.

5.1.3 Generalization

Generalization refers to code-sharing relationships. When most OO developers think of generalization, they think of class (or implementation) inheritance. If an OO language supports class inheritance, then a developer can create a hierarchy of classes and inherit code down branches of the hierarchy. Visual Basic 6.0 does not support class inheritance. This leads some OO purists to say that Visual Basic is an object-based language and not a truc OO languagc. If one insists that a OO language must support class inheritance, then, of course, Visual Basic isn't an OO language; it's an object-based language. But rather than quibble with purists or emphasize the negative, it's probably better to emphasize the positive. Visual Basic is a component-oriented language. It doesn't support class inheritance, but it does support interface inheritance, which is probably more important for component-based development.

In our general discussion of objects in Chapter 2, we spoke as if each object had a set of methods. In fact, a composite object contains many different objects, each with its own set of methods. Similarly, many Visual Basic objects are composite objects. Each Visual Basic object can support several interfaces. The initial interface that a class module supports describes the attributes and methods the developer creates when he or she creates the class. If the developer wants the class to support any additional interfaces, he or she simply names the interface and indicates that the class implements it.

Remember that an interface is simply a collection of one or more method signatures. Somewhere, however, there must be an interface implementation object that has the code that implements the interface. In some cases, Microsoft may provide both the interface definition and the implementation code. In other cases, Microsoft or someone else may define an interface, but not define the implementation, leaving the actual writing of implementation code to the developer. You can't change interface descriptions once they're created, but you can create more than one implementation for a single interface. In this case, the functionality of the COM object will vary according to which implementation of the interface the specific COM object points to (see Figure 5.1).

In an OO language with class inheritance, you might inherit a method and then modify it. In this case, the superclass and the subclass would both have the same interface, they would both support the same set of method names, but the two classes would provide different behavior in the case of at least one method. Visual Basic does not allow a developer to change

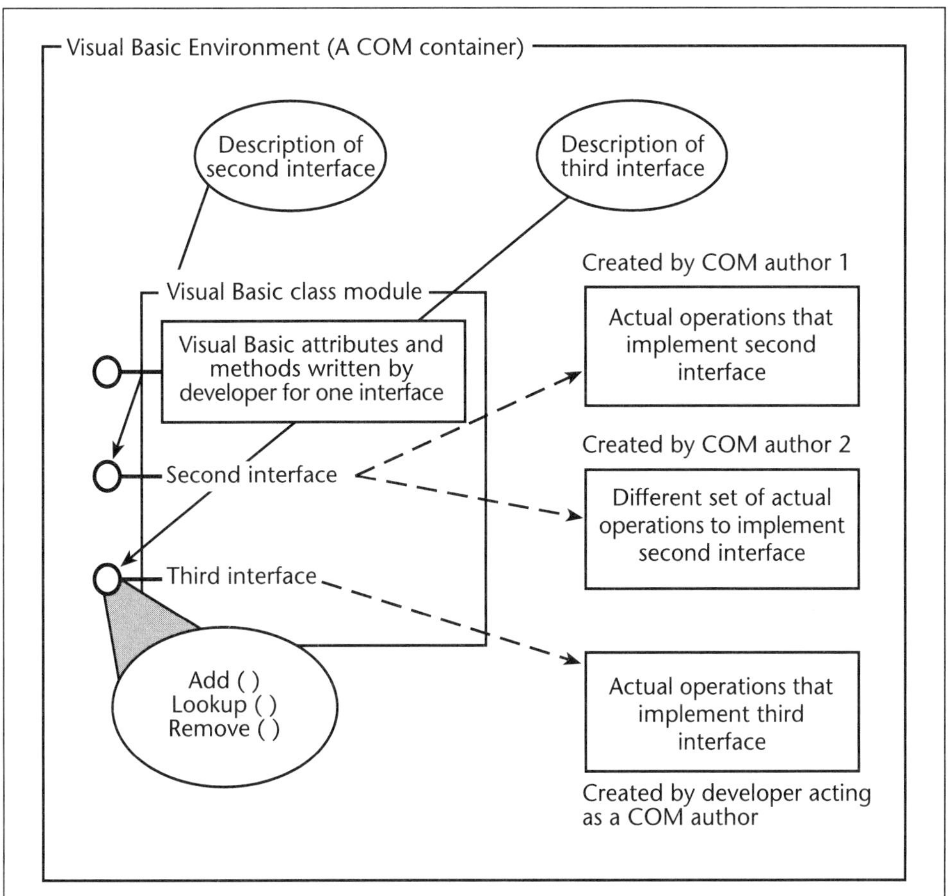

Figure 5.1 *A Visual Basic class module with COM interfaces.*

an interface once it's been used. If a developer needs slightly different behavior, he or she must use another interface or create a new implementation of the earlier interface class, as in Figure 5.1.

The techniques by which an interface is associated with a specific class module are referred to as aggregation and containment. We'll consider both of these in a moment when we discuss COM. In effect, Visual Basic has borrowed most of its interface concepts from techniques developed for COM.

Most OO languages come with extensive class libraries to facilitate rapid development. Microsoft's Visual C++, for example, comes with Microsoft Foundation Classes, an extensive C++ class library. Visual Basic does not come with a class library, as such. It does, however, come with a library of interface classes, organized as COM components. The ActiveX controls for GUI development are the most obvious, but a growing number of other ActiveX components are available to handle other aspects of application development. Database access, for example, can now be handled by ActiveX database components.

5.1.4 Polymorphism

Many developers think of polymorphism as a characteristic of class inheritance. By specializing subclasses, and then routing messages to either the super- or subclass at run time, one can create very dynamic and flexible programs.

One can achieve most of the same functionality by creating and incorporating multiple interface classes within an object module. In this case, polymorphism is achieved by routing messages to alternative implementations of a single interface.

5.1.5 A Component Development Language

You could develop an entire OO application with Visual Basic, using only class modules written in Visual Basic. In fact, however, you will probably never do that. Instead, you will supplement the classes you develop in Visual Basic with COM components that you draw from the COM library that comes with Visual Basic. In COM terms, Visual Basic is a container in which you can run COM components. The obvious example is that every Visual Basic developer normally uses ActiveX controls to create GUIs.

Equally important, you will often create a class module or a set of class modules in Visual Basic, and then decide to turn those classes into COM objects, thus creating a new ActiveX component. You aren't forced to do this, but if you are developing a distributed Internet application, it will probably be more efficient.

Thus, we return to the point where we began. Visual Basic 6.0 supports the development of object-based applications. But it is even better at mixing objects and component techniques to create what most would call component-based applications.

5.2 Microsoft's Component Object Model

We have already discussed how different people use the word "component" in different ways. To a Smalltalk programmer, a component is simply a composite Smalltalk object—an object that contains other objects. To Microsoft developers, however, a component is a module that supports one or more standard interfaces and uses communication protocols provided by Microsoft's COM. In effect, COM is a high-level language for manipulating components. Some OO purists would always use the term "component" to describe a COM entity, arguing that COM isn't really an OO system. Others tend to use the term "object" when they are talking in abstract terms and then use the term "component" to describe something like ActiveX or an ActiveX DLL. We'll generally refer to abstract entities as "COM objects" and more specific examples as "COM components," but there is no real technical difference between the two terms. (COM objects are instantiations of classes, which COM refers to as "Factories.")

As with an object in an OO language, everything inside a COM object is hidden from every other component. The COM standard specifies exactly how the interfaces are to work. Moreover, the COM standard provides for message passing between components. Microsoft's Interface Definition Language (IDL) is a neutral language that can pass messages between COM objects without regard to the language in which the internals of the component were programmed. Thus, one COM component created in C++ can be used in a

Visual Basic application and respond to messages from Visual Basic objects or from other components written in Visual J++ (see Figure 5.2).

A component system, as we mentioned earlier, is made up of components and an environment or container in which the components function. Many products supported by Microsoft can serve as COM containers. Visual Basic, Excel, and Internet Explorer, as well as a number of more specialized environments, like ActiveX EXEs and Active X DLLs, are all examples of containers. Whatever else a container includes, it must include or provide access to the COM library, which provides a way of handling communications between any COM components placed in the container. In addition, most containers provide services. The services provide functionality that would otherwise have to be included in each individual

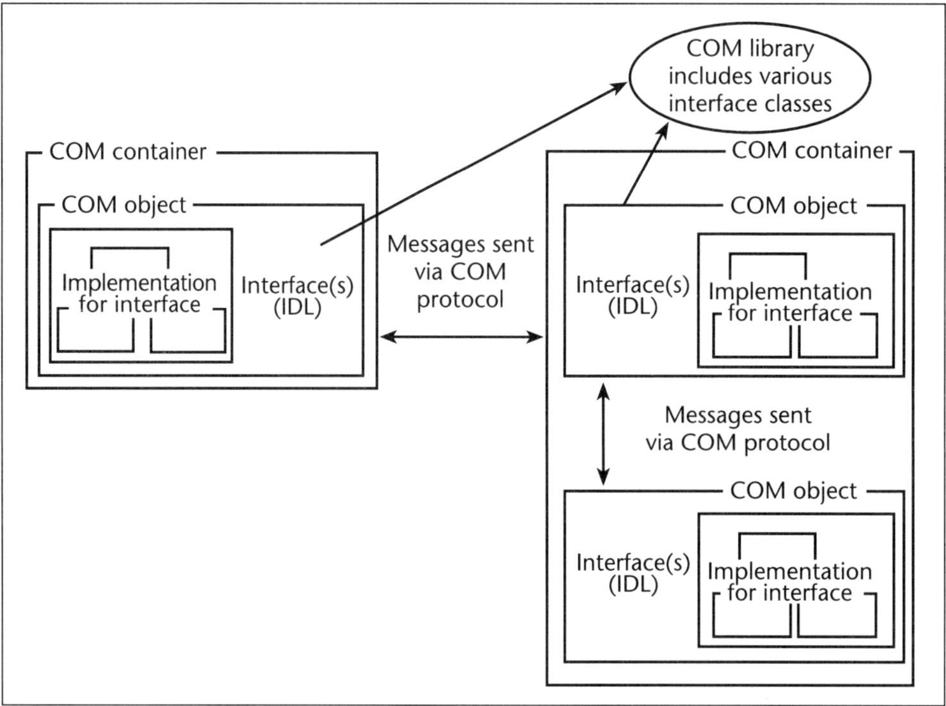

Figure 5.2 *Message passing in the COM component system.*

COM component. In some cases, the services are part of the Windows operating system. In other cases, the services are themselves packaged as COM components that reside in the container.

Keep in mind that components can be embedded within other components. Thus, you might use ActiveX controls to create an interface and then turn the entire interface into an ActiveX EXE component, which you could subsequently embed in a still larger ActiveX EXE component.

The internals of a COM object aren't important, as far as COM is concerned, as long as the component provides the services described by the interfaces. Thus, a component could contain a DOS Basic procedural routine or a legacy COBOL program. Similarly, the component could contain C++ or Visual Basic code. Object technology has always emphasized using encapsulation to combine older code with object-oriented code. Microsoft's approach to components makes this a particularly effective strategy.

When you are not using a COM object to encapsulate legacy code, but developing a new COM object from scratch, you will probably find that it's easier to create the new object's internals by means of Visual Basic or C++. Object technology is the ideal way to implement COM objects.

If you develop COM objects in Visual Basic, then when you indicate that you want to develop a new project, the environment will present you with a dialog that will ask you to choose a project type. You can choose a standard EXE, an ActiveX EXE, an ActiveX DLL, an ActiveX control, or an ActiveX Document DLL or EXE. Most writers refer to ActiveX DLLs, ActiveX EXEs, and ActiveX controls as ActiveX or COM components. Again, the key to all this is that components can be nested within components to almost any depth, so it can get confusing fast. In effect, calling something a COM or ActiveX component largely depends on context.

COM objects are packaged in a binary format. Thus, users can only access the interfaces; they can't examine the implementation. This makes it easy to use COM or ActiveX components in a wide variety of situations without regard for the language in which the COM component was originally implemented.

5.2.1 COM Objects, Interfaces, and Implementations

To minimize the confusion, we'll use the term *COM object* to refer to a basic module that combines one or more COM interfaces with implementations of those interfaces. Even this can get confusing, since COM objects usually don't include the code that implements their interfaces, but, instead, have pointers to the code that does the implementation.

A *COM interface* is a set of method signatures. Each signature indicates the name of the methods, any datatypes that must be passed with the message to drive the method, and any datatypes the method will return. The COM interface method signatures are specified in Microsoft's IDL. IDL is a C-like language used for specifying interfaces. Thus, you can specify an IDL interface for an object that is implemented in Visual Basic as easily as one implemented in C++. Using IDL assures that COM components implemented in different languages can communicate with each other without difficulty.

A COM interface is represented as a circle attached to the UML object rectangle. This interface symbol is usually called a lollipop. A single COM object can support any number of COM interfaces. COM interfaces are indexed in the COM library.

In conventional OO languages, developers sometimes use classes that include methods, but no code to actually implement the methods. These classes are referred to as *abstract classes*. In Java, if one class inherited from an abstract class, the subclass would inherit the method names, but no specific implementation code. The developer of the subclass would need to write the code that would implement the method names (signatures) inherited from the abstract class. This approach is typically used when a developer wants a number of classes to respond to the same set of methods, but each in a different way.

Some writers describe COM components as abstract classes. In many cases this is exactly how a COM component works. The component only specifies method signatures. The COM component author creates a new COM object that implements the interface class. The author creates the code to implement each method described in the COM interface class. The author can use any type of code he or she wants to implement the method signatures. COM does not care about how an interface is actually implemented; COM is only concerned with the interfaces and communications between the interfaces. Using this approach, several ActiveX object developers could implement the same COM interface, each using different code. In this case, a developer who creates an application that will use a specific COM component must specify the implementation of the interface to be used for each particular case.

Unlike abstract classes in other OO languages, however, COM interface classes are not limited to simply specifying method signatures. In some cases Microsoft, or another author, will create a COM interface class and include code to implement some or all of the method signatures described by the interface. Most of the elementary interfaces that are used in ActiveX development come with their interfaces already defined. In this case, when several different COM objects use these interface classes, they will be using the same implementation (see Figure 5.2).

Figure 5.2 illustrates one way of diagramming a COM object. The COM object itself is diagrammed as a rectangle. The various interfaces are represented by lollipops attached to the side of the box. (As we will see later, in UML and the visual modeling tools we will use, the box and lollipops together form a component diagram. In UML, component diagrams are only used to represent physical entities. If you wanted to show what lies inside the component, you would use other UML diagrams, like class diagrams, to show classes, attributes, and methods used to implement the COM object.)

COM objects inherit interfaces by one of two ways. In one case, they provide a pointer to the interface class. This is called *containment* or *delegation*. In the other case, they actually incorporate the interface class within the COM object that supports the interface. This is called *aggregation*. In either case, the COM object must implement methods that point to or call the methods of the interface class. Containment is the more common approach, but aggregation is preferred when problems involving reference counting (garbage collection) make containment ineffective.

Remember throughout this discussion that no matter how methods and code are handled within COM, when you write a Visual Basic application, you either create a class and write Visual Basic code to implement the methods included in a class, or you use a COM interface and let the component provide the implementation. As a Visual Basic developer, you aren't concerned with how the COM object implements the interfaces it provides.

Each interface provides one or more methods. The COM object contains any values associated with attributes used by the interface. A COM object must always be implemented inside a container or "server," which is represented by the box around the COM object and its interfaces in Figure 5.2. One container type is a dynamic-link library (DLL), which is loaded as needed; another is an executable (EXE) process. The method code is contained in the container. Data inside the COM object can only be accessed via one of the methods supported by one of its interfaces.

If this seems a bit complex, remember that when we normally discuss objects, we simply assume that they are written in a language that provides the environment when they are executed. Thus, a COM object has an environment, and since it's interpreted, it needs a run-time engine.

Microsoft offers a number of different ways to provide all this functionality—a number of different COM object types and a number of different containers in which to execute them. Thus, a discussion of ActiveX may make it seem as if ActiveX is more complex than a C++ class, but that's simply because ActiveX discussions invariably involve a good deal of detail about the specifics of implementing the objects, and because ActiveX components are designed so that they can be written and run in a number of different environments.

5.2.2 The COM Library

Every system that supports COM must implement the *COM library*. In effect, the COM library contains the functionality that provides the basic behaviors of the COM object-based system. The COM library provides the basic interface classes for the COM system (e.g., *IUnknown* is a COM interface class) and the code to implement the methods in that interface. It also supports other basic interfaces. In addition to the basic interfaces, Microsoft has created a wide variety of additional interfaces and DLLs to support them. Developers can also define additional interfaces and define the code to implement the methods associated with those interfaces.

COM interfaces are binary. They are defined in Microsoft's IDL. COM doesn't care what language the method code is written in; other COM objects only interact with the IDL of the interface. By keeping a clean distinction between the interface and the underlying code, COM makes it possible for component vendors to create and sell components in binary form without revealing the underlying code to buyers.

5.2.3 Establishing Communications

Each COM object is an instance of a specific class (or factory). To access a COM object, a "client," which might or might not be another object, begins by contacting the COM library. The COM library, which we'll refer to as "COM," checks with a system registry to locate the appropriate factory. Then COM sends to the factory and asks it to instantiate an object. At the same time, COM obtains a pointer to one of the new object's interfaces and passes that pointer back to the client that originated the request. Using this pointer, which usually goes to the COM object's IUnknown interface, the "client" can query the COM object to learn what other interfaces it supports and then establish pointers to whatever interfaces the client needs. The client establishes one pointer per interface that it wants to use. Each interface, of course, can support many different methods.

Figure 5.3 illustrates how a COM object can be invoked. (This figure and several others used in this chapter are modified after figures from David Chappell's popular book *Understanding ActiveX and OLE,* which we highly recommend.) When a "client" invokes a COM interface method, it seems as if it is evoking a local procedure or function. In fact, however, the code that gets executed could be running in a library, a

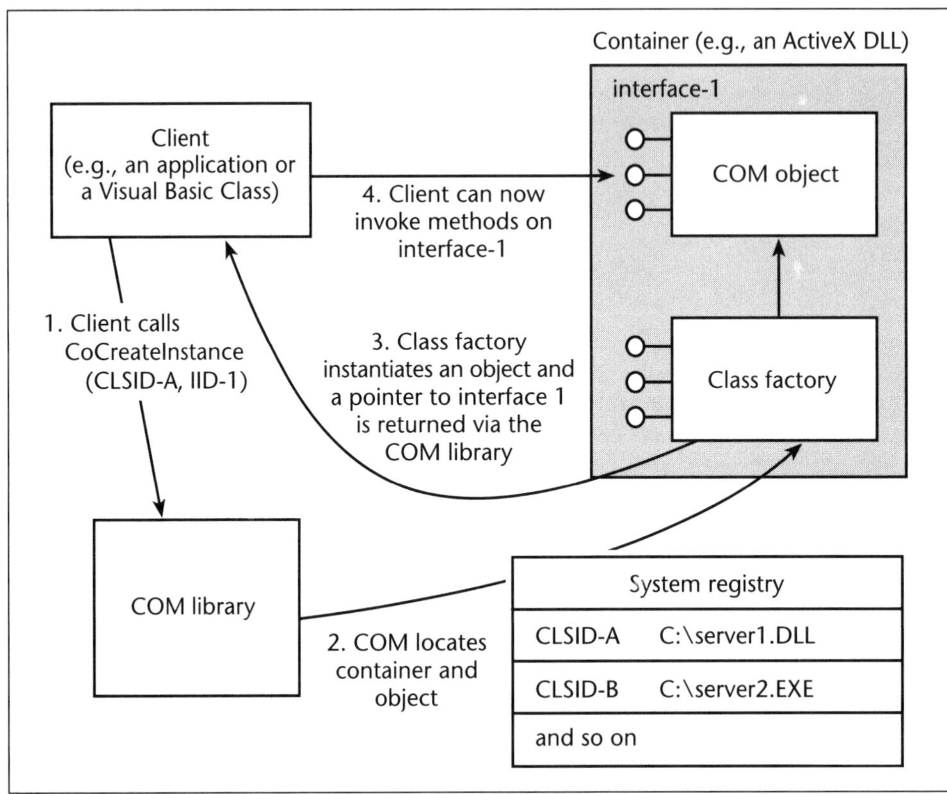

Figure 5.3 *Creating a COM component (modified after Chappell).*

separate process, or even in the operating system. Thus, the actual method code is not contained within the interface nor is it inside the COM object. Instead, the method code is contained within the server.

The procedure we have outlined can get a bit complex. COM provides an alternative, called *monikers*. A moniker is a COM object that has a single purpose: it knows how to create and initialize another COM object. Monikers aren't required, but, once the monikers are in place, they simplify the instantiation process for the COM objects they represent.

The COM system is an interpreted system, and it supports a version of garbage collection. In effect, COM keeps track of when a component is created and tracks all references to the component. When the reference count falls to zero, COM disposes of the component. (Reference counting is handled by the methods *AddRef* and *Release,* which are on the *IUnknown* interface.)

COM does not support class inheritance, but it does support two different ways of modifying an object for reuse. One approach is called containment (or delegation). In this case one COM object acts as the client of another object. This second object is called the *outer object,* and the original object is called the *inner object.* In effect, the outer object adds whatever modifications are needed for the new application. When a new client needs some functionality, it contacts the outer object. The outer object either provides the desired functionality, or it uses its own pointers to the inner object's interfaces to obtain functionality from the inner object and passes that functionality on to the new client.

A second approach to reuse is called aggregation. Aggregation, in effect, encapsulates the original object inside a new outer object and presents both the inner and outer object interfaces to any new client.

COM also provides *structured storage,* a way of making COM objects persistent. There are several different ways the data contained in a COM object can be stored on disk. In simple cases the data is stored in a file. In more complex cases, data from different programs are stored within a single file that is internally divided up to allow separate cells for different types of data.

The COM system provides a technology for creating COM objects. OLE components and ActiveX controls are two examples of COM objects.

5.3 Distributed COM

Applications use COM to access components in linked libraries, in other applications, or in the operating system. COM is currently available on all Microsoft operating systems. COM, however, is designed to function only on a single platform.

To allow applications to transparently access COM objects on other platforms, Microsoft is currently in the process of rolling out Distributed COM. DCOM is currently available on Windows NT (Release 4.0) and on Windows 95/98. (In effect, DCOM is designed to replace WinSoc as the way to link applications on various Windows platforms.)

It might be useful to step back a bit and discuss all this in more abstract terms.

The technology for Remote Procedure Calls (RPCs) became popular in the mid-eighties. Developers were already familiar with making calls between two processes written in the same language and running on the same machine. In effect, one procedure, running in one process, called another procedure, running in a second process. As developers began to deal with applications that were distributed on different machines in a network, however, they began to need a mechanism for calling procedures on other platforms. At the same time, people wanted to make calls from one language to another. RPC technology was developed to solve these problems.

To solve the problem of communicating between different languages, RPC developers created an independent language that could be used to represent the calls that were passed between platforms. This language was referred to as an Interface Development Language (IDL). An IDL wasn't a complete programming language, but was adequate to encode the information in the calls that were passed between procedures.

Different specific approaches can be used, but the essence of an RPC is that the call, in one language, is translated into an IDL call. That call is then transmitted over the network and then translated into the language of the target procedure. In a similar way, the response is translated into IDL and returned to the initial procedure. Obviously, mechanisms are needed to translate between the various programming languages and IDL. Similarly, mechanisms are needed to keep track of where the remote procedures are located, and to bundle and send IDL code from one platform to another. Directories are used for the first purpose, and the mechanisms for handling IDL transmission are usually called "stubs" and "skeletons." Figure 5.4 illustrates DCE's popular RPC mechanism.

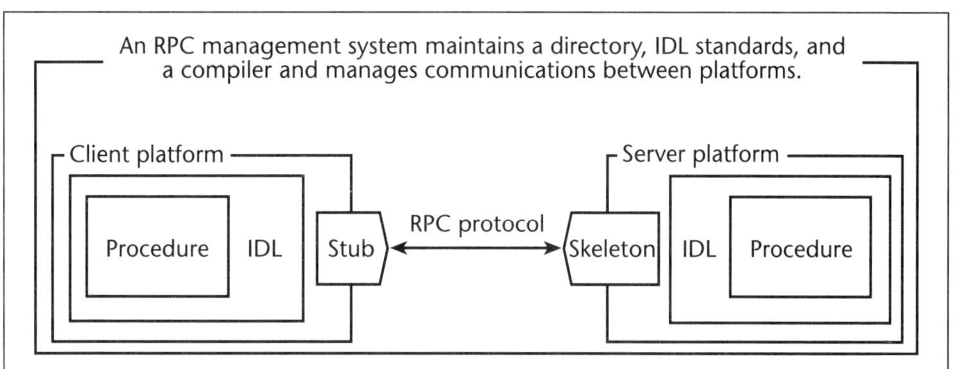

Figure 5.4 *A Remote Procedure Call (RPC) system.*

The RPC mechanism is based on a synchronous approach. The procedure on the client is waiting while the remote procedure call is made, and continues only after a response is received. The best known RPC system is the Open Software Foundation's Distributed Computing Environment (DCE) RPC. Microsoft uses a slight variation on the DCE RPC mechanism.

There is a sense in which an RPC system provides the basis for a component system. Procedures, encapsulated by IDL code, communicate with each other by means of the RPC environment.

In the nineties, everyone has been focused on objects because they offer greater flexibility and they are easier to maintain. Thus, several different groups have been exploring how to extend the basic RPC mechanism to support objects and to pass messages between objects on different machines. And, in the process, components have been developed. Most people refer to an object-oriented version of an RPC mechanism as an Object Request Broker (ORB). Figure 5.5 shows an overview of a generic ORB. DCOM is an ORB that supports COM distribution on multiple platforms.

A quick glance will show that this diagram is very similar to the one we used to describe an RPC mechanism. RPCs are designed to communicate between processes; ORBs are designed to pass messages between objects. Just as an RPC approach requires a neutral IDL, like the DCE IDL, so any ORB requires

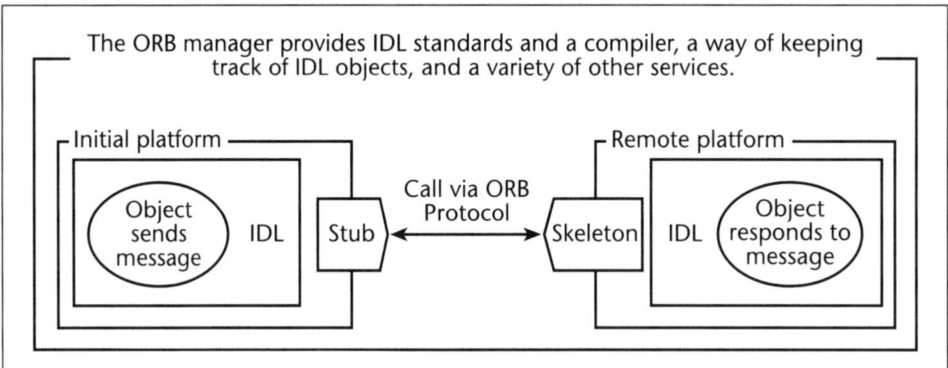

Figure 5.5 *A generic overview of an Object Request Broker (ORB) system.*

a neutral IDL to assure that objects written in one OO language can communicate with objects written in another language. Similarly, an ORB system requires an indexing system to locate objects on other platforms and a system of stubs and skeletons to handle the actual network communication process.

Because of polymorphism (the possibility that multiple objects of the same class might exist) and the variety of packages in which objects and components might be packaged, an ORB can get quite a bit more complex than an RPC system, but the basic concepts are the same.

As we have already discussed, a component system doesn't pay attention to what's inside the component package. Thus, you could wrap a procedure or an object inside a COM component. In most cases, however, objects are used to create the functionality that is then packaged within a component. And IDLs and RPC mechanisms are used to handle communications between platforms.

Microsoft has made arrangements with a number of vendors to make COM and DCOM available on UNIX, AS400, and mainframe platforms. These versions will become available in the course of 1998 and 1999.

When a client uses DCOM to look for a component, the process appears to be very similar to using COM. The client calls on COM to help it obtain a pointer to one of the component's interfaces. COM checks the local system registry to find out where the component is located. COM then goes to the local system registry on the appropriate platform, arranges to have the class factory instantiate a COM object, and then gets a pointer to one of its interfaces and returns information about the pointer to the client. Using that pointer, the client then determines what interfaces the COM object supports and sends appropriate messages. (See Figure 5.6.)

DCOM supports several network protocols, including TCP/IP and NetWare's IPX/SPX. In addition to supporting the static linking mechanism I have described above, DCOM also supports a dynamic option. In this case, rather than relying on a local registry to find an object, the client can query all the platforms at run time and dynamically choose the COM object it needs.

As in COM, DCOM can use monikers to simplify the creation of objects. DCOM also keeps track of references to objects on other platforms and eliminates them when the reference count drops to zero.

Because DCOM was developed by Microsoft, it provides good access to Windows and Office. For example, DCOM is designed to work with Microsoft Word and Excel. Similarly, some of the COM interfaces provide services that Windows developers will find very useful. For example, the Open Database Connectivity (ODBC) interface built into Windows provides one way to access relational databases. The COM ODBC interface (OLE Database or, more recently, COM DB) allows this functionality to be accessed from COM objects in a systematic way. A source of data can be modeled as a DataSource object and then have a command object specified for it. This service is available for use with DCOM in Windows NT 4.0 and Windows 95/98.

We noted earlier that DCOM is an ORB and that all ORBs were initially based on Remote Procedure Calls, which are synchronous. Synchronous message systems, however, don't work very well when lots of clients are trying to interact with a server more or less simultaneously. Let's consider some alternatives.

Figure 5.6 *Linking to a Distributed COM component (modified after Chappell).*

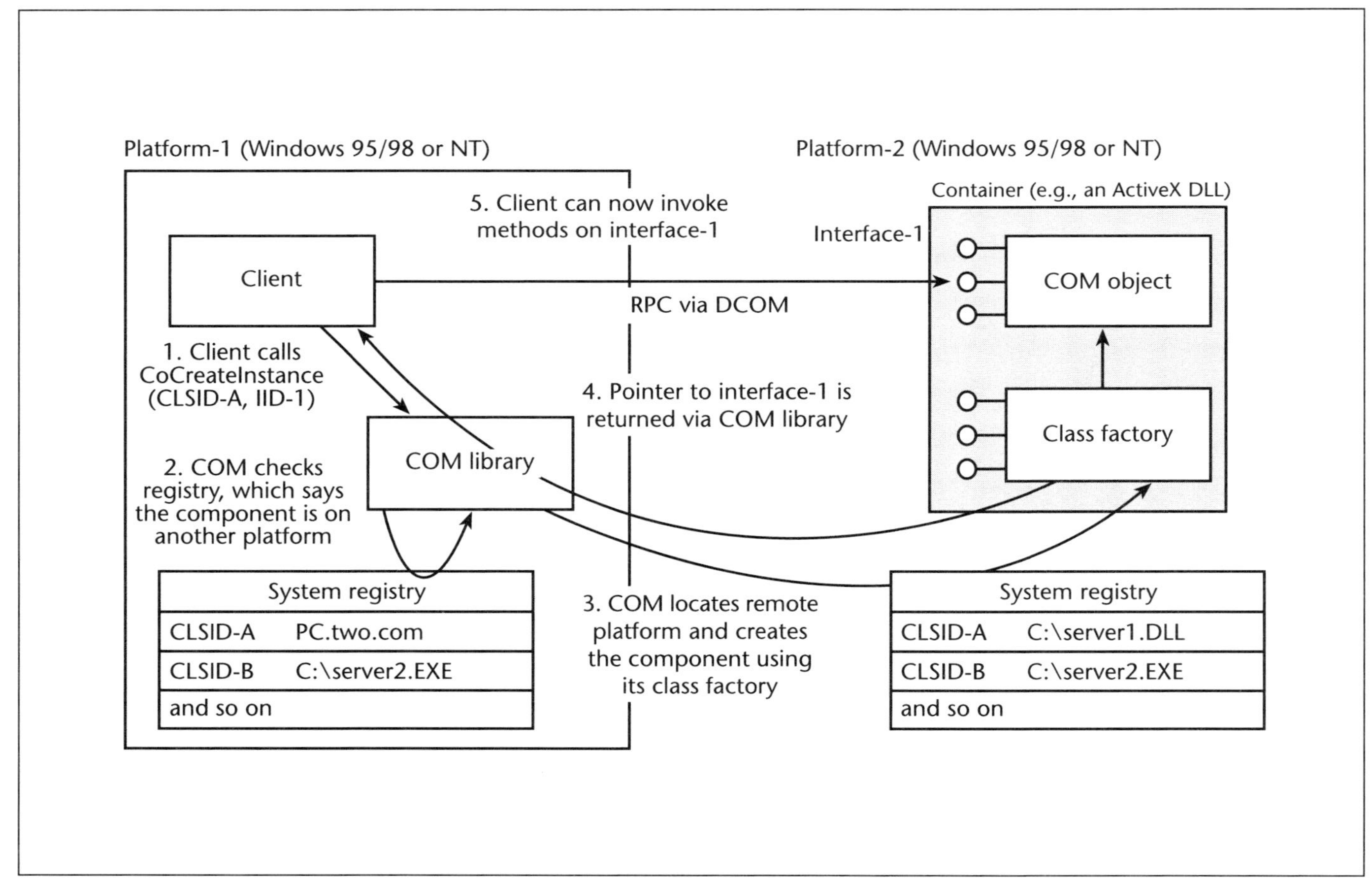

Figure 5.7 is starting to show up in lots of articles, and it provides one way of thinking about the options.

In effect, Figure 5.7 has focused many managers on the object transaction monitor (OTM), and most of the ORB vendors are now rushing to explain how they, too, are in fact offering an OTM. We've placed the names of some of the leading vendors of each type of product in the four cells of the matrix in Figure 5.7.

Although widely used, there are some things about this matrix that should cause some concern. For one thing, it's not obvious that data integrity increases as you move from RPCs to transaction processing monitors (TPMs). TPMs certainly guarantee that data has been handled correctly when it is updated, but they tend to be asynchronous systems. Consider the situation in which a message is waiting in a queue on an asynchronous TPM while another transaction is taking place

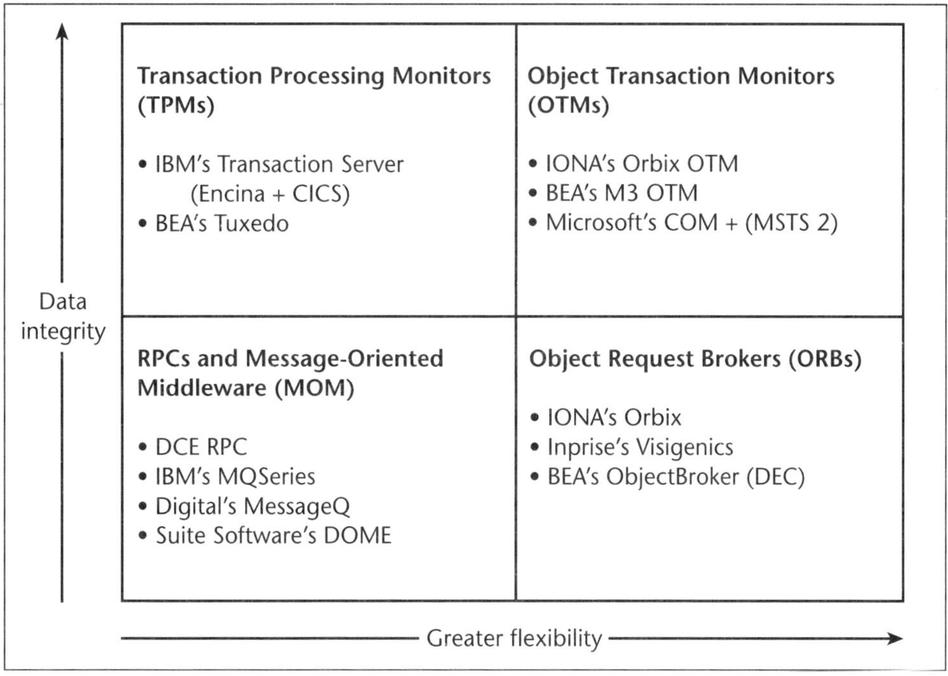

Figure 5.7 *The Object Transaction Monitor (OTM) matrix.*

using data that the message waiting on the queue is intended to update. With a synchronous RPC connection, you are more likely to update messages in sequential order and, thus, avoid certain types of data integrity problems. It might be better to stress that RPCs are slower, MOMs are usually faster, and TPMs are faster still. In other words, you might want to replace the data integrity arrow on Figure 5.7 with an arrow labeled "greater speed."

The other thing that bothers us is that the matrix ignores database options. Whenever you are shown a matrix that is designed to analyze a market, you should always ask yourself what the third axis would be if you could add one more axis. In this case, we would probably add an axis to capture the difference between (1) middleware that is independent of the application layer and (2) database, 4GL, or ODBC-based middleware. Oracle8 includes support for messaging and queues, and Oracle has plans to support CORBA in its management system.

In spite of these qualifications, however, we want to focus on ORBs, TPMs, and OTMs. In passing, however, we would stress that, for many companies, the Internet and middleware problems these technologies are designed to solve can be solved just as well with a database solution. This is an especially important option when you consider the new Internet server products that support transactions and ODBC integration and the greater familiarity of most developers with database approaches.

At this point, however, let's consider each of the four cells on the object transaction monitor matrix shown in Figure 5.7 to be sure we understand what's involved.

We looked at RPCs and ORBs a few pages ago, so we'll concentrate on the other categories.

MOMs

Message-oriented middleware (MOM) technology was developed to deal with asynchronous problems. In effect, a queue is placed between the client and the server. Messages, whether originated by an object, component, or a procedural system, are sent to the queue. The queue attempts to deliver the message to the target platform and continues to try until it succeeds. Similarly, responses are routed to the queue and then to the original process when that process is ready to receive them (see Figure 5.8).

This approach keeps messages flowing, even though two platforms may not be available for a direct connection. On the other hand, it isn't an approach you would want to use with a sequentially oriented application, since the initiating process has no way of knowing when the target might get the message.

An RPC system is like a phone call. You either get the other party and talk with them, or you don't. A MOM system is like a phone system that includes answering machines. You call the person you want to talk with. If the answering machine answers, you simply leave your message on the answering machine and figure the person you are calling will get back to you when they can. In many cases, the person may call back when you are out and leave a message on your answering machine.

One of the problems with MOM products over the last few years is that the vendors all supported proprietary approaches.

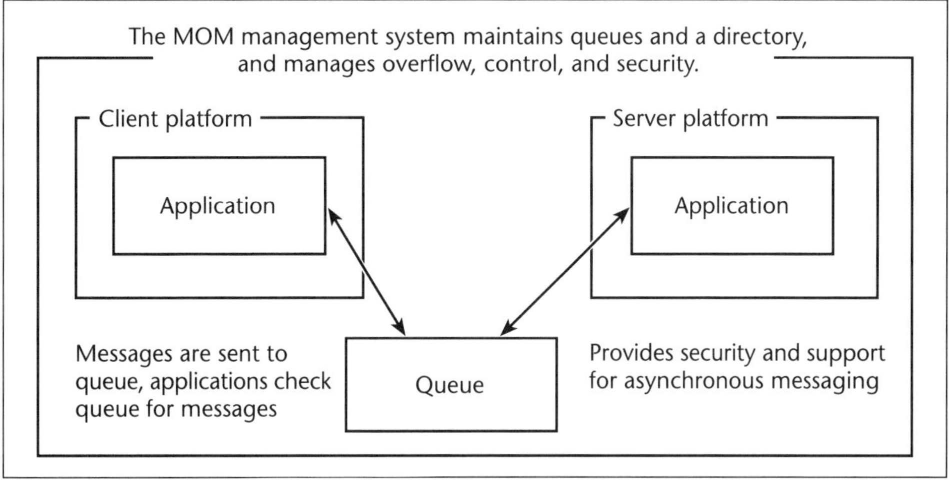

Figure 5.8 *A generic message-oriented middleware (MOM) management system.*

In 1995 they organized a vendor group and have been working to standardize on CORBA since then.

Transaction Processing Monitors

Transaction processing requires that a system handle lots of clients and that it do so with next to no errors. A transaction processing monitor makes this possible. Bank card terminal (ATM) systems that debit and credit bank checking and savings accounts provide a good example of transaction processing systems. A customer enters information into an ATM and offers to deposit a check in exchange for updating his checking balance. Rather than simply sending information to the bank mainframe saying, "Update Mr. X's checking account," the system relies on a transaction processing monitor. In effect, the information is sent to the monitor. The monitor communicates with the mainframe and determines that the account is there and can be updated. Then it processes the transaction in two phases. The mainframe is updated, and the check is accepted and a receipt given. If either side of the transaction fails, the entire transaction is rolled back.

Figure 5.9 provides an overview of a generic transaction processing monitor system. Transaction processing monitor systems are designed to handle large numbers of transactions while also ensuring that no data is lost or entered incorrectly. In other words, TPM technology provides the maximum data integrity while simultaneously scaling up to handle huge flows of data. IBM's CICS system is the best-known TPM system and is routinely used by banks to handle interactions between bank mainframes and hundreds of ATM terminals around the clock.

The first TPM systems were designed to link mainframes to dumb terminals and to communicate between known languages in known locations. Hence, interface languages were not required, and any bridges that were needed were handbuilt. A TPM system could be a synchronous system, but in fact most are asynchronous and, hence, most incorporate a queueing system within the TPM system.

In the era of client-server systems, several companies introduced more flexible TPM systems. Good examples are IBM's Transaction Server (based on Encina) and BEA's Tuxedo.

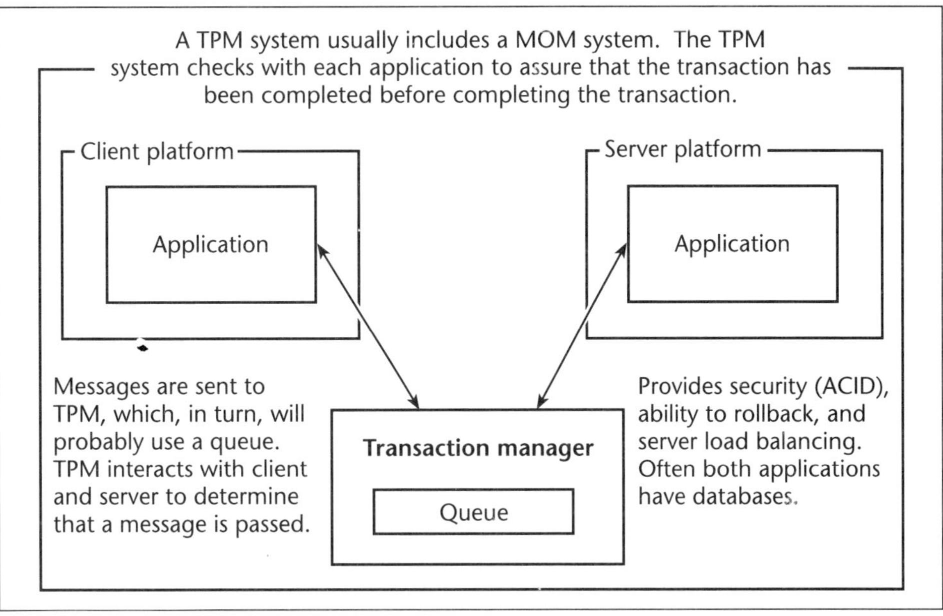

Figure 5.9 *A generic model of a transaction processing monitor (TPM) system.*

Object Transaction Monitors

We have finally arrived at the top right cell in the matrix—the new blend of technologies that are currently being referred to as object transaction monitors. This type of product is necessary if companies are going to use objects or components on Internet-based systems and want to handle large numbers of clients at once. More to the point, this approach is required if companies want to process financial transactions over the Internet.

Although it may be necessary, it isn't trivial. We have already noted that ORBs are based on RPCs and were largely conceptualized in terms of synchronous linkages. You could combine an ORB and a TPM and keep the interaction synchronous, but if you make it asynchronous, as most will, you introduce lots of technical problems.

The main difference between traditional TPM systems and object-oriented TPM systems is the presence of state in objects. In other words, a procedure is just a operation, but an object is both a set of operations and attributes with associated data values. When you combine an object system and a TPM system, you have to decide how to deal with state. ORBs keep each object's state in memory from the time the object is activated until the server explicitly destroys it. When large numbers of clients access many server objects, memory quickly fills and the system starts to page, which leads to sluggish response times. Any system that combines TPMs and ORBs needs to develop a way of managing client and server state.

If you ignore these technical details, however, the combination is obvious and straightforward. Objects are given interfaces via an IDL. Stubs, skeletons, and the other elements of a request broker are added to a system that includes a TPM with a queueing (MOM) system between the client and the server. Figure 5.10 illustrates a generic object transaction monitor system.

There are already two CORBA OTMs on the market and more will follow. Microsoft introduced an early version of a transaction server in 1997 and has been working on a MOM product to handle message queueing.

COM+ combines Microsoft Transaction Server 2.0 and message queueing with DCOM. Thus it will soon be possible to create asynchronous distributed COM applications.

5.4 COM Component Types

COM components take a number of different forms. VBXs, OLE objects, and ActiveX components are each examples of COM components that we'll consider in more detail.

5.4.1 *OLE*

OLE components are made up of one or more COM objects. OLE components were originally designed to modularize elements that could be used in the construction of compound documents. Thus, a spreadsheet could be an OLE component that could be inserted into a Word document. If you keep this

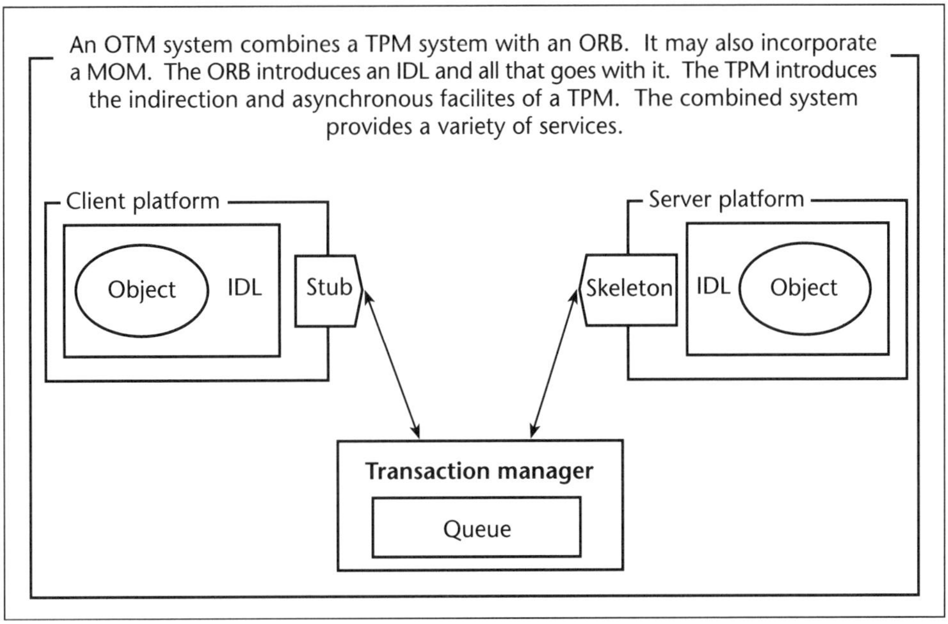

Figure 5.10 *An overview of an object transaction monitor (OTM) system.*

basic model in mind, it goes a long way toward explaining Microsoft's container/client/server vocabulary. The Word program/document became the container into which you placed the OLE component. The OLE component (a specific spreadsheet) had interfaces, but its methods were part of its server, the Excel program. By the end of 1995 Microsoft had taken to using the term OLE to refer to a wide variety of different components and techniques.

The idea of reusable binary components began with Visual Basic extensions (VBXs) that were developed in Microsoft's Visual Basic language. In this case, the VBX component functioned like a COM object, and Visual Basic provided the server or container. VBXs, however, were limited to Visual Basic. Although VBXs could serve a variety of purposes, they are primarily used to provide interface functionality.

Later, Microsoft developed OLE controls (which were usually written in Visual C++ and were often called OCXs). Like VBXs, an OCX had to support a large number of interfaces to assure that it would interact with other OCXs. Unlike VBXs, they could be written in other languages and run in other servers or containers, although Visual Basic and Visual C++ are the most commonly used containers. Several other vendors offer development packages that provide libraries of OLE controls.

When you look at OLE systems, there is often a clear distinction between the OLE component and its container (or document). The spreadsheet component that you inserted in the Word document relied on methods that were part of the Excel container (program), for example. When you turn to controls, however, there is essentially no difference between the container and the OLE object. The container and the object are conceptually independent, but, for practical purposes, they function as a single unit. Imagine a control to put a button on the screen. The code that puts the image on the screen and manipulates it is in the container while the interfaces are part of the OLE control component, but they are almost always treated as one unit. A control runs in the address space of its container. Events represent a message-passing mechanism used by components to contact their containers.

The first specification for OLE controls required that they support a wide variety of interfaces to assure they could be easily manipulated by users.

5.4.2 ActiveX Controls

When Microsoft decided to get serious about the Internet in late 1995, they decided to incorporate some minor changes and repackage the control aspects of the OLE technology under the name ActiveX. OLE has now reverted to its earlier usage, in the sense that the term "OLE components" now refers to modules used in compound document development. "ActiveX components," on the other hand, now refers to COM components that are used primarily for Internet development, and especially for the development of interface elements for Web browsers. (See Figure 5.11.)

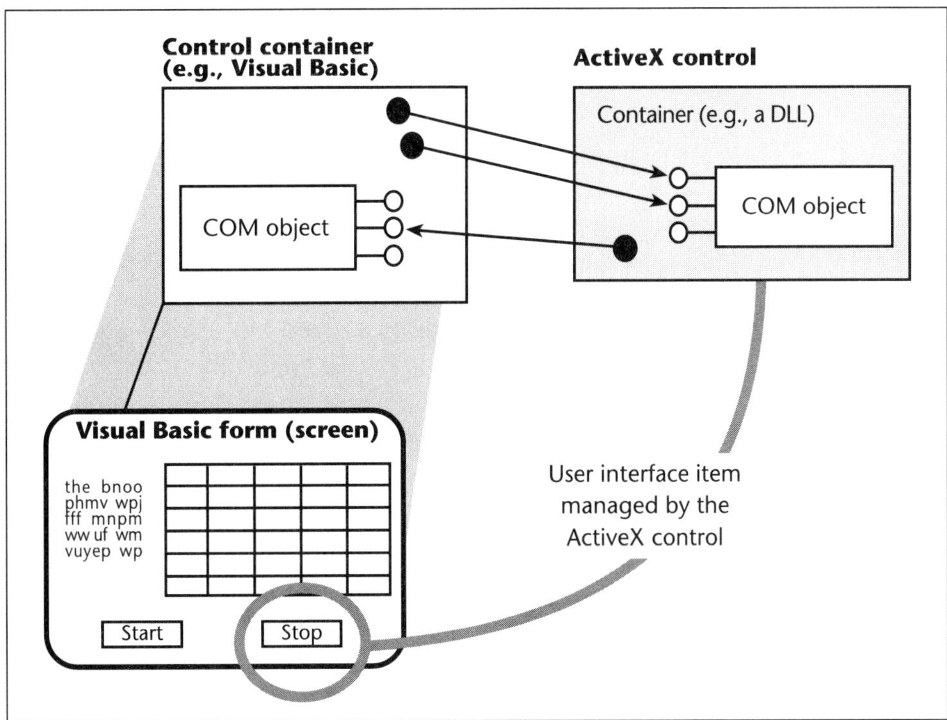

Figure 5.11 *An ActiveX control (modified after Chappell).*

Figure 5.11 shows an ActiveX control that is being used to provide a button for an interface developed in Visual Basic. The Active X control's server, in this case, is a DLL. The container is Visual Basic, which, in this case, contains other COM objects that help determine how the control will be positioned on the screen, and so on. The great majority of ActiveX controls are built as in-process servers. This means that they're implemented as DLLs with no separate local servers.

In the course of repackaging OLE controls for the Internet, Microsoft reduced the number of interfaces normally required of a component. They did this for two reasons: First, they eliminated some elements of COM that were specifically tied to Microsoft platforms to make ActiveX controls more generic. Second, they reduced the number of interfaces required to make it easier to move ActiveX controls across the

Web. Even with their reductions, the 28.8K limit on most Internet traffic makes ActiveX components time-consuming to load.

Figure 5.12 provides an idea of the actual interfaces that might be involved in the situation described in Figure 5.11. Notice that the container, Visual Basic, contains COM components, and that the ActiveX control also is a container and contains COM components. Also notice that the various interfaces (always identified by an initial *I*) include interfaces that were originally developed when the technology was still being referred to as OLE. If you calculate that each interface contains 5 method descriptions, then the container would have some 40 methods and the ActiveX control would consist of about 75 methods.

ActiveX components aren't restricted to a browser in the way that Java applets are. By their very nature, they need to be able to access system components to perform their tasks. To provide users with security when they download ActiveX components, Microsoft relies on *licensing*. All a license really tells the user is that the component was developed by a specific vendor and hasn't been changed since then. Microsoft argues that this is, in effect, what people currently rely on when they buy software programs—the reputation of the vendor and the fact that the package hasn't been messed with since it left the factory.

At the same time that a container attempts to create a new COM component, it checks an interface to determine if it is licensed to use that component. Some controls are sold with global licenses, for example, and others are licensed for specific machines, and so on. This, along with their binary packaging, provides security to the vendor, which is important for the creation of a market for components.

There are already a large number of VBX and OCX controls that you can buy from vendors, and there will soon be large numbers of ActiveX controls, as well. Appendix D provides a list of some of the Internet sites you can check to obtain information on ActiveX controls, or to buy them.

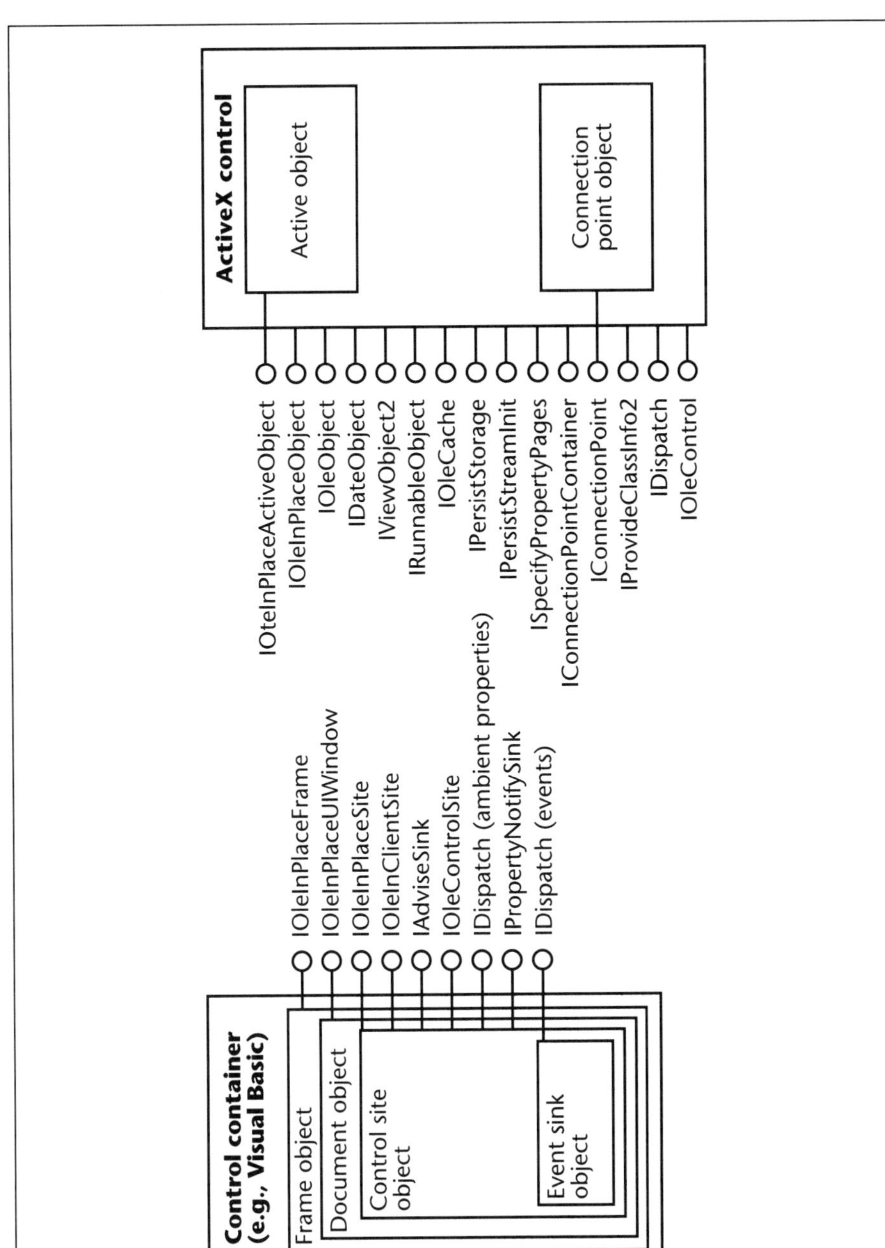

Figure 5.12 *Typical ActiveX control and control container interfaces (after Chappell).*

5.4.3 ActiveX Components and the Internet

Although ActiveX can be used for any Windows interface development, it is and will increasingly be tailored for Internet (or for intranet) development.

In Windows NT 4.0, there are special containers called Office Document and Office Binder. These are ActiveX containers that you can use to create generic containers for other ActiveX components. For example, instead of importing an Excel spreadsheet into a Word document, you can import both an Excel spreadsheet and a block of text into an Office Document. In a similar way, Microsoft's Internet Explorer 4.0 is a container into which you can import ActiveX controls.

The Internet Explorer browser is itself an ActiveX component that is designed to contain other components. The browser loads other components, including an HTML viewer, only as needed. If the browser wants to display HTML pages or a Java Virtual Machine component, the browser finds the appropriate components it needs to interpret HTML or a Java applet. Similarly, Internet Explorer (which is currently built into Windows 95/98 and Windows NT) can load a variety of other ActiveX components, including Excel or Word documents.

The current version of Netscape Navigator does not support ActiveX components; however, when Netscape announced that it would begin to focus more on tools for intranet applications, they also announced that future versions of its intranet development tools would support ActiveX components. In addition, SUN's JavaBeans component model is designed to encapsulate ActiveX components.

Figure 5.13 illustrates how the Microsoft Internet Explorer interface is based on a frame (container), which, in turn, is organized by a Web browser object. Other COM components or ActiveX components, including spreadsheets from Excel and text from Word, can be incorporated into a browser interface. Similarly, all of the various elements that make up the Microsoft Internet Explorer are COM components or ActiveX components.

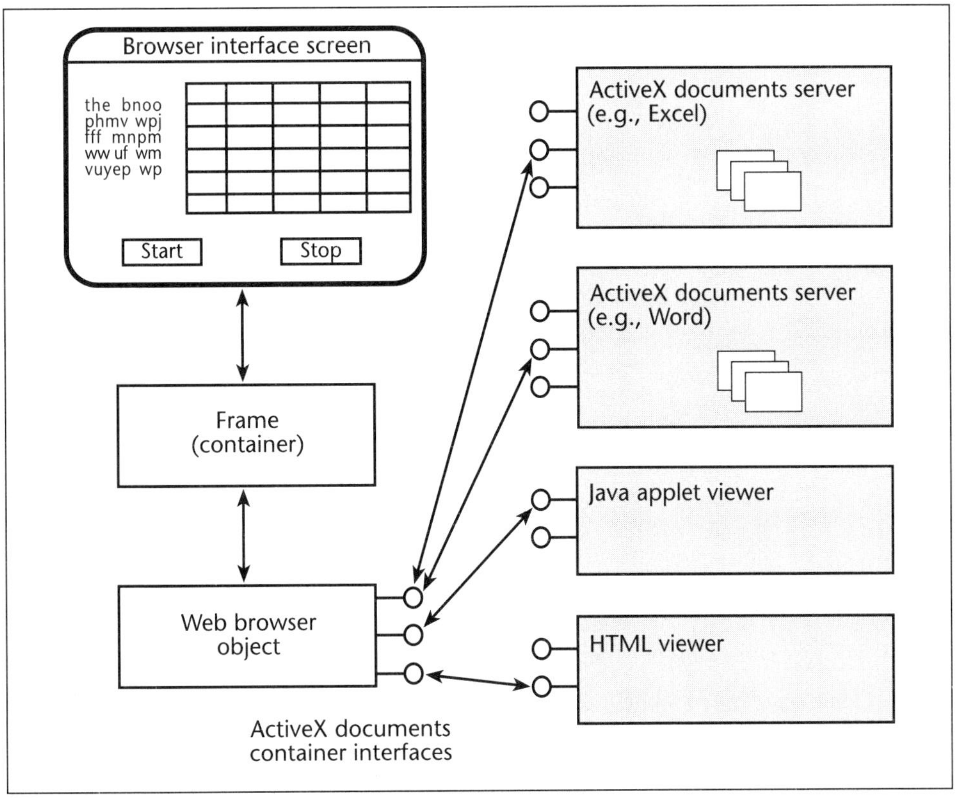

Figure 5.13 *Microsoft's Internet Explorer 4.0 is assembled from separate COM components (after Chappell).*

Microsoft created Visual Basic Scripting (VB Script) as a way to add functionality to Internet components. HTML supports the use of scripts embedded in components like Java applets and ActiveX components. A new version of VB Script, called ActiveX Scripting, has been tailored to support ActiveX components. The HTML viewer, if loaded into the Internet Explorer 4.0 container, can serve as a host for the ActiveX Scripting engine, which is also an ActiveX component. The ActiveX Scripting engine can then interpret any ActiveX scripts contained in any ActiveX controls loaded on the browsers.

If you want to learn more about either Visual Basic or COM, we've recommended some good books in the Bibliography at the end of this book.

5.5 COM+ and MTS 2.0

In the fall of 1998, Microsoft released the latest update to its COM system, which is often called COM+. In the spring of 1998 there was speculation that the new release of COM would include a run-time library and, perhaps, some features like inheritance that would help Visual J++ developers. The run-time library is still coming, but it will be in a later release. The release that occurred in the fall of 1998 included features that we considered earlier in this chapter. Microsoft Transaction Service (MTS), which had been released as an independent product, has been combined with COM so that COM can handle transactions and asynchronous communications. Similarly, Microsoft Message Queue (MSQS) has been added to COM to further facilitate asynchronous systems development. Along with MTS, COM+ includes load balancing—a process that shifts tasks between servers to maximize the efficiency of servers when they handle lots of transactions. COM+ also includes data caching and a new publish and subscribe mechanism that supports the use of events. Taken together, the new COM+/MTS package makes it a lot easier to build enterprise systems that can handle lots of simultaneous clients—just what's needed by anyone that wants to build Internet systems for e-commerce.

5.6 Infrastructure and Business Components

Visual Basic 6.0 and the COM component model support both infrastructure and business components. This distinction isn't technical, but refers rather to the use to which the component is put.

GUI components like ActiveX controls and COM components designed to access databases are good examples of *infrastructure components*. EXE and DLL components that capture business logic and represent actual things or concepts in a company, like an Employee, Plant, or Order component, are properly termed *business components.*

To date, Microsoft has focused almost entirely on using ActiveX and COM technology for infrastructure components. Only infrastructure components are packaged with current Microsoft packages like Visual Basic or Visual Studio. As Microsoft continues to ramp up for enterprise development, however, there are signs that Microsoft will put more emphasis on business components and evolve ActiveX and COM to better support business component development. An early effort is the Microsoft OLE Industry Solutions program. In this case, Microsoft is working with company groups from a number of specific industries to identify specific COM components that might speed application development within each specific industry.

5.7 Microsoft Repository

Visual Studio 6.0 comes integrated with Microsoft's new Microsoft Repository 2.0 and with Visual Component Manager, a tool that lets you examine the contents of the repository. Unlike a conventional database manager, a repository is especially designed to store components and information about application development efforts. More importantly, you can create components or application elements in one tool, store them in the repository, and then later retrieve them with another tool. Thus, you could develop a Visual Basic application, store it in the repository, and later access it in a Java development tool.

The latest version of Microsoft Repository supports versioning and is thus a major improvement over the first version of the repository. Using the versioning facility, you can create and store different versions of an application. More importantly, different individuals can check out and modify the same component, and the repository will keep track of all this for you.

If you are building a new application from scratch and working on your own, this will not make much difference to you. If you develop one application and decide to save the components for use in a subsequent project, however, or you are part of a team that is developing a large application, then the Microsoft Repository will probably play a major role in your development effort.

The Microsoft Repository consists of five parts: repository databases, a repository engine, a type information model, several specific tool information models, and several generic tools used with the repository (see Figure 5.14). In addition, there are the application development tools that use the repository. The repository engine will sit on top of any ODBC database. At the moment, Microsoft is demonstrating and shipping the repository using their own SQL Server RDB. The repository engine actually stores and retrieves objects and relationships from the database.

The metamodel is an abstract definition of all the types of information that the repository can handle. In effect, the repository can handle objects and components and relationships between them and all of the documentation needed to define a system.

A tool information model is an instantiation of the metamodel designed to interface between one or more specific tools and the repository engine. For example, the Microsoft Development Object (MDO) model is the tool information model that specifies the types of data of interest to Visual Basic programmers. Using the MDO in conjunction with a repository-aware VB product allows programmers to store VB information in the repository or to examine other VB data that has already been stored in the repository. Someone using the repository can select which of the various tool information models they want to include in their implementation.

Another information tool model is UML, which was developed by Rational, working in conjunction with Microsoft and several other vendors. The current version of Rational Rose for Visual Basic can use the UML model to store and retrieve UML data types in the repository.

Microsoft refers to its metamodel as the Type Information Model (TIM). In fact, Microsoft's Repository TIM is a version of Microsoft's Component Object Model (COM), and the only type that the Microsoft Repository actually stores is an

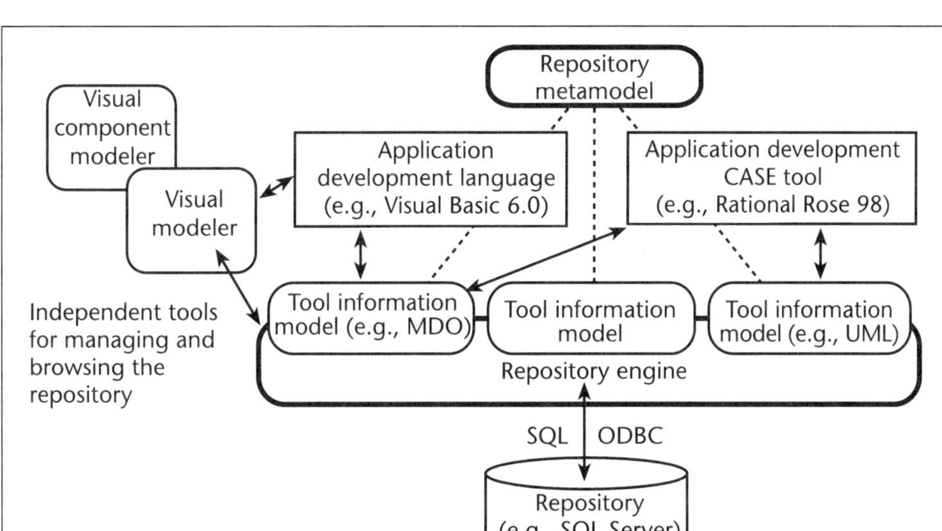

Figure 5.14 *The overall Microsoft Repository architecture.*

ActiveX component. In effect, the Microsoft Tool Information Model maps between tool metamodels by converting each tools construct to an ActiveX component. One "tool metamodel" that TIM supports is the OMG's UML notation. In effect, a developer can create UML diagrams in any of several CASE products and then store the resulting diagrams in the Microsoft Repository.

In addition to integrating the repository with its own development tools, Microsoft has worked hard to develop close relationships with a wide variety of other tool vendors. In February of 1997, at a general demonstration of the Microsoft Repository, five vendors who had been working with Microsoft demonstrated full cross-tool interoperability with each other's tools and with Microsoft's Visual Modeler, each putting data into the repository and retrieving data entered by other tools. The vendors involved in the demonstration included Logic Works, Popkin Software, Rational Software, Select Software, and Texas Instruments. As a result of this demonstration and a review of the repository specifications, some 40 vendors, including all the major OO CASE vendors, agreed to support the Microsoft Repository effort.

Rational Software has announced that they will migrate from their current proprietary repository and eventually use Microsoft's Repository as the native store for Rational Rose applications.

Microsoft Repository runs on both Windows NT and Windows 95/98. Microsoft has a deal with Platinum Technology that calls for Platinum to implement the repository on some non-Windows platforms at some point in the future.

6

Development with a Visual Modeling Tool

You may remember when Computer-Aided Software Engineering (CASE) tools were popular in the 1980s, and you might imagine that all CASE tools disappeared at the end of that decade. Those earlier CASE tools were primarily designed to develop traditional COBOL applications for mainframes, and they have, indeed, largely disappeared. Or you may be completely unfamiliar with CASE tools. In fact, there is a new generation of OO development products, called either OO CASE tools or, more often, visual modeling tools, that offer developers an excellent way of developing UML-based applications. Most vendors now prefer to refer to them as visual modeling tools, and we'll use that designation.

Visual modeling tools are software environments designed to facilitate the development of notation-based applications. They depend on diagrams that allow the developer to represent the analysis and design of the application. Once the developer has created diagrams to represent the application, the visual modeling tool then generates some or all of the code for the application. Visual modeling tools rely on OO notations, support OO methodologies, and generate OO code. There are a number of popular visual modeling tools. During the past half-dozen years, while a number of different OO methodologies have been competing with each other, most OO modeling tools supported several OO methodologies (e.g., Booch, Rumbaugh, Martin and Odell, and Jacobson) and generated one or more of the popular OO languages, such as Smalltalk or C++. Now, with the standardization of UML, all of the popular OO modeling tool vendors are in the process of introducing new versions of their products to support UML. (For a while, at least, most will support UML in addition to other methodologies and allow users to convert diagrams they may have developed in notations other than UML.) Similarly, the popularity of the Internet and Visual Basic has led many vendors to introduce versions of their products that support ActiveX components and generate Visual Basic code and HTML. And, perhaps most important of all, objects and components seem likely to make visual modeling tools the environment of choice for developers who want to assemble applications from preexisting components or business objects.

We believe that visual modeling tools offer a superior way to develop large object- or component-based applications. Before trying to justify that statement, let's take a very high-level look at how visual modeling tools work.

6.1 Visual Modeling Tools

Figure 6.1 provides an overview of a generic visual modeling tool. We have overlapped the various tools and utilities that make up the whole to suggest that different tools have different ways of arranging the various capabilities included within the tool.

In the center we show an environment that is usually presented as the main window of the tool. It provides the developer with a view into the tool and the various menus that

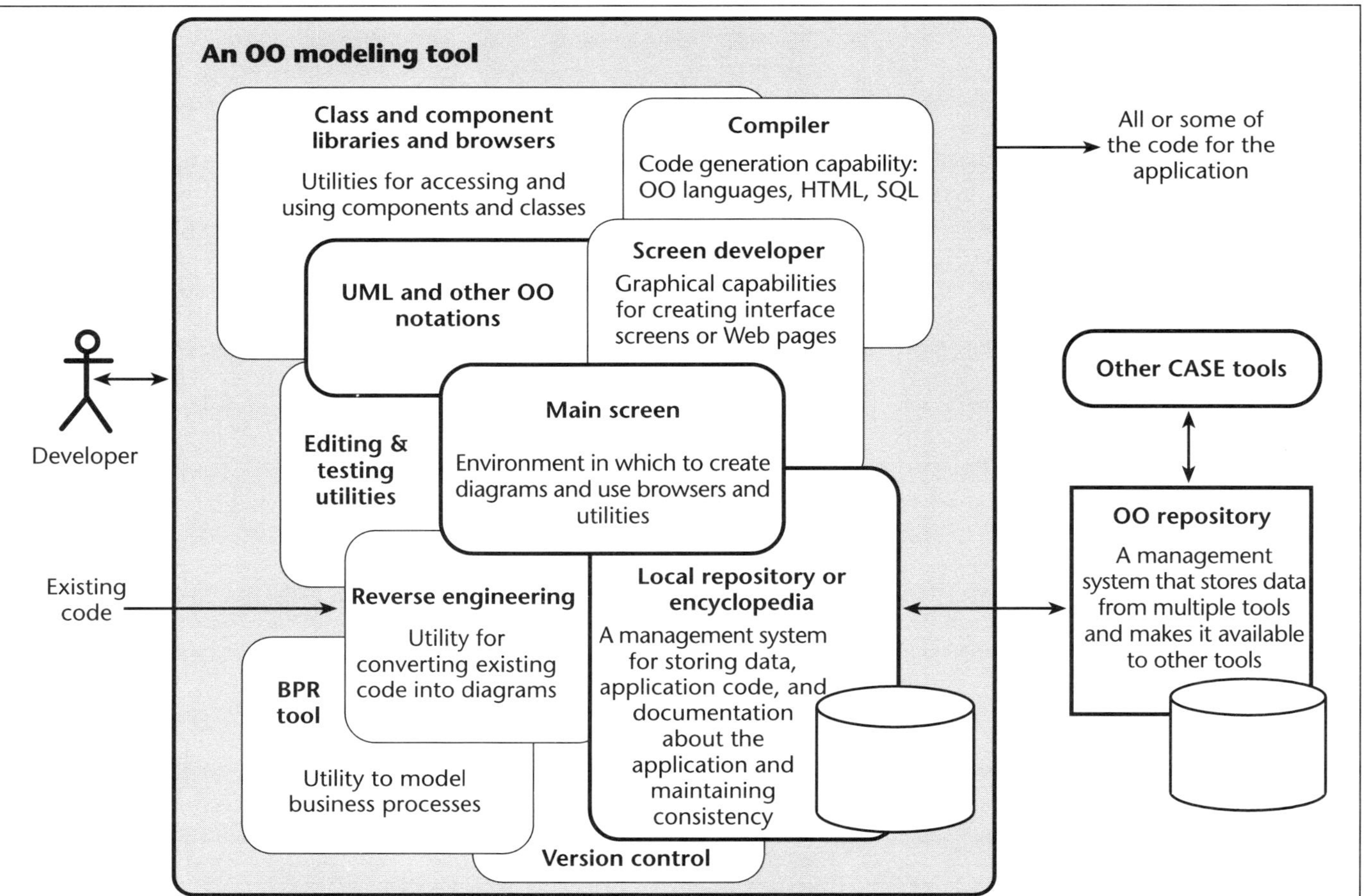

Figure 6.1 *The architecture of a typical OO modeling tool.*

allow the developer to access other capabilities. This environment lets the developer access special windows in which they can create different types of UML diagrams. If the tool supports multiple OO notations, it may allow the developer to change a diagram from one notation to another. When the developer moves from one diagram to another, the tool will usually "suggest" some of the structure necessary for the subsequent diagram. The tool can do this because it stores all the information about the application in a local repository. The repository management tool assures that names and diagrams are kept consistent.

In addition to supporting the development of OO diagrams, most visual modeling tools include facilities for developing screens (or Web pages). Most of these facilities rely on internal, or externally accessible, collections of GUI components or classes.

Visual modeling tools also provide editing and testing utilities and compilers. Some modeling tools can run applications from the tool environment, while others simply generate code that can be run anywhere. Most visual modeling tools can generate all types of code, from C++, Java, and Visual Basic 6.0, to HTML and SQL.

Some visual modeling tools provide reverse-engineering utilities that can convert existing code into diagrams. This is important if you create diagrams and then generate code and subsequently modify the code. In that case, you want to be able to put the code back into the modeling environment and recapture any changes you have made. Similarly, BPR facilities provided by some visual modeling tools allow the developer to model business processes in workflow diagrams and then convert them into object models within the visual modeling environment.

Finally, most visual modeling tools provide some kind of version control. This allows several developers to work on a single application simultaneously. Depending on how the control is set, a single developer can either select a module of the application to work on and lock it so no one else can access it, or several developers can work with the same module and then modify it according to some set of priorities.

The heart of a modern visual modeling tool is its *repository*. This is where the definitions, diagrams, and documentation for an application are maintained. The repository maintains internal consistency and alerts the developers to any potential problems. All visual modeling tools have their own repositories. Some use flat files, some use relational databases, and some use OO databases.

Recently, IBM, Microsoft, and Unisys have all introduced generic object repositories that can store information from multiple tools. All three repositories support UML, and most visual modeling vendors have announced they will support these repositories. Microsoft has based its repository on the Common Object Model (OLE, ActiveX). IBM and Unisys are both supporting an Object Management Group effort that will result in an alternative standard object repository model. Any of these repositories guarantees companies that if they use one visual modeling tool today and decide to use another later, they will be able to port their earlier applications to the new tool.

Let's see if we can summarize the advantages of visual modeling tools. They aren't especially useful for small, one-of-a-kind applications because it requires an effort to learn how to use a visual modeling tool effectively. On the other hand, if you are faced with a larger, more complex application, and especially if you are trying to develop an application with a team of developers, visual modeling tools can significantly reduce the time it takes to develop the application, while simultaneously improving the quality of the result. Moreover, increasingly, developers that plan to reuse components will use visual modeling tools to see how the components can be integrated with their new application.

Visual modeling tools decrease development time, once you know how to use them, because they provide an automatic way to move from one diagram to another and from diagrams to code. Moreover, since they manage the entire application, they assure that names and data types are maintained in a consistent manner. Similarly, they provide an orderly way for different developers to work on separate versions of the application while staying in sync with each other.

As developers increasingly usc components and business objects for application development, visual modeling tools provide the ideal way to coordinate the development of diagrams and the insertion of components and business objects into the overall application.

One of the reasons the older CASE tools failed was because IBM failed to deliver a universal repository (the AD/Cycle Repository) that it had promised by 1989. IBM failed because the world of software development was changing so fast that no one knew what would be needed by the mid-nineties. IBM started working on its repository in the mid-eighties. It was designed to support CASE tools that generated COBOL for mainframe applications. By the late-eighties, however, companies were moving from mainframes to client/server applications, to OO languages, and to windows-based GUIs. IBM's basic design simply wasn't flexible enough to handle all the extensions and enhancements that companies began to ask for. On top of that, as companies moved from COBOL-based mainframe applications to client/server systems, the market for tools to develop mainframe applications collapsed.

Now, near the end of the nineties, the world of software development seems to be settling down around a new paradigm. Development will increasingly be done with objects and components in languages like C++, Java, and Visual Basic. A wide variety of different platforms will be networked by TCP/IP, and the Internet will be used to solve distribution problems that frustrated earlier client/server developers. Applications will be more graphical and will depend on components to make interface development easier. And corporate applications will increasingly rely on the reuse of business objects to facilitate large-scale enterprise development.

In recognition of this, the object repositories recently introduced by IBM, Unisys, and Microsoft can do exactly what IBM had wanted to do at the end of the eighties. Today, a company can develop an application in UML and Visual Basic, incorporate ActiveX components, and store the resulting product and documentation in an object repository. Later, another visual modeling tool can withdraw some or all of that application and modify it for use in another application. This combination of a standard object notation, UML, visual modeling tools, an active components industry, and new object repositories has laid the foundation for a new generation of visual modeling tools. The fact that object repositories and libraries of components and business objects already exist, guarantees companies that this time the visual modeling products will be able to live up to their potential. This is why, in addition to discussing the use of UML in the development of a Visual Basic application, we decided to illustrate how UML could be used with two visual modeling tools to develop the same application.

6.2 Microsoft's Visual Modeler 2.0

There are a number of good visual modeling tools available. We decided to use Microsoft's Visual Modeler 2.0 and Rational Software's Rational Rose 98. We chose Visual Modeler because it comes with every copy of the Enterprise Editions of Visual Basic and Visual Studio. (If you don't have the Enterprise Editon of either product you can download Visual Modeler from the Microsoft Web site.) We chose Rational Rose because it is a natural extension of Visual Modeler.

In 1996 Microsoft and Rational Software worked together to create a lightweight version of their Rational Rose Visual Basic product. Rational contributed its knowledge of CASE tools and UML, and Microsoft helped with the developer interface. Microsoft termed the new product Visual Modeler. The first version of Visual Modeler generated Visual Basic code. The current version, Visual Modeler 2.0, supports both Visual Basic and C++ code generation.

The current version of Visual Modeler supports a limited set of UML symbols and the generation and reverse engineering of Visual Basic and C++ code. Visual Modeler is highly integrated with Visual Basic 6.0, and you need the language on your machine to use Visual Modeler. In Visual Basic, you can use the Addins menu to install the Visual Modeler interface and the Tools menu to start the reverse-engineering operation against a current project.

In an introductory booklet, Microsoft positions Visual Modeler this way: "Visual Modeler provides modeling tools for the analysis, design, and implementation of component-based applications." They also say: "Typically, we expect that developers will start using Visual Modeler by 'reverse-engineering' existing applications. This way, they can get a visual layout of the application's structure to easily determine where, or if, it needs enhancements or changes."

The developer interface on Visual Modeler is almost exactly like the Rational Rose 98 Visual Modeler and is tailored for three-tiered development. It is also tailored for development based on the use of ActiveX components. Visual Modeler is also designed to work with Microsoft's new Microsoft Repository.

If you open Microsoft's Visual Modeler and load an object model of one of the sample applications, you get a screen like the one shown in Figure 6.2. The first thing to notice here is the indented outline (the Browser) on the left side of the screen. Visual Modeler divides everything you might want to do into three high-level categories: *Logical View, Component View,* and *Deployment Model.* Each of these is subdivided into diagrams (the little hierarchy and component figures), packages (file folders) of classes, and dialog boxes that show the details of a class (e.g., *Customer*). The main class diagram appears within a larger context, in which the application is divided into three-tiers, including *User Services, Business Services,* and *Data Services.* (In effect, each of these areas are packages and the contents of each are represented by package icons on the outline to the left.) A developer can move classes into whatever tier he or she wants. By clicking on any class on the diagram you can reach a menu that allows access to a dialog box that describes the class.

The association lines on class diagrams can be solid to show a semantic relationship or dashed to show a dependency.

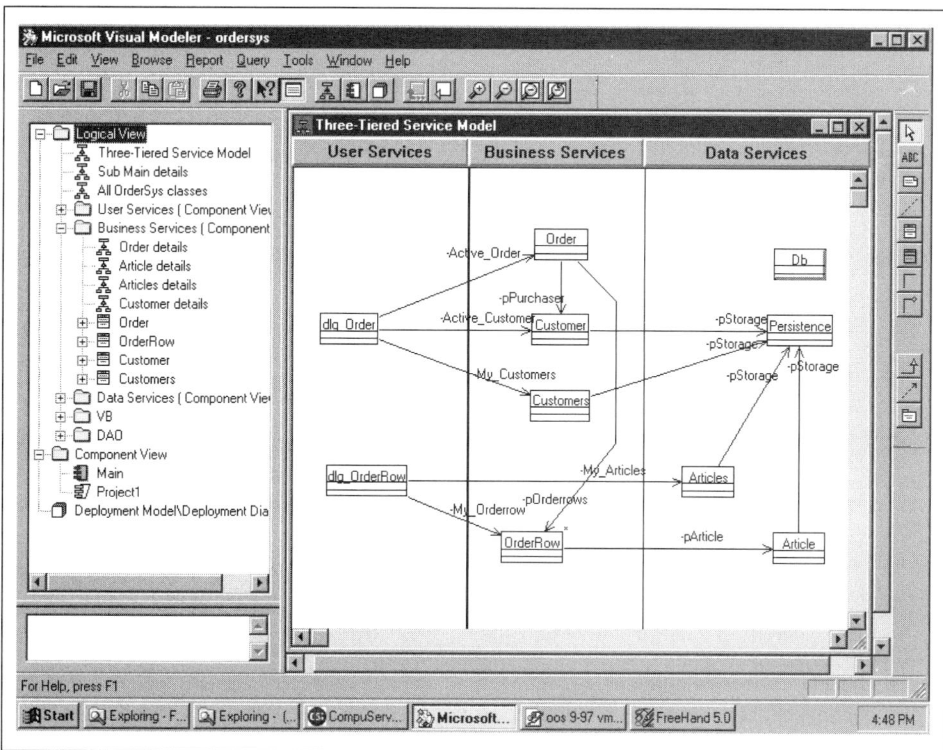

Figure 6.2 *A simple class diagram in Visual Modeler.*

They can be adorned with arrows to show the direction of flow, with diamonds to show aggregations, and with asterisks or numbers to show the multiplicity of an association. Inheritance can be shown, but is confined to special situations in Visual Basic. Class utilities and association classes can be shown. Classes can be expanded to show the attributes and methods. Attributes can be shown to be public, private, or friend (protected in UML). Stereotypes are introduced to allow developers to designate methods as <<get>>, <<set>>, or <<let>>. Most of the more elaborate UML class notation, beyond these basics, are unavailable in Visual Modeler. Visual Modeler supports UML component notation, including the extensions for indicating threads of control, and deployment notation.

Figure 6.3 illustrates a detailed look at the Order (Form) visual interface (*dlg-Order*). This class is pictured on the class diagram, but is, in fact, an ActiveX control. The developer identifies the type as "control," which, in turn, means that Visual Modeler won't generate Visual Basic code for this class. Thus, Visual Modeler allows the developer to create applications that incorporate ActiveX components and to reverse engineer applications that include components. You can drag-and-drop a COM component on the Visual Basic Component Diagram. Visual Modeler will automatically reverse-engineer the component and model it for you, giving you the Visual Basic extensibility classes you can use.

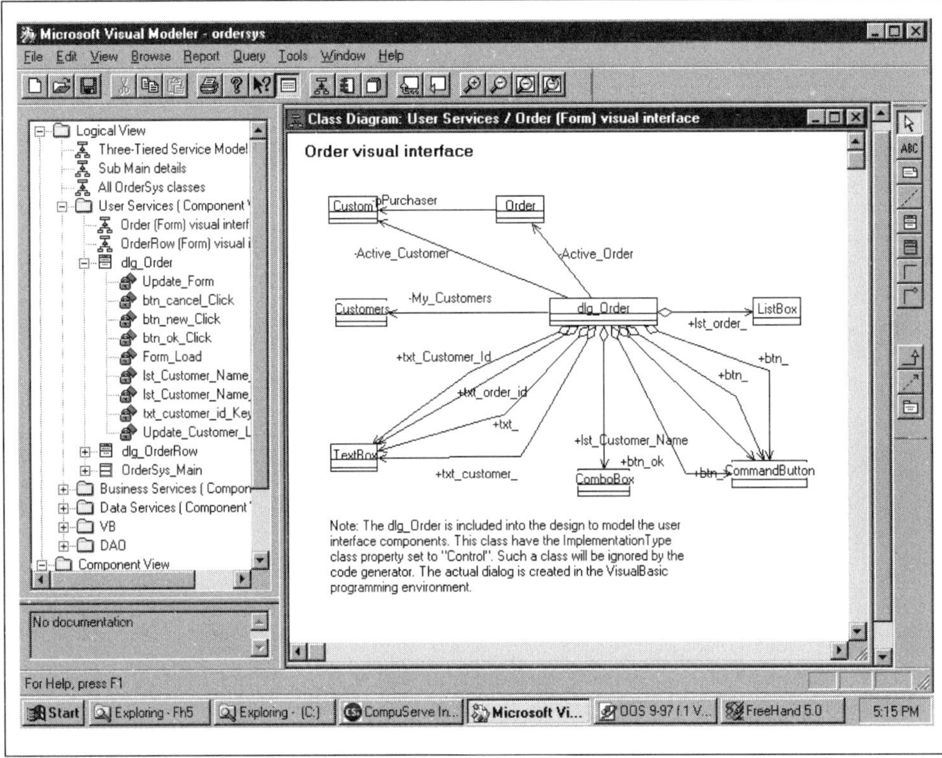

Figure 6.3 *Visual Modeler's Order (Form) interface.*

Visual Modeler does not provide an environment in which to create ActiveX components, but Visual Modeler is running on top of the Visual Basic programming environment in Visual Studio 97, and you can easily create an ActiveX control in that environment.

Visual Modeler provides *wizards* for creating classes and for generating code and reverse-engineering code. For the simple tasks we tested Visual Modeler with, the wizards were easy and efficient. When you do reverse engineering, the main screen shows a hierarchical browser diagram of the Visual Basic code with modules, forms, and ActiveX references shown. The developer can examine the code units, select units to reverse engineer, and assign units to a tier for display on a class diagram. The entire reverse-engineering process is simple and very intuitive.

In discussing Visual Basic, we mentioned that there are some awkward things about the language as far as an OO developer is concerned. The need to work around the lack of class methods is a good example. Problems associated with Forms is another. Visual Modeler allows the developer to design an OO application in UML and then generates Visual Basic code that incorporates the work-arounds. This is controlled by tables that specify Visual Basic stereotypes for UML constructs. Most of these are set as defaults, but the developer can modify them as needed, just as the developer can modify the link between class and the Visual Basic stereotype "class module" when using an ActiveX component and set it to "control" instead.

Visual Modeler, like Rose, comes with its own flat-file repository. In addition, Visual Modeler is designed to integrate with the Microsoft Repository. Since many other visual modeling tools, including all the major OO CASE products, are scheduled to work with the Microsoft Repository, at some point in the future you should be able to move classes from a tool like Rose or Paradigm Plus (written in another language) into Visual Modeler and generate Visual Basic code from them.

Figure 6.4 indicates which UML diagrams that Microsoft's Visual Modeler supports. The only diagram that it supports

Rational's UML Documentation 1.0	Rational's Rose 98	Microsoft's Visual Modeler
• Use case diagram	• Use case diagram	
• Class diagram	• Class diagram	• Class diagram
• Sequence diagram	• Sequence diagram	
• Collaboration diagram	• Collaboration diagram	
• State diagram	• State diagram	
• Activity diagram		
• Package diagram	• Package diagram	• Package diagram
• Component diagram	• Component diagram	• Component diagram
• Deployment diagram	• Deployment diagram	• Deployment diagram
	[3-tier diagram]	[3-tier diagram]

Figure 6.4 *Diagrams supported by UML, Rose 98, and Visual Modeler.*

that results in code generation, and is supported during reverse engineering, is the class diagram. The package, component, and deployment diagrams are only used for documentation.

Since many procedurally oriented developers seem to prefer sequence (event-trace) diagrams to class diagrams, we suspect that many Visual Basic developers won't find Visual Modeler as much help as they might expect when it comes to analyzing new applications. On the other hand, anyone new to OO development should enjoy being able to generate a class diagram from existing Visual Basic code and see exactly how the various classes and ActiveX controls are related.

Visual Modeler is a powerful adjunct to the Visual Basic programming environment rather than as a full-scale CASE tool itself. It provides a very nice way of visualizing an application that is a mix of classes and components. It clearly wouldn't be much help for a complex development task when you need all the additional perspectives that other UML diagrams offer, but it will probably be very useful to developers that want to quickly load existing Visual Basic code and get an overview of its class model. More important, it can help Visual Basic developers generate OO code without having to worry about some of the work-arounds they would have to deal with if they did it by hand. This tool is a step toward a new generation of component browser and assembly tools that will begin to appear in the next few years.

And the best news: for all practical purposes Visual Modeler is free—it comes with Visual Studio 6.0 and with Visual Basic 6.0.

6.3 Rational Software's Rational Rose 98

Microsoft's Visual Modeler was designed for Microsoft by Rational Software. In effect, Microsoft's Visual Modeler is a "lite" version of Rational's Rose for Visual Basic. In 1998, Rational Software introduced a new version of its modeling tool, Rose 98, which combines the features of Rose for Visual Basic, Rose for Java, and Rose for C++. Using Rose 98, you can develop diagrams and then generate or reverse engineer any of three languages: Visual Basic, Java, or C++.

Consider Figure 6.5, which shows a Rose screen with the same class diagram that we showed in Visual Modeler. The first thing you notice is how similar the two screens are. Rose uses the high-level class diagram frame that divides the application into three business tiers. It also uses a browser that divides all the modules into *Logical View, Component View,* and *Deployment Model.* Then consider what's different. Rational has added a fourth high-level view, the *Use Case View.* Similarly, on the top tool bar, in addition to the icons for class, component, and deployment diagrams, they have inserted buttons for use

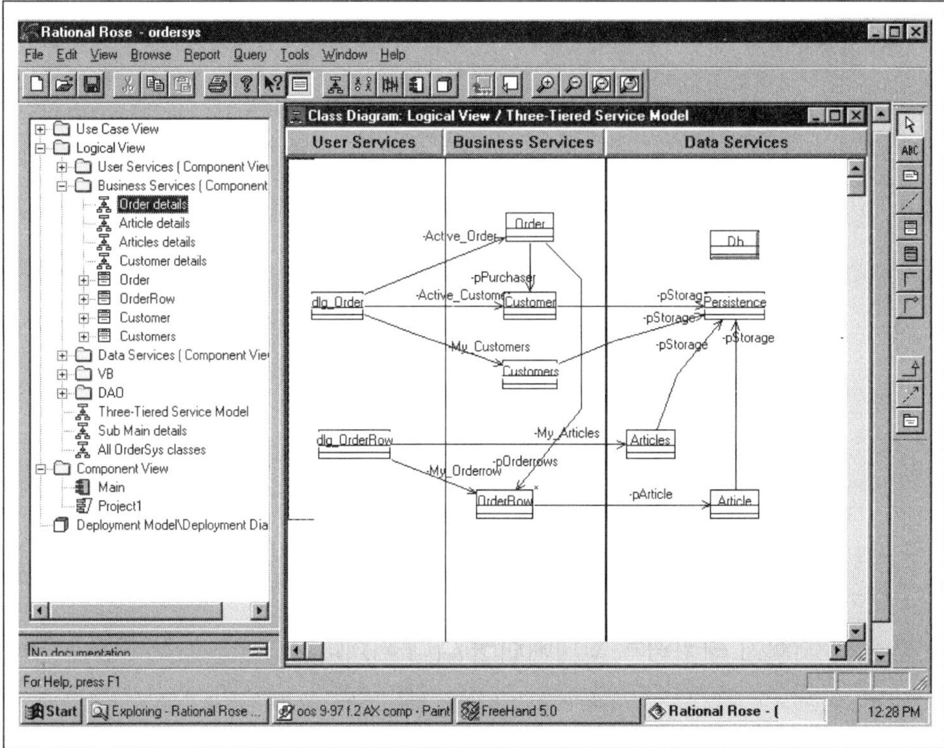

Figure 6.5 *A class diagram in Rose.*

case diagrams and for interaction diagrams (i.e., for sequence and collaboration diagrams). Rose also supports state diagrams. Since state diagrams are only used when you want to study the changes in a single class, this diagram is accessed from a menu when you are already looking at a class diagram.

A glance back to Figure 6.4 makes this point. Visual Modeler only supports one type of analysis diagram: the class diagram. Rose 98 supports five: use case diagrams, class diagrams, state diagrams, sequence diagrams, and collaboration diagrams. Rose 98 doesn't support activity diagrams, which was the last diagram added to the UML notation.

Figure 6.6 illustrates two of the additional diagrams supported in Rose: a use case diagram and a sequence diagram. With this set of diagrams, a developer is in a much better position to analyze a complex application from several perspectives.

If you were to examine the pull-down menus of Rose 98, you would also find that Rose 98 supports three different notations: UML, Booch, and OMT. Moving from one diagram to another is as fast as clicking the switch. This probably won't mean too much in this specific tool, since there aren't that many Visual Basic applications that have previously been developed in one of the older notations, but it's still a nice feature.

As with Visual Modeler, a developer must use Rose 98 in conjunction with Microsoft's Visual Basic 6.0. Similarly, Rose 98 supports the generation of Visual Basic code for classes, attributes, and method names, and the reverse engineering of Visual Basic code. In addition, Rose 98 generates all the other

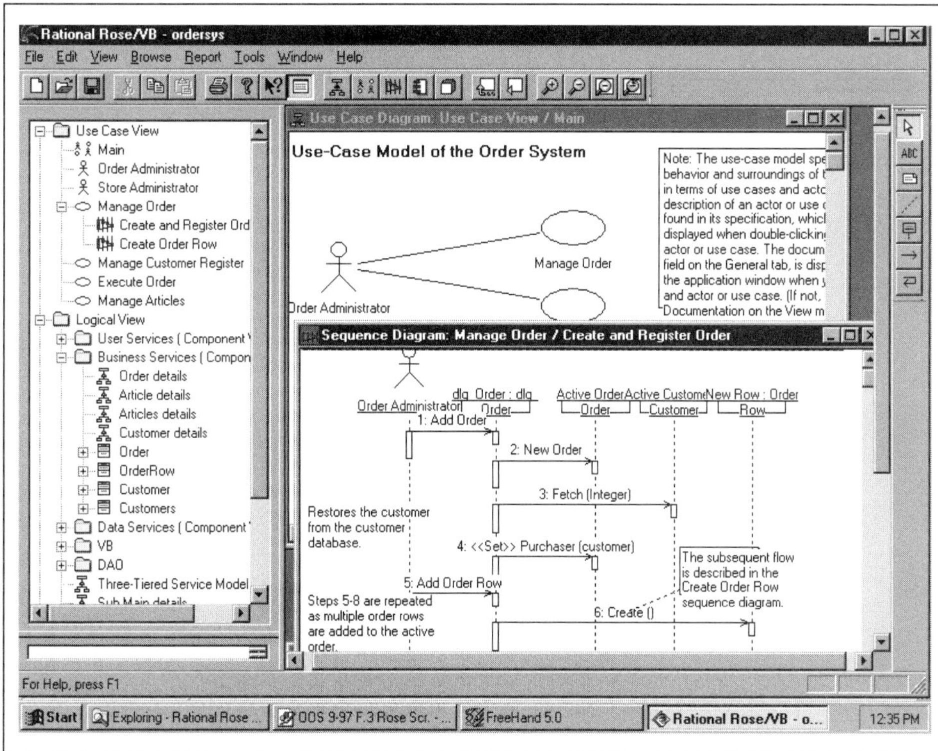

Figure 6.6 *Rose 98 with use case and sequence diagrams.*

Visual Basic elements including forms, property pages, and so on. And, like Visual Modeler, a developer must select options to determine how methods are interpreted in Visual Basic.

Figure 6.7 illustrates the diagrams supported by Rational Rose 98 and indicates which diagrams can generate others, which can update others via the repository, and which are involved in code generation.

In both Rational Rose and Microsoft's Visual Modeler it is only the class and component diagrams that are actually involved in capturing code or generating code. In other words, if you reverse engineer an existing Visual Basic application, all you get is a class and a component diagram. You don't get sequence or collaboration diagrams, and so on. Thus, if all you want to do is generate Visual Basic code, you only need to create a class and a collaboration diagram.

The additional diagrams in Rational Rose do allow you to refine the class diagram indirectly by adding information to the repository, which in turn updates the class diagram. Thus, you can add a method to a sequence diagram, and that method will appear on subsequent class diagrams. The component diagram tells how you are going to group the classes.

You might have expected that Rose 98's dynamic diagrams would allow for a more comprehensive code generation, but that isn't the case. Thus, even though you spell out quite a bit of detail on a sequence diagram about how a method is to work, you can only generate method names, not actual procedural code.

If you create a sequence diagram, you can use that to automatically generate a collaboration diagram and vice versa. You can't use Rose 98 to generate any other complete diagrams. For example, you can't use a class diagram to generate a basic collaboration diagram, or a package diagram to generate a component diagram.

If you create a use case diagram and then want to create a use case description of a generic scenario for one of the use cases, you can use a description block in Rational Rose. In most cases, however, it will prove too small, and you will need to move to a text processor, like Microsoft Word, to create your use case descriptions. (This external file can be linked to

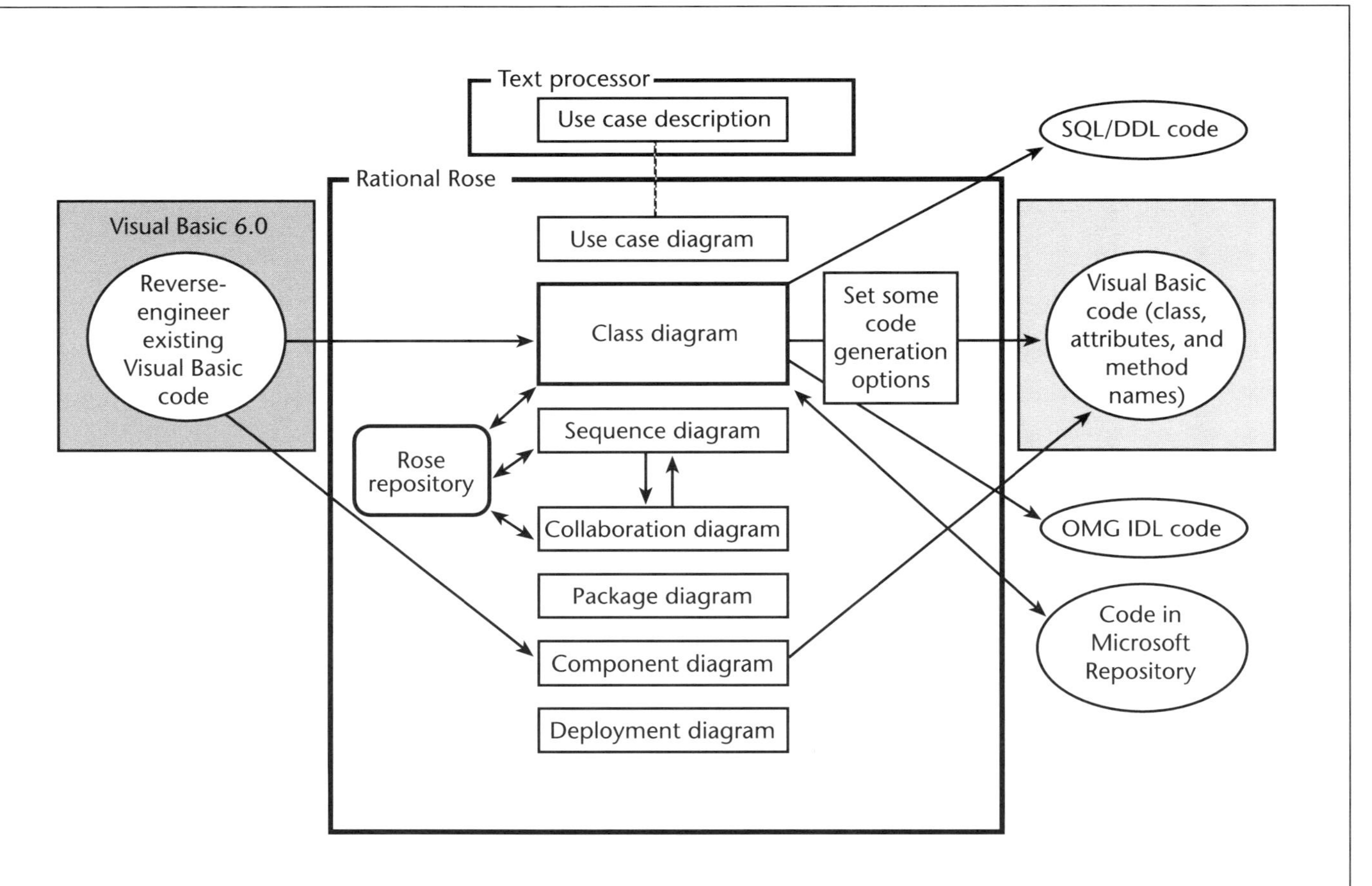

Figure 6.7 *Rose diagrams used to generate code.*

your use case descriptions. (This external file can be linked to the use case diagram via Rose, but it's still a bit of a hassle.)

You can author an Active X component in Rose 98 by setting the stereotypes of a component to represent it as an Active X DLL, but it's a rather indirect approach compared with Visual Basic or tools specifically designed to generate components.

One last thing to note on Figure 6.7: You can't simply generate Visual Basic code from a class diagram. Unlike a pure OO language in which all methods are represented the same way, Visual Basic supports a variety of different procedural statements. The developer must set some code generation options in dialog boxes associated with the class diagram in order to let the compiler know how to convert different methods, and so on.

You can print copies of any diagrams to serve as a kind of documentation, but you can't make changes to a sequence diagram and then see the changes reflected in a class diagram or in code that is generated.

Anyone who first learned about CASE tools by using Texas Instrument's Information Engineering Facility (IEF) or IntelliCorp's OO modeling tool PowerModel, as we did, will think that Rational Rose 98 is a relatively weak tool. IEF and PowerModel keep all the different diagrams in sync with each other and use the information on the dynamic diagrams to generate all the code needed to run an application. To be fair, however, they generated COBOL for mainframes. None of today's popular visual modeling tools attempt anything like what IEF or PowerModel could do. Instead, tools like Visual Modeler and Rose use diagrams to generate classes, attributes, and method names and leave the task of writing the specific method code to the developer.

The best defense we might offer is that, as developers move toward more extensive component-based development, they will use OO CASE tools less for code generation and more for the arrangement of components. Both Rose 98 and Visual Modeler can reverse engineer code that includes ActiveX components and generate code that incorporates ActiveX components. The tools don't actually generate the ActiveX components, of course, since they are already complete modules of code. If an application were largely made up of components, then obviously you would not be as concerned with generating code as with arranging the links between components and creating a few new classes for the new application.

Rose 98 will generate SQL and database code to store persistent classes in a relational database. Rose 98 has its own flat-file repository, but it also supports the Microsoft Repository. It not only supports ActiveX components, but it also supports JavaBeans and the OMG's CORBA middleware.

One of the areas where Rose 98 is clearly superior to Visual Modeler is in providing support for team development. Different developers can lock segments of an application while they work on them, and the tool maintains versions to assure smooth updates. Clearly, if you were working on a corporate application of any size and were concerned with maintenance, you would want to use Rose 98 and not Visual Modeler.

Rose 98 uses its own repository, but you can also store information in Microsoft Repository. Thus, a developer could create an application in Visual Modeler, store the application in Microsoft Repository, then use Rose 98 to access the application from Microsoft Repository, and then modify the application in Rose 98.

Rational Software and Grady Booch started the effort to create a single OO notation. By recruiting first James Rumbaugh and then Ivar Jacobson, Rational acquired the expertise to create the Unified Modeling Language, which was formalized by the OMG in 1997. One of Rational's considerable achievements was getting Microsoft to embrace UML and use it in their Repository and in Visual Modeler. The market has rewarded Rational for its creative efforts by making the Rational Rose line of OO CASE tools the best-selling products in the CASE market. Moreover, Rational Rose 98 with its new interface and support for multiple languages is the best OO CASE environment Rational has produced.

Rational Rose 98, Enterprise Edition, is available for Windows 95/98 and Windows NT. A single unit currently costs $3,600. For more information, check the Rational Web site at *www.rational.com*.

6.4 Developing an Application with Visual Modeler

If you download a copy of Visual Modeler and load the software on your computer, and then double-click the Visual Modeler icon, you will arrive at the main window, which will appear as it does in Figure 6.8. We won't go into all the items on the Visual Modeler menu. Instead, just to provide you with a high-level orientation, we'll consider how we want to use the Visual Modeler tool and then consider some of the menu items we would use to accomplish each task.

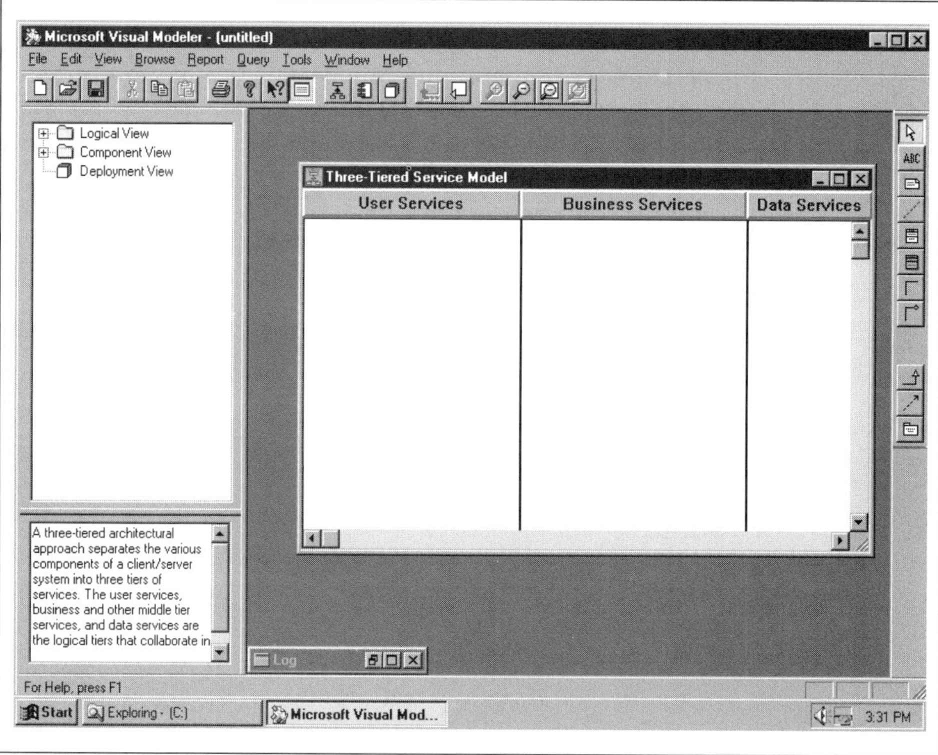

Figure 6.8 *The main window in Visual Modeler.*

Our overall task will be to use our generic, iterative OO methodology to create a Visual Basic Web application. We've broken that task up into six general steps:

1. Create a new project in Visual Modeler.
2. Analyze the application by creating UML diagrams.
3. Generate the code needed for the SalesWeb application.
4. Enhance the application in Visual Basic.
5. Reverse engineer the code back into Visual Modeler.
6. Convert appropriate classes to components.

Step 1: Create a New Project in Visual Modeler

To begin the actual development process, we start by creating a new model that will contain the diagrams, code, and other information that we will enter about our SalesWeb application. As we create new diagrams, Visual Modeler will check with the information already in our model to assure that it's consistent with what we have already entered.

You create a new SalesWeb model by clicking on the New option in the File menu (see Figure 6.9). We won't take advantage of it in our example in this book, but Visual Modeler makes it easy to reuse code from previous application development efforts. If you had previously created class diagrams in prior models made in Visual Modeler (or Rational Rose), you could reuse these classes rather than having to create them from scratch.

Step 2: Analyze the Application by Creating UML Diagrams

The second step is the heart of our SalesWeb analysis and design effort. We create UML diagrams to describe the problem. In fact, as you will see when we actually develop some diagrams, as we place an element in a diagram, we not only can place a box on the screen to represent a class, but also specify some of the class's attributes and operations, indicate

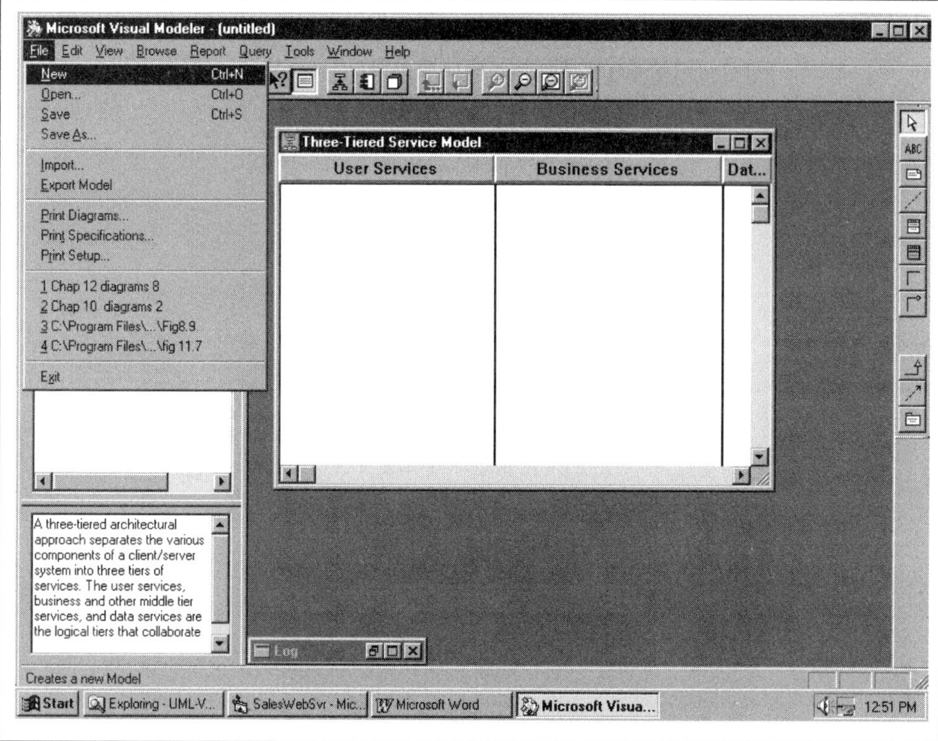

Figure 6.9 *Creating a new application in Visual Modeler.*

whether they are public or private, assign them a data type, and so on.

We won't go into the details of how we create UML diagrams or how we move from one diagram to another at this point. We'll consider the generation of diagrams and what gets transferred from one diagram to another when we consider specific UML diagrams in subsequent chapters.

If we had already done a previous application or if our company had a database of business objects, we could use those in our application. Similarly, we will be able to use Visual Basic classes and components when we create screens for our application.

Step 3: Generate the Code Needed for the SalesWeb Application

To generate Visual Basic code in Visual Modeler, you can use the Code Generation Wizard to define the mapping between components in your model and Visual Basic code. If you choose not to define the mapping, Visual Modeler will use a set of preestablished code generation options to translate your classes, properties, and methods into code.

Step 4: Enhance the Application in Visual Basic

Once you have generated Visual Basic code, you can run the application in user environments and test it. If necessary, you can modify it.

Step 5: Reverse-Engineer the Code Back into Visual Modeler

When you are satisfied with the application code you have generated, you can then reverse engineer the code back into Visual Modeler. You can refine your model, and then generate code again. Known as "round-trip engineering," this iterative process of modeling, implementing, and refining continues until your application is finally complete.

Step 6: Convert Appropriate Classes to Components

Once you are satisfied with the class structure of an application, you should consider which, if any, classes can be grouped together and converted into components. Components form the natural modules or packages of a Visual Basic application. In addition, components are easier to reuse in other applications. On the other hand, components are more difficult to modify, so you should develop them until you are sure that your application is in final form.

6.5 Creating an Application

In Chapter 7, we'll begin to consider UML diagrams and create an application. As we create each diagram, we'll return to Visual Modeler or to Rational Rose and explain how each diagram would be created in one or the other visual modeling tool. Whenever we can, we'll use Visual Modeler. Whenever we are considering diagrams that are not supported by Visual Modeler, we'll switch to Rational Rose.

The Visual Basic code we generate can be examined using either tool. Obviously if you load it into Visual Modeler, you'll only be able to examine some diagrams, while if you load it into Rational Rose, you'll be able to examine all the diagrams we discuss in this book. But, in either case, you can create the application using either tool, and you can examine the code using either tool.

7

Use Case Diagrams and Ideal Object Models

Ivar Jacobson introduced use cases in *Object-Oriented Software Engineering: A Use Case Driven Approach*, a book he coauthored. The book also introduced a general OO methodology, usually called OOSE. In OOSE, you begin with use cases and then proceed to develop a complete OO application. In the last two years, many different methodologists have embraced use cases as a way to do an initial analysis of the problem to be modeled. In 1996 Ivar Jacobson joined Rational Software and was part of the team that developed the UML notation. Thus, use cases are now a part of UML.

Many developers employ use cases as a way to do a requirements analysis, which is what we are going to do. Then we'll proceed to develop what the old OOSE methodology called *ideal object models*. An ideal object model is the first step in the transition from the use case model to a class diagram. We'll rely on use cases to help us specify system requirements. We'll use the ideal object models to get an overview of the kinds of classes we are likely to need when we switch from use cases to class diagrams. Once we develop rough versions of the ideal object models, we'll switch to UML class diagrams, in Chapter 9, to refine our understanding of the classes we'll need in our final system.

A use case approach requires that you begin by creating one or more use case diagrams and then create a use case description (or scenario) for each use case–actor relationship you identify. Later, both the use case diagrams and the use case descriptions can be used to generate an ideal object model. Or you can move directly from the use case descriptions to UML class diagrams. We'll consider the steps in order.

7.1 Use Case Diagrams

A use case diagram provides a functional description of a system and its major processes and places a boundary on the problem to be solved. It also provides a graphic description of who will use the system and what kinds of interactions they can expect to have with the system. In use case modeling, entities outside the problem area that are going to use the application are called *actors*. Processes that occur within the application area are called *use cases*.

A rectangle with rounded corners represents the application or system. An application can have one or more use cases. Things inside the rectangle are to be included in the application to be developed, and those outside are to be excluded. The name of the system or application to be developed is written just inside the top left corner of the system rectangle.

An actor may be a person, another software application, or a hardware device. All are represented by a little stick figure of a person. Although it's unnecessary, most developers tend to place people who will use the system on the left of the diagram. Hardware, other applications, and systems personnel who will use the system are typically placed on the right side of the diagram.

The use case itself is represented by an oval. The name of the use case is written inside the oval (or, sometimes, below the oval). A use case is not a class or object. It is a process that satisfies some need of a user of the system.

A line connects the actors and the use cases they interact with. You can label these interaction lines. Later, a written description of the interaction between the use case and the actor will be prepared. This written scenario is called a use case description.

An initial use case diagram is an abstract model of the system. An actor describes types of users, and a use case describes a generic process that satisfies the needs of those who will use the system. (See Figure 7.1.)

Use case diagrams can go beyond simply representing isolated processes and can show relationships between processes. We won't go into these advanced use case diagramming techniques in any detail, since most developers simply rely on basic use case diagrams.

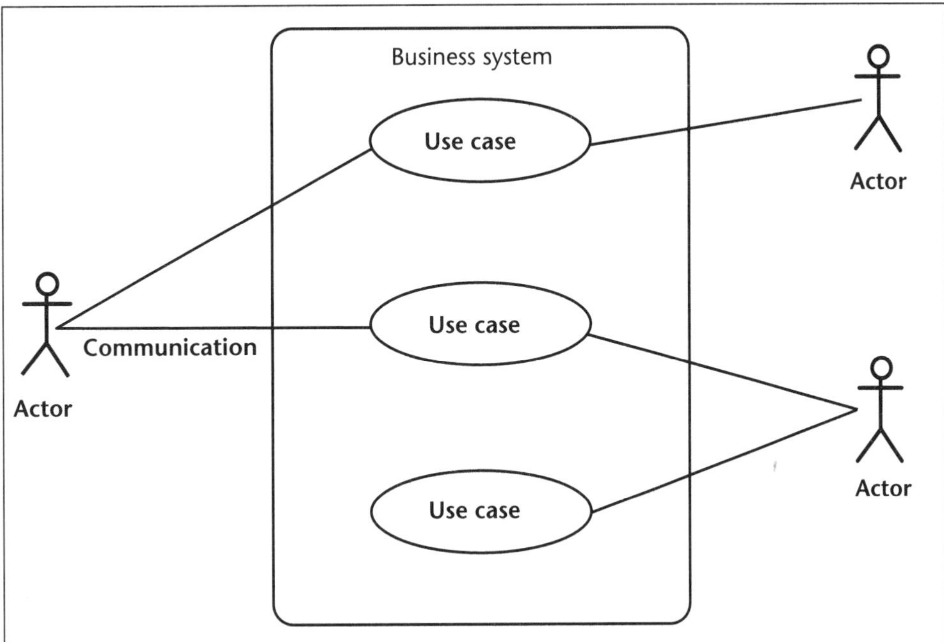

Figure 7.1 *A use case diagram.*

7.2 Moose's SalesWeb System

In order to have something concrete to discuss as we consider developing an OO application, we'll use an imaginary problem. We'll assume Moose's Furniture is an established office furniture supply company that sells to companies throughout North America. Moose's maintains a central warehouse facility, and that facility is managed by a database application that was developed many years ago. Moose's also has a general accounting and billing system that they maintain at corporate headquarters. Both applications were written in COBOL, and both rely on small IBM mainframes and DB2 relational databases. At the moment, the accounting system evaluates and approves orders, then passes them to the warehouse department to be fulfilled. When the order is actually shipped, the warehouse inventory system not only updates its own inventory, but it passes the shipping information to the accounting system so that the accounting system can initiate billing.

Until recently, the corporate sales staff, which is divided into eight regions, relied on paper, fax machines, and clerks to transmit orders from the field and to maintain records on the performance of salespeople in the regions. The larger regions had regional offices, and salespeople often maintained desks there, but in most regions the salespeople operated out of their homes. The salespeople call on office furniture companies, individuals, a few large corporate customers, and some governmental agencies.

In 1997, Moose's management group decided to conduct a Business Process Reengineering (BPR) study of its sales process. A team of salespeople, managers, accounting people, inventory people, and information systems analysts was assembled. The current sales/order fulfillment process, described in the activity diagram shown in Figure 7.2, was broadly defined and included activities that occurred in the sales department, the accounting department, the manufacturing department, as well as activities that used information systems. (We won't consider activity diagrams in detail until later in the book. Activity diagrams are commonly used by BPR teams to represent the flow of business processes.) The common thread that

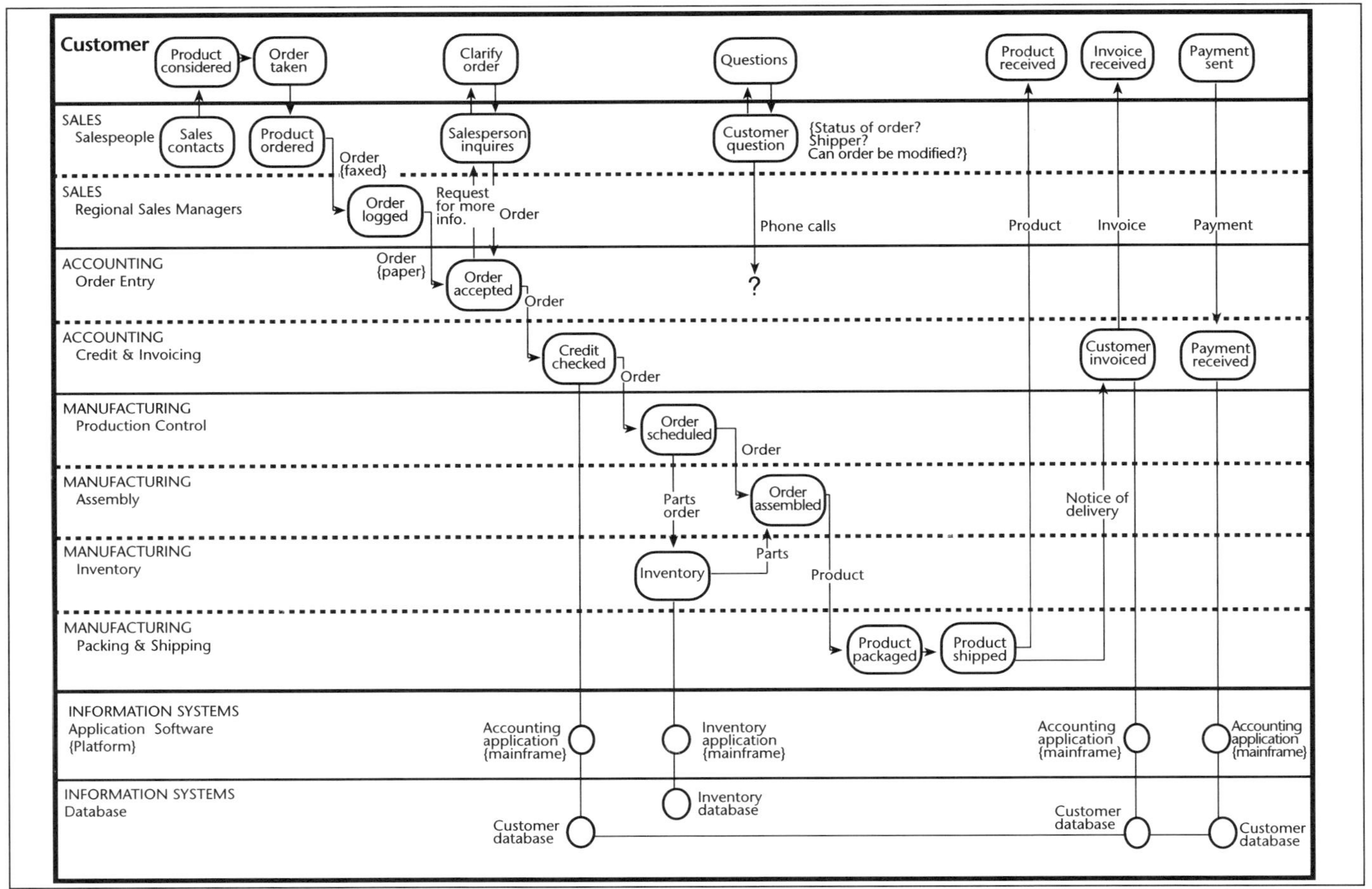

Figure 7.2 *Moose's current sales process.*

tied them all together was a sales process that began when a customer placed an order for new furniture and ended when the furniture was delivered and the company received payment for the order. (Some companies refer to this process as the order fulfillment process.)

The workflow shown in Figure 7.2 leaves out lots of details. An entire additional workflow diagram could be constructed just to show how an order is assembled or how an order is accepted. Similarly, a separate diagram could be developed to show how regional sales managers and salespeople negotiate annual and quarterly sales goals, how sales managers log orders against quotas, and how sales managers and regional managers meet to discuss how salespeople are performing.

What this high-level workflow diagram did show Moose's BPR team, however, was that interactions among salespeople, their managers, and accounting were all being handled by faxing paper forms back and forth. It also highlighted the fact that when customers asked salespeople questions, salespeople were often at a loss to find someone within Moose's who could answer the customers' questions. The paperwork was often in transit between one department and another, and in any case, it was impossible to identify who might have a specific order, since each department had several people working in parallel. (Several company surveys showed that this problem was a considerable source of irritation to both customers and salespeople.)

A survey of several dozen sales organizations, conducted by a BPR consulting company, indicated that as a result of their approach, Moose's employed more regional sales managers than did their competitors. Moreover, it was obvious that the regional sales offices where salespeople met to fill out forms, get the forms reviewed by sales managers, and then fax them into accounting were a major overhead cost. In addition, many argued that the time the salespeople spent traveling between their homes and the regional offices could be better spent visiting potential customers. Finally, everyone complained that the process took too long.

One key breakthrough came when the BPR team decided that salespeople should send the same order to both accounting and inventory at the same time so that order fulfillment and billing could then proceed in parallel. Accounting was a little nervous about the possibility of accepting orders from uncreditworthy customers. But they agreed that if they could check and be sure that the customers were known and were ordering within approved credit limits, parallel processing would significantly speed things up while exposing the company to only minor risks.

Eventually, after several different versions had been studied, the BPR team arrived at the workflow diagram pictured in Figure 7.3. At first glance, the new organization might appear more complex because there are more lines going up and down the chart. In fact, the new design relies on letting salespeople, accountants, and inventory people interact directly with the existing computer systems—in effect, letting them communicate with each other via computer postings. The new design assumes that the accounting and inventory systems will be tied together and pass information back and forth. More important, it assumes that regional sales offices will be closed and that regions will be consolidated so that fewer sales managers will manage more salespeople.

The BPR team decided that salespeople should be given laptop computers with modems. Henceforth, salespeople will be able to enter orders while they are at a customer's site, get approval and shipping dates, and then submit all the "paperwork" automatically. To facilitate this, Moose's decided to set up an Internet server that can interface with the salespeople in the field and with the existing mainframes that run the legacy accounting and inventory applications. Since the sales system could keep track of how each order was handled and when, salespeople could contact the sales system directly to find out the status of any given order.

The BPR team also assumed that a new software package would allow managers and salespeople to create sales quota agreements on-line and then allow both managers and

Figure 7.3 *Moose's new sales process.*

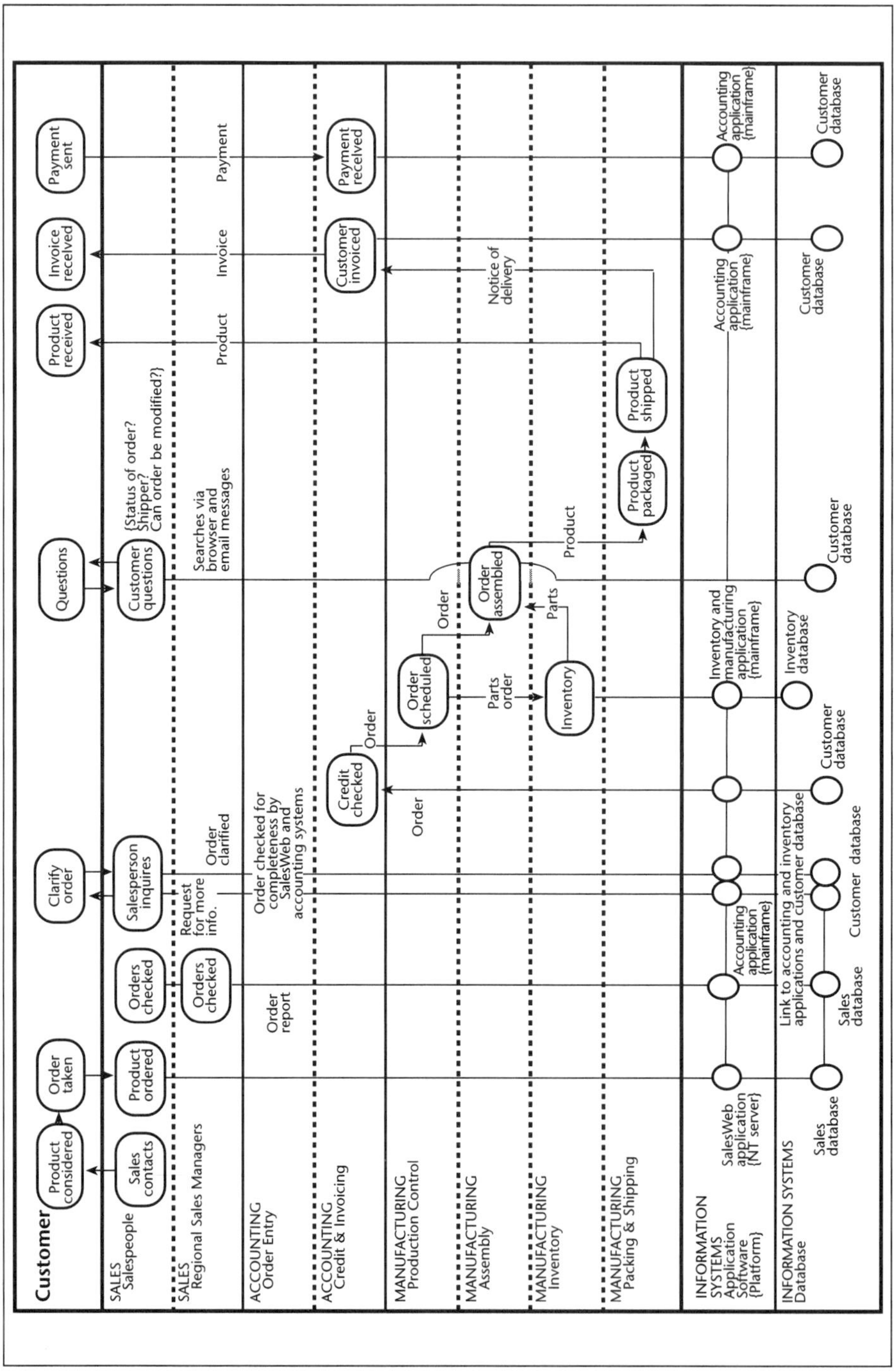

salespeople to track their progress toward fulfilling their quotas by checking the on-line quota system.

The BPR team came up with a long list of changes they wanted to make and tasked different managers with preparing to implement different aspects of the system. The only subset of the BPR effort that we will follow from this point on is the effort involved in developing a software application that would sit on the new Internet server and on salespeople's laptops and allow them to report sales orders and check their success in meeting their quotas. The task also included an interface to let regional managers check on the success of individual salespeople or all the salespeople within a region in meeting their sales quotas.

The BPR team that handed the assignment to a Moose's information systems (IS) group didn't try to pin down lots of details. They didn't consider, for example, whether the salespeople should have an application on their laptop machines or simply have a browser. It was assumed that the sales application development team would conduct their own analysis and design effort and figure out the answers to these and other questions. The BPR team did specify that when a salesperson contacted the server, the server, in turn, would contact the accounting system and verify that the customer was placing an order within the credit limits established by the accounting system before the order was passed to the inventory system for processing.

In addition, the BPR team considered allowing some of Moose's customers to link directly with Moose's system to place their orders. In the end it was decided that neither Moose's nor their customers were ready for that change yet, but the BPR group asked the IS team to use techniques that would facilitate customer access at some point in the future. The IS group decided that this request suggested that they use Internet technology and Visual Basic 6.0. A Visual Basic application would run on any of the desktop machines that the company was acquiring and could be served by the NT machines that the company was acquiring to replace its UNIX servers. In any case, if the people in the field used browsers, it wouldn't make any difference what kind of hardware the customer had. Moreover, Visual Basic, being an OO language, would facilitate rapid development and reasonably rapid alteration when the time came to modify the application to support customer access.

Moose's IS department created a sales application development team to undertake the software development effort. The team accepted the assignment and decided to undertake a use case analysis as a preliminary step before beginning a more detailed OO analysis phase. Before proceeding to use case analysis, however, the IS team spent quite a bit of time trying to come up with a good name for the system they planned to develop. Someone suggested the Moose's Distributed Sales Reporting and Management System—MDSRMS—but everyone agreed that didn't have any pizazz. Finally Annie Moose, the company's CEO, suggested they call it the SalesWeb System, and everyone agreed that that name was the one they should use.

7.3 A Use Case Diagram of the Moose's SalesWeb System

Figure 7.4 provides a high-level use case diagram of the simple sales system that Moose's BPR team assigned to the SalesWeb software development team. The large round-cornered rectangle, labeled "Moose's SalesWeb System," defines the boundary around the problem. Things outside the boundary are not going to be part of our application development effort. In our diagram we show four actors. One is the salesperson. Another is the regional sales manager. The other two represent computer systems that the SalesWeb system will interact with. One is Moose's existing accounting system, and the other is the existing warehouse inventory system.

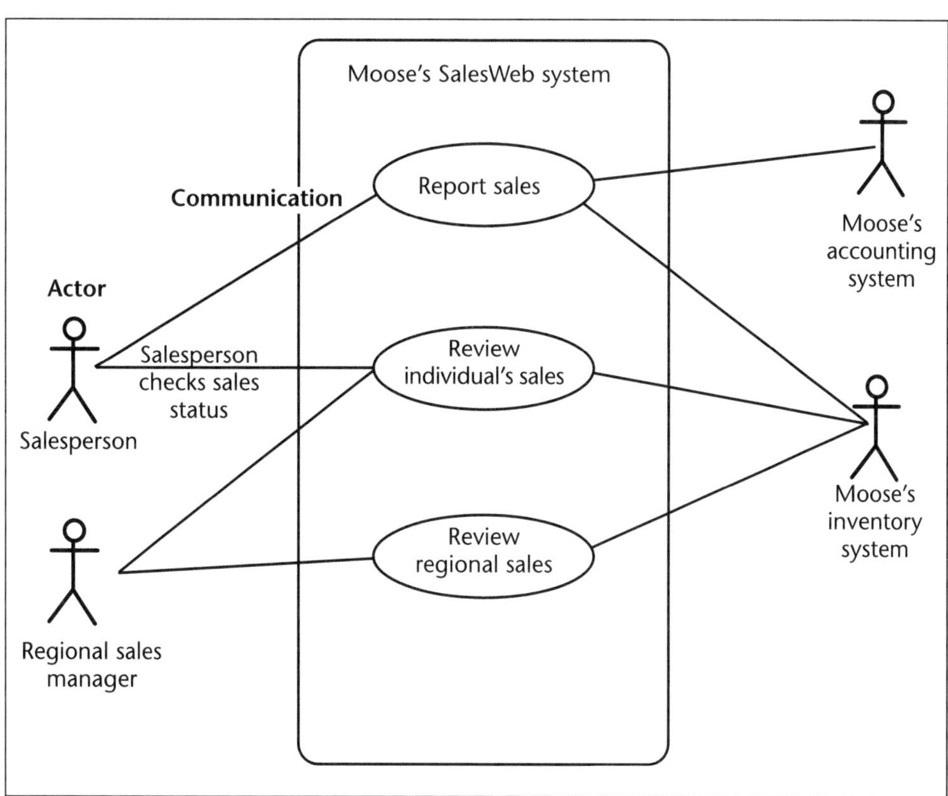

Figure 7.4 *Use case diagram of SalesWeb system.*

The use case diagram in Figure 7.4 shows three use cases: *Report Sales, Review Individual's Sales,* and *Review Regional Sales.* Each of these use cases is a process that could contain several classes. Some of the classes that will need to be modeled might occur in more than one use case. So, again, don't think of use cases as classes or objects. They are processes that occur in response to a stimulus by an actor. The same actor can be involved in more than one use case. We sometimes speak of the relationship or communication between an actor and a specific use case as a role. In this example, one role the salesperson can perform is to submit a new order. Another role involves checking a report of his or her sales performance.

7.4 Clarifying Our Vocabulary

One of the problems that any software development effort faces involves deciding what to call things. It's easy to get into a lot of confusion if things aren't clear. In the real world, the SalesWeb developers would have to work lots of these details out for themselves. To simplify things for you, however, we'll try to be a little more explicit before proceeding any further.

Figure 7.5 provides an expanded diagram that combines a use case and some icons to illustrate all of the elements that will occur as we talk about our sales system. On the left side of the diagram we can see the customer who wants to order furniture. Then there's the salesperson who will submit the order. The salesperson will use a laptop that will either have an application or a browser. In any case, the laptop will have some kind of client software. In the middle section is the

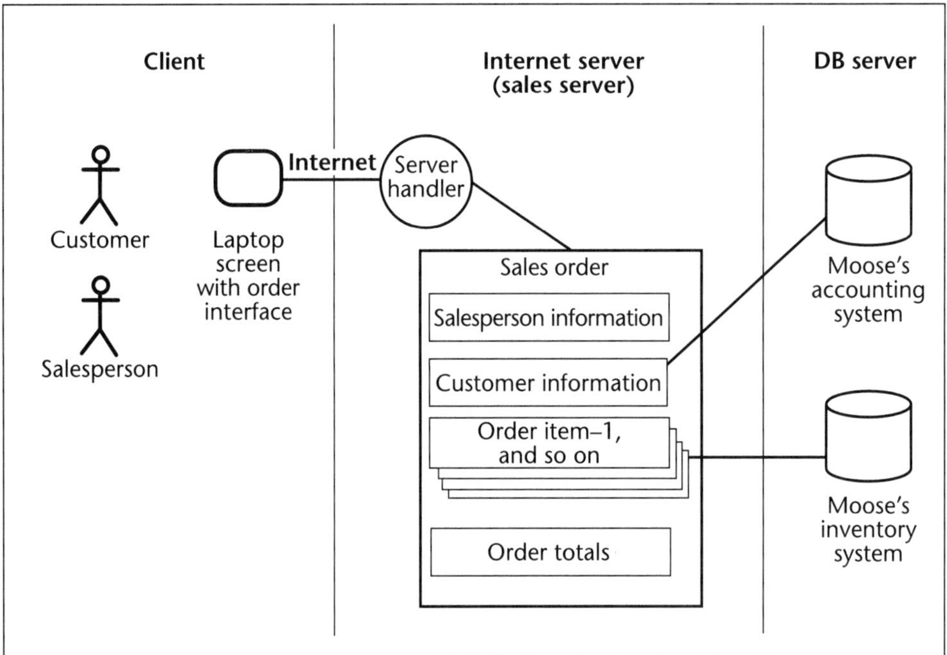

Figure 7.5 *A diagram of the elements of the Moose's sales system.*

Moose's Internet server. Some kind of handler class will deal with salespeople who want to sign on and, if appropriate, create a sales order. The sales order itself will consist of at least four parts. There will be information about the salesperson placing the order. There will be information about the customer who wants to place the order. This information will include some data on the customer's credit limit, which will be obtained from the legacy accounting application/database. There will be information on each of the furniture items the customer wants to order. For each item that is ordered, there will be information on the type of item; the style; decisions about colors, fabrics, or finishes; the number of the item desired; the cost of a single item; and a total for the single item. There can be anywhere from one to dozens of furniture items on a single order. As the order is entered, the legacy inventory application/database will need to be checked to determine whether the items are in stock and when they can be shipped. Finally, there will be a section of the order that totals all the items, adds taxes and shipping costs, and gives total cost for the entire order. Independent of the server, on the right side of the diagram, are the mainframe legacy applications and databases that the sales application will need to access for information, approvals, and so on.

In writing descriptions in this book, it would be easy to confuse the real customer with the information about the customer that will be listed on the sales order. We'll use "customer" to mean the actual person or company ordering furniture. We'll use *Customer Information* to refer to the class that contains information about the customer that is included in the sales order. (In a real-world situation OO developers would never name a class *Customer Information*. They would simply call it *Customer*. After all, each of our objects will contain information, and it would be silly to attach "information" to the name of each class. We're writing an introductory book, however, and we don't want to write sentences that make it hard to tell whether we're talking about a real person or an object. So we'll allow ourselves this awkward name just to make things a little easier on the reader. We hope it won't upset OO programmers too much.)

There will be some kind of interface on the salesperson's laptop that will resemble an order form. It shouldn't be confused with the *Sales Order* object on the server. Moreover, the *Sales Order* on the server will probably be a compound object that will contain other objects, including one or more *Item Ordered* objects.

We'll use "salesperson" as a term that applies to both the actual salesperson and to the software module that sits on the salesperson's laptop machine. Thus, *Salesperson* will refer to the software module, including the sales order form, that is displayed on the salesperson's laptop. We could just as well call this module the client module, but we want to avoid terms that suggest computer architecture in favor of those that suggest how it might ordinarily be talked about. Salespeople submit sales orders. So sales orders originate from salespeople.

During the analysis phase we'll ignore the possibility of a *Sales Handler* class, since that's a software construct, and we'll simply combine its functions with the *Sales Order* class. On the other hand, we'll break the *Sales Order* class itself down into a *Customer Information* class and an *Item Ordered* class.

Initially we'll talk about *Accounting* and *Inventory* as if they were classes. When we get to the design phase, we'll get more explicit about the fact that they are really legacy applications.

Having clarified our vocabulary a bit, let's return to our use case analysis of the Moose's SalesWeb application.

7.5 Use Case Descriptions

A use case description provides a generic, step-by-step written description of the interaction between an actor and a use case. In Figure 7.4 we showed eight interactions: two between the salesperson and two use cases, two between the regional manager and two use cases, one between the Report Sales use case and Moose's Accounting system, and three between Moose's Inventory system and all three use cases.

To complete the use case analysis, you would need to write up eight descriptions. There is no correct level of granularity for use case processes, but you should try to choose processes that result in clear written descriptions. A salesperson might report a new sale and then proceed to see what her status relative to her quarterly quota was, all in a single session. To simplify things, assume that these are two independent transactions: one to report the sale and another to check performance against the quota. Also, don't consider the details of how the transaction will be implemented on computer hardware. Don't assume, for example, that the salesperson will contact the company via a browser. It could just as easily be done by an application on the salesperson's laptop that initiated a direct Internet link to the company's server. Similarly, the salesperson could create the sales order before contacting the company's server, or she could contact the server and then create the sales order while on-line. These are design details and should be ignored during analysis. If you describe the scenarios cleanly, focusing only on business classes, it will work equally well no matter how you decide to implement the application when you turn to the design phase of the effort.

A use case description is a generic scenario. It talks about salespeople, not a specific salesperson, and it talks about the generic steps in reporting a new sale, not about a scenario in which a specific salesperson starts to report a sale and then realizes that she has entered the wrong customer number, or decides to abort an entry so she can answer an incoming phone call. Later, we'll need to write lots of specific scenarios. We'll create them by working through specific variations of the generic sequences we'll describe in our use case descriptions.

Figure 7.6 illustrates a use case description for one of the interactions shown in our simple SalesWeb use case diagram—the generic scenario for any salesperson reporting a new order. Our description assumes a generic salesperson and describes a typical way in which the salesperson would report a new order. If we wanted to explore more possibilities, we would write con-

Use Case Description of the Report Sales Interaction

Normal sequence:

0. Salesperson turns on laptop, brings up SalesWeb program, and chooses Report Sales Order from menu.
1. Salesperson enters name, employee number, and PIN.
2. Sales Order checks to see if name, number, and PIN are valid.
3. Salesperson enters customer name and address on sales order form.
4. Sales Order checks customer information to find out customer status.
5. CustInfo checks Accounting to determine customer status.
6. Accounting approves customer information and supplies customer credit limit.
7. CustInfo accepts customer entry on Sales Order.
8. Salesperson enters first item being ordered on sales order form.
9. Salesperson enters second item being ordered, etc.
10. When all items have been entered, Items Ordered are checked to determine availability and to check pricing.
11. Items Ordered checks with Inventory to determine availability and to check pricing.
12. Inventory supplies all availability dates (when it can ship), approves prices, adds shipping and taxes, and totals order.
13. Complete sales order appears on salesperson's screen.
14. Salesperson can print order, check with customer, etc.
15. Salesperson submits the approved Sales Order.
16. Sales Order is submitted to Accounting and Inventory.

Alternate sequences:

The salesperson's name, employee number, or PIN is not acceptable. SalesWeb displays a message indicating that something is wrong and asks the user to reenter name, number, and PIN. If the user reenters the wrong name, number, and PIN three times in a row, the SalesWeb system signs off and notifies the SalesWeb manager of the attempt to enter.

The salesperson enters a part of the sales order and then asks the SalesWeb system to save the document as an incomplete order. SalesWeb saves the incomplete order, setting it aside so that the salesperson can access the incomplete order from the SalesWeb menu whenever her or she signs on in the future.

The salesperson enters an order for a company, and the order exceeds the credit limit Moose's has established for that customer. SalesWeb makes an effort to increase the customer's sales limit by checking on past behavior, payment status, etc. If unsuccessful, the order is saved while the customer calls a representative at Moose's accounting department.

Figure 7.6 *Step-by-step description of use case: Report Sales.*

crete scenarios that described specific salespeople and the steps they might take to report different kinds of concrete orders. For example, we might describe a step-by-step scenario of how Bill Jones reports the sale of 16 items of furniture to Ace Office Supplies, a long-time Moose's customer. We might also describe how Bev Smith reports a sale of 10 items to Harmon Associates, a small company with no previous credit history with Moose's. Or, we might describe an interaction in which Tina Washington signs on and reports a sale and then immediately proceeds to review her sales-to-date to see if a previous order she placed has shipped yet. In describing the steps in these concrete examples, we would, in effect, draw on our knowledge of two different use case descriptions, since Tina uses two separate processes.

Some developers are satisfied to create generic use case descriptions. Others not only write use case descriptions for each interaction, but go on to write several concrete scenarios as well. Our SalesWeb example is reasonably simple, but it would probably require several concrete scenarios to assure that we really understood all the ways the system would need to respond to support Moose's salespeople and their managers. The more complex the problem, the more scenarios we need to assure that we haven't overlooked important details.

7.6 Instances of Use Cases as Test Cases

If you develop a concrete scenario from a description of an interaction between some hypothetical salesperson and the system, in effect you have a high-level test case that you can later use to determine whether the application you have built provides the functionality that you agreed to deliver. The scenario describes a set of inputs and expected outputs you should be able to demonstrate with the final version of the new application. Thus, some developers continue working with use cases until they have a dozen specific test cases that everyone involved in the project agrees will provide a good test of the desired functionality of the system to be developed. In this sense, the use case analysis can be used later in the development cycle and isn't simply something you only use during the requirements phase of the effort.

7.7 From Use Cases to Ideal Object Models

Many developers abandon the Jacobson approach to OO development as soon as they have created a use case diagram and written up the use case descriptions of the interactions. From the use case diagram, they move to class diagrams, to begin analyzing the actual classes they will need for their application. Before doing that, however, it's often worthwhile to develop an ideal object model of each of the use cases. (In fact, in UML terms it would be a class model.) The development of ideal object models is especially useful if you are new to OO development, since it suggests some of the classes you will probably need to develop when you turn to class diagrams.

In his OOSE methodology, Jacobson suggests that you convert your use case diagram into an OOSE object model following a series of steps that we'll describe below. The first object model he suggests you develop is called an *ideal object model*. This model is developed during the analysis phase of the development cycle and describes an ideal system that would accomplish all of the requirements identified by the use case diagram.

Later, when you switch to design, you begin to constrain the ideal model so that it will work in the actual environment in which you will field your application. The real object model that Jacobson uses during the design phase is different from the ideal object model. It uses different icons (rectangles instead of circles) to indicate that it is a design model and reflects the constraints of the environment for which it is being developed.

We won't consider Jacobson's real object model in this book; clearly that is being superseded in UML by UML class diagrams. We will, however, take a few minutes to review Jacobson's approach to the development of an ideal object model.

An ideal object model is not an official part of UML. Instead, ideal object notation is done by means of UML stereotypes—extensions of UML for special purposes. Stereotype terms are always indicated by guillemets («»).

7.8 The OOSE Ideal Object Model

The key to Jacobson's approach to converting a use case to an ideal object model is to assume that there are three broad types of classes. Jacobson originally had slightly different names for them, but UML provides the three "stereotype" names that we will use. (Recall that UML stereotype names are more or less official extensions of UML that allow UML to provide special functionality.) In this case, the extensions are designed to allow OOSE developers to create ideal object models while still working within the general confines of the UML notation. UML provides both names and alternate icons for three special types of classes: interface classes, entity classes, and control classes.

7.8.1 «Interface Classes»

Interface classes interact with things outside the application. An interface class might be responsible for screens the user sees or for controlling the interaction between the application and another software application or a hardware device.

The names of stereotype terms are always written within guillemets (or angle brackets) on UML diagrams. The UML OOSE stereotypes provide both a small icon and a way of using the stereotypes with a conventional class diagram. Figure 7.7 shows the three terms, the three small icons, and the three classes, one for each type of ideal class. The small symbol for the interface class is a circle with a "T" extending to the left. (The stick figure of an actor is also a stereotype of a class, but since it is also used in the UML use case diagram, the actor is usually represented exactly as it is in a regular UML diagram.)

7.8.2 «Entity Classes»

Entity classes keep track of information. These classes are usually identified with the major elements of the problem as users currently describe it. They include things like forms, orders, checks, and accounts. Later, we'll see that the information stored in these classes usually needs to be stored in databases because we need them whenever we run the application. The small symbol for an entity class is a circle.

7.8.3 «Control Classes»

Control classes manage processes that transcend the various specific entity classes that are involved in the process. Control classes are commonly used to deal with transactions. These

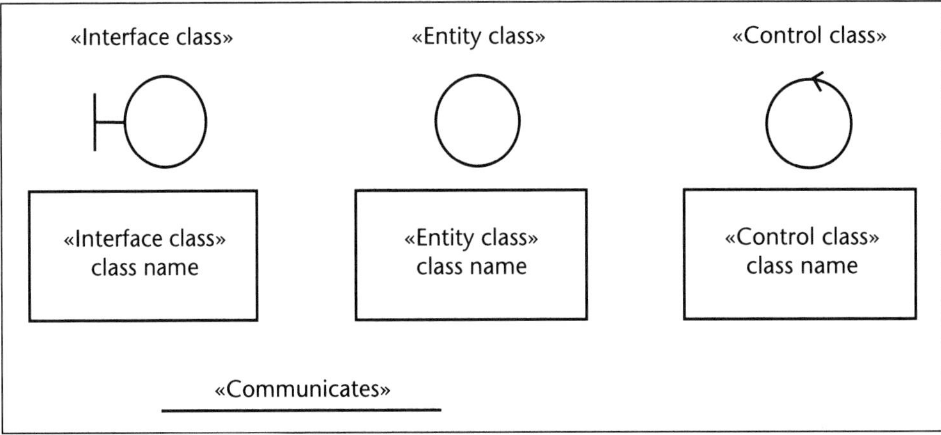

Figure 7.7 *Icons for OOSE ideal object stereotypes.*

objects generally don't keep track of information that needs to be stored between uses of the application. Instances of control classes are created, they manage a transaction, and then they are discarded. (Classes that provide this type of functionality in other OO methodologies are often called handlers.) The small symbol for a control class is a circle with an arrow inserted at the top to suggest rotation or processing.

Classes in ideal object models can be related to each other by means of association lines that are often labeled "communicates." An association line simply means that the objects of the two classes will send messages to each other. In other words, the objects will rely on each other for support in getting things done.

7.8.4 Identifying Classes in Use Cases

As we have already stressed, there is no one-to-one relationship between classes and use cases. Several classes are typically involved in the process that is described by a use case. Some classes are used by several different use cases. When we start to identify the classes associated with a use case, we don't expect that we'll develop a unique set that only applies to that single use case. Nevertheless, you have to start somewhere, so one place to begin is to pick one of the use cases you have described and identify the main classes that will be involved in the process represented by that use case.

Jacobson suggests that you begin by creating an interface class to handle each of the interactions between the use case and the actors outside the system. Then, he suggests that you create at least one control class to manage the use case. If the interfaces are complex, he often creates one control object to handle each interface class. Finally, he suggests that you create entity classes for each of the major things that the process seems to involve. In other words, you create an entity class for each collection of data the use case will need to keep track of.

7.9 An Ideal Object Model for the Report Sales Use Case

Figure 7.8 illustrates a first cut at creating an ideal object model for the Report Sales use case. In this example, we've kept the oval for the Report Sales use case and placed the name for the use case near the top of the oval. We have eliminated the system rectangle since we are only looking at part of the system. We created one interface class to represent the interface between the salesperson and the core of the application and labeled it *BrowserInterface.* We created a second interface object to handle interactions between our SalesWeb application and Moose's two existing applications: the accounting system and the inventory system. We labeled that interface object *CorporateInterface.* We created one control class, *SalesWebHandler,* which will control the overall server process and generate sales objects as needed. And we created a *SalesOrder* object to clearly maintain information on the

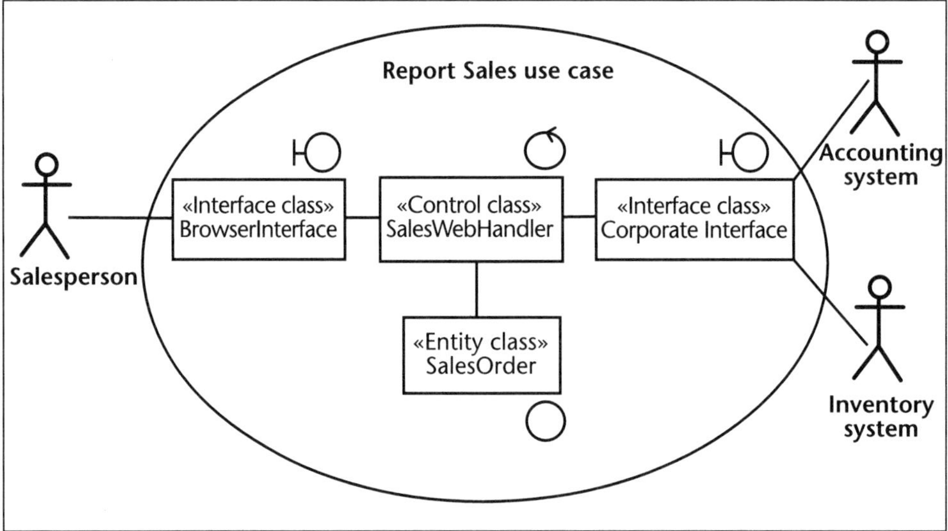

Figure 7.8 *Ideal object model for the Report Sales use case.*

customers who are buying products from Moose's and the items they are buying. We could have converted the *Salesperson* actor into a class, just as we could have converted the accounting system and the warehouse inventory system into classes, but to keep things simple we left them as they were on the original use case diagram.

All these objects are very high-level objects, and we could probably break our application out a little more. Figure 7.9 represents a second cut at our ideal object model. In this case, we added two entity objects, *CustomerInfo,* to keep track of customer information, and *ItemOrdered,* to keep track of items on the *SalesOrder* (and we changed *SalesOrder* into a control object to handle the *CustomerInfo* and *ItemOrdered* objects).

As you can see in Figure 7.9, ideal object models can get rather complicated in short order. Imagine doing an ideal object model for a system with 25–30 objects. In our opinion, ideal object models do a nice job of suggesting the basic high-level objects a system will probably need to have. At the same time, the ideal object approach tends to focus the developer's

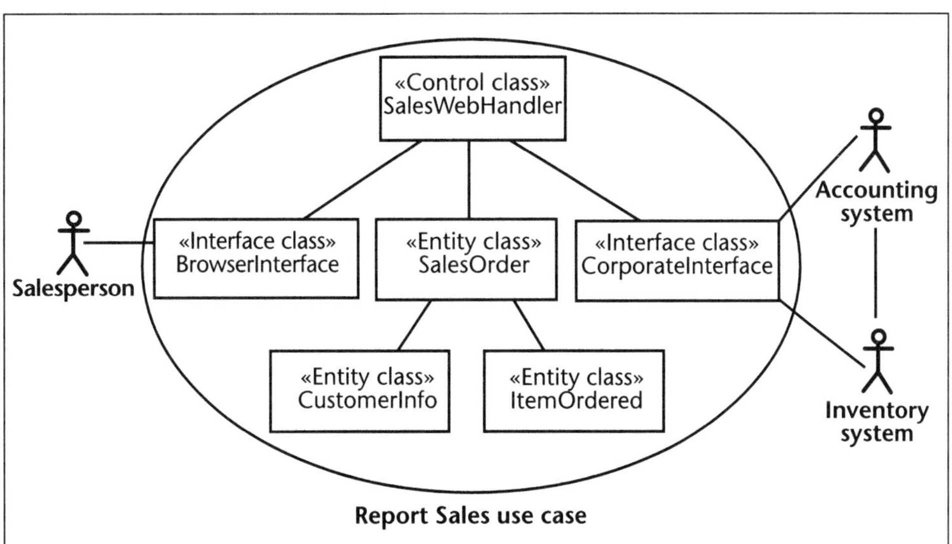

Figure 7.9 *An ideal object model of the Report Sales use case with some additional classes illustrated.*

attention on infrastructure classes (interface and control objects) more than on business objects (control and entity objects). From our perspective, you should either skip ideal modeling altogether, or, once you've developed a model like the one shown in Figure 7.9, you should switch to a UML class diagram. In the process, you should temporarily "forget" the infrastructure objects (both interface objects and the generic handler) and focus on the business objects. When we get to design, however, we'll come back to those infrastructure objects.

7.10 Creating Use Case Models with a Visual Modeling Tool

So far, we've been discussing use cases and ideal object models as if you would be drawing them on a sheet of paper with a pencil. In fact, most OO modeling tools support the creation of use cases.

Since Visual Modeler doesn't support use case diagrams, we'll use Rational Software's Rational Rose 98 to illustrate how you could create the use case model we've described above and how you could also create an ideal model of the Report Sales use case. We've already seen how you can access Microsoft's Visual Modeler tool. You can access Rational Rose 98 in almost exactly the same way.

Figure 7.10 shows the opening window in Rational Rose 98. From here select "Use Case" from the "Browse" menu. When the "Select Use Case Diagram" dialog comes up, choose "New" and click "OK". This brings up a box that will ask you to identify the name of the diagram you want to create, Type in "SalesWeb" for the name. This will give us a window like the one shown in Figure 7.11.

At the moment, the SalesWeb Use Case View window is blank. On the right you see a number of buttons that show the notational elements you will need in order to create a use case diagram. If you are unsure what any specific button

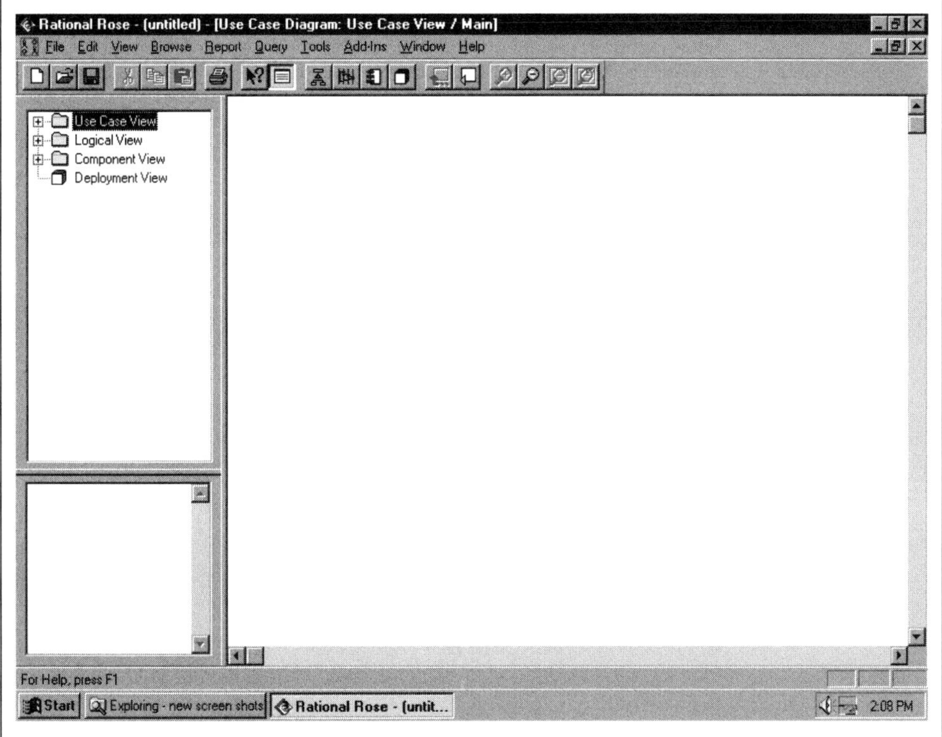

Figure 7.10 *Opening window in Rational Rose 98.*

means, you can rest the cursor arrowhead on it, and text will appear, briefly describing the function of that button.

We'll begin by clicking on the lowest button from the top on the right-hand side of the palette—use case—and then use the crosshair cursor to place our first use case within the business system box. When we click on a location our first use case icon will appear. Give it a name by simply typing the words "Report Sales" and clicking on the new icon. We'll repeat this process and create two more use cases: *Review Individual Sales* and *Review Regional Sales.*

Now, we'll create some actors. Click on the send from the lowest button on the palette, actor.

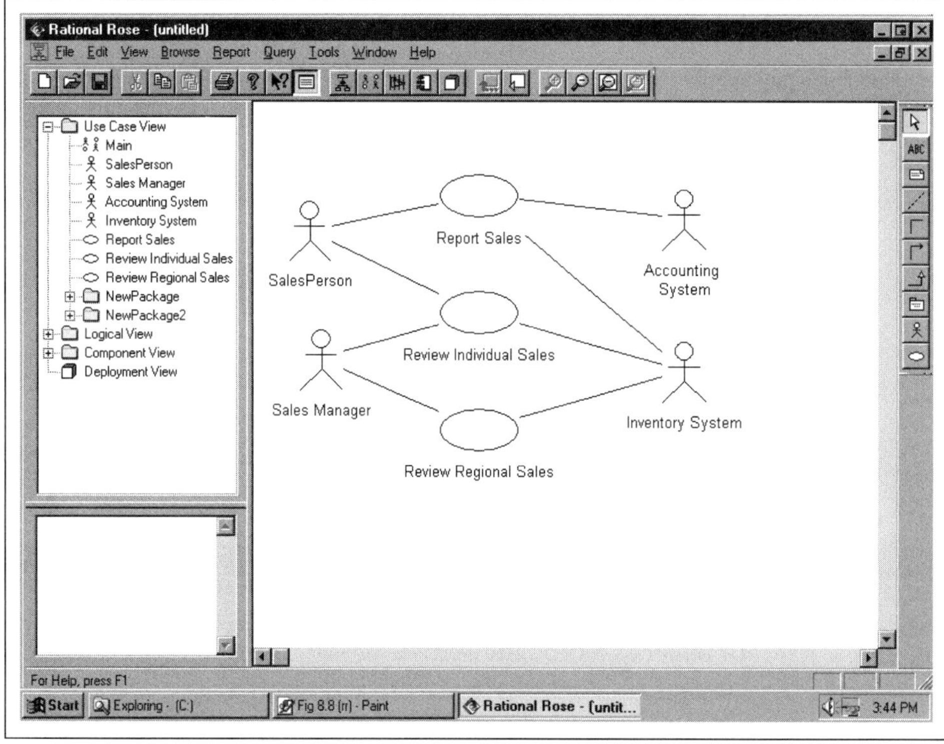

Figure 7.11 *Rose 98 window showing a use case diagram.*

We do this by clicking on the fifth button down on the left side of the menu buttons. Then we move our cursor to the left of the Report Sales icon, and click. As soon as you click, the stick figure representing the actor will appear on your diagram, and you can just start typing to name the actor. Type in Salesperson. Next, click on the fifth button from the top in the palette to the right, association. Now using the cursor, first click on the Salesperson actor, then, holding down the mouse button, position the mouse pointer over the Report Sales use case, and release the button. A link will appear. Repeat the process to link the *Salesperson* to the *Review Individual Sales* use case. Using this same approach, you'll create actors to represent the sales manager, the accounting system, and the inventory system.

In official UML we would enclose our three use case icons within a "business system" box, which we would title "Sales-Web." Our links would travel out through the business system box to our actors. However, Rational Rose 98 does not provide the ability to create the business system box, so we will leave it out.

Now the screen will look like the one in Figure 7.11. We've created the same use case diagram in Rational Rose 98 that we created by hand as Figure 7.4. Next we would want to create a use case description. Rational Rose 98 allows users to type in their use case description in a text window that appears in the lower-left corner of the screen.

You can create ideal object models with Rational Rose 98 in one of two ways. You can move into the class diagram and create classes, or, better, you can create ideal models within the use case environment of Rational Rose 98 by changing the stereotype of the actor symbol to represent interface, control, and entity classes. In fact, if we were working in an OO modeling tool, we'd probably just draw an ideal model on a piece of paper as a thought exercise and then move on to creating a class model in the tool's class diagramming window.

8

CRC Cards

There are many different ways to approach OO analysis. Some developers begin by preparing BPR workflow diagrams to describe the task in a sequential manner. Many prepare detailed use case diagrams and descriptions or scenarios before they begin to develop UML class diagrams. Others prefer to create only a very general use case diagram and a minimal set of descriptions and then proceed to class diagrams. Still others rely on CRC cards as a way of analyzing the classes involved in an application. They consider CRC cards as an alternative to use case diagrams or as a supplement to use case diagrams. CRC cards are not an official part of the UML notation. They may be recognized as a stereotype at some point, but in the meantime, they are an informal and very useful way for people to begin to develop an OO business model.

Recall that CRC stands for Classes, Responsibilities, and Collaborators. CRC cards are usually 3-inch × 5-inch lined index cards. You use cards to represent classes and write information about the classes on the cards. CRC cards are normally used by a group of five to seven people who work together to identify the classes in an application and then talk through scenarios to assure that they understand the characteristics of all the classes. In other words, developers can use the cards when they meet with end users or subject matter experts.

For those just beginning OO development, we suggest you start with a limited use case analysis like the one we described in Chapter 7. Then, we suggest you work through a CRC session like the one we describe in this chapter. Prepare your first UML class diagram only after you have first done use cases and CRC cards. Later, you may decide you would rather skip CRC cards, but on the first few tries, it will probably help.

Use cases describe processes and the actors that interact with the processes. Use cases and use case descriptions form the basis for scenarios. Ideal object models identify some of the major classes that are likely to be needed to implement a use case.

CRC cards constitute another, more informal technique for identifying and defining the characteristics of the classes that make up an application. In effect, you develop use cases to define the overall scope of the application and to generate scenarios that will describe the uses of the application. Then, you use CRC cards to actually work through scenarios and refine your understanding of the classes that will make up the application. Once you have the informal descriptions of the classes, you are ready to create your first UML class diagram.

Analyzing the classes needed for an application by means of CRC cards has some distinct advantages over simply starting with a UML class diagram. To begin with, because it's informal, it's a good technique to use with domain experts, user representatives, and other nonprogrammers who should have input during the initial definition of the system. Equally important, it's a great way to help programmers who are more familiar with procedural analysis make the transition to OO analysis. The OO approach really is different. When you are getting started, it's important to be sure everyone has the OO mind-set. CRC cards are a concrete way of understanding exactly what OO development is all about.

To use CRC cards, there are two things you need to know. First you need to know the physical layout of a CRC card. Then you need to know the steps in a CRC development session. We'll consider each in turn.

8.1 The Layout of a CRC Card

Figure 8.1 illustrates the front and back of a CRC card. Some people omit attributes or superclasses and subclasses, but we'll cover them all. At the top of each card you write the class

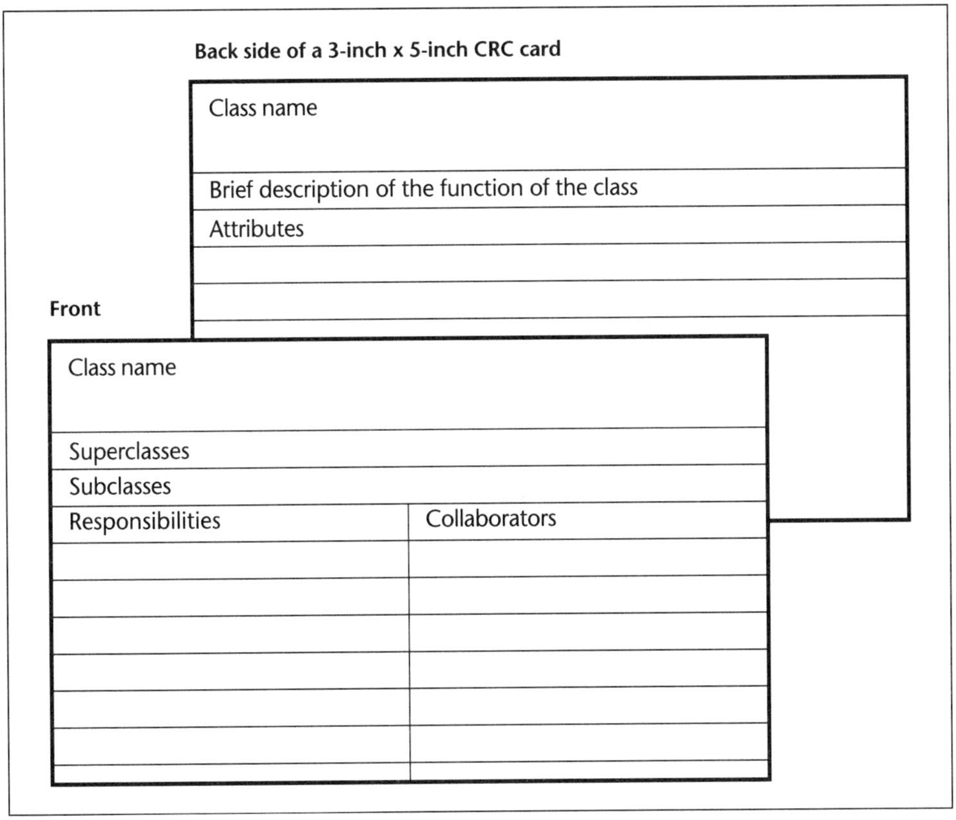

Figure 8.1 *The two sides of a CRC card.*

name for the class the card is to describe. Classes are generic descriptions of sets of objects. There is the class customer, and then there are specific objects of customers: Bill Hong, Emily Fernandez, and Eden Zoll. Class names are generally nouns. Simple, well-chosen, descriptive nouns will make the entire effort easier to understand. The class description is a simple statement about the overall function of the class.

One of the great things about 3-inch × 5-inch index cards is that they are so cheap and informal. If you try one name and decide it isn't right, you can simply tear up the card and make another. Similarly, if you find you have two cards for two different classes and subsequently find that they are really just different names for the same class, you choose one and throw the other away.

Responsibilities are operations and knowledge that the system maintains. A responsibility is usually a short phrase. It must include a verb. Thus, submitting an order, checking whether an item is in inventory, verifying a customer's credit limit, or knowing which customers have credit limits of over $10,000 are all responsibilities. A *collaborator* is the name of another class that is used to perform a specific responsibility. For example, a salesperson would need to collaborate with an authorization class to verify a customer's credit limit. Each responsibility can be associated with zero to several collaborators. The same collaborators can be associated with more than one responsibility. *Attributes* describe values that the object of the class will store. Thus, the authorization class will include the attribute customer credit limit.

When we considered class hierarchies in Chapter 2, we said that relative to any one class, the class above it in a hierarchy is its superclass, and the classes that are below it and inherit from it are its subclasses. In a multiple inheritance system, one class could have more than one superclass. If you plan to work in Visual Basic and find yourself listing more than one superclass on a CRC card, don't worry about it. Chances are you'll find that one or more of the superclasses can actually be interface classes.

In Visual Basic, as in ActiveX, you can't inherit from a superclass, but you can inherit from interfaces. Interfaces have become popular since the CRC approach was first developed. In general, interface classes are infrastructure classes, and CRC doesn't focus on infrastructure classes. We suggest you ignore interface classes and don't mention them to users or consider them yourself, if you undertake a CRC exercise. On the other hand, if you want to include interfaces, consider that they are, in fact, other classes that collaborate with a container class, and for analysis purposes, you might just as well consider them another class.

8.2 The Steps in a CRC Session

Here's a brief overview of the steps that occur in a typical CRC session:

1. Assemble a group.
2. Review requirements.
3. Brainstorm a list of classes.
4. Review the list of classes.
5. Prepare CRC cards.
6. Develop a description of each class.
7. Brainstorm responsibilities and collaborators.
8. Generate specific scenarios.
9. Talk through several scenarios.
10. Add superclasses and subclasses.
11. Repeat the process.

We'll consider each step in turn and work through our simple SalesWeb example at the same time.

8.2.1 *Step 1: Assemble a Group*

An ideal group has five to seven members. It should include someone familiar with object technology to act as a facilitator. It should certainly include domain experts and users who know what they want from the system, and it should include developers.

If you are working alone, you are going to have to play all the roles. If you don't have to work with groups, you'll probably give up CRC cards after a while. We suggest, however, if you are new to OO programming, that you try CRC cards once or twice when you are getting started, even if you have to do it by yourself.

8.2.2 Step 2: Review Requirements

The CRC session should only be scheduled after a requirements statement has been developed for the project. Similarly, use case diagrams and documentation should already have been completed before the session. The session begins by reviewing the requirements statement and the use case diagram and documentation to assure that everyone agrees on the overall goals of the project.

8.2.3 Step 3: Brainstorm a List of Classes

The group should develop a list of likely classes. Usually the domain experts can come up with a good list without too much prompting. You can also examine the use case descriptions, looking through the step-by-step scenarios to identify nouns that might refer to potential classes.

Don't forget that use cases refer to processes, not objects. A use case can contain several or even hundreds of classes, and the same classes can occur in many different use cases. If you created an ideal object model of your use case, that should suggest some potential classes. (Keep in mind, however, that you'll generally want to ignore the interface classes and any classes, such as handlers, that simply coordinate the work of other classes.)

Someone should write the names of the classes that the group identifies on a blackboard, chart paper, or some other media.

8.2.4 Step 4: Review the List of Classes

Consolidate the list of classes by eliminating names that are too abstract or too specific for the initial effort. Focus on a subset of the list if the list is too long. A group of five people is bound to disagree about what to call things. Moreover, there will be misunderstandings about the meanings of words. This is the time to talk them out. Well-chosen class names will make all future discussions more productive.

Some of the classes proposed by the group will be high-level abstractions. Some will be very specialized. Both should be avoided during the initial effort. Thus, in the case of our SalesWeb application, you will probably not want to get into the various details involved in ordering a specific item on a sales order during your first CRC session. It will be sufficient to think simply that the salesperson fills out a sales order and identifies furniture items to be purchased. You won't need to identify different types of furniture, such as desks and chairs, or consider order details such as price, number, and so on. If you can get the middle-level classes identified and sorted out, you can always go back later and identify opportunities for higher-level unifications or subclasses. Similarly, as you get closer to design, you can always generate more specialized classes as they prove necessary. Even if you limit your classes to those that fall along the middle of the potential class hierarchy, you will often find that there are lots of classes. In this case, you want to find some criteria that will allow you to focus on only a portion of the middle of the hierarchy. For example, you might only consider sales to furniture stores and ignore, for the moment, direct sales to companies. You could also ignore the possibility that sales of over a certain amount might allow stores to receive discounts.

Figure 8.2 illustrates a class hierarchy. The classes at the top are very abstract. Classes lower down in the hierarchy are more concrete. The classes at the bottom of the hierarchy are very specialized. We have circled the classes that fall along the middle, and then we have circled a subset of those in the middle.

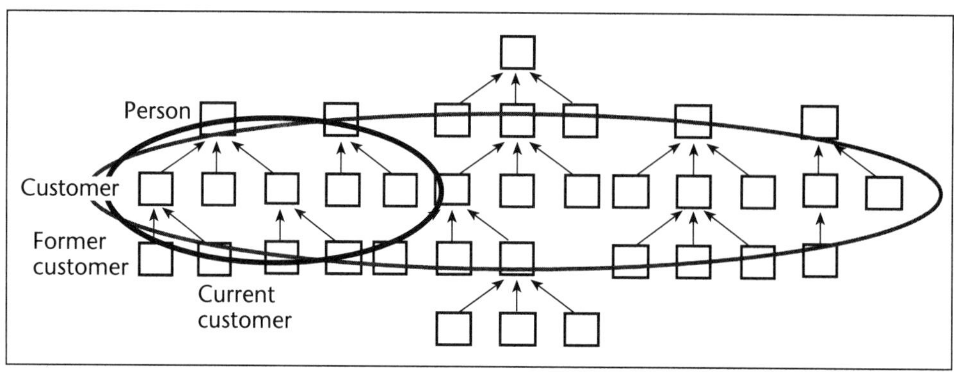

Figure 8.2 *The classes within a hierarchy on which you should initially focus.*

Of course, everyone has a slightly different idea of what constitutes middle-level classes. One rule of thumb is that you should identify all the classes you need to "process" the scenarios. So, if you're unsure, wait until you start working with the scenarios and add or subtract as appropriate. Ideally, you would like to start with between 5 and 10 classes. If you discover a lot more (and any big application will probably involve a lot more), you need to figure out how to subdivide the middle-level classes into some groups. Focusing on just the classes involved in one specific use case is one way to subdivide a large application.

When preparing CRC cards, always ignore interface classes that are used to manage screens, databases, or classes that are, in effect, really part of a process being performed by outside software applications or hardware devices. In other words, focus on business classes.

One of the great advantages of OO development is the ability to modularize the effort and work on one part of an application at a time. Developing your initial model will offer enough challenges, and you don't want to allow yourself to be overwhelmed by trying to consider too many classes at once. Pick a subset of classes. Once you have figured out how they work together, you can easily go back and add others until you have a complete model.

8.2.5 Step 5: Prepare CRC Cards

Once everyone agrees on the list of classes, write the class names on 3-inch × 5-inch cards and give one or more cards to each member of the group. Each person with a card acts as the representative of that class/object as you work through scenarios.

8.2.6 Step 6: Develop a Description of Each Class

Before going any further, write a brief description of each class on the back of the respective CRC cards. This is the final test where everyone agrees on the meaning of each class name. If technical people are present, this can become quite complex, but it's important to be sure you understand what the class really does. People often make assumptions about class names based on the ordinary meanings of the words. Later, they find that technical people use a seemingly ordinary word in a much narrower or more specialized way.

Figure 8.3 illustrates how we might have defined some of the classes that we found in the use case description we created in Chapter 7 (Figure 7.6). Remember that we are ignoring interface and database access classes as well as handlers that simply sequence activities. We won't concern ourselves with the details of how the accounting system and the warehouse inventory systems work, but we will represent them as two classes, since they will have responsibilities in several scenarios.

8.2.7 Step 7: Brainstorm Responsibilities and Collaborators

Some prefer to move directly to scenario walk-throughs. Others prefer to record obvious responsibilities and collaborators on the various CRC cards before the scenarios begin. It's easy to use scenarios to learn that you must add responsibilities. It's harder to realize that you have added unnecessary responsibilities. Thus, it is better to list only those responsibilities you

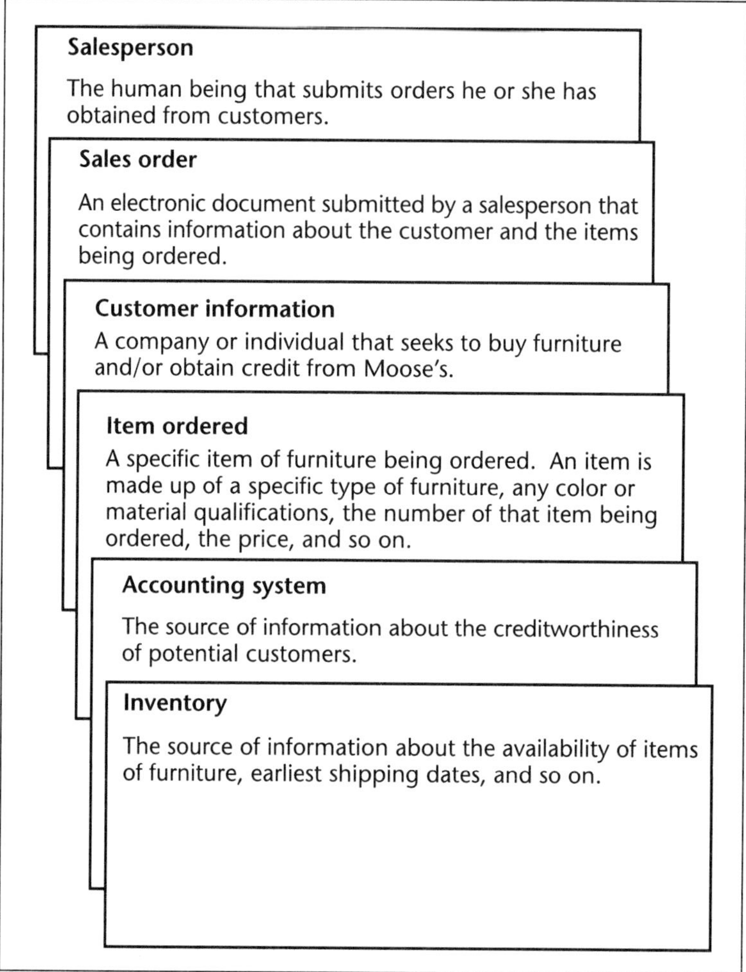

Figure 8.3 *An initial set of CRC cards for the SalesWeb example.*

are sure of and leave doubtful responsibilities until you begin to work through scenarios.

Responsibilities are described by phrases that begin with verbs. They either involve actions (order, check) or states (approved, available). In most situations one class will call on another class to perform some task. The responsibility of the second class is to perform the task. Don't bother to add another responsibility indicating that the second class must notify the first class that it has completed the task; answering back is assumed.

There are no correct answers about which class will perform which task. In many situations, either of two classes could do the task equally well. As a general rule, you want to keep classes independent and minimize interaction. Thus, if you find two classes exchanging lots of messages to accomplish some general task, it's probably better to give more responsibility to the second class. Then, once the first class has asked the second class to do something, the second class can do lots of work and only respond when the task is done. This is just like a manager giving an assignment to an assistant. You want to delegate enough responsibility to avoid having the assistant return to ask questions every other hour.

The exception to this generalization occurs when the first class has the task of maintaining some overall control of the flow of a transaction (a handler) and needs to be able to control exactly when the second class should begin to perform step two and then step three, and so on.

8.2.8 Step 8: Generate Specific Scenarios

At this point, you will want to walk through several scenarios to see how the classes work in an application. The best way to get scenarios is to begin with the use case descriptions. Remember that each use case description is a generic version of a scenario. The same use case description can be used to generate a number of different specific scenarios.

Pick a use case description and then let one person talk through a specific scenario of the description. For example, in Figure 8.4 we have listed the Report Sales use case description we listed in Figure 7.6 on the left and then provided two specific scenarios on the right.

Note that in this example, since it is simple and since we assume that it's going to be done across the Web, we're inclined to assume lots of other things. We have the salespeople signing on to their laptops. We probably shouldn't. We simply did it to remind you of how the application is going to work.

Figure 8.4 *Use case description of Report Sales and two scenarios.*

	Normal sequence		Scenario 1		Scenario 2
0.	Salesperson turns on laptop, brings up SalesWeb program, and chooses Report Sales Order from menu.	0.	Salesperson Curtis Clyde turns on his laptop and accesses the Report Sales Order form.	0.	Pooks Rutherford turns on her laptop and accesses the Report Sales Order form.
1.	Salesperson enters name, employee number, and PIN.	1.	Curt enters his name, employee number, and PIN.	1.	Pooks enters her name, employee number, and PIN.
2.	Sales Order checks to see if name, number, and PIN are valid.	2.	The system recognizes Curt and lets him continue.	2.	The system indicates that the entry is wrong and asks Pooks to reenter her number and PIN.
3.	Salesperson enters customer name and address on sales order form.	3.	Curt enters Harmon Assoc. as the customer.	3.	Pooks enters her name, employee number, and PIN correctly.
4.	Sales Order checks Customer Information to find out customer status.	4.	The Sales Order checks with Customer Information concerning Harmon Association.	4.	The system recognizes Pooks and lets her continue.
5.	Customer Information checks Accounting to determine customer status.	5.	The Customer Information class checks with Accounting to see about Harmon Associates.	5.	Pooks enters Morrissey Office Furniture as the customer.
6.	Accounting approves customer and supplies customer credit limit.	6.	Accounting approves Harmon Assoc. and sets its credit limit at $5000.	6.	The Customer Information class checks with Accounting to see about Morrissey Office Furniture.
7.	Customer Information accepts customer entry on Sales Order.	7.	Harmon Associates information is displayed on the sales order.	7.	Accounting approves Morrissey and sets its credit limit at $50,000.
8.	Salesperson enters first item being ordered on sales order form.	8.	Curt enters the type of desk that Harmon Associates wants to buy and indicates that that's the only item on this order.	8.	The Morrissey information is displayed on Pooks' screen.
9.	Salesperson enters second item being ordered, and so on.	9.	Sales Order checks with Item Ordered to determine availability, and so on.	9.	Pooks enters several desks and chairs that Morrissey wants to buy and then indicates that the order is complete.

Normal sequence

10. When all items have been entered, Sales Order checks Item Ordered to determine availability and to check pricing.
11. Item Ordered checks with Inventory to determine availability and to check pricing.
12. Inventory supplies all availability dates (when it can ship), approves prices, adds shipping and taxes, and totals order.
13. Complete order appears on salesperson's screen.
14. Salesperson can print order, check with customer, and so on.
15. Salesperson submits the approved Sales Order.
16. Sales Order is submitted to Accounting and Inventory.

Scenario 1

10. Item Ordered checks with Inventory.
11. Inventory provides the availability (immediate) and price ($1500), adds shipping and taxes, provides a total, and estimates when the order will arrive at the customer's site.
12. Curt prints the order, shows the complete order to the purchase order manager and Harmon Associates (Paul Harmon), and gets his approval.
13. Curt approves the order.
14. The Sales Order is forwarded to both Accounting and Inventory.

Scenario 2

10. Sales Order checks with Item Ordered to determine availability, and so on.
11. Inventory provides availability and price, and so on.
12. Pooks prints the order and shows it to Mr. Morrissey.
13. Mr. Morrissey insists he needs the desks sooner.
14. Pooks queries about rush ordering the desks.
15. Item Ordered/Inventory indicate that they can't be rush ordered.
16. Mr. Morrissey says he'll have to get the desks elsewhere.
17. Pooks modifies the order to eliminate the desks, gets approval for the chairs, and submits the order.

Figure 8.4 *Continued.*

In an ideal world, analysis ought to focus on the logical organization of a system without regard to how it will be arranged when it is actually developed. It would be better to imagine a salesperson, an order form, someone who would approve customers, and so on, all in a single room. Once you have the classes worked out, you can figure out where they will be physically located when an actual order is processed.

Since we went halfway and talked about the salesperson signing on with a laptop, it seems awkward to have the laptop talking with *Sales Order.* In fact, as we'll see when we get to design, we'll have a *Sales Handler* that will always be active on the server. The laptop will access the *Sales Handler,* which will approve access and then cause the *Sales Order* to create an instance of itself, and so forth. None of this makes too much difference with a simple system like this because you can maintain a good overview of what's happening. When you start analyzing much larger systems, however, and have to deal with dozens or hundreds of classes, then it's very important to be more precise about these things.

8.2.9 Step 9: Talk through Several Scenarios

Each person takes the card(s) they are responsible for and makes entries on it as their class card becomes involved in a scenario. One person begins by describing a scenario. For example, suppose the group begins by walking through Scenario 1 from Figure 8.4. The walk-through begins with the person with the *Salesperson* CRC card beginning the dialogue, which then runs as follows:

> *Salesperson*: I'm Curtis Clyde. I want to enter an order from Harmon Associates for an executive desk. I turn on my laptop and access the Report Sales Order program and choose the Report Sales option. I now have a sales order form on my computer screen. I enter my name, employee number, and PIN. My laptop sends information over the telephone to the SalesWeb system.
>
> *Sales Order*: I need to determine whether the name, employee number, and PIN match those of someone I

can work with. I check my table of salespeople and identify Curtis Clyde. I tell Curt to go ahead.

Salesperson: I enter the name Harmon Associates on the order form on my screen.

Sales Order: I can see anything that the *Salesperson* enters on the order form. When I see that Curt has entered a customer's name, I ask *Customer Information* to verify the customer and to find out what the customer's credit limit is.

Customer Information: I check with *Accounting* to see if Harmon Associates is OK and to find out what their credit limit is.

Accounting: I check my tables when asked and then tell *Customer Information* that Harmon Associates is an established customer and that we've approved them for a credit limit of $5000, all of which is currently available.

Customer Information: Once *Accounting* tells me Harmon Associates is OK, I pass the information on to *Sales Order.*

Sales Order: I highlight the name Harmon Associates on the order form and show the current credit limit.

Salesperson: Once I see the customer's name highlighted and see the credit amount, I enter the first (and only) item that Harmon Associates wants to buy—an executive desk.

Sales Order: As soon as I see that the *Salesperson* has entered an item, I ask *Item Ordered* to check on its availability, price, delivery date, and so on.

Item Ordered: I check with *Inventory* to find out about availability, and so on.

Inventory: I check my database tables and determine that we have an executive desk like the one Harmon Associates wants, and that it is available to ship. Using zip codes, I determine when it could arrive at the Harmon Associates site. I also provide information on the current price of the desk, shipping costs, taxes, and so on.

Item Ordered: I pass the information from *Inventory* on to *Sales Order.* If there had been more than one item ordered, I would have done the math to figure out the total cost of the order.

Sales Order: I display the information about the executive desk on the order form.

Salesperson: Once I have the information about availability, I check with the guy at Harmon Associates to be sure it's OK, then I press Submit.

Sales Order: Once the *Salesperson* tells me to submit the order, I send copies of the order to *Accounting* and *Inventory*.

We can stop now, since *Accounting* and *Inventory* are legacy systems that are outside the scope of this development effort. They already know how to process orders once they are received. They ship and bill.

In considering this dialogue, remember that we are using CRC "class" cards, but we are talking as if they are passing messages to each other. In other words, we are acting as if each class is an object. The class *Customer Information,* for example, is, for the purposes of this dialogue, the object Harmon Associates.

Also keep in mind that we are talking about objects sending messages to each other. An actual system creates objects at run time and only maintains them as long as they are needed. Try to avoid falling into procedural terms and beginning to think of "calling an object" as if objects were a block of procedural code that always exists. It might be easy to think this way about a *Sales Handler,* if we were including one in our example, since it will have some kind of permanence. But even the "permanent" *Sales Handler* will in fact be a class that will create an object of itself to handle each specific call from each *Salesperson*. Indeed, the *Sales Handler* might easily have a dozen objects of itself in existence at one time if the server it is on is equipped to handle several salespeople calling at the same time. The *Sales Order* is a better example of an object. An object of the *Sales Order* class is created when a new order is entered. It accumulates information, updates the accounting and inventory systems, and then ceases to exist.

Next, consider that we have already experienced some problems as a result of assuming we know about the architecture of the system. We might decide to store the *Sales Order* class on each salesperson's laptop and have it send to get authorizations as needed. We could even make it an applet, have the salesperson use a generic Web browser, and then download the *Sales Order* applet whenever a salesperson contacted the server. As it is, we're assuming that an application on the laptop machine initiates the link between the laptop and the server. But whether you know this or not, you should ignore architectural issues at this point. Assume that everything is taking place on a single computer and that all of the classes are available to each other. This is an ideal system that we are analyzing at this point. We'll take design issues into account later. For now, you simply want to know what the key objects are and what each one will be responsible for accomplishing.

Now consider the actual events that occurred. *Salesperson* sent a message to *Sales Order* containing his name, number, and PINs. *Sales Order* returned a message approving it. *Sales Order* must have a table listing the salespeople and their numbers and PINs. *Sales Order* might store this information in a database and access it as needed (largely depending on how many salespeople there are), but we don't need to concern ourselves with that. At a minimum, the object derived from *Sales Order* will need attributes to store the values for *Salesperson*'s name, *Salesperson*'s number, and *Salesperson*'s PIN.

Salesperson sent another message giving the customer's name. Thus, the *Sales Order* object will also need an attribute to store the customer's name. The *Sales Order* object then sent a message to the *Customer Information* object, to check on the status of the customer. The *Customer Information* object will also need a slot to store the customer's name, and it will generate a message to the accounting system to determine the creditworthiness of Harmon Associates and their credit limit. Thus, the *Customer Information* object will also need an attribute for credit limit, and so on.

By working your way through the dialogue, you can begin to see which classes need to be able to send messages to which other classes. You can also see which classes need to have attributes that will allow them to access or to store data (names, numbers, etc.).

The individuals responsible for each CRC card should write these things down as they take part in the dialogues. When people holding CRC cards have to ask someone else for help, that is a trigger for writing down a responsibility on their cards. Similarly, if they ask for or receive a data item, they need to enter an attribute name to remind them that they will have to be able to store that data item.

8.2.10 Step 10: Add Superclasses and Subclasses

To keep this example simple, we haven't begun to consider the possibility of creating new classes or subclasses yet, but this will probably arise if the participants make the dialogues a little more detailed than we have so far. For example, the address to which a bill is shipped is not always the same as the address to which the furniture will be shipped. It might be in the case of an individual but probably won't be in the case of a large company. Hence, we'll need to have one attribute for billing address and another for shipping address. Accounting will be interested in the first, and inventory will be interested in the second. In addition, an address isn't a simple data type. It usually involves several fields. In fact, in most OO systems, address would be an object in its own right. In effect, *Sales Order* or *Customer Information* will be compound objects and include within them another object, *Address*. (Or, since we are using Visual Basic, this may be handled via interfaces. In other words, *Sales Order* or *Customer Information* would support an address interface.)

Since a billing address and a shipping address are very much alike, we might create one class for address and then create two subclasses: one for customers whose billing address and shipping address are the same and another for customers with two or more addresses. We might, for example, get an order from a company that wanted office furniture delivered to all six of its regional offices.

We won't go further into this issue at the moment. We are primarily using this superclass/subclass relationship to give us an opportunity to show inheritance. In reality, there are several ways this could be solved, and we'll certainly consider it

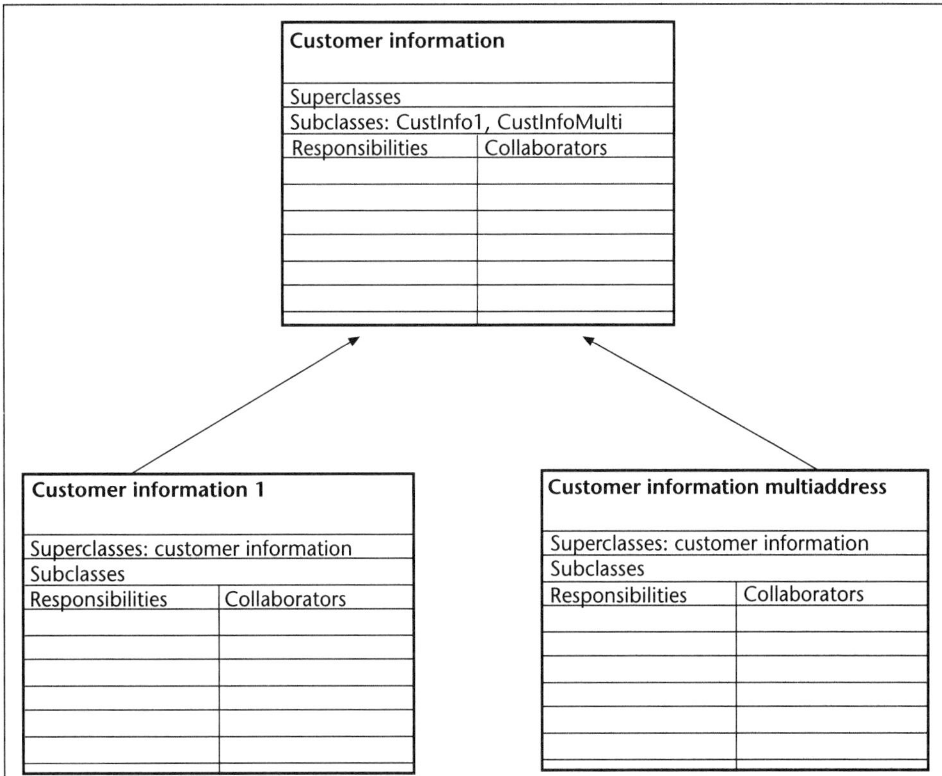

Figure 8.5 *The customer information class and its subclasses.*

further when we get to the design phase of our effort. Meanwhile, we'll assume that our team has decided to subdivide the *Customer Information* (*CustInfo*) class into two subclasses: *CustInfo1,* which supports a single address, and *CustInfoMulti,* which will support two or more addresses. (See Figure 8.5.)

Using a similar kind of logic, we might decide to subclass the *Item Ordered* class into subclasses that describe more specific groups of furniture. Consider that some furniture items are simple, while others come in a variety of woods, paints, and coverings. Desk chairs, for example, can be ordered in a wide range of fabrics or leathers, and the finish on chairs can be various colors. It's easy to imagine that it would make sense to subclass *Item Ordered* into a number of subclasses, one for each major type of furniture. They might all inherit some general characteristics (as, for example, the shipping address) but might diverge as we began to consider the different types of decisions the customer would have to make before we could provide information on availability or price. Standard oak desk chairs might be in stock, but desk chairs in rare woods might be a special order. These are issues that will come up if you are working with users who know about furniture. The smart Inventory system card holder will ask lots of questions of the *Sales Order* CRC card holder before he or she is willing to speak about availability or provide a firm price. At this stage, if possible, put off worrying about possible subclasses. Assume we are only going to develop a small prototype system to establish that the overall design of the SalesWeb system will work. Ask everyone to agree to limit the furniture available to two items for now. The point is that you will have to deal with all these issues, but at the moment you are only trying to decide on the main classes you will need and the most important attributes and responsibilities each class will need to accommodate. Keep things as simple as you can.

Assuming you stick with the initial set of classes, each member should now have a reasonably good idea of the responsibilities, attributes, and collaborators for his or her class. We show the set of CRC cards we came up with below.

Class: *Salesperson*

Responsibilities	**Collaborators**
Initiate sales order report	*Sales Order*
Enter customer name	*Customer Information*
Enter customer address	*Customer Information*
Enter items to be ordered	*Item Ordered*
Indicate that order is complete and acceptable	*Sales Order*

Attributes

Customer name

Customer address

Item-1 (type, style, size, wood/fabric, number)

Class: ***Sales Order***

Responsibilities	**Collaborators**
Recognize/authorize salespeople	*Salesperson*
Ask *Customer Information* to check customer credit	*Customer Information*
Update salesperson's screen with credit limit	*Salesperson*
Ask *Item Ordered* to check item availability	*Item Ordered*
Pass item information to *Salesperson*	*Salesperson*
Pass final approval on to *Customer Information*	*Customer Information*
Pass final approval on to *Item Ordered*	*Item Ordered*

Class: ***Customer Information***
Subclasses: ***Customer Information1, Customer Information Multi***

Responsibilities	**Collaborators**
Obtain customer credit approval	*Accounting*
Pass credit approval to *Sales Order*	*Sales Order*
Pass final approval to *Accounting*	*Accounting*

Attributes

Customer name

Customer billing address

Customer credit limit

Class: ***Customer Information1***
Superclass: ***Customer Information***

Responsibilities

Set shipping address equal to billing address

Class: ***Customer Information Multi***
Superclass: ***Customer Information***

Responsibilities

Establish shipping address

Attributes

Customer shipping address

Class: ***Item Ordered***

Responsibilities	**Collaborators**
Determine availability of item	*Inventory*
Pass availability to *Sales Order*	*Sales Order*
Pass final approval to *Inventory*	*Inventory*

Attributes

Type of item

Style of item

Characteristic-1

Characteristic-2

Number needed

Price per unit

Shipping cost

Applicable taxes

Total price

Class: ***Accounting***

Responsibilities	Collaborators
Know customers	*Customer Information*
Know credit limit of customers	*Customer Information*
Determine whether limit can be raised	*Customer Information*
Process order	*Customer Information*

Attributes

Customer

Credit limit

New order

Class: ***Inventory***

Responsibilities	Collaborators
Know items in inventory, price	*Item Ordered*
Calculate shipping charges	*Item Ordered*
Calculate arrival date	*Item Ordered*
Estimate time if item is ordered	*Item Ordered*
Arrange to ship items once approved	*Item Ordered*

Attributes

Item number

Type of item

Style of item

Characteristic-1

Characteristic-2

Number needed

Price per unit

Shipping cost

Applicable taxes

Total price

Of course, a real CRC group would have come up with different names, and you could probably add a few more. In any case, if the group runs through a half dozen additional scenarios, they will surely add several more and modify some of these.

For example, someone might argue that the *Sales Order* class would need to keep track of the time and date. It would be an additional responsibility and another pair of attributes. You probably wouldn't want the *Sales Order* class to actually calculate the time or date. Instead, you'd probably create a separate class to provide time and date information upon demand. Hence, the *Sales Order* class would simply have the responsibility to record the time and date of the transaction. It would do this by asking the *Time-and-Date* class for that information. We've ignored this detail in our analysis effort, but eventually it will need to be added.

8.2.11 *Step 11: Repeat the Process*

So far we have only been considering scenarios generated by a single use case, Report Sales. Once the CRC group is satisfied that they have exhausted all the possibilities of this use case, they should proceed to the other two use cases.

In dealing with the review of individual sales and the review of group sales, for example, we would probably find we needed to add a class to handle sales quota information and another to handle keeping track of which salespeople belong to which region. This wouldn't expand the number of classes too greatly, but it would undoubtedly lead to the discovery of some additional classes and to additional responsibilities for the classes we have already identified.

8.3 CRC Cards and Object-Oriented Thinking

We hope this brief exercise has been sufficient to give you an overview of how to use CRC cards and to convince you that it's a good way to start learning to think like an OO analyst.

By letting cards be objects and having them ask each other to take responsibility for knowing and doing things, you are already a long way toward the mind-set of someone who routinely thinks in an OO way. Moreover, once you have completed your set of CRC cards, it will be easy to create your first UML class diagram.

We have described CRC cards and CRC sessions as a technique that can be used by a group to learn about objects while developing a list of classes that will occur in a specific application. It won't be as effective as an individual exercise, but if you are new to OO development and are working alone, it will probably still be worth working through one or two personal CRC sessions just to familiarize yourself with this popular way of identifying classes and their characteristics.

8.4 CRC Terms versus UML Terms

We have not yet introduced the UML vocabulary for class modeling, but suffice it to say that it's somewhat different from the vocabulary used in developing CRC cards. CRC is not an official part of the UML notation, so its terms vary slightly. Figure 8.6 illustrates which terms are associated with which. Later, when you consider creating a UML class diagram, if you are uncertain of the correct analogies, check this figure.

CRC cards, since they require that you enter both attributes and operations (or responsibilities), are like UML classes. On the other hand, you develop CRC cards in the context of specific scenarios in which you pretend that actual people pass actual data from one card to another. In that sense, during a scenario, you are acting as if the cards were objects. Classes never really interact with each other. They are templates that are used to generate objects. When an application is run, objects are generated as needed from classes, and data is stored in objects. Hence, CRC cards have some of the characteristics of UML classes and some of the characteristics of objects.

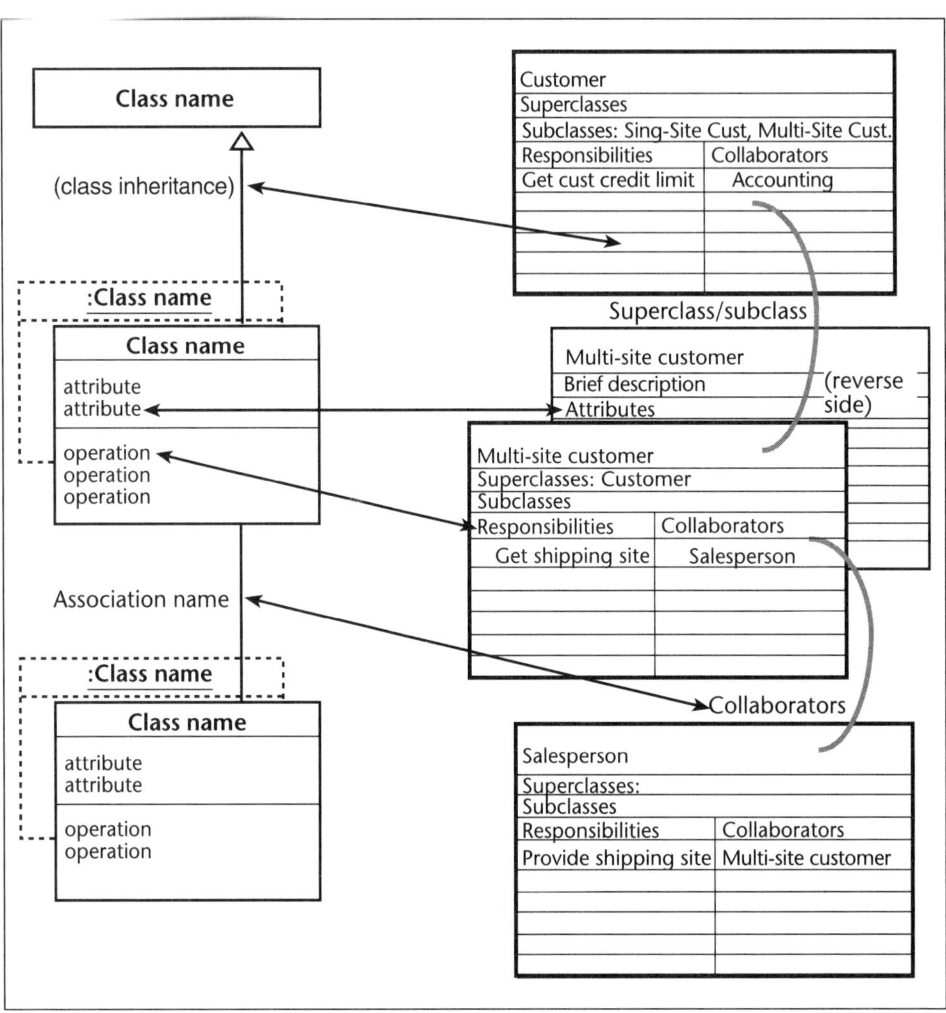

Figure 8.6 *Relationships between UML and CRC terms.*

The other relationships are straightforward. Attributes mean the same thing in both systems. UML operations are CRC responsibilities. Superclass and subclass relationships in CRC describe class inheritance relationships in UML. And collaborators in CRC are simply classes that have associations in UML. In effect, collaborators pass messages to one another, and that's exactly what associations indicate in UML.

9

UML Class and Object Diagrams

A complete set of hand-drawn UML static structure diagrams is made up of anywhere from one to hundreds of specific class and object diagrams. Most of the diagrams will be class diagrams. Some will be very high-level views of the system, while others will describe specific subsections of the overall model. Some will be very detailed. A few might show how specific objects would interact. If the system is large, you might decide to partition it into packages and then develop different class diagrams for each package.

In general, dividing an application into packages is something you leave for the design phase of a project. If you are doing a relatively simple application, like the SalesWeb application we are focusing on in this book, you would probably develop an overall object model of the entire application and worry about subdividing the classes into packages at a later time. If the application is very large, however, you might decide to focus initially on a small part of the overall application. In that case, you might begin by creating a diagram of the possible packages in the system and then select one package and create class and object diagrams for that package first. Whatever you do, you will probably go through several iterations, and any decisions you make at the beginning can be modified as you learn more about the system you are developing. (UML package diagrams are discussed in Chapter 13.)

However you begin, keep in mind that class diagrams and object diagrams are both static diagrams. They picture classes and their relationships with other classes and, in some cases, relationships between objects. They are fundamental because you need to define what you are dealing with before you can describe when or how those things might change.

You begin the analysis effort by creating a simple class diagram that shows the core classes that you anticipate will be in your first prototype system. You then enhance and expand that initial class diagram throughout the first analysis phase. Later, you continue to expand the class diagram throughout the design phase, constantly adding more details to the class diagrams until they are ready to serve as the primary source of information when you begin to write code (or use an OO modeling tool to generate code) during the prototype phase. After testing your first prototype, you return to the analysis phase again, when you begin the second prototype cycle. You begin the second round by modifying your high-level class diagram to incorporate things you learned during your first prototyping cycle. Then, if you are going to focus on new classes during the second prototyping cycle, you start by expanding your class diagrams to describe them. And, as before, you then proceed to expand and fill in details on those new class diagrams throughout the analysis and design phases of the second prototype cycle, which ends when you implement and test your second prototype. You keep repeating this process through one prototyping cycle after another until you complete your entire application.

Thus, to begin any UML development effort, you must first learn to create and then enhance class diagrams. To keep things from getting too complex, we'll begin by introducing a few basic class diagramming terms. Then we'll develop a simple class diagram. After that, we'll develop a simple object diagram.

9.1 Class Diagramming Basics

The UML class diagram shows classes and the relationships between classes. The simplest way to represent a class is to draw a rectangle and place the name of the class inside the rectangle. UML suggests that class names begin with capital letters.

Later, when you want to add more details, you draw a larger rectangle and divide it into three horizontal compartments. In the top section you indicate the name of the class, in the second section you list the attributes of the class, and in the lower section you list the operations that the class can perform. Attribute and operation names usually begin with lowercase letters.

9.1.1 *Attributes (Properties)*

Each attribute must have a name. Descriptive names are best. Because the attributes of one class are usually hidden from the attributes of other classes, you can use the same attribute name in more than one class. If you do this, we recommend you do it in a consistent way so you'll be able to remember what the attribute stands for, no matter what class it occurs in. If an attribute name is made up of more than one word, most OO languages require that you link them with hyphens or underscores so they form a single unit. (Visual Basic, for example, allows underscores.) Some developers prefer to combine two words and capitalize the first letter in the second name. Thus, *part_number* and *partNumber* are examples of attribute names.

When you create your first class diagrams, you will probably start by listing the names of a few attributes—just those that are needed for the prototype you are working on. As you learn more about the application, you may specify the data type of the value that can be associated with various attributes. Similarly, if there are default values associated with the attribute (e.g., an initial value that the attribute is always set at), you may want to list them. For example:

```
attributeName : data_type = default_value
```

UML provides a whole collection of symbols that you can use to indicate different characteristics of an attribute, but we'll ignore them for the moment. In fact, you won't need them for most small to midsized development efforts.

9.1.2 Operations (Methods)

Operations are modules of procedural code that respond to messages by providing information or by causing something to happen. Initially, you only specify the names of the operations. By the time you get to design, you may want to create some pseudocode to document what each operation will do. You don't usually get around to writing Visual Basic code for the operations until the prototyping phase of the cycle.

Operation names, like attribute names, should be descriptive. If they involve more than one word, they should be linked into a single unit by an underscore or by capitalizing the first letter in the second word.

As you refine your model, you may decide to identify operations that have associated arguments or parameters, or you may want to list the arguments that are associated with specific operations. If you simply want to indicate that an operation can have one or more parameters associated with it, you put opening and closing parentheses after the name of the operation. If you want to go further and specify the argument or arguments associated with the operation, you can list it (or them) within the parentheses.

You may also want to specify the data type of any results you expect the operation to return. If you indicate a result type, you do it after the argument list, for example:

```
operationName (argument1, argument2) : result_type
```

As with attributes, there are additional UML symbols you can use to indicate specific characteristics of an operation, but we'll ignore them for the moment. Figure 9.1 illustrates the generic form for the class notations we have just discussed.

9.1.3 More on Attributes and Operations

Earlier, we mentioned that attributes were generally private but could be public (although this would be very bad OO programming). When you see an attribute listed within a class box with no special symbol in front of it, you assume the attribute is private. If you want some attributes to be public and others private, UML suggests that you put a – in front of the names of private attributes and a +$ in front of public attributes.

More useful is the distinction between public, protected, and private operations. Again, recall that the default is always public operations. If you need to discriminate, you should

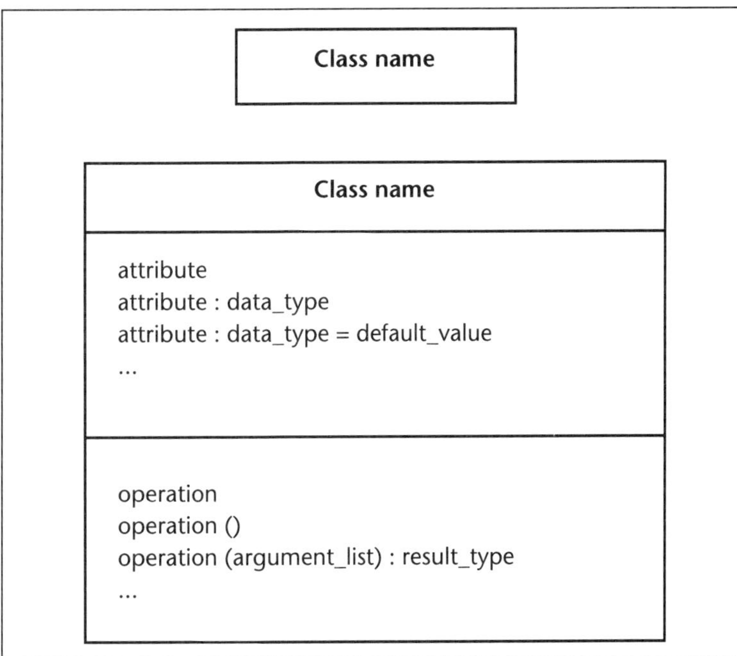

Figure 9.1 *Basic UML notation for classes.*

place a + in front of public operations, a # in front of protected operations, and a – in front of private operations, for example:

```
+performOperationX (argument1, argument2) : result_type
-performStep1OfOperationX [a private operation]
```

9.1.4 Associations

An *association* documents a physical or conceptual connection between two or more classes. If one class has the responsibility of telling a second class that a social security number is valid or invalid, for example, the two classes have an association. The most generic association is represented as a line between two classes. An association is naturally bidirectional. In other words, an association implies that the objects of one class will send messages to operations associated with the objects of the second class and that the second class's objects will respond when appropriate.

The line representing the association can be given a name. The association name is written just above or below the line connecting the two classes. (Association names begin with uppercase letters.) The association name may be omitted if the association represents a single, obvious relationship between the two classes.

In some cases you will want to provide names for the roles played by the individual classes making up the relationship. In UML, these are referred to as *roles,* and they are written just under or just over the association line. The role name on the side closest to each class describes the role that class plays relative to the class at the other end of the line, and vice versa. Role names are written in all lowercase letters. (See Figure 9.2.)

In the example shown in Figure 9.2, you can see that the role of the *Sales Order* is that of being made up of parts being ordered. The part, in turn, is included in a *Sales Order.* In effect, made_up_of and included_in are the two roles involved in the Contains association. Indicating roles is especially critical when an association exists between two objects of the same class. In this case the association line begins and ends on the same class rectangle, as we've illustrated in Figure 9.3. The

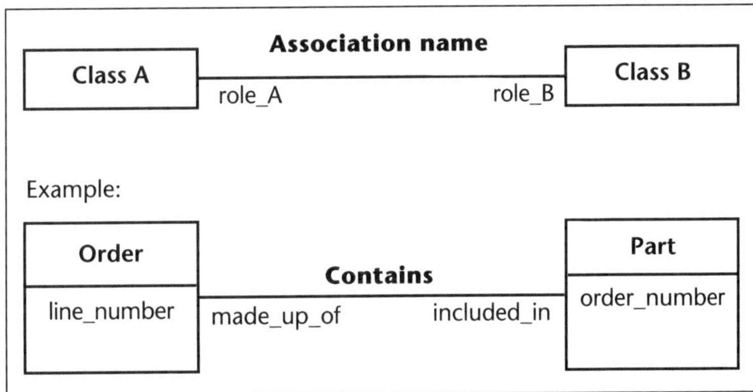

Figure 9.2 *Basic notation for an association.*

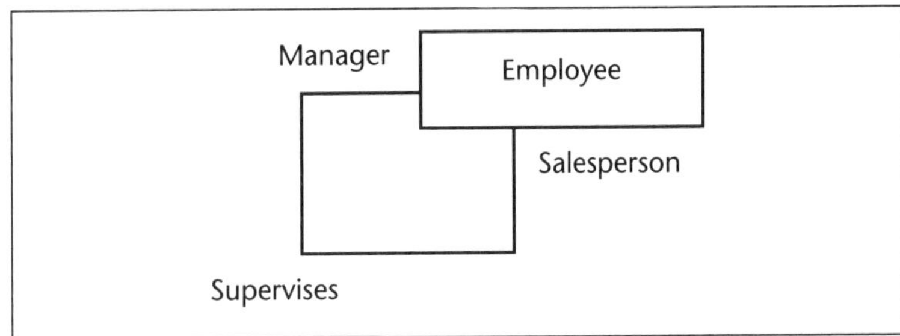

Figure 9.3 *Notation for a self-referencing association.*

association illustrated by this "loop" is between various objects of the *Employee* class and involves supervision. Some objects of *Employee* are managers, while other objects of employee are salespeople who are supervised by sales managers. Role names are usually necessary to clarify this kind of relationship.

The Multiplicity of an Association

UML also provides a way to indicate the multiplicity of an association. *Multiplicity* refers to how many objects of one class can relate to each object of another class. Multiplicity isn't something you worry about when you are first creating a class diagram. As you expand the diagram, however, it's important to discriminate, at a minimum, between associations that only involve one object and those that involve many objects.

Figure 9.4 provides an overview of the symbols available in UML to indicate multiplicity. An unadorned line between two classes, as we showed in Figure 9.2, indicates one and only one object on each end of the association. An asterisk above one end of a relationship line indicates that zero or more objects of that class can be linked to objects of the class at the other end of the line. Obviously, there should be an asterisk on the end of the association line in Figure 9.2 where it touches the part class. Several objects of the part class can belong to a single order object. A single order, on the other hand, can own many different parts. Similarly, an asterisk should be added at the "salesperson" end of the association line shown in Figure 9.3. One manager can supervise many salespeople, but each salesperson has only one manager.

To indicate more precise relationships, you can place numbers over the line. For example, 0..1 indicates that zero or one object can be involved, 0.. * indicates that zero to many objects can be involved, and 1–3, 5 indicates that one, two, three, or five objects can be involved.

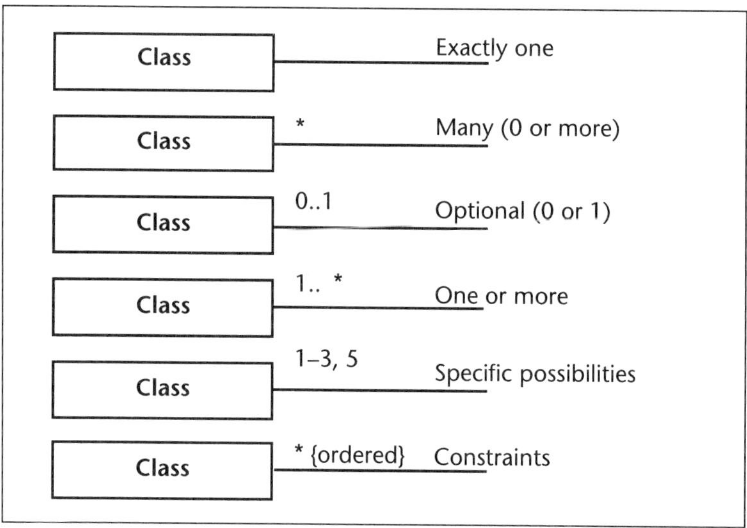

Figure 9.4 *Notation for multiplicity of associations.*

In some cases the class that will be represented by many objects will order those objects in some particular way. If it is important to indicate this, UML suggests you place the word "ordered" within braces (squiggly brackets) above or below the association line, close to the asterisk, as shown in Figure 9.4. (This is a specific example of the use of braces to include information about constraints on a diagram. Information within braces can be included on any diagram to indicate that constraints apply. We'll consider constraints in more detail a little later in the chapter.)

In most cases you will either have a plain line or a line with an asterisk at the end—these are the two most common multiplicities to note.

Association Classes

At times you may want to think of an association as an object in its own right and to imagine it has its own attributes. This is especially useful when there is an association between many objects and many other objects, and the attribute (or attributes) that describes the relationship is not a characteristic of either of the classes being linked but, rather, a characteristic of the linkage itself.

You can include a single attribute or multiple attributes and operations within an association class, as shown in Figure 9.5.

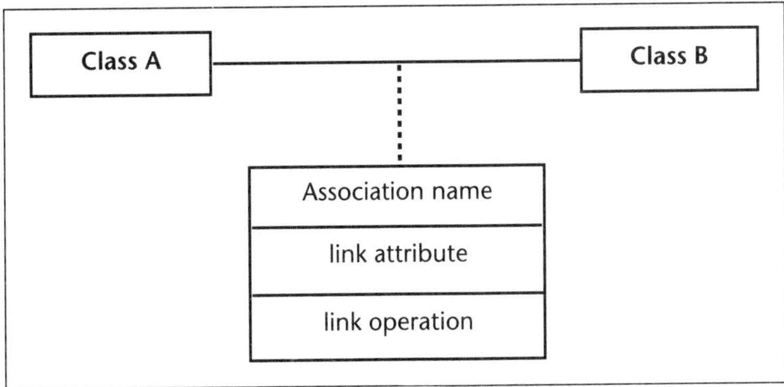

Figure 9.5 *An association class.*

Consider our earlier example where the association defined a relationship between objects of employee who were managers and those who were salespeople. Now imagine we wanted to add the attribute *supervisorsTitle.* It wouldn't properly be an attribute of employee, so it would be better to simply attach it to the association itself. We might also decide we wanted to add an attribute, *numberSupervised.* And we might decide to add an operation that would determine which employees were supervised by which managers.

Dependency Relationship

In Figure 9.5 we linked our association class to the regular association line with a dotted line. A dotted line denotes a dependency. A dependency indicates that one of the elements will change when the other changes. This can occur as a result of the fact that a message is sent, but it can also involve more abstract relationships. As we examine other diagrams, we'll see that dependency relationships are used to suggest a relationship without getting too specific about it.

Qualified Associations

In some cases you may want to qualify a specific association. This occurs when one class is linked to another in a one-to-many relationship and you want to specify the nature of the association more precisely. Thus, the *SalesManager* class is linked to many objects of the *Salesperson* class. Sometimes a manager will want to see how all of the salespeople reporting to him or her are performing. At other times a manager might only want to examine how one salesperson is doing. In that case the association could be qualified by the specific salesperson's name or employee number. You could show that specific or qualified association as we have in Figure 9.6. The

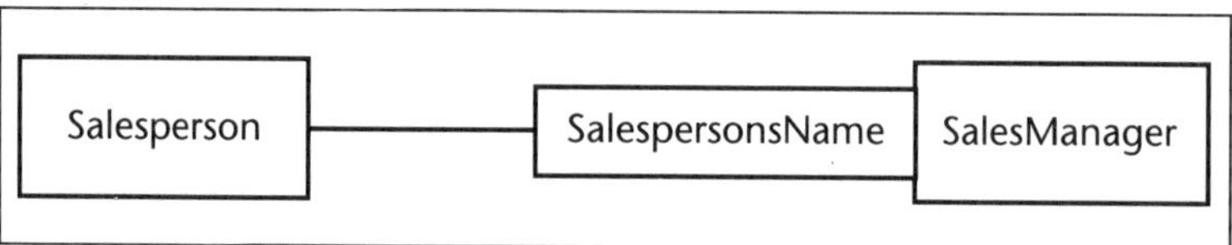

Figure 9.6 *Notation for a qualified association.*

discriminatory attribute is placed next to the source class (*SalesManager*) from which we want to navigate to the qualified association.

Note that once you have qualified an association you no longer need to use an asterisk to indicate that there is a multiple relationship. The qualification says that this association is going to function as a relationship between a single object of the *SalesManager* class and a single object of the *Salesperson* class. The single object of the *Salesperson* class will be governed by a specific salesperson's name.

9.1.5 *Generalization*

Generalization refers to a relationship when one class shares its properties, methods, relationships, and constraints with another class. Generalization can be implemented by either class or interface inheritance.

UML indicates generalization by means of hollow-headed arrow. The arrow always points towards the superclass. (See Figure 9.7.)

Class or Implementation Inheritance

Class inheritance refers to a situation in which one class inherits the code of its superclass. Most OO languages support class inheritance. Visual Basic doesn't support class inheritance, but you should understand it since the concept is so

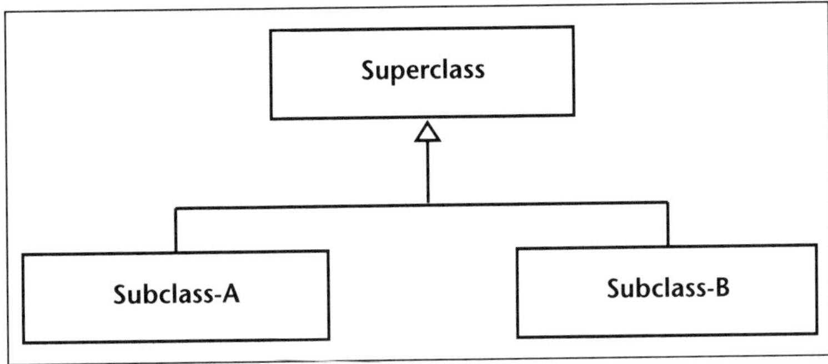

Figure 9.7 *Notation for generalization.*

important to most OO languages. C++ and Java support class inheritance, and COM may do so in a future release.

Class inheritance is good for two things. In some cases you find that you want to create a number of classes that are similar in all but a few characteristics. In other cases you will find that someone has already developed a class that you can use, and all you need to do is modify that class. We'll consider both possibilities.

Imagine that we decided to create a class for each of the furniture items that Moose's sells. All of the furniture items would have certain things in common—a stock or item number, a price, an availability number or date, and so on. In fact, whole groups of items would have things in common. For example, all desk chairs would either have wheels or not, would either have padded seats or not. Whole lines of chairs would have common fabric or leather options. In developing our first prototype we might very well just use a generic class called *FurnitureItem,* or *Item,* but when we began to refine our application, we would probably take some time to create classes for the different furniture items. The most effective way to do that would be to create a class hierarchy. The top class would be *FurnitureItem* or *Item.* That class would have subclasses that divided the actual furniture items into groups. And each of those groups would probably have classes that represented the specific furniture items stocked by Moose's. When it came time to identify the attributes and operations, we would begin with the superclass and work down. If an attribute or operation is identified in the top item, it wouldn't have to be identified again in a lower class, since lower classes always inherit all of the attributes and operations of their parent classes.

In creating a UML class diagram, you usually begin by showing only a top-level class, like *FurnitureItem,* and how that class relates to other classes, for example, *Sales Order* and *Inventory.* Later, if you subclass furniture, you still tend to leave the links between the high-level *FurnitureItem* and *Inventory* as they were; otherwise, you would need to show links between each of the subclasses and the *Inventory* class. Thus, associations are, in effect, inherited, just like attributes and operations are inherited.

Once you have subclassed a class, as a rule, the actual objects used in an application are instantiated from the subclasses. In that case, the only function of the superclass is to serve as a template for the subclasses. Developers sometimes refer to the high-level class, which is only used as a template for other classes, as an abstract class.

If you have been doing OO development for any period of time, you will usually have some classes that can be reused when you create a new application. In most cases, however, the older class will need to be modified in some way before it's ready to use in the new application. To keep things neat, the best way to do this is to leave the older class as it was and simply create a subclass of the older class. Then, make whatever modifications you need to make in the subclass. You can modify a subclass by adding new attributes or operations that don't exist in the superclass. Or you can use the name of an attribute or operation in the subclass and define it differently from the way it's defined in the superclass. Since objects always use the attributes and operations in their parent class, if you overwrite an attribute or operation in the subclass, it is the attribute or operation that will be used by the object. If you don't overwrite attributes or operations, the object will inherit them from the superclass via the subclass.

You can easily develop small OO applications without any form of generalization. Once you become involved in reuse, or you find yourself considering writing a new class that will have operations or attributes just like or very similar to those in another class, you should consider using generalization.

Creating classes that can be reused in other applications can get very complex, because you need to keep the superclasses' attributes and operations generic. It's too complex to consider in this book, but it is important if you intend to develop a lot of OO applications. If you do, you should certainly study some books on developing code for reuse.

Interface Inheritance

An object model that incorporates generalization can also be implemented with interface inheritance. In this case, instead of directly incorporating the code superclass into the subclass, the subclass contains the interface supported by the superclass and a pointer to the superclass.

In some cases, the superclass may be both an interface and an implementation. In other cases, the superclass may only be an interface, and the developer will have to write the code to implement the superclass interface.

In Visual Basic, generalization is spoken of as implementation. In effect, any class can implement one or more interfaces. Implementation, or interface inheritance, isn't as powerful as class inheritance. It's more appropriate for infrastructure relationships than for business objects. You can still create complex business objects and plan to reuse them in their entirety, but it's a lot more work to do this in Visual Basic than it would be in Java or C++.

In this book, our diagrams will indicate generalization. The same diagrams could be implemented in either C++ or Visual Basic. In our sample code, we will implement the generalization relationships by means of interface inheritance. If a C++ developer were dealing with the same problem, he or she would more likely implement the relationships via class inheritance.

9.1.6 *Identifying Aggregations*

An aggregation refers to part-whole relationships. In effect, aggregation suggests that some classes are contained within another class, and indeed, some notations allow you to literally place the part classes inside the class that represents the whole. This can get messy fast, however, and in reality, the classes usually aren't contained but are simply organized by the fact that messages go to the class representing the whole, which then passes them on to classes representing parts, and vice versa.

An aggregation relationship is indicated by placing a small diamond at the end of the association line that runs between part classes and the whole class, pointing at the whole class. Figure 9.8 illustrates two ways to diagram a whole-part relationship. UML refers to the type of aggregation represented by placing one class inside another as a composite class.

9.1.7 Constraints and Notes

Constraints are functional relationships between elements of a class or object model. A constraint sets limits on the values that one of the elements can take. A constraint can limit the value an attribute can take, or it can limit the value that an operation can accept. It might limit the number of objects of the class that can exist at any point in time. For example, it may be a matter of policy that no corporate sales order can exceed $200,000 without the explicit approval of the vice president of accounting, or that salespeople may not enter sales orders for individuals or companies outside their sales region. If you identify a constraint that you want to remember, you can write it in braces below the class involved. (Constraints can

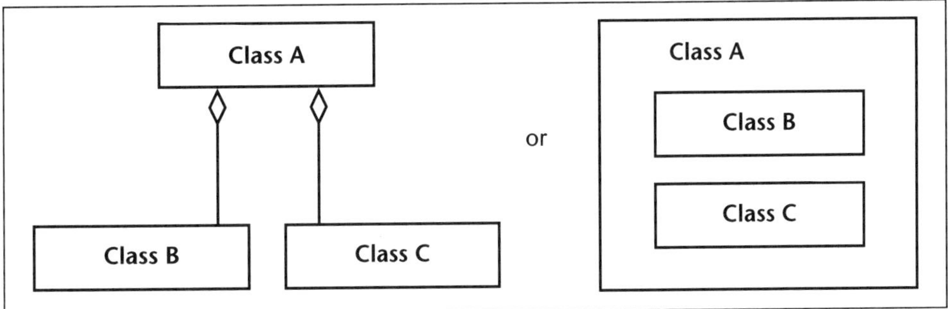

Figure 9.8 *Notation for an aggregation (whole-part) relationship.*

also be noted on the various other OMT (Object Management Technique) diagrams in a similar way, between braces.)

UML also allows developers to write notes on diagrams by putting them in rectangles with a dog-eared right corner. Thus, if you discover something that is more complex than a constraint—perhaps an explanation of why you handled a specific aspect of the problem in a particular way—and you want to be sure to remember it, you can simply write it in a box off to one side of the diagram. Figure 9.9 illustrates both the use of a note and the specification of a constraint.

9.2 Diagramming Objects

Occasionally you will want to diagram objects of classes to clarify some particular situation. Some developers create an object diagram for each sequence diagram that they create. In this case they probably use collaboration diagrams. Object diagrams are used for more informal analysis.

UML indicates an object as a rectangle—the same way it indicates a class. You can tell the difference, however, by noticing the way the name is written inside the rectangle. UML offers you three ways to name an object:

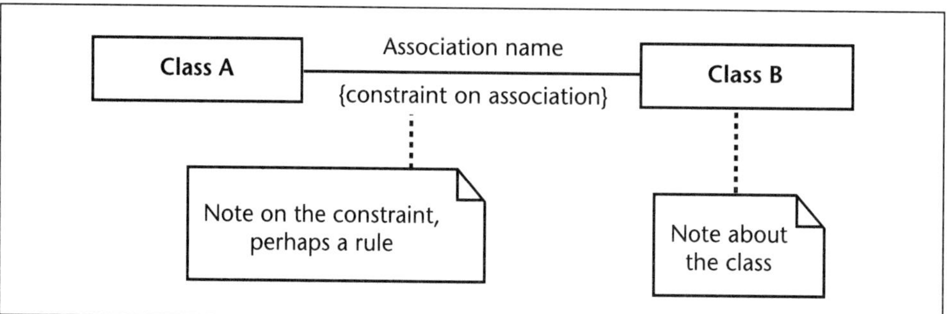

Figure 9.9 *Notation for a constraint and for notes.*

1. You can simply write the class name, preceded by a colon and underlined:

   `:Class Name`

   This can be used to refer to "generic" examples of an object—in other words, any object of the class.

2. You can write the name of the specific object, underlined and followed by a colon:

   `object name:`

3. You can write the specific object name followed by the class name, thus:

   `object name:Class Name`

You can also expand the size of the rectangle and include attributes and values associated with the object, as shown in Figure 9.10. This is useful if you are creating a diagram and want to show how messages will result in changes in attributes.

There is never an occasion in which you would enter the name of an operation inside an object rectangle. Operations are always associated with classes and accessed by objects when needed.

If you want to show that an object has been instantiated from a class, you use a dashed line with an arrow pointing to the class from which the object derived. This is also shown in Figure 9.10.

Notice that the instantiation line is a dotted line. This is an example of a dependency relationship. Solid lines show associations or links—relationships that are based on semantic relationships. Dependencies are relationships that aren't based on message passing but on some other relationship. In this case, the object is an instance of the class.

Just as classes are related by associations, objects are related by links. In effect, a link is an instantiation of an association. Or, conversely, an association represents all of the links that could occur between objects of the two related classes. Links are also represented by lines. There is no need to indicate multiplicity when you are diagramming objects. If one object relates to several objects of another class, you can actually

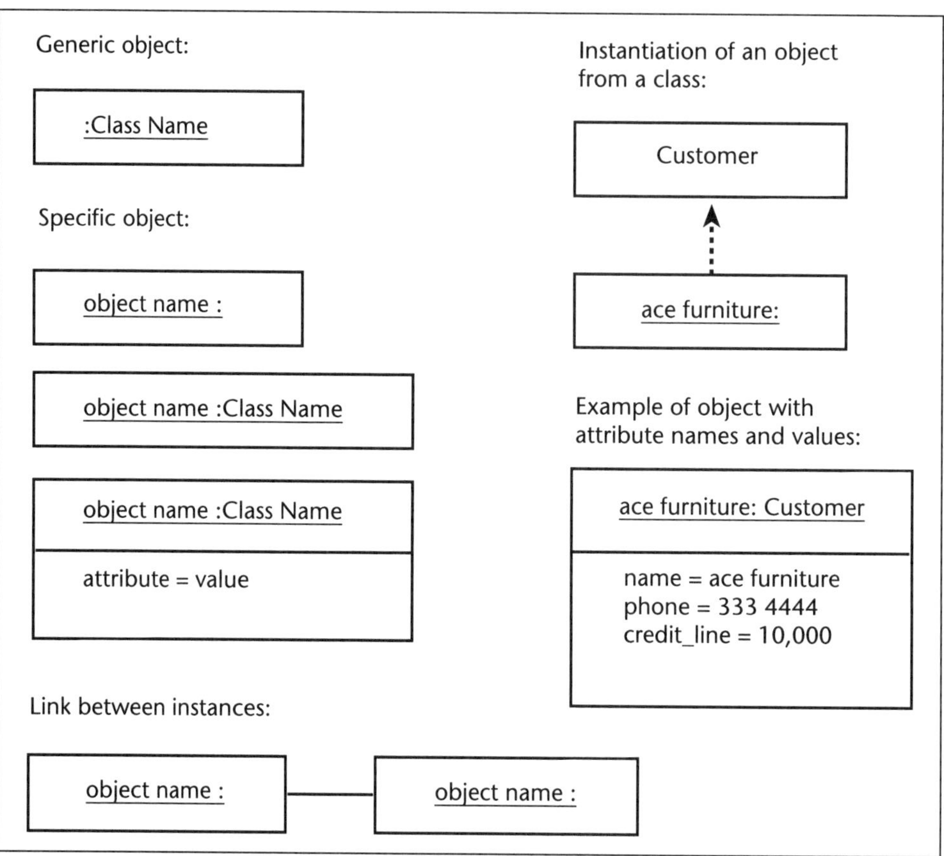

Figure 9.10 *Basic UML notation for objects.*

show the existence of multiple objects relating to single objects. Indeed, whenever you are trying to figure out the multiplicity of a particular association between classes, you can usually draw an object diagram to clarify it. Figure 9.11 illustrates an object diagram and the related class diagram.

9.3 Creating a Class Diagram

Your first class diagram should be a very simple affair that shows the major classes in your application and the obvious associations between them. Later, you can redraw it, adding

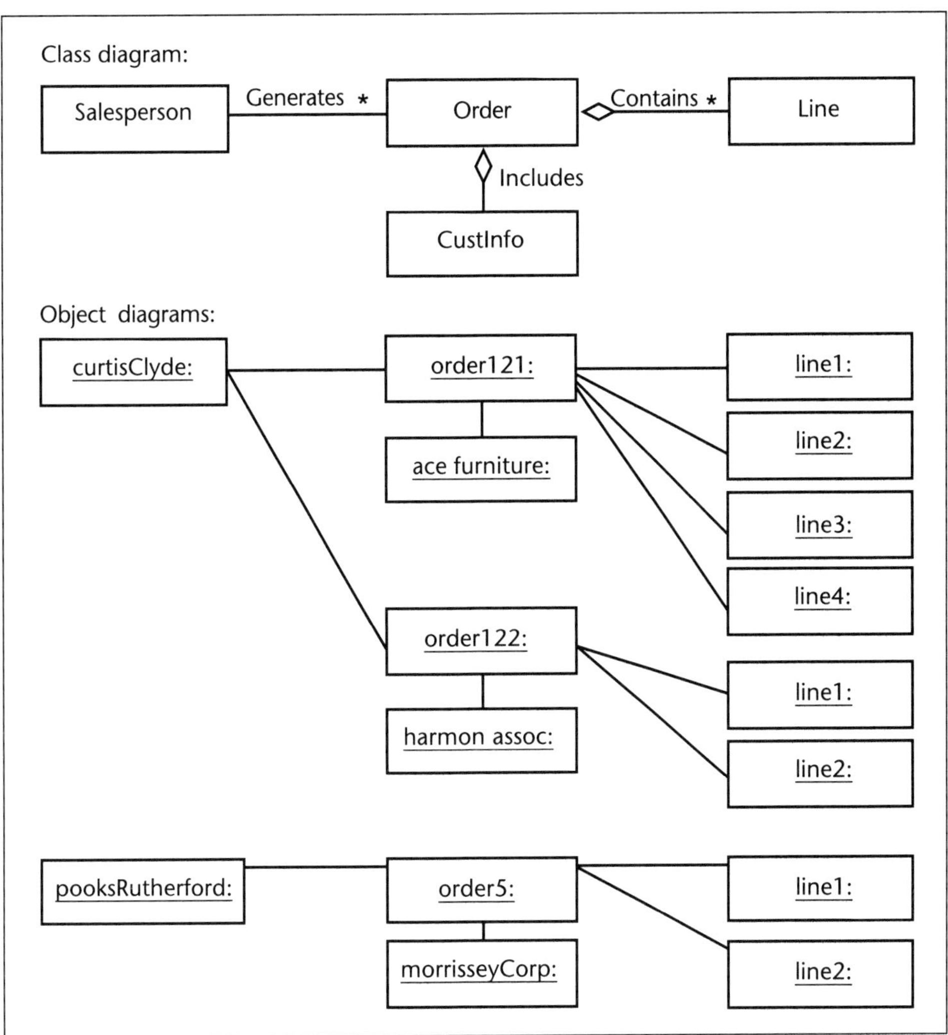

Figure 9.11 *Class and object diagrams.*

attributes to the classes, indicating multiplicity for the associations, and adding new classes as you identify them.

When you develop BPR workflow charts, high-level use case diagrams, or CRC cards, you tend to look at the whole system. You need to do this simply to know what the whole system will have to include. Once you get an overview, however, in most cases you'll want to focus on a subset of the entire application and develop a prototype of that before moving on to other subsets of the application. Earlier we said that we would focus our first prototype on the Report Sales use case. Thus, we're ignoring other potential classes, such as *Regional Sales Manager, Quota,* and *Regions.* During the second prototype phase, our SalesWeb development team can go back and add classes, attributes, and relationships to handle the two other use cases. For the moment, we're only working with scenarios that involve reporting sales, and our first class diagram will only be a model of the sales-reporting portion of our application.

Since we've developed a use case analysis of our SalesWeb system and created use case descriptions and an ideal object model, we already have an idea of the classes that should appear in our first OMT object diagram. We also worked with CRC cards, so we have another version of the classes that might be in our application. We've listed the results of the two separate approaches below.

Ideal Object Model Classes	**CRC Classes**
Salesperson	*Salesperson*
Browser Order Interface	
SalesWeb Handler	
Sales Order	*Sales Order*
	Address
Customer Information	*Customer Information*
	CustInfo1
	CustInfoMulti
Item Ordered	*Item Ordered*
	(subclasses for different types of items)
Corporate Interface	
Accounting System	*Accounting* System
Inventory System	*Inventory* System

There is quite a bit of overlap between the two approaches and some differences that we'll need to resolve. In a real CRC effort, the participants would probably have come up with different names than what we chose during our use case analysis, and this would be the time to decide which names to use from now on.

The ideal object model, by emphasizing interface objects and objects to handle coordination tasks, creates classes that we will need when we get to design but which we can ignore during analysis, when we are primarily concerned with business objects such as *Salesperson, Sales Order,* and *Item Ordered.*

The CRC approach, which tends to include end users and subject matter experts in the process and which emphasizes business classes, messages sent (responsibilities), and attributes, is more likely to generate more superclass/subclass relationships. It's also likely to lead to people suggesting more practical new classes, such as address and time stamp. All of these issues would come up at some point during analysis and design. If we were working with a larger project, we might want to be more systematic about putting off certain considerations until design. Since we are working with a small problem, we are ignoring side issues until they occur.

Let's review both lists and focus only on the major business objects, ignoring all the subclasses for the moment, except the distinction between customers with a single address and those with multiple addresses. We're keeping this one inheritance relationship at this point only so we can show the UML notation. Thus, we arrive at this list: *Salesperson, Sales Order, Customer Information, CustInfo1, CustInfo-Multi, Item Ordered, Accounting,* and *Inventory*—eight classes to represent on our first UML class diagram. Since we're going to be constructing a UML diagram, we might as well convert these names into UML style. From here through the remainder of the book we'll place all class and object names in italics in the text to make them more obvious. We'll also combine multi-word names into a single name and eliminate some letters, as shown below.

Salesperson	*Salesperson*
Sales Order	*SalesOrder*
Customer Information	*CustInfo*
Customer Information1	*CustInfo1*
Customer Information Multi	*CustInfoMulti*
Item Ordered	*ItemOrdered*
Accounting	*Accounting*
Inventory	*Inventory*

Initially, we could just use a large sheet of paper and put the classes on one at a time as we begin identifying the associations between them. As a general rule, with a simple diagram, we think of events as flowing from left to right, so we'll put the *Salesperson* class, which provides the initial stimulus, at the top left of the page and go from there. We have one generalization relationship, so wherever we put *CustInfo* we'll want to leave enough room near it for the two *CustInfo* subclasses.

Associations indicate high-level relationships between classes, which will be implemented, at lower levels, as messages that will flow between the objects of the various classes. At this point, assuming you've done a CRC card exercise, you can consult your cards to see who was collaborating with whom. Or you can review the use case description and any scenarios you developed for the Report Sales use case to see what relationships will need to exist between classes. It's not important that you find them all at this point; you can continue to add associations as you go.

Most of the input to the system will enter via the *Salesperson* class. It will need to interact with the *SalesOrder* class to get signed on, and then it will provide all the customer and item information that will drive the other classes in the application. The input that doesn't come from the *Salesperson* class will come from the accounting and inventory databases, which will provide information on creditworthiness and item availability.

Figure 9.12 shows our initial UML class diagram of our simple SalesWeb system for inputs from the field sales staff of Moose's Furniture. In thinking about this diagram, try not to think of it as a procedural diagram; it describes the logical relationships between the various items, not the flow. (We chose an example that's easy to think of in procedural terms because we wanted an example that was easy to understand. On the other hand, if you have an application that involves changing a Web browser page around as the user clicks on one thing or another, that will be a lot harder to think of in procedural terms, since you'll never know where the user is likely to click next. Class diagrams are designed to show logical relationships, and they only incidentally suggest a procedural flow in some cases.)

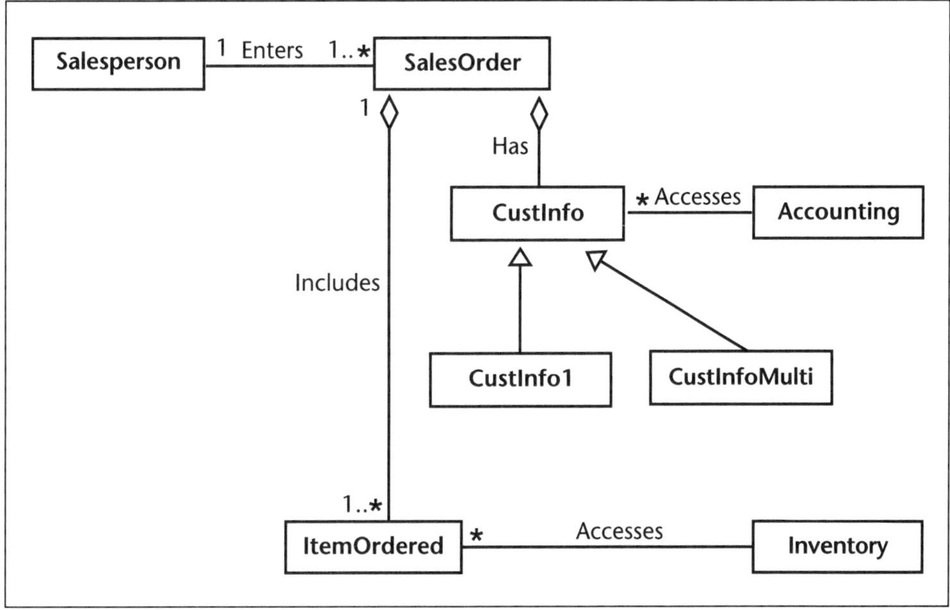

Figure 9.12 *Initial UML class diagram of the SalesWeb application.*

In Figure 9.12 we've connected our classes with lines to show associations. The associations should largely match the responsibilities and collaborators we identified in the earlier CRC exercise. We've given names to the associations, although other people might prefer different names. We've also included numbers and asterisks to show where relationships could involve one or more objects. And we've used diamonds to show whole-part relationships (aggregations). The figure in the next section will help clarify this.

9.3.1 An Object Diagram

Rational Software's UML documentation does not have an object diagram, as such, but you can create object diagrams by creating a collaboration diagram, ignoring arrows and numbers that show the flow of messages and events. Whatever they are called, there will be occasions when you will want to draw diagrams that show objects and their relationships.

Figure 9.13 is a UML object diagram of the same set of classes we've been discussing. Of course, being an object diagram, it deals with objects of classes and shows the multiple relationships more clearly. We also substituted a slightly different type of UML notation for an aggregation. We've shown the objects that are parts of an aggregation inside the bolder rectangle, which represents the whole class. (UML calls this particular way of representing an aggregation a composite object.) Notice that although we show the superclass *CustInfo* accessing *Accounting* in Figure 9.13, in fact, it will be an object of one of the two subclasses of *CustInfo* that actually accesses *Accounting.*

Using this object diagram, we can talk our way through the problem. Once a single salesperson, Curtis Clyde, initiates a transaction, he can submit one or more sales orders. In Figure 9.13 we show Curt submitting two sales orders. The orders might be given numbers so Curt can keep track of them, in which case there will be an attribute of each *SalesOrder* called number. Otherwise, the system will simply assign a system-

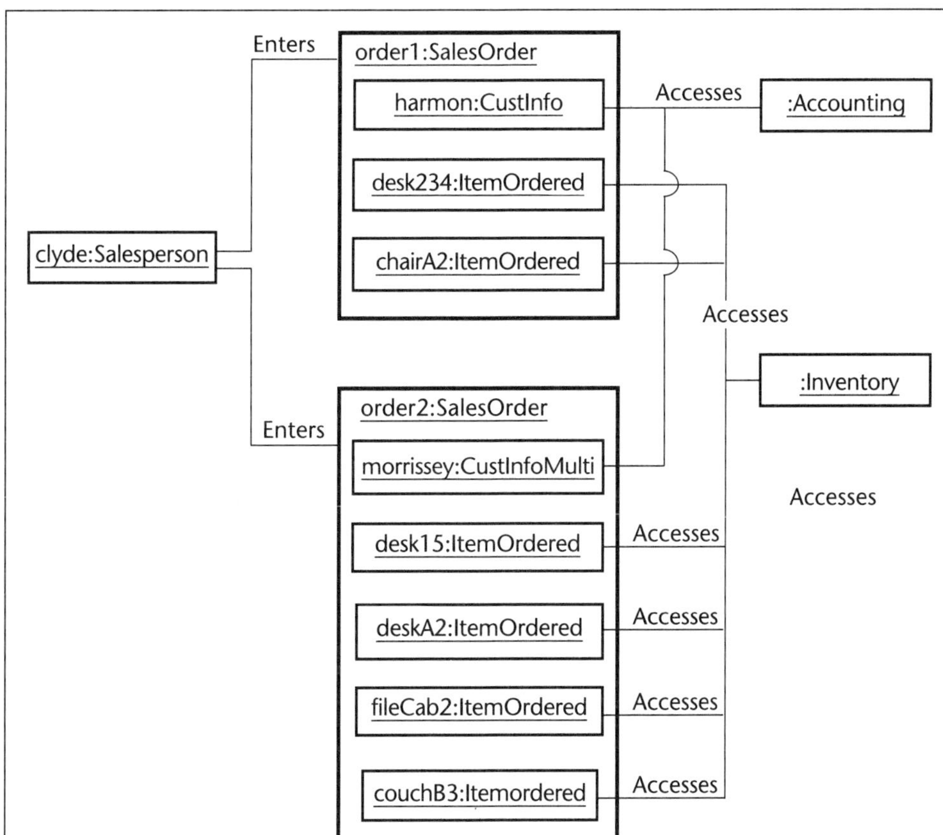

Figure 9.13 *Initial UML object diagram of the SalesWeb application.*

designated number to each instance of *SalesOrder* that it creates. A single *SalesOrder* object is made up of one *CustInfo* object and can have from one to many *ItemOrdered* objects. The number of *ItemOrdered* objects depends on how many different types of furniture the customer is ordering. *Accounting* can receive information requests from different *CustInfo* objects. Similarly, *Inventory* can receive availability and pricing requests from many different *ItemOrdered* objects.

9.3.2 A More Elaborate Class Diagram

In Figure 9.14 we have expanded the initial class diagram and included some of the attributes of several of the classes. We've taken these from the attributes we identified via our CRC card exercise. Assuming some knowledge of design, we know that *Accounting* and *Inventory* are legacy systems, and we will not have to create them but only interface with what already exists. Thus, to simplify our task, we've left them on the diagram but haven't bothered to generate attributes and operations for them. So far we've been using a phrase to explain what a method would do. At some point, however, you will need to determine specific names for the attributes and methods and use those names on your class diagrams. Following are some we've decided on.

Attributes:

orderID	The unique number of each order submitted
custName	The name of the customer ordering items
custBillAddress	The billing address of the customer
custShipAddress	The address to which the items are to be shipped
custCreditLmt	The maximum amount the customer can order on credit
itemName	The catalog name of the item
itemNumber	The catalog number of the item
itemStyle	The catalog style of the item
itemPrice	The price of one unit of the item
numOfItems	The number of units of an item being ordered
salesTax	The sales tax on the item
shippingCost	The shipping cost of the item
totalCost	The total cost of the order

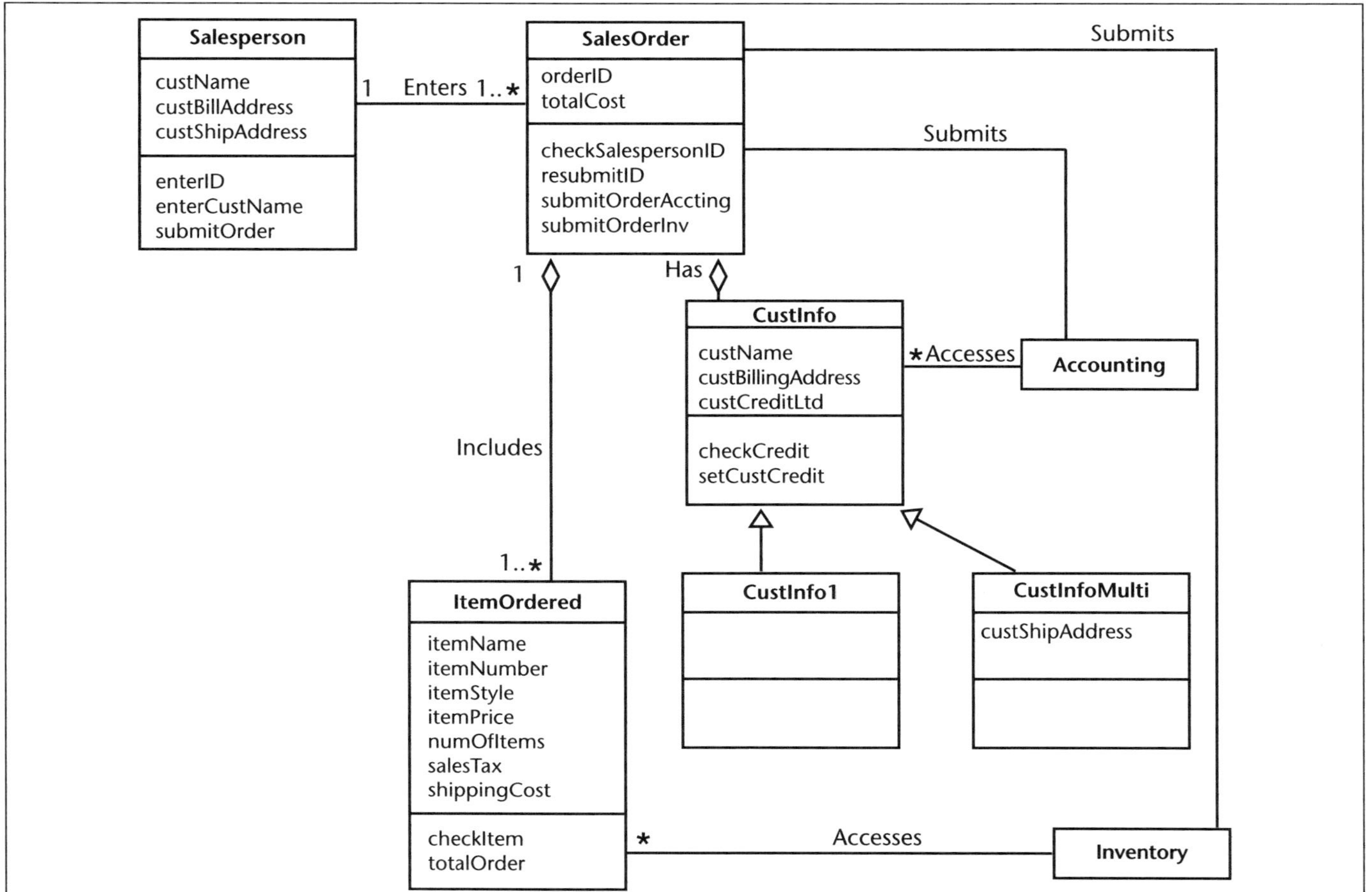

Figure 9.14 *The second cut of a UML class diagram of the SalesWeb application.*

Operations:

enterID	Enters salesperson's name and ID
checkSalespersonID	Checks to see if salesperson and number is acceptable to the system
resubmitID	Asks the salesperson to reenter name and ID
enterCustName	Enters customer name
checkCredit	Checks customer credit
setCustCredit	Sets customer credit
enterItem	Enters item number 1
checkItem	Checks item availability and price
enterItem	Enters item number 2
checkItem	Checks item availability and price
totalOrder	Totals items and adds shipping and tax
submitOrder	Submits completed/approved order
submitOrderAcct	Order information sent to *Accounting*
submitOrderInv	Order information sent to *Inventory*

In the process of entering the attributes and operations listed above, we were forced to think again about which object would do what and decided that while the *CustInfo* and *ItemOrdered* objects would contact the *Accounting* and *Inventory* systems for specific information, the *SalesOrder* itself would actually submit the final order. No individual item class will know the total of all the item classes. Clearly, that attribute and the operation to do it should reside on the *SalesOrder* class. Hence, *submitOrderAcct* and *submitOrderInv* required that we establish associations between the *SalesOrder* class and both the *Accounting* and *Inventory* systems.

At this point, you could think about adding more attributes, more operations, and perhaps a couple of additional classes. Similarly, you could begin to consider inheritance issues and think about breaking out subclasses for the *ItemOrdered* class. Given the small size of our application, however, we probably have a pretty good first approximation. So it's about time to switch and use some dynamic models to refine our understanding of the relationships between the classes we've identified. Before doing that, let's pause to consider how we would have created the class diagram shown in Figure 9.14 in an OO modeling tool.

At various points we've mentioned other things you could do to the SalesWeb application. We've suggested creating a class for addresses and for date and time stamps. We've also talked about breaking the *ItemOrdered* class into a hierarchy that would classify the various types of furniture that Moose's stocked. If you were to do these things during the first cycle of your application development effort, you would need to add the items onto your class and sequence diagrams and perhaps generate other diagrams, besides, to be sure you understood each addition. To keep our application simple, we'll assume that all of those additions are to be put off until the next cycle. Thus, we'll assume that the class diagrams we have developed so far are the ones we will carry forward into the design phase of the first cycle.

9.4 Creating UML Class Diagrams with a Visual Modeling Tool

Up to this point we've described the development of class and object diagrams as if we were simply drawing our diagrams on paper. And, of course, our example is so simple that we could easily do that. However, as we considered more complex problems, the diagramming would become more tedious. A visual modeling tool provides a way to automate the diagramming process and also reduces the effort involved in generating other diagrams or code.

Let's consider how we would have generated our initial class diagram in Microsoft's Visual Modeler. We saw in Chapter 6 how you could access the Visual Modeler tool. The Class Diagram button is on the horizontal tool bar, just to the right of the button that is depressed in Figure 9.15. If you simply clicked on this button and accepted the default, you'd be presented with a screen divided into three vertical panels: User Services, Business Services, and Data Services. This division of classes into tiers can be quite useful, but it is a design issue rather than an analysis issue. To avoid considering it now, we'll double click on the class diagram button on the horizontal tool bar, and chose a <new> class diagram. In this case, we will be given a single panel without vertical divisions.

Figure 9.15 shows Visual Modeler with the Class Diagramming window open. Notice that the buttons on the vertical

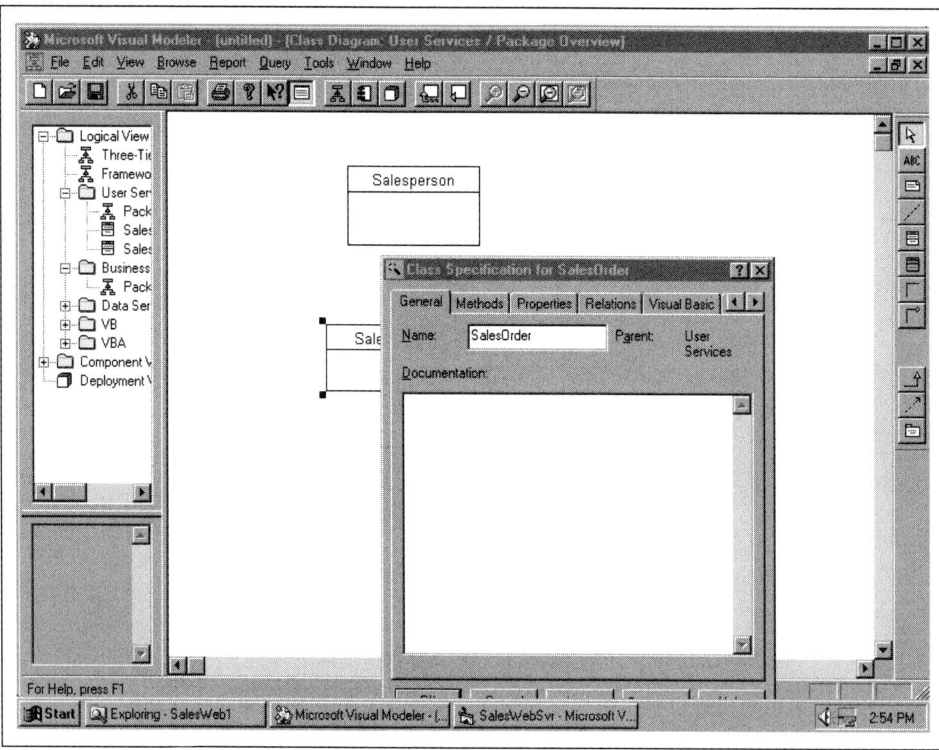

Figure 9.15 *Visual Modeler screen with the Class Diagramming window open.*

tool bar on the right of the screen are the UML class diagramming elements we have been discussing in this chapter. By pressing on the fifth button down and then clicking anywhere on the screen we get a simple class rectangle. In the case of Figure 9.15, we have already done that twice and created two classes: *Salesperson* and *SalesOrder*. We have also double clicked on the *SalesOrder* box and caused a Class Specification window to open. Using this window we can enter methods, properties, relationships, and other characteristics of the *SalesOrder* class.

Using Visual Modeler, if we just place the class boxes on and arrange them more or less as in Figure 9.12, we get Figure 9.16. Assuming that once we had placed all the class boxes correctly, clicked on the association button and then drawn a line between the *Salesperson* class and the *SalesOrder* class, and then double clicked on the line, we would get

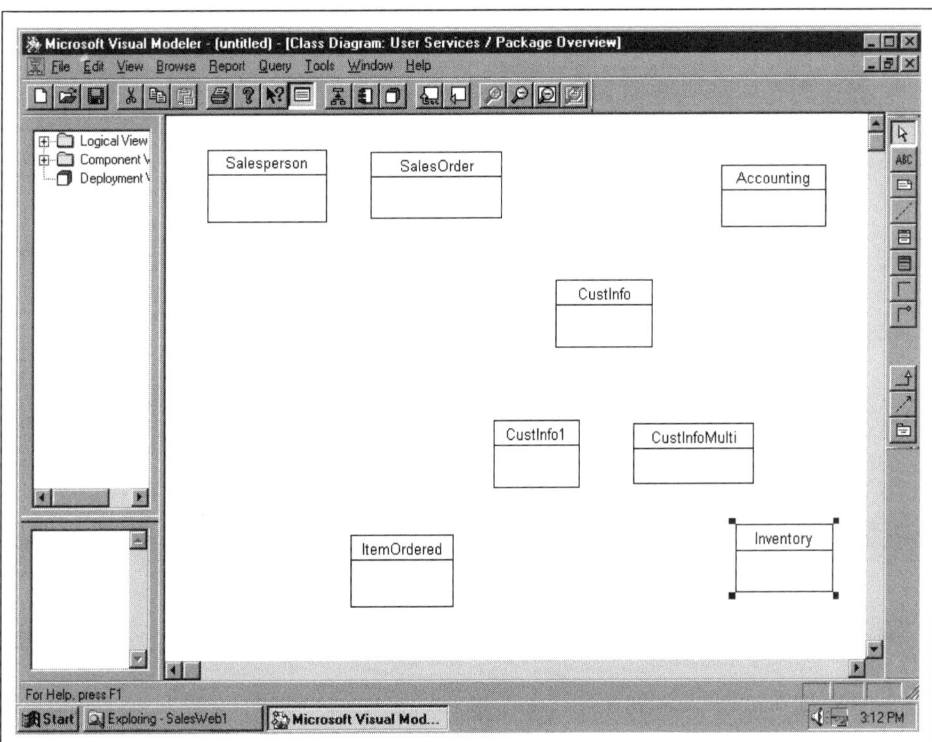

Figure 9.16 *Visual Modeler screen showing all basic SalesWeb classes.*

another window asking us to name the association. (See Figure 9.17.) Using this window, we can indicate the role of the association. In Figure 9.17 we have just entered the role "Enters", which will subsequently be placed on the association line.

If you look at the menu of buttons on the right, you won't see an aggregation symbol. You create an aggregation by drawing an aggregation association line between two classes. Assuming we now work through the diagram and define all the associations, we end up with the diagram shown in Figure 9.18, which is reasonably close to Figure 9.12.

Now, let's assume we're prepared to move on and add attributes and operations to enhance Figure 9.18. To convert it into Figure 9.14, we start providing more information on each class.

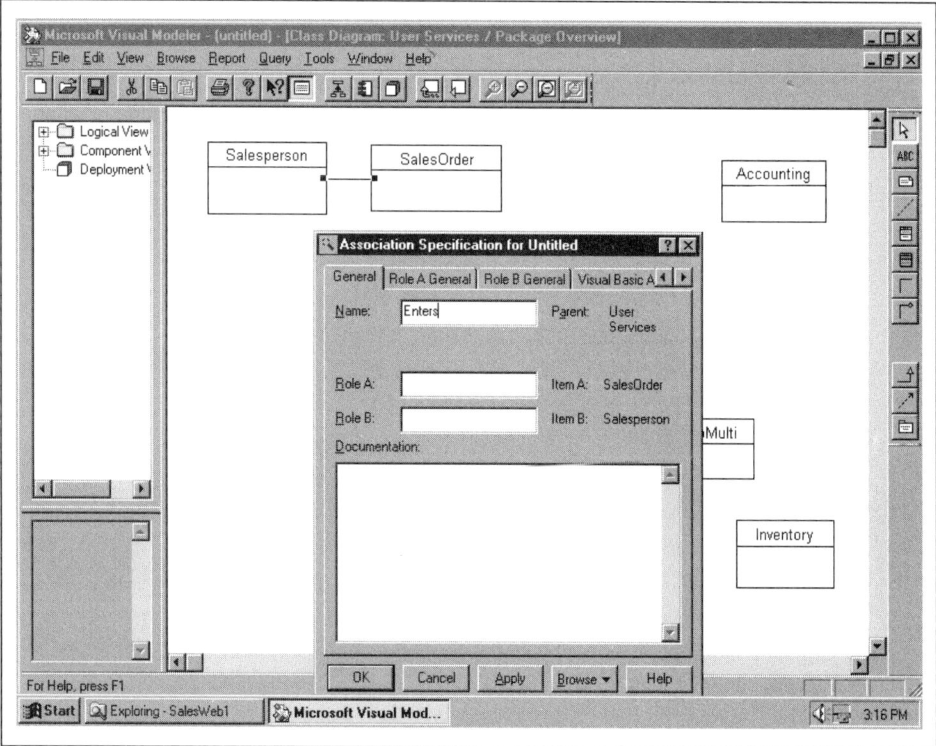

Figure 9.17 *Visual Modeler screen showing dialog box for naming associations between classes.*

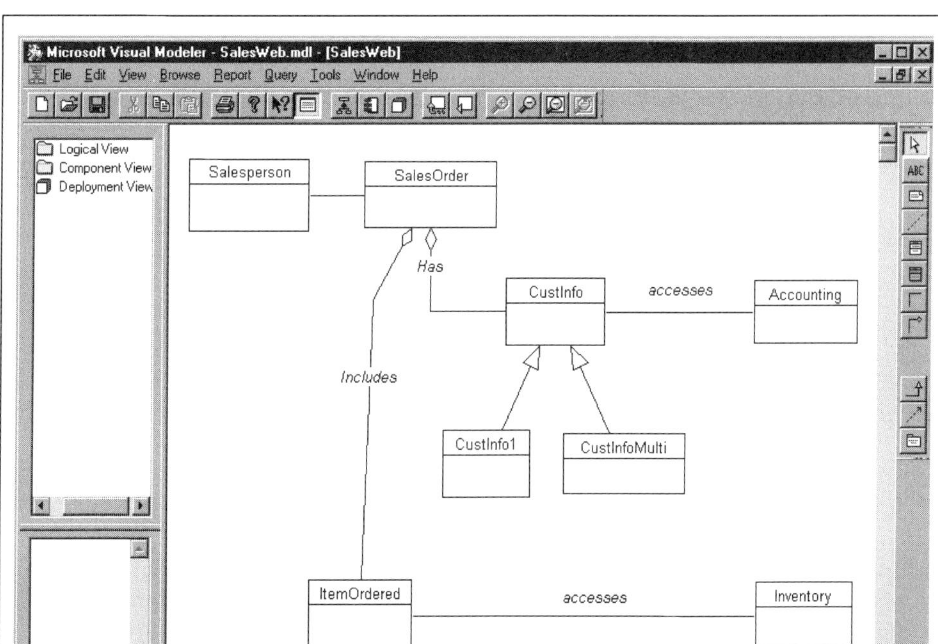

Figure 9.18 *Visual Modeler screen showing initial SalesWeb class diagram.*

Let's begin with *Salesperson*. We highlight *Salesperson* and double click on the class box. This brings up the Class Specification box that allows us to enter information about the class. In Figure 9.19 we have entered the names of the attributes (properties) and operations (methods) we identified in Figure 9.14. In each case, Visual Modeler is making assumptions about things like whether the attribute is public or private. You can see the symbols for attribute and private shown on the left-hand side of the Class Specification box and could change them if you wanted. Similarly, by highlighting any item and choosing Visual Basic, you could check the assumptions Visual Modeler was planning to make when it generates code. You could change any of those assumptions too, if you wanted. At this

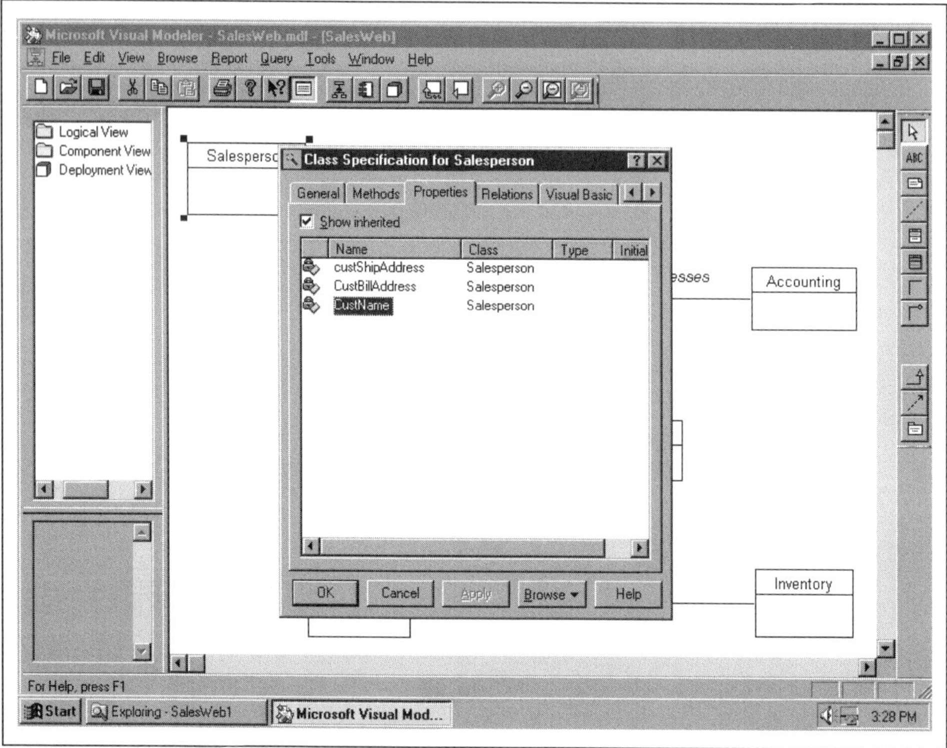

Figure 9.19 *Visual Modeler screen showing Class Specification box that allows us to enter information about the class.*

point, however, it's best to ignore such details and revisit them during the design phase of the project.

Figure 9.20 is a Visual Modeler diagram with all the information that we had on our earlier Figure 9.14. Once we've saved the diagram in Visual Modeler, we can recall it whenever we want. Similarly, we can print out a copy whenever we need to. Moreover, unlike our hand-drawn diagrams that we have to redraw when we want to enhance them or change them, we can modify our Visual Modeler class diagram by changing something on the diagram or changing a class definition and then reprinting the entire diagram.

Notice that, in addition to indicating the names of the attributes and methods we have entered for each class, the

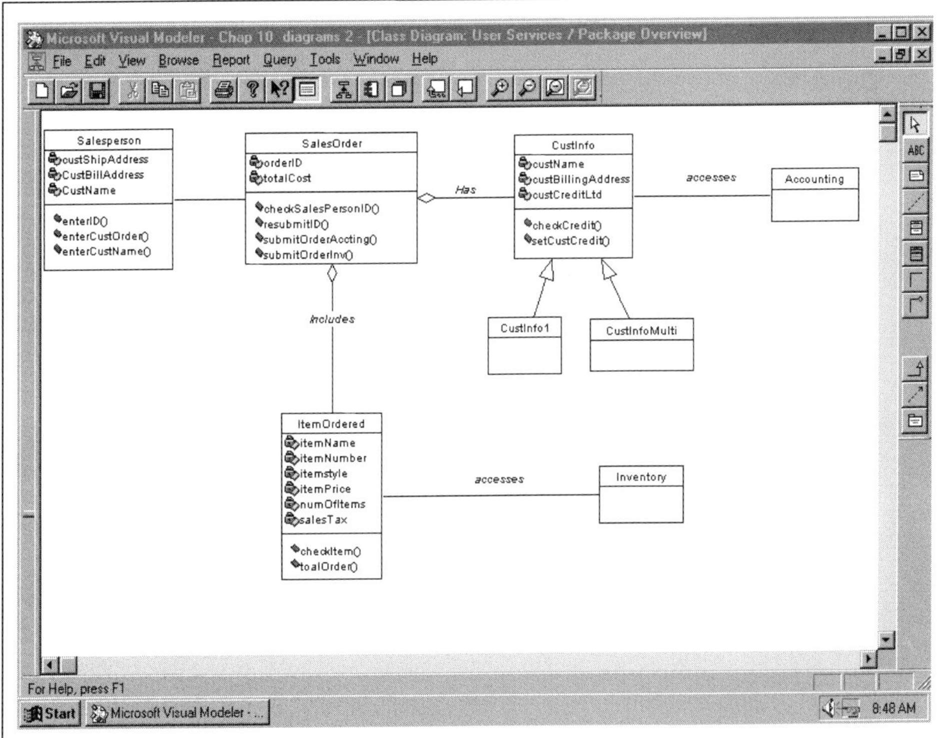

Figure 9.20 *Visual Modeler screen showing SalesWeb class diagram with some attributes and operations.*

diagram incorporates symbols to indicate that a name refers to an attribute or a method and also adds a little lock icon to indicate that the property is private and cannot be accessed by another class. We didn't set those when we entered the properties and methods; we simply accepted the defaults. We could, of course, open the Class Specification box for any class and modify them at any time we wished.

A project that depended on hand-drawn UML diagrams might easily produce a dozen class diagrams in the course of even a simple application like SalesWeb. When we develop the application with Visual Modeler or Rose 98, we really only have one class diagram that we simply keep enhancing as we refine our definitions of the classes, relationships, attributes, operations, and other characteristics of the application. If we print each version of the diagram, we have a historical record as well as a final version of the diagram, ready to generate code.

If we created one class diagram and wanted to save it, while creating another slightly different version of that class diagram, we would need to start using the version control feature of Visual Modeler and indicate which version each diagram was associated with. We won't worry about that sort of thing as we develop our simple application, but it would prove valuable to a team working on a more complex application.

When we use Visual Modeler or Rose 98 we are entering information into a repository that will later be used to generate code. If we create a class on a class diagram, Visual Modeler or Rose 98 will, on command, generate all the Visual Basic code necessary to define a class.

When we discussed Microsoft's Visual Modeler and Rational Software's Rose 98 earlier, we saw that the two products had an almost identical interface. Since both support UML class diagrams, if we had used Rose 98 screens in this section, they would have looked almost exactly like the Visual Modeler screens we actually used. Moreover, you would have developed the diagrams in exactly the same way. Thus, we won't show any Rose 98 screens until we come to another UML diagram, like the use case diagrams, that Visual Modeler won't support.

10

UML Sequence and Collaboration Diagrams

The UML class and object diagrams provide a static view of a system. Using the class diagram you systematically identify the classes in the system, define their attributes and operations, and describe their relationships with one another. When you look at a class diagram, however, there is no sense of starting at one point and working through the system in any order.

Often it's useful to diagram a system in a way that indicates the order in which things occur. UML offers two sets of diagrams that can be used to show the dynamics of a system. The first set, the sequence and collaboration diagrams, show how the objects in a system send messages to one another. These diagrams provide a macro-level analysis of the dynamics of a system. The second set, the state and activity diagrams, which we'll consider in the next chapter, focus on workflow processes on a specific class and show how that single class changes as it receives and sends messages.

10.1 Approaches to Diagramming

Sequence diagrams (sometimes called event trace or interaction diagrams) provide a more detailed view of the interaction between the objects of the major classes in the system or between the objects of some subset of classes. They provide specific information about the order in which events occur and can provide information about the time required for each activity. Collaboration diagrams combine object diagrams, numbers, and arrows to show the sequence of events traveling over the links connecting the objects. A collaboration diagram is similar to a Booch object diagram.

In developing an OO application, you always need to develop class diagrams. You will probably also always need to prepare one or more sequence diagrams. You may not always need to develop state or collaboration diagrams; it depends on the complexity of the system you are developing.

Most developers begin their analysis effort by preparing use case descriptions and scenarios. Then they move on to either class diagrams or sequence diagrams. As a general rule, subject matter experts—people who are already familiar with the problem to be automated—prefer to do class diagrams first. They usually find it easy to identify all the major business classes that will be needed in the application.

Programmers who aren't subject matter experts, on the other hand, normally find it easier to start with a sequence diagram. To develop a sequence diagram you also need to specify classes, but since you specify the classes in the process of spelling out the activities that will occur, programmers often find that this more "procedural" approach is an easier way to begin to understand a new system.

There's no correct order in which to proceed; it depends on the system being developed and the inclination of the developer. The simple SalesWeb system we are considering could be modeled equally well either way. We've rather arbitrarily begun by developing class diagrams, but we could just as well have started by developing sequence diagrams. Either way, you'll soon discover whether the classes you identified in the class diagram are really workable when you consider them in a dynamic context.

We'll consider sequence diagrams before collaboration, since we generally find them the more useful. We'll start developing our sequence diagram by using the classes we identified when we created class diagrams in the previous chapter. Before converting our SalesWeb class diagram into a sequence diagram, however, we'll need to define the basic sequence diagram conventions used in UML.

10.2 Sequence Diagrams

A sequence diagram is a graphical way to illustrate a scenario. Sequence diagrams are among the most popular UML diagrams and are used in conjunction with class diagrams to capture most of the information about a system. They show the sequence in which objects pass messages to each other. Sometimes they also show how long an object takes to process a message. Some other uses are to show when objects are created and destroyed and to note when messages are synchronous or asynchronous.

10.2.1 *Sequence Notation*

To create a sequence diagram, you begin by identifying a set of classes that will probably be involved in a scenario. The diagram itself can be concerned with either generic objects *(:CustInfo)* or specific objects *(Chou Furniture: CustInfo)*; you can use either.

Once you have identified the objects involved in the scenario to be described in your sequence diagram, you list the objects in a line along the top of a page and drop a dotted line beneath each object. (See Figure 10.1.) The dotted lines are referred to as lifelines. You should list the objects more or less in the order they are used in the scenario. The leftmost object should be the one that provides the stimulus that starts the scenario. If you can figure it out in advance, go ahead and list the objects in order. If you aren't sure, begin at the top left and list the first object, and then ask what object comes next. In other words, work your way through the scenario, listing each new object, in turn, as it enters the scenario.

Figure 10.1 illustrates the minimum notation needed to create a sequence diagram. The line on the left often represents an actor or event that is outside the system boundary. In other words, it might be an individual or an input from some other system. Something represented by the left-hand line provides the initial stimulus that leads to events. Similarly, the right-hand line often represents the outside boundary of the system. If it does, it is understood that events reaching the right-hand line pass to systems that lie outside the focus of the current effort.

A sequence diagram can depict many different event sequences. In each case, events within a sequence that occur

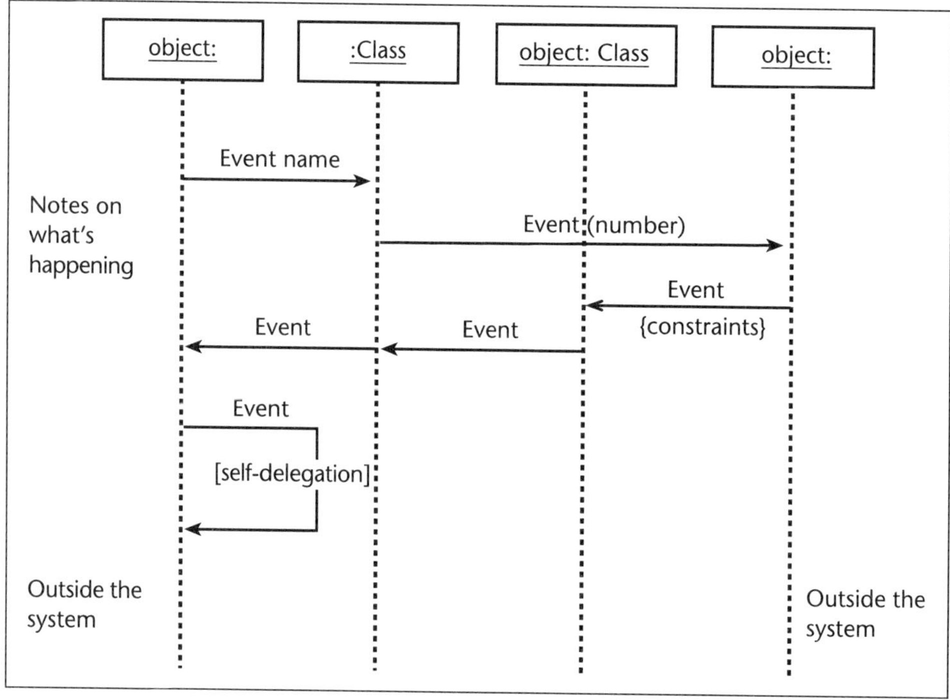

Figure 10.1 *Notation used in a sequence diagram—1.*

lower on the chart are understood to occur later in time than those that occur higher on the chart. Some developers are very informal about this and simply move all the event arrows down by a small set amount. Others try to capture information about how long things take to occur and space the arrows to show the difference between long and short time durations. In some cases, developers will actually note the interval of time between an incoming and an outgoing arrow.

An event arrow connects objects. In effect, the event arrow suggests that a message is moving between those two objects. An event line can pass over an object without stopping at that object. The event stops at an arrowhead.

Events are given names, which can be a phrase or an operation or message name. Some developers record additional information after the event name. For example, if the message is sent three and only three times, you might record a 3 in parentheses after the event name. This could be used in an application that asks a salesperson for his or her identification number three times before the session is terminated by the sales server.

Constraints are listed within braces. Information—for example, a rule or condition that determines when an event fires or succeeds—is indicated by the event line within square brackets.

Sometimes an event is a message passed between two different objects of the same class (i.e., self-delegation). This can be represented by an event arrow that begins and ends on the same object as the last arrow on the leftmost object in Figure 10.1.

Some developers place notes on the left-hand side of a sequence diagram to remind themselves or others of what's happening at different points in the sequence diagram. For most purposes the notation shown in Figure 10.1 will be adequate to show the initial sequences you will want to diagram.

Figure 10.2 is a slightly more complex version of Figure 10.1. In this case we have added tall, thin rectangles that lie on top of the dotted lines below the object rectangles. These rectangles indicate when the object is active. They are called activation lines. We have also added times to indicate how long each object is active.

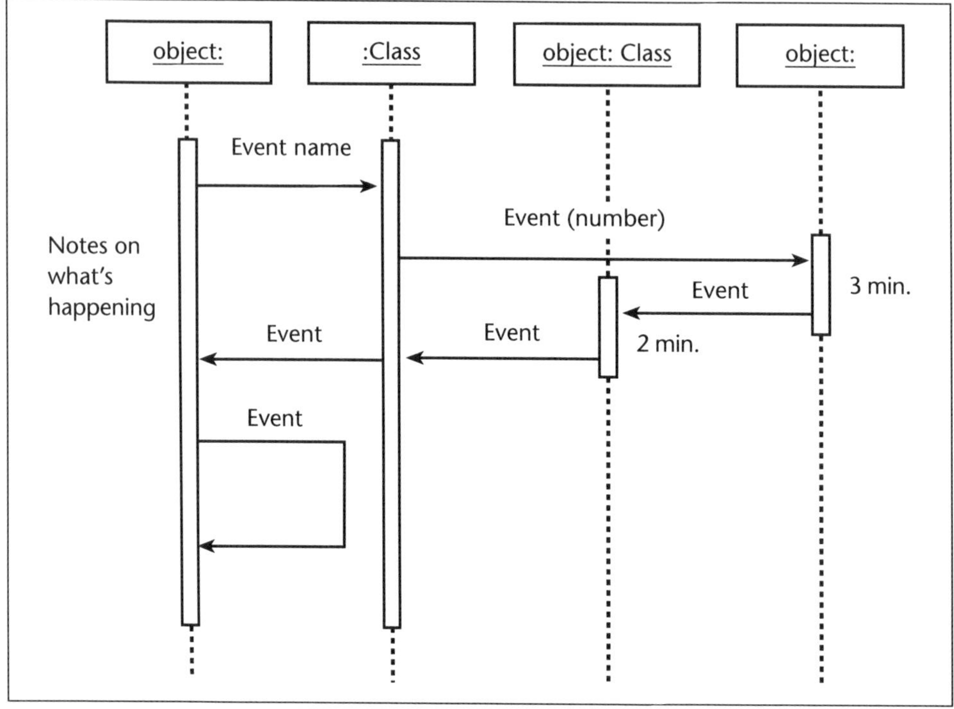

Figure 10.2 *Notation used in a sequence diagram—2.*

In some cases several objects are active simultaneously, even if they are only waiting for another object to return information to them. In other cases an object becomes active when it receives a message and then becomes inactive as soon as it responds.

In Figure 10.2 the two objects on the left side of the diagram are active throughout. The object on the right side, however, becomes active only when it receives a message and then becomes inactive soon after it responds.

Figure 10.3 shows a still more complex version of a sequence diagram. In Figure 10.3 the third object in the diagram was created by the second. The event arrow leading to the third object rectangle rather than to the tall rectangle below it indicates the creation of that object. Similarly, the bold "X" at the bottom of the lifeline of the third object indicates that the object is terminated at that point.

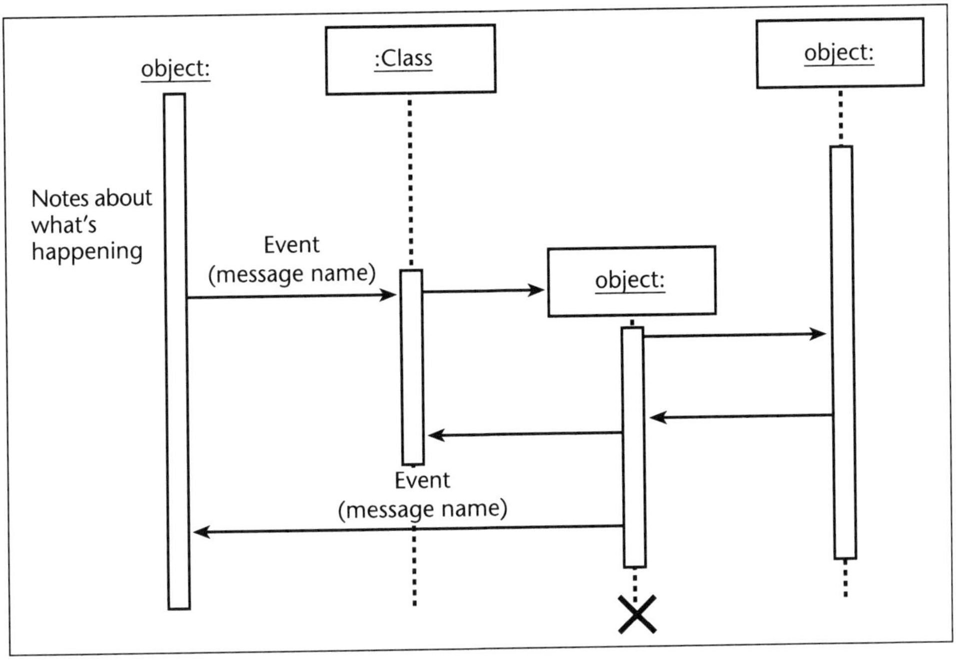

Figure 10.3 *Notation used in a sequence diagram—3.*

Most developers don't bother to show when objects are created or destroyed, especially during the analysis phase, but it's sometimes useful to do this if the system is complex and it's important to keep track of exactly which objects exist at any specific point in time.

In Figure 10.3 the left-hand object isn't a software object. It could be a customer who is entering information via a computer screen. In this case, you can leave the rectangle off the name, leave out the dotted line, and have a continuous tall activation rectangle instead to indicate that the source of the stimuli isn't a real software object.

10.2.2 Creating a Sequence Diagram

Let's consider how we would prepare a sequence diagram for a scenario we considered when we did the CRC exercise. We'll diagram Scenario 1 from Figure 8.4. In this scenario, Curtis

Clyde, one of Moose's salespeople, wants to report an order that he received from Harmon Associates for a new desk.

Figure 10.4 shows how we would diagram that scenario. You wouldn't normally enter both the class name and the object name at the top, but we did it in some places to make things a little clearer. The object names would probably be best, but the "class names" would be acceptable, as long as you understand that you are using the class name to stand for a generic object in this diagram.

If we were going to continue to work on this example, we would probably do several more sequence diagrams as we added classes (e.g., additional Item classes or an Address class) or break some of the events out into more detail. And, of course, as we embark on subsequent cycles and keep enhancing our prototype, we'll keep doing new sequence diagrams to capture new functionality.

10.3 Collaboration Diagrams

The collaboration diagram provides a second way of showing the sequence in which events occur. In effect, a collaboration is a cross between an object diagram and a sequence diagram. As in an object diagram, objects are shown in rectangles, connected by lines that indicate links between them. (Recall that lines connecting classes are called associations, while lines connecting objects are called links. In both cases they represent the fact that messages will flow between objects.) Unlike object diagrams, however, numbers, operation names, and arrows are placed over the links to indicate the flow of specific messages. Thus, although there is no axis to indicate time, as there is in a sequence diagram, the numbers assure that we can actually follow the events or messages in sequence as they move from object to object. In a complex diagram several messages could pass back and forth across the same link.

Some developers may prefer to use the collaboration diagram in place of a simple object diagram and hence capture

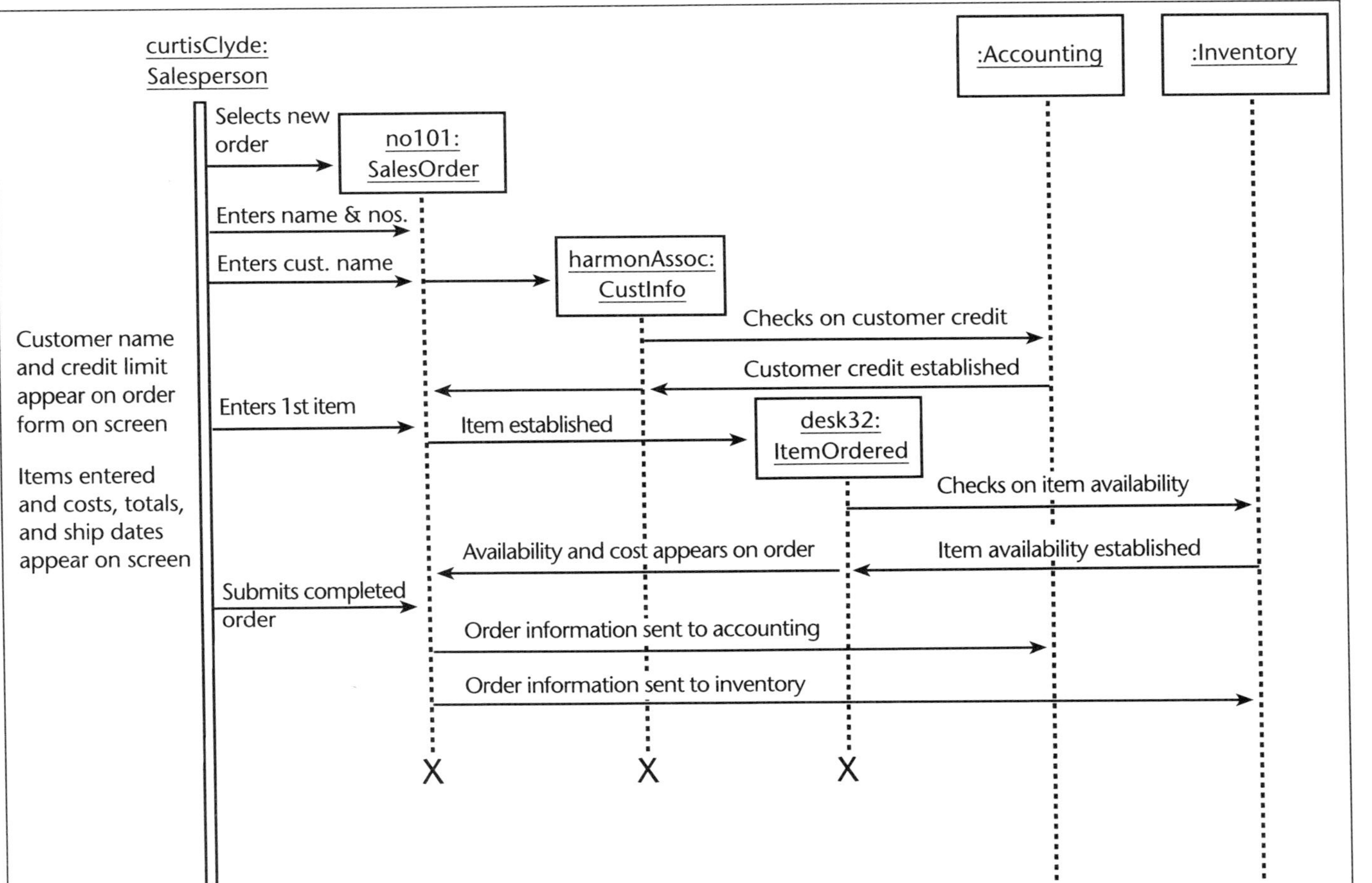

Figure 10.4 *A sequence diagram of Scenario 1 from Figure 8.4.*

not only the objects involved in a scenario, but also the use of specific operations and some of the data flow. As with all the diagrams, different types of applications will favor different diagrams. The collaboration can get awfully complex and messy rather quickly, but it may be ideal for developers who want to analyze a narrowly focused scenario in a great deal of detail.

10.3.1 Collaboration Notation

Figure 10.5 illustrates the basic notation used in collaboration diagrams. Objects are represented as rectangles with either object or object:class names. If appropriate, you can also show the attributes associated with an object.

The lines between the objects are links. Each link can be labeled with one or more operation names. Each operation name is preceded by a number to indicate the order in which the operation is executed. An arrow, either after or beside the operation name, indicates the direction of the flow. (The operation being executed always resides on the object the arrow is pointing away from.) The reason we don't show returns is that, in most cases, this is an automatic response and not the result of a new operation being executed in the target object.

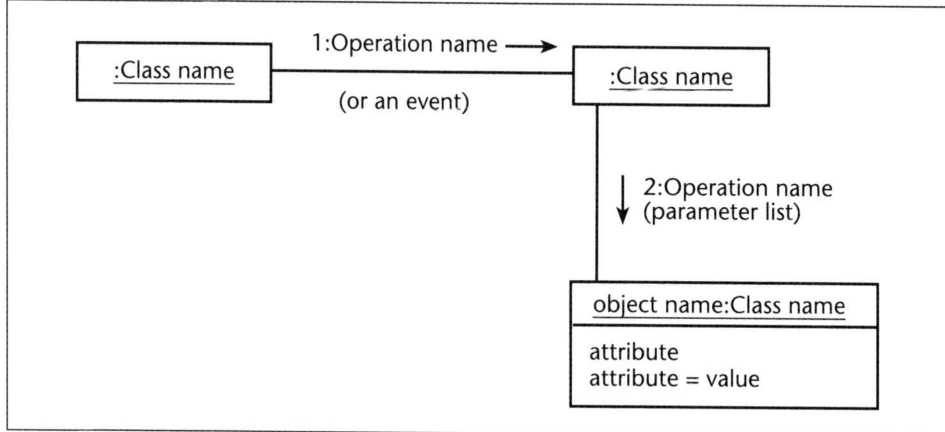

Figure 10.5 *UML collaboration notation.*

You don't need to show numbers or asterisks on a collaboration diagram because it's an object diagram, and you can actually show multiple objects if you wish.

10.3.2 Creating a Collaboration Diagram

Now let's consider how we might apply the collaboration notation to our SalesWeb problem. We'll start by looking again at our first class diagram of our SalesWeb application (Figure 9.12). That gives us an overview of the classes and their relationships. Next we might look at Figure 9.13, which is an object diagram of Figure 9.12. That suggests one specific scenario we might want to consider in more detail. In fact, we'll develop a collaboration diagram to illustrate the top sequence, involving a sales order for Harmon Associates.

Finally, we might look at Figure 10.4, which is a sequence diagram of a series of events that rely on the structures described in Figures 9.12 and 9.13. By combining all of the insights we got from each of these three diagrams, we arrive at the collaboration diagram of Scenario 1, which we've illustrated in Figure 10.6. Here, as with our second class diagram, we use the attribute and operation names that we decided on in Chapter 9.

This collaboration shows a generic *SalesOrder* entry scenario, much like the one we discussed earlier as Scenario 1. We've eliminated numbers and asterisks, since this is really an object diagram and doesn't need them. If we wanted, we could show more than one object of any class involved in this sequence. And, as we already noted, we didn't bother to make the legacy applications, *Accounting* or *Inventory,* into objects. Similarly, we didn't bother to trace the return of values, although in most cases the object on the receiving end of the arrow would, sooner or later, obtain a value that it would pass back, ultimately to the *:SalesOrder* object, which would display it on the salesperson's computer screen.

The key things shown in Figure 10.6 are the operations that are invoked to pass information and the order in which the operations are used. You could capture this same information on the sequence diagram by simply using the operation names, rather than the phrases we used there.

If we had created several different scenarios, and felt the need, we could do one of these diagrams for each scenario, just as we could do a different sequence diagram for each scenario. We could also have gone into a lot more depth with this diagram. We could, for example, have shown the attributes and the values that were being changed when specific methods were executed.

One important thing to keep in mind is that all these diagrams are just tools to help you understand the system you are developing. There is no value in doing diagrams for their own sake. You should do them when you have a specific purpose and a specific audience in mind. They document information or communicate it to others. You will probably use some, such

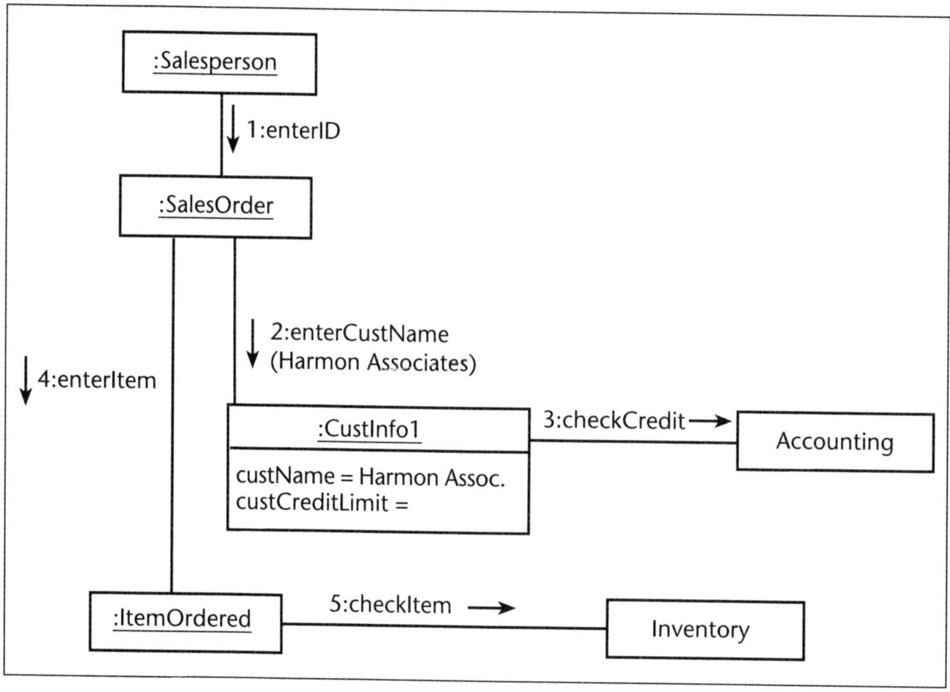

Figure 10.6 *UML collaboration diagram of the SalesWeb application.*

as the sequence diagram, every time you develop an application. Others, such as the collaboration diagram, are only useful occasionally, when you encounter a special problem that can best be clarified by means of a collaboration diagram.

10.3.3 *Collaboration Diagrams and Patterns*

Patterns describe ways of solving recurring problems. Thus, many different OO applications require that developers use a time/date stamp. A pattern describes an especially good way to accomplish this. There are books on OO patterns that every OO developer should acquire and study in order to assure that he or she is acquainted with proven ways of solving common, recurring problems. We'll go into the use of patterns in more detail, in Chapter 14, when we consider design and coding, which is where the topic is more appropriate. We only mention it here to point out that most books that describe patterns rely on something like collaboration diagrams to illustrate the patterns in their catalogs.

10.4 Creating Sequence and Collaboration Diagrams with a Visual Modeling Tool

In Chapter 9, when we were developing class diagrams, we used Microsoft's Visual Modeler. Visual Modeler doesn't support most of the UML diagrams. It's especially unfortunate it doesn't support sequence diagrams, since so many developers find them especially useful. In any case, Rational Rose supports all the UML diagrams, so at this point we will switch back to Rose to consider how we would develop each of the diagrams we have considered in this chapter.

We show a sequence diagram that we developed in Rose in Figure 10.7. Notice on the tool bar that there is a button for interaction diagrams: A set of four vertical lines with arrows moving to the right and then back to the left. By pressing on this button you get a screen that asks what kind of interaction diagram you want to create. Choosing sequence diagram gives you a blank screen and a palette of tools like the ones on the right-hand side of the screen on Figure 10.7. Using those tools it is easy to create the diagram shown in that figure.

Whenever you create a sequence diagram (or a collaboration diagram), you are also creating the other diagram and only need to switch between them to see the alternative representation. Thus, if we switch from the sequence diagram to a collaboration diagram, we get Figure 10.8.

As with class diagrams, Rational Rose 98 gives you a large "drawing space" so that you can create very large drawings. In

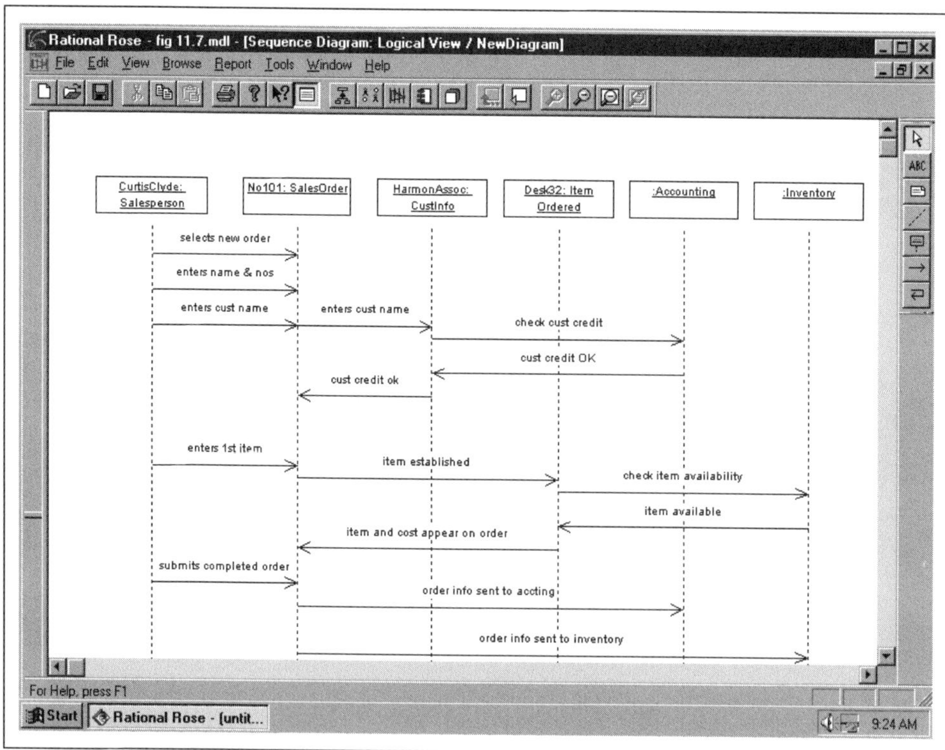

Figure 10.7 *Sequence diagram developed in Rational Rose.*

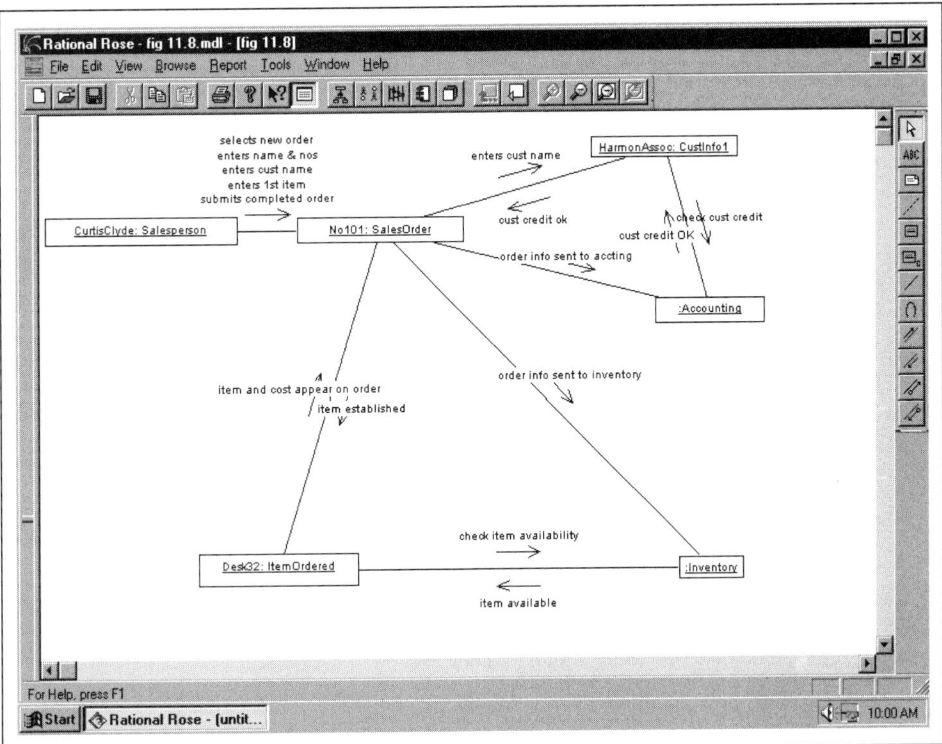

Figure 10.8 *Collaboration diagram developed from sequence diagram in Figure 10.7.*

addition, since Rose 98 maintains dynamic links once they are established, you can move objects around, and the lines connecting them will remain attached. If you were drawing these diagrams by hand, you would make mistakes and find yourself starting over to put in a new object between two others. With Rose 98, you can easily insert a new object without having to start a new diagram. When you work by hand, you usually end up with lots of different sequence diagrams, representing different options or different stages in your analysis of the problem. Since you can keep modifying and enhancing diagrams so easily in Rose 98, you tend to end up with only one diagram of each type—the final diagram with all the details.

Indeed, if there's a problem with Rose 98, it's the reverse of having too many versions of the sequence diagram. If you keep adding details you will soon end up with a sequence diagram that's useful for developers but too complex to show users. Sometimes you have to remember to save early versions of diagrams just to document how you started or to remind yourself of an alternative you considered and rejected. This is easy enough. It's simply a matter of using a function key to copy everything on one diagram, starting a new diagram with a different name, and pasting all the objects from the first diagram onto the second diagram.

11

UML State and Activity Diagrams

So far, we have considered use case, class, and object diagrams, which provide us with an understanding of the static, logical relationships in our application. We have also looked at interaction diagrams, including sequence and collaboration diagrams, which provide us with a dynamic view of how objects interact with one another. Now we'll turn to a third group of diagrams, collectively called state diagrams. State diagrams are designed to show us how one specific object changes state as it receives and processes messages. Compared with the earlier diagrams that provide us with overviews of our entire application, or at least views of a number of different classes or objects, state diagrams are narrowly focused, fine-grained diagrams that are good only for analyzing very specific situations.

As we commented earlier, Rational's documentation treats activity diagrams as a special type of state diagram. This may be logically correct, but in reality, activity diagrams are just the opposite of state diagrams. A state diagram focuses on activity within a specific class. An activity diagram, on the other hand, describes activities and flows of data or decisions between activities. In effect, activity diagrams are the diagrams used in most workflow analysis tools. They provide very broad views of business processes. Or they can be used to break out the activities that occur within a use case. Activity diagrams commonly show lots of different activities that will be handled by lots of different objects.

We'll consider both state and activity diagrams in this chapter, but keep in mind that they are very different diagrams used for very different purposes. Activity diagrams provide overviews of procedural flows. State diagrams provide precise information on changes in the values associated with a specific class.

11.1 State Diagrams

State refers to the set of values that describe an object at a specific moment in time. In other words, the state of an object is determined by the values associated with its attributes. As messages are received, the operations associated with the object's parent class are invoked to deal with the messages. As these operations are executed, they often change the values of attributes contained by an object.

Imagine we had a *:CustInfo* object that contained the name of a company. If the *:CustInfo* object received a message (*getCustName*) asking for the name of the company, an operation contained in the *CustInfo* class (e.g., *returnCustName*) would be invoked. That operation would check the attribute *custName* and then pass the value associated with that attribute back to the object that sent the message in the first place. In this case the state of the *:CustInfo* object would not have been changed.

Now assume that the same *:CustInfo* object received a message (*updateCustName*) that included a parameter (Harmon Corp.):

```
updateCustName (Harmon Corp.)
```

In this case, the object would invoke an operation from its class that would modify the value associated with the *cust-Name,* changing it from Harmon Assoc. to Harmon Corp. In the process, the state of the *:CustInfo* object would have been changed.

State diagrams are sometimes called state-transition or Harel diagrams. (The diagrams are derived from the statecharts that David Harel originated. They were originally developed for modeling process control systems.) These diagrams provide a detailed look at one specific class. In effect, by showing successive state changes, they illustrate the life cycle of a class, showing every state the class passes through as events occur.

Sequence diagrams need not be too complex and are useful to assure that you have a good overview of the messages passed between a number of different objects. State diagrams must be more precise and provide a narrow but exact view of what happens to one object as it receives successive messages. Many development efforts avoid state diagrams. Most complex applications, however, will probably have a few classes worth analyzing in this kind of detail. And almost any process control application will require that you prepare several state diagrams.

Some developers use a single state diagram to describe the state changes in several closely related classes simultaneously, but such a diagram can become very complex, very quickly. At least initially, you should probably stick with modeling a single class in a single state diagram.

There is certainly no reason to prepare a state diagram for each class in your system. Indeed, many developers create rather large systems without bothering to create any state diagrams at all. State diagrams are useful when you have a class that is very dynamic. In that situation, it is often helpful to prepare a state diagram to be sure you understand each of the possible states an object of the class could take and what event (message) would trigger each transition from one state to another. In effect, state diagrams emphasize the use of events and states to determine the overall activity of the system.

11.1.1 State Diagram Notation

States are represented as rectangles with rounded corners. The name of the state is placed inside the box. Events are shown connecting states with an arrow to indicate the new state that results from the transition in a value.

An event occurs at an instant in time when a value is changed. A message is data passed from one object to another. At a minimum, a message is a name that will trigger an operation associated with the target object. The message name may also be accompanied with values. For most practical purposes, you can think of the message and the event that the message causes as the same thing and use the terms as synonyms. This is convenient, since you have already created names for operations, and those names are generally used to describe the messages they send. Those names are generally also used to describe the events that result when the messages are received by target objects.

For example, a message might look like this:

```
CustInfo.setCustName (Harmon Assoc.)
```

or

```
CustInfo.getCustName : string
```

In the first case, the operation *setCustName* (which is part of the *Salesperson* class) has generated a message (which is also called *setCustName*) for an object of the class *CustInfo*. The message, which includes the parameter Harmon Assoc., will trigger an operation associated with the *:CustInfo* object to set "Harmon Assoc." as the value of its *custName* attribute.

The second message *getCustName* is a message sent by some object to an object of the *CustInfo* class to determine the value associated with the target object's *custName* attribute. The return_type linked to the message name requires that the data returned by the target object be a string data type.

Unlike a message, which seeks to determine the value associated with an attribute, the name of a state often refers to the name of an attribute and the value associated with it. Thus, at one point, the name of a state of *:CustInfo* is *custName* =

Harmon Assoc. Then, after receiving a message telling the object to change the name to Harmon Corp., the name of the state of *:CustInfo* becomes *custName* = Harmon Corp.

You can be very precise about the names of events in state diagrams, but most developers aren't. Instead, they simply use a short phrase to remind them of the nature of the message, state, or state change indicated by a single event arrow.

A state is a box with rounded corners that describes an object and one or more of its attribute value tuples at one instance in time. The name of the state is placed in the top compartment of the round-cornered box. The state variables (or the state variables of substates if the box represents a high-level view) are listed in the second compartment of the box. The operations associated with the state are listed in the lower section of the box. In some cases the operations are described by a phrase. In other cases, one or more of four reserved words are used to identify the nature of the actions stimulated by the operations.

The following are four reserved action descriptions:

entry	a specific action performed on the entry to the state
do	an ongoing action performed while in the state
on	a specific action performed as a result of a specific event
exit	a specific action performed on exiting the state

For example, Figure 11.1 illustrates a state of the object *:CustInfo1*.

In most cases, state diagrams, like initial class diagrams, don't show the attributes and actions within a state and focus more on the overall changes in states and the changes in substates. Figure 11.2 illustrates the basic high-level state notation and the notation of states and substates. Notice that it shows several state boxes. In the top case, two states are connected by an event arrow.

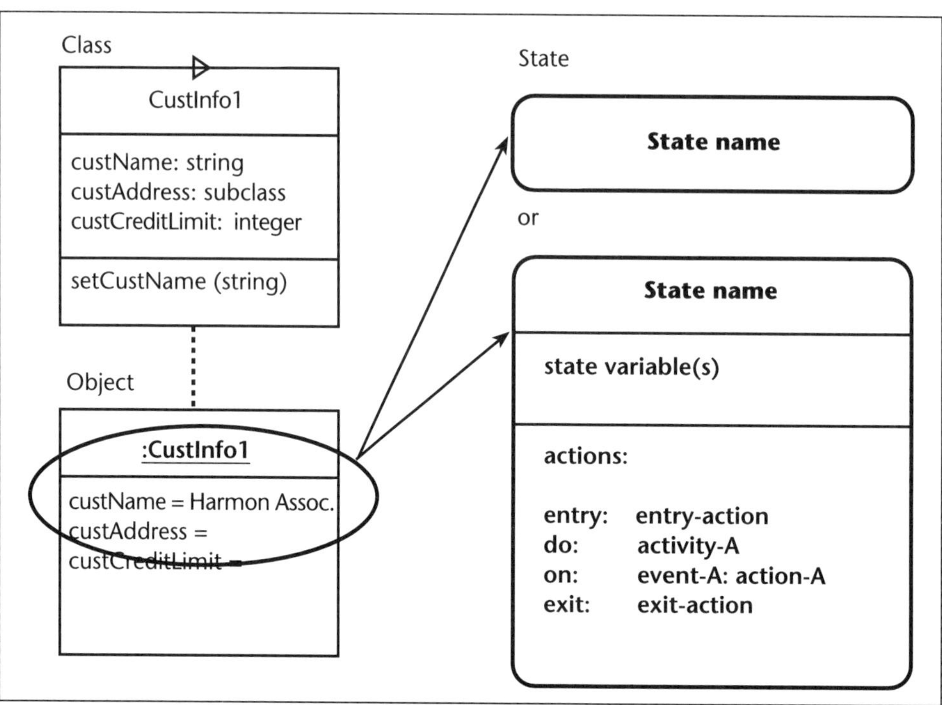

Figure 11.1 *A state describes the value of an attribute of an object at a point in time and the actions that occur while the object's attribute maintains that value, or when it changes the value.*

In some cases, a black dot is used to indicate where the system starts. If a starting point is indicated, the first state that occurs is sometimes called the initial state. A black dot inside a circle is used to signify when the state transitions end. Some systems, such as software programs, do not normally have a start and finish (in the sense that these terms are often used with physical systems). The program code resides on a hard disk and simply transitions back and forth between on and off. (A state description of a lightbulb would be the same. A lightbulb has two states: on and off, and it simply transitions between them until the lightbulb is worn out.)

It is sometimes useful to include additional information in state diagrams. You can expand the state box and include information on actions that are stimulated by the state change (as in Figure 11.1), or you can include additional information with the event name by placing the information in parentheses after the event name.

When things become more complex, it's often useful to do layered state diagrams with one group of states placed within another, as illustrated in the lower example in Figure 11.2. In

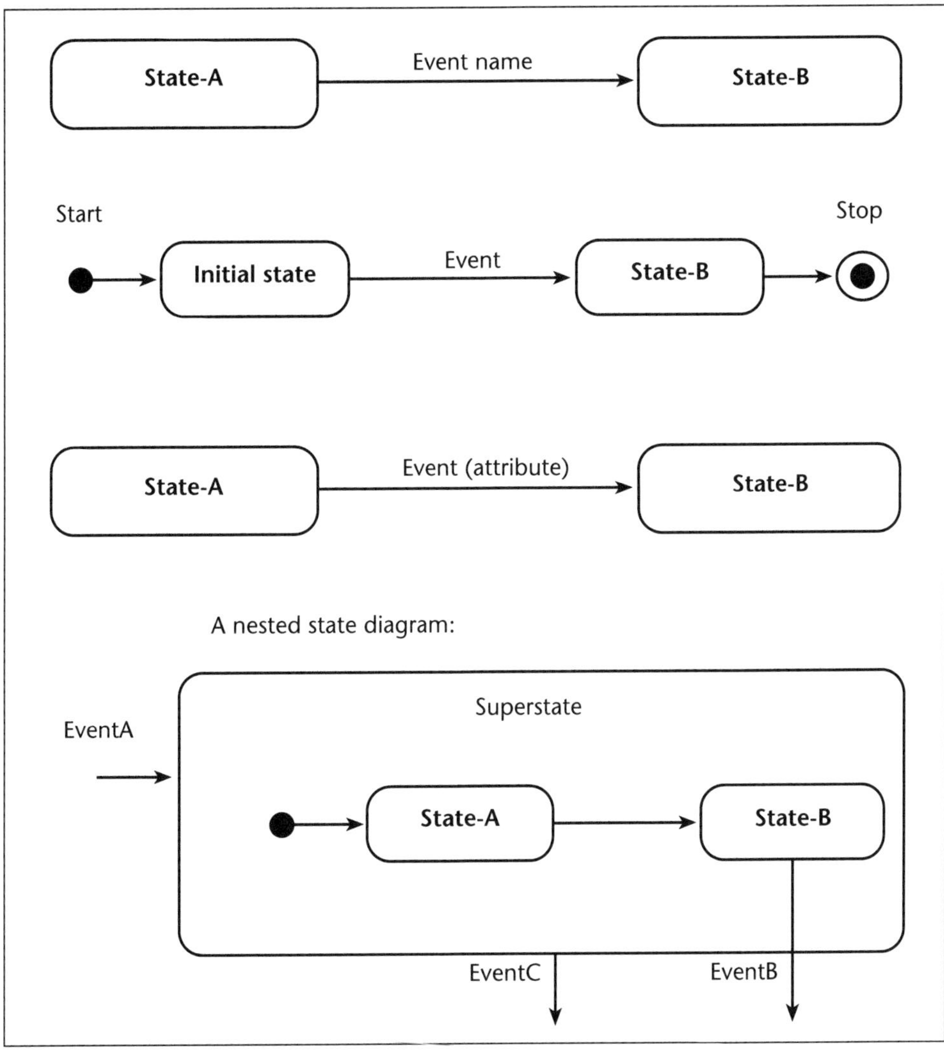

Figure 11.2 *Basic notation for state diagrams.*

this case the superstate (one object) is triggered, which in turn triggers a series of state changes in another object. Imagine a state diagram that showed an object of our *SalesOrder* class, with an object of the customer class contained within it. The object of the *SalesOrder* class would be the superstate, and the object of the company class would be shown inside.

Even more complex nesting structures are possible, especially when you have systems that may be doing things in parallel. In effect, you show one superstate, then subdivide the superstate box into two or more compartments. Within each compartment of the superstate diagram, you draw a state diagram that shows one of the series of state transitions that are going on simultaneously. Imagine that our object of the *SalesOrder* contained three objects of the *ItemOrdered* class and that each object was simultaneously sending a message to the inventory application to determine the availability and price of the item.

11.1.2 Creating a State Diagram

To clarify all this before going on to a more elaborate example, consider a class designed to model a light switch. The class itself might be modeled as we show in Figure 11.3. In addition, we could draw a simple sequence diagram of an object of the light switch class. In effect, the inputs come from a user class, and the results of changing the light switch are communicated to a light class. (Notice in this case that the user is a person who physically moves a switch, and thus the initial stimulus for a state change is an event that the object registers and not a message, as such.)

Figure 11.4 shows how we could represent the states of a generic instance of the *LightSwitch* class by using a state diagram. Notice that our system is so simple that the diagram doesn't show a start or stop condition. In effect, the light switch is always running and always in one of its two states. The key here is to realize that both the states represent the same instance of the *LightSwitch* class, and the only thing that is changing is the value associated with the attribute switch status. The events that connect the two states of the

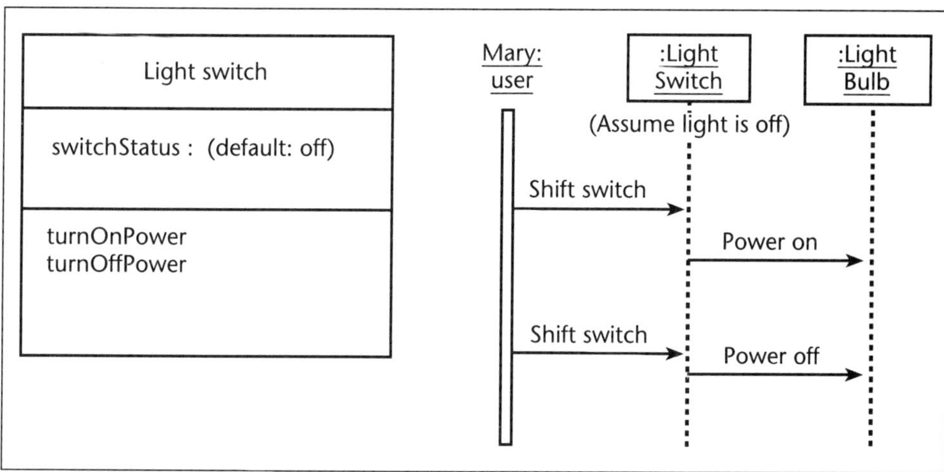

Figure 11.3 *Overview of the light switch class and an event trace.*

:LightSwitch object come from an outside class, but here they are only used to show that an event has triggered a state change. The operation that would allow electricity to flow is captured by placing the "do" comment under the value of the right-hand state of the instance.

Having looked at a very simple situation, let's turn to our SalesWeb application. Most of the classes in this application are not worth the kind of analysis that goes into a state diagram. As you continue to develop the system, the one class that might merit a state diagram is the *SalesOrder* class. In

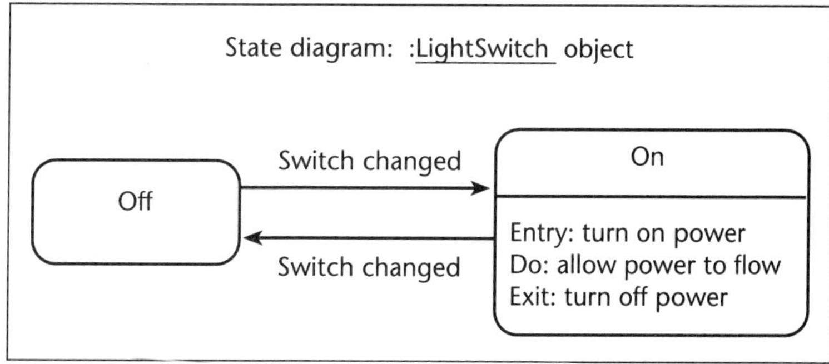

Figure 11.4 *State diagram of the :LightSwitch object.*

Figure 11.5 we've drawn a very high level state diagram for an object of the *SalesOrder* class.

To create this, we began by going down the sequence diagram for Scenario 1 (Figure 10.4) and examining all the inputs to the *:SalesOrder* object. Some came from the *:Salesperson* object, and others came from objects to the right of the *SalesOrder* line. Some were repeating events that had already occurred. Taken together, they gave us a good start. Next we would have examined Scenario 2, and so on. In other words, we would keep reviewing scenarios and looking for changes in the attributes of the *:SalesOrder* objects that were stimulated by outside events or which caused outside events, and then work out what must be going on inside the object.

By using the sequence diagram and supplementing it with state diagrams, and the activity diagrams we'll consider next, you can gradually capture all of the dynamics contained in the scenarios and, in effect, determine each of the operations you will need to create when you move to the prototyping phase.

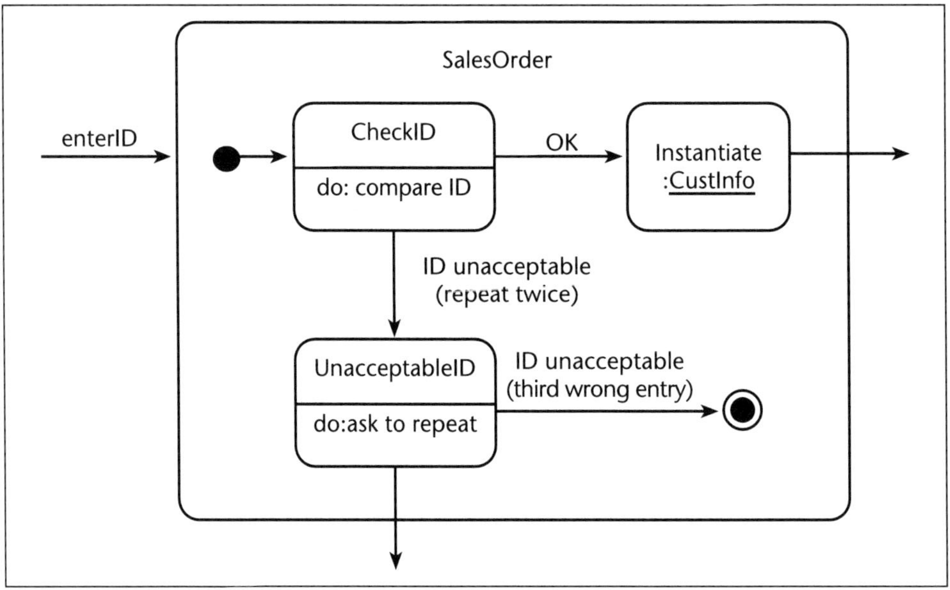

Figure 11.5 *A state diagram for an instance of the* SalesOrder *class.*

11.2 Activity Diagrams

Activity diagrams are used to model the flow of activities in a procedure. In UML, activities are called states, and thus, activity diagrams are associated with state diagrams. Two good examples of activity diagrams are the workflow diagrams we used in Chapter 7 when we first discussed Moose's sales system.

In an activity diagram, the states are usually termed activities. Events are generally referred to as transitions. Diamonds are introduced to allow the developer to show what happens when a transition can have more than one consequence. Activity diagrams tend to be drawn without placing them inside some larger frame. Bars are used to show when several streams of events must come together before the next activity can occur. You can use the state symbols for beginning points and end points, but they usually aren't necessary.

Unlike state diagrams that focus on the events occurring within a single object as it responds to messages, an activity diagram can be used to model an entire business process or to provide a high-level view of what's going on inside a use case. Thus, activities could easily represent a module of several different classes. More to the point, an activity describes the performance of a task and isn't directly related to objects. In that sense, the activity diagram is much more like a workflow diagram or the use case diagram, neither of which describes objects, as such. This is probably why activity diagrams were left out of the Booch and OMT methodologies. Many OO developers use activity diagrams, however, to get an overview of how some process works, and thus they have been included in the UML documentation. As far as we are concerned, the best example of an activity diagram is the workflow diagram we used in Chapter 7. For completeness, however, we'll consider how UML formally defines an activity diagram in this chapter.

Figure 11.6 illustrates the basic symbols used in a UML activity diagram. Since we've already considered a large-scale activity diagram in Chapter 7, we'll focus on a small-scale activity diagram at this point. Specifically, we'll consider an activity diagram that focuses on the activity within a specific object.

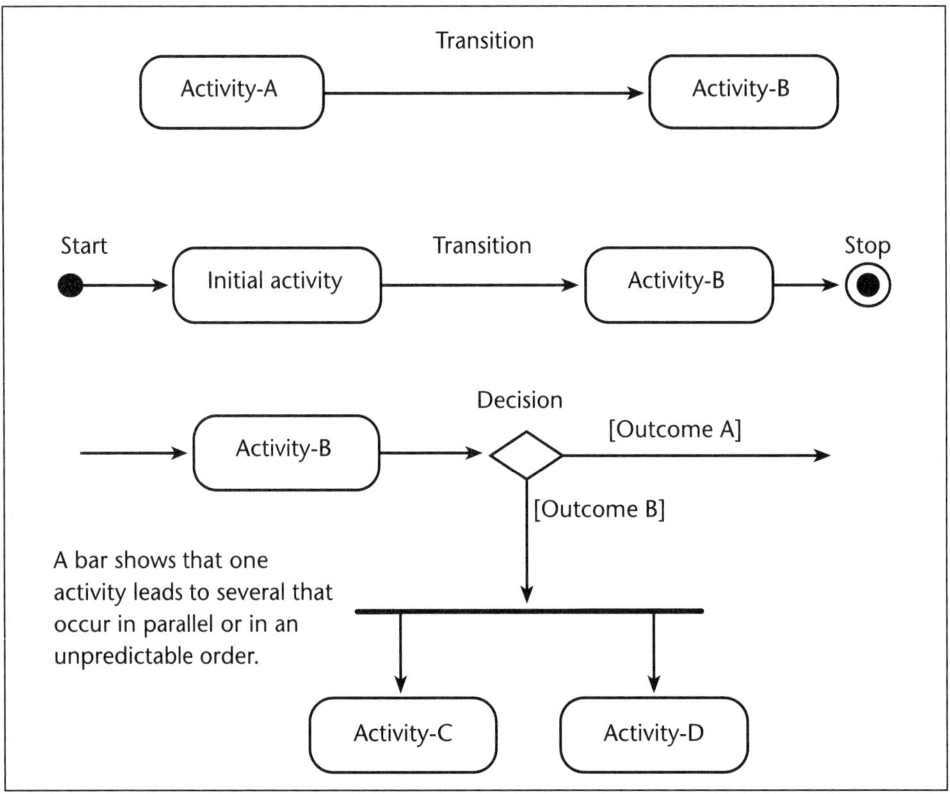

Figure 11.6 *Basic notation for an activity diagram.*

Figure 11.7 shows how we would represent an object of the *CustInfo* class as an activity diagram.

11.3 Creating State Diagrams with a Visual Modeling Tool

Having now considered how we could describe an object's states in terms of either a state diagram or an activity diagram, let's consider how we could create a state diagram using Rose 98. Click on the "SalesOrder" icon in the class diagram, then

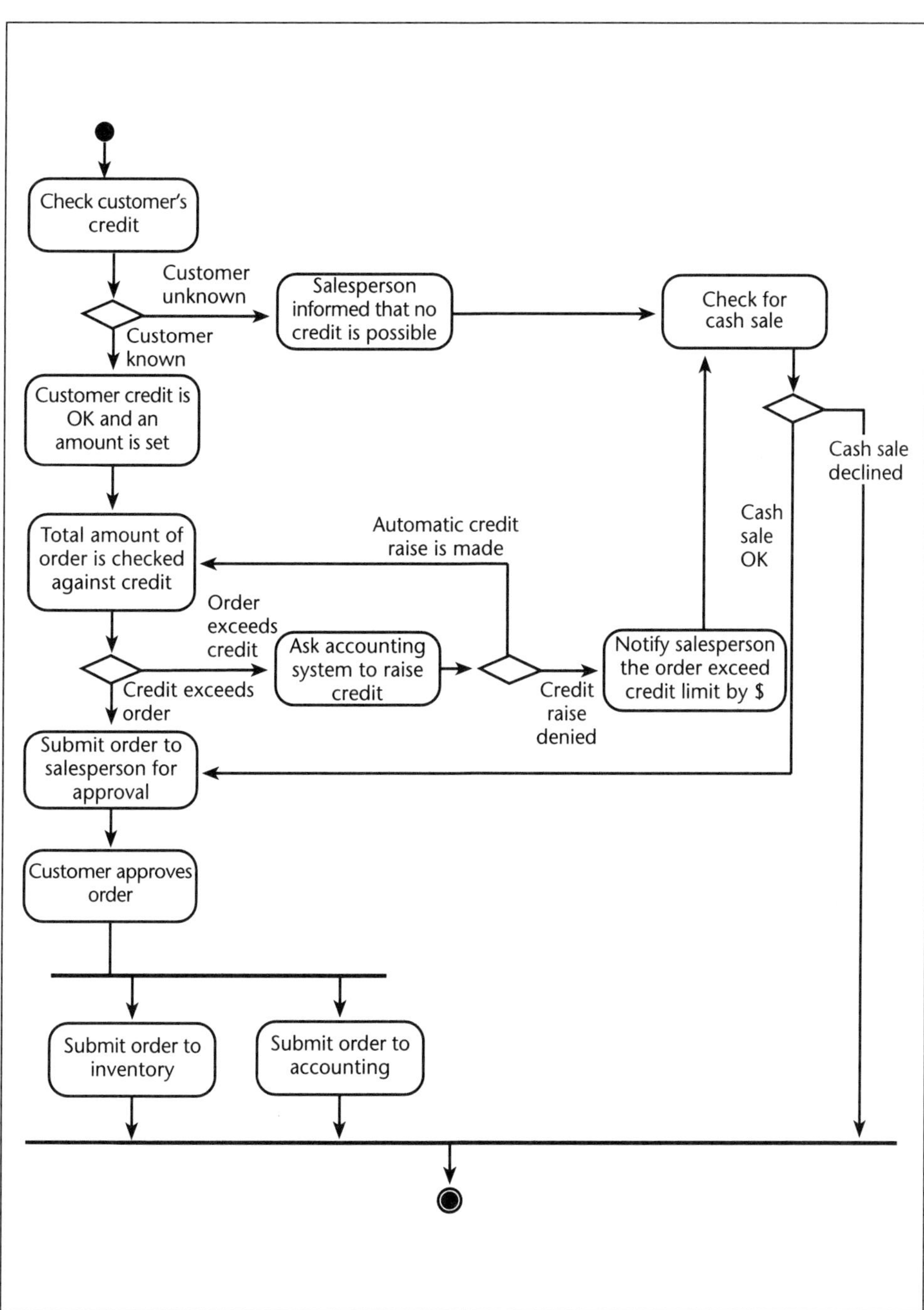

Figure 11.7 *An activity diagram for the* CustInfo *class.*

select "State Diagram" from the "Browse" menu. A blank state diagram will come up.

Using tools available on the palette that Rose 98 displays, we quickly create the diagram shown in Figure 11.8. First, click on the "State" button on the palette at the right of the screen (the fourth button from the top). Now draw a box of the state box as shown in Figure 11.8 and type in "SalesOrder" as its name. Inside the box, follow the same steps to create states named "Check ID", "Instantiate: CustInfo", and "UnacceptableID".

Next, click on the "Start State" button (fourth from the bottom of the palette). Position the start state as shown in the diagram. Click on the "End State" button (third from the bot-

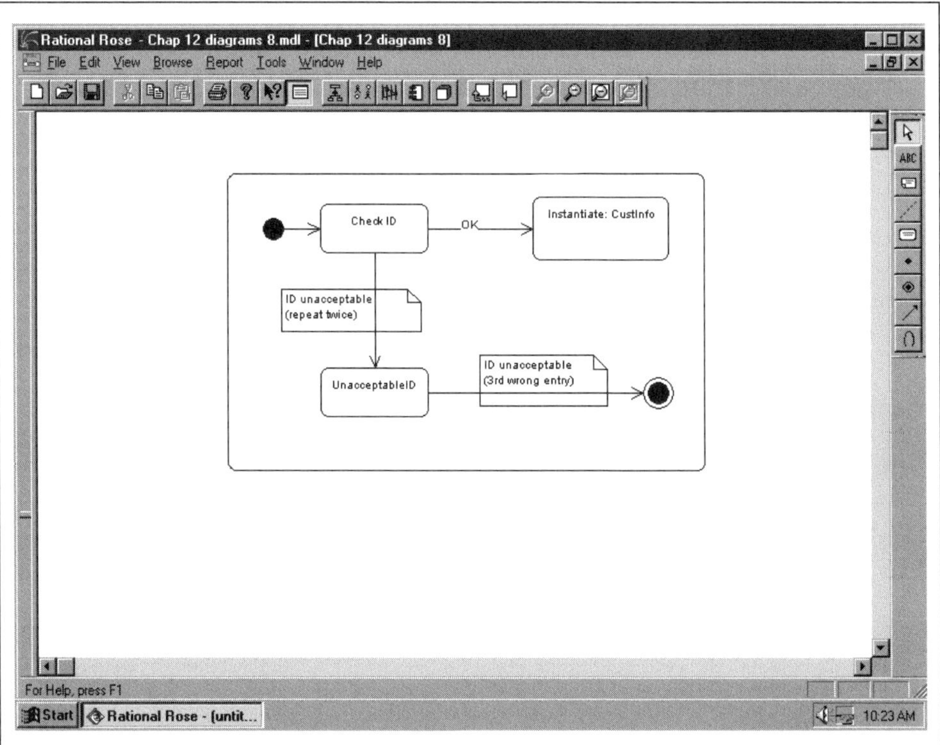

Figure 11.8 *State diagram created using Rational Rose 98.*

tom of the palette), and position a new end state as shown in the figure.

Click on the "State Transition" button on the palette (the second from the bottom). Now click on the "CheckID" state, and, keeping the mouse button held down, drag the line to the "Instantiate..." state and release the mouse button. An arrow will now indicate a transition between the states. Click on the arrow, and type "OK" to label the state transition.

Following the same steps, create the state transitions "ID unacceptable (repeat twice)" and "ID unacceptable (3rd wrong entry)" as shown in the diagram. Finally, create an unlabeled transition from the start state to the "Check ID" state.

Unfortunately, we can't use Rose 98 to create an activity diagram, since activity diagrams are not supported by Rose 98.

12

Designing an Object-Oriented System

Thus far, we have tried to talk in abstract, logical terms about analyzing a problem. We've been trying to find a clean, ideal solution to the problem that was described in the requirements statement and the use case diagrams. Now it's time to shift from creating a model for an ideal system to creating a design that can be implemented in the actual environment in which you will run your application.

UML doesn't make a sharp distinction between analysis and design notation. Indeed, one of the best features of the OO approach is the lack of any difference between the diagrams and constructs you use during analysis and those you use during design. The same UML diagrams that you used during analysis will continue to be used and enhanced as you proceed to make the more concrete decisions typical of the design process. There are, however, three implementation diagrams that primarily capture information about the architecture of an application that we will discuss in the next chapter.

Keep in mind that if you are developing your application using a cyclical, iterative methodology, once you have created the diagrams to describe your prototype at the end of the first iteration, you will have all those diagrams to consider when you begin to enhance your system during the second iteration. Thus, any distinction between analysis and design that we have maintained up until now will have vanished when you begin your second analysis phase.

In this chapter, we want to pull together some general ideas about how to proceed to develop your system. We assume that once you get to design, you will continue to use your existing UML diagrams. Thus, our concern here is not so much to teach you new UML notation, although there will be some, but to provide you with practical suggestions about how to complete the effort that you began with the diagrams created during the first analysis phase of your development effort. Moreover, since the emphasis in design is on tailoring an abstract design to a specific language and environment, and since that's hard to do in an abstract way, we will organize our discussion around the problems of moving our SalesWeb application from an abstract model to a concrete Visual Basic 6.0 application.

12.1 Moving from Analysis to Design

We suggested that during at least the first analysis phase you start by developing an object model that describes the entire application. Then, once you have that overview, we suggested you choose a portion of the entire application to develop in more detail. In the case of our SalesWeb application, for example, we chose only one of the use cases, Report Sales, and created diagrams for just that portion of the application.

Different prototypes will suggest very different designs. In some cases you will be working on a prototype that will require that you develop an elaborate infrastructure to support its implementation. In other cases you will have avoided the necessity for an elaborate infrastructure effort on the first cycle. Whatever you do, when you consider design for the first time, you should develop at least a general view of the overall architecture you will need to implement the final system, even if you then proceed to implement only a part of the final infrastructure during the first phase.

During the first design phase you will need to elaborate the portion of the overall application you have selected to develop first. Even then, however, you will need to decide how complete you want to make your first prototype. For example, you may decide to create flat files to simulate links to a mainframe database, rather than actually linking with the mainframe during the first development phase. In one sense, this is design. In another sense, it is merely deciding on tactics to guide your iterative development process.

Figure 12.1 is another version of our general cyclical development model. It reminds you where you are in the overall process, and it suggests some of the things you must accomplish during any design phase.

We have listed some of the tasks that must be accomplished during the design phase of an OO development project on the right side of Figure 12.1. We used bullets, rather than numbers, because we didn't want to suggest that these are steps that should be followed in a specific order. Depending on the nature of the application, the experience of the developer, or the size of the development team, these tasks could be handled in a different order, or even in parallel. We will work our way through them in more or less the order we have suggested in Figure 12.1, beginning with a consideration of application architectures and the introduction of two new UML diagrams—the deployment and the package diagrams—in Chapter 13. Then we'll proceed to a discussion of elaborating the business model in Chapter 14.

Before getting into any details, however, it is useful to consider how much time you might spend in the design phase. Most methodologists who have studied OO development have concluded that OO development is different from more conventional development. OO development rewards the effort spent on analysis and design and leads to a reduction of

Figure 12.1 *An iterative approach to OO development.*

Key activities for the design phase:

- Settle on the overall architecture of the application.
  - 1, 2, or 3 tier
  - location of major modules
  - inter-tier communications
- Create UML deployment and package diagrams.
- Elaborate the business object model to incorporate infrastructure classes. Extend all classes to include needed operations. Extend UML class, sequence, state, activity, and collaboration diagrams.
- Consider opportunities for reuse of COM components. Create UML component diagrams as needed.
- Design GUI screens.
- Design database and linkages, as needed. Elaborate UML deployment diagrams, etc.
- Generate initial code from Visual Modeler or Rational Rose 98, after establishing settings for methods, components, and so on.

the time spent on coding. This occurs in large part because lots of problems are solved in analysis and design that would otherwise be solved during coding—and, of course, because of reuse. If you spend time during the design phase and locate several components that will provide 30% of the functionality you need, you won't have to write that code later.

Figure 12.2 suggests the balance of time spent in different phases in an OO development effort. These times are approximate and will vary depending on the nature of the application. Still, they emphasize that lots of time is typically spent in analysis. And, more to the point for this chapter, they emphasize that most of your time should be spent in design.

In the analysis phase you consider the object model in the abstract. You work out the logical relationships between the business objects. In the design phase you determine the physical architecture of the system. This in turn suggests the infrastructure objects you will need. And the infrastructure objects

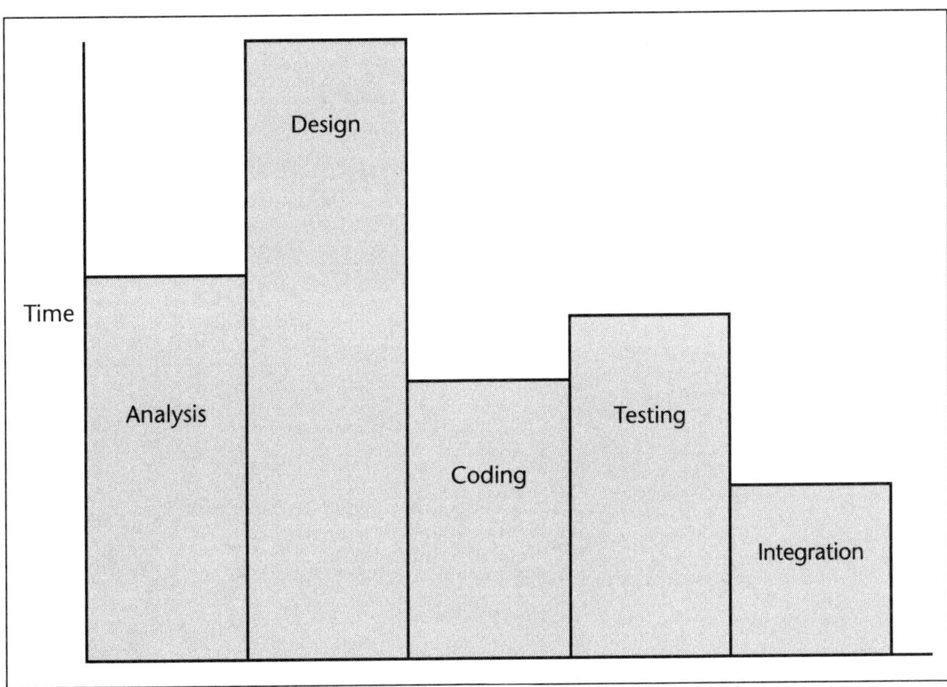

Figure 12.2 *Time required in different activities of OO development (after Booch).*

suggest lots of different operations that will be needed to handle the communications between all the new objects. By the same token, during design you decide what classes and components you can reuse, and they also suggest changes in your object model. And, of course, you design the user interfaces during this phase, and that also takes time.

If you did a good job of analyzing the business model during the analysis phase, you probably won't need to change too many of the classes you have already developed. You will, however, need to develop several new classes and lots of new operations to create a complete application. Then, finally, you will need to worry about lots of really detailed issues involved in obtaining the performance you will require.

Since this book is intended to introduce you to the UML notation, we do not provide a detailed prescription for designing OO applications. More important, our goal is to give you an overview and assure that you don't get lost in the details. Hence, we won't go into great depth about the various different design issues. We do, however, want to make some general comments and suggestions in the next two chapters.

13

Choosing an Object-Oriented Architecture

What hardware will your application run on? Will the application run on one machine or be distributed across many platforms? How will your application software be modularized? Does the system have to perform within certain time limits? Are existing COM objects or other applications going to be incorporated into or used by the system? What databases will be used by the system? These are the kinds of questions you must ask when you begin to think about how to create a concrete design for an application.

Some of these questions may already have been answered. Your company may own equipment or have adopted standards that determine or constrain the answers to some of these questions. The fact that you are using Visual Basic in the first place suggests that your system will be designed to run on Windows 95/98 and NT platforms. Similarly, your BPR team may have answered some of these questions when they designed the new business process your application will support. You may even have spelled out some of the design characteristics of the system when you created your initial requirements specification or when you made presentations to users before the project began. Whatever has gone before, when you begin the first design phase, you must reconsider the issues raised by these questions and come up with a firm design.

Of course, the conclusions you reach are not irreversible. The whole point of developing an application by means of successive approximations is to allow you to test alternatives before you finalize the entire system's design. Most developers start with an idea of how to develop their system, complete a few classes and test a portion of the idea, and then modify the idea as necessary. Similarly, if your first approximate or sub-application is intended to test the infrastructure and your plan for integration, and something doesn't work as well as anticipated, then during your next cycle you may decide to revise the design and test an alternative. Given all those qualifications, when you end your initial design phase, you should have a good approximation of your final design—if only in order to test it to see if it really works.

This book is not a comprehensive or detailed treatment of system design, so we won't go into many of the points that apply equally to conventional and OO development and are treated in many other books. (We recommend some of the best of these books in the Bibliography.) We will comment on a few of the considerations that you will face during development in order to clarify how these issues might affect the way you develop and extend the diagrams you are creating to document your system design. And we'll discuss how we might modularize our simple SalesWeb system.

13.1 Dividing an Application into Tiers

Let's start with a basic consideration: will our application run on a single machine or on multiple machines? And, if on multiple machines, will it use a two-tiered or three-tiered architecture?

Many small Visual Basic applications are designed to run on a single machine. The user loads the entire application onto his or her computer, including data in flat files or a local database, and then runs it. It's the simplest possible design because you don't need to worry about interfaces between one platform and another.

Increasingly, however, systems are designed to run on multiple machines. If you are creating a multiplatform system, your primary choice is likely to be between a two- and three-tiered architecture. Some developers call a two-tiered system a simple client/server system, and they call a three-tiered system a complex client/server, or distributed system. Internet systems can be two-tiered systems, but generally, they are three-tiered systems.

13.1.1 A Two-Tiered Design

A *two-tiered system* places a portion of the application on user platforms and the rest of the system on a server. Usually, three basic modules are created: (1) the user interface screens and associated logic, (2) the business logic of the application, and (3) the database and associated logic. A typical simple client/server system puts the user interface and the business logic on the client platform and puts the database and associated logic on the server portion of the system, which is usually a database server.

Many simple Internet systems use a two-tiered approach. In some cases the Internet-based client/server systems arrange things just as we described above. Internet protocols are simply used to transport information between client machines and the database server.

In other cases, the two-tiered Internet application assumes that the user has a Web browser. The server has the user screens, the business logic, and the database. The user signs on via the Internet, and the screens and some or all of the business logic are downloaded over the Internet. (Interestingly, that's just the way mainframe systems used to work with dumb terminals. Everything was on the mainframe, and the user screens and some logic were downloaded to the user's terminal, as needed.)

Figure 13.1 illustrates a simple two-tiered Internet-based system. In considering Figure 13.1, bear in mind that the tiers are, in fact, the platforms. The network hardware and software that links the client and server platforms are middleware. We'll consider connections between tiers in a moment.

13.1.2 A Three-Tiered Design

More complex applications typically rely on a three-tiered design. A *three-tiered design* separates the business objects and their operations or business rules from both the user interface and from the database portions of the system and from any other legacy applications that might be used. A typical three-tiered design puts the screen interface on the user's machine, the business logic on an intermediate server, and leaves the

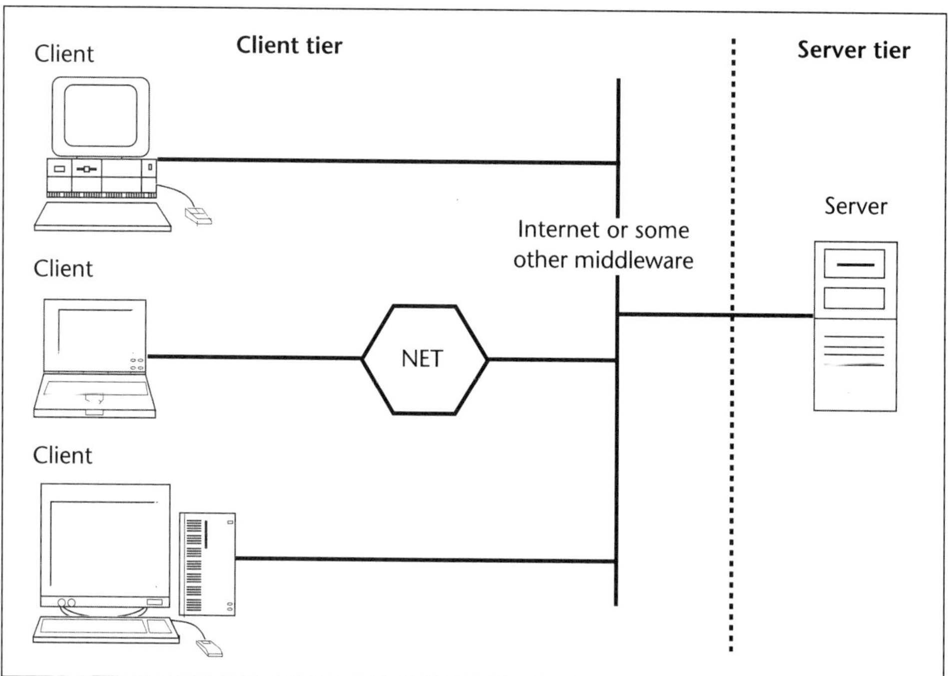

Figure 13.1 *A two-tiered client/server system.*

legacy applications and databases on whatever machines they currently reside on.

Larger Internet applications tend to be three-tiered systems. This usually means that a new Internet application must be designed to connect to both browsers and existing company databases or legacy applications. Three-tiered Internet systems may keep the user screens on the Internet server and download them when the user connects to the server. In this case, we assume that the user has a Web browser on his or her machine. Or there may be small applications that reside on the user machines and that initiate the contact with the Internet server. Figure 13.2 illustrates a three-tiered system. Again, the tiers are platforms, and the wiring and software in between the platforms constitute middleware.

If you develop a two-tiered system, you only have to develop an interface between the two tiers. Moreover, if you are going to rely on the Internet, you might also rely on the user having a browser, in which case you might only have to develop an applet and a server application, and ignore concerns about what kinds of machines the users have.

A two-tiered system tends to be a new system. It's easier to develop, but it's harder to maintain. If you know that your system is going to grow, or if your system will need to interact with existing databases or other applications, a three-tiered design is cleaner and easier to enhance and maintain.

A three-tiered system will require at least two interfaces: one between the user and the Internet server and another between the Internet server and a database server or any other application on other platforms. Most large distributed systems, in fact, require several "backend" interfaces, since they typically link to multiple legacy applications and multiple databases. In any case, client/server or distributed systems bring up the possibility that different parts of the application will be written in different languages or that they will be running on different kinds of platforms. Either or both will make application interfaces more complex.

You might initially design and implement a two-tiered system that later evolves into a three-tiered system. This typically occurs when additional business logic is added to the server tier, for security reasons, or to better distribute the processing load.

Figure 13.2 *A three-tiered distributed system.*

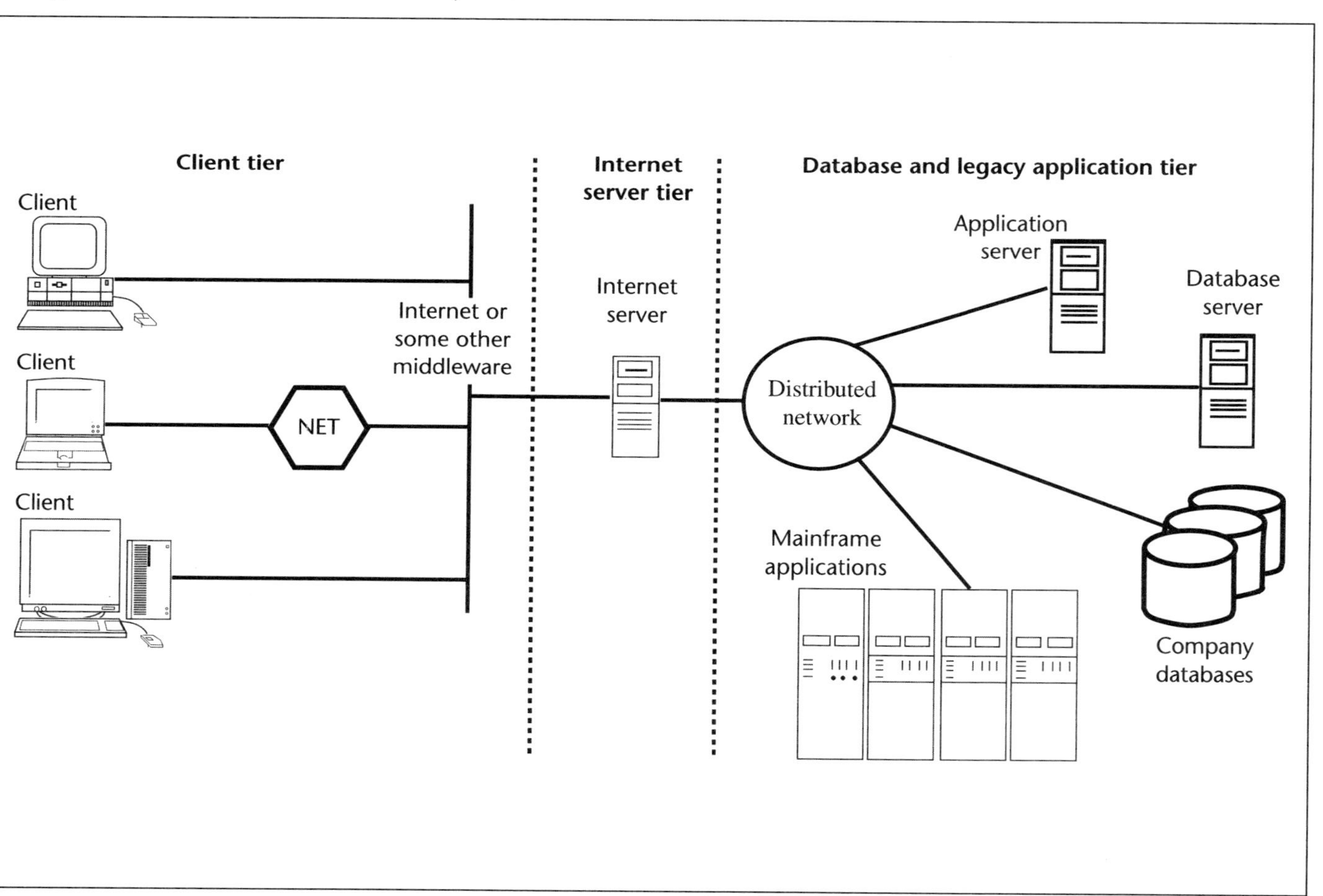

13.2 Assigning Packages to Tiers and Platforms

UML refers to a module that serves to group several objects together as a *package*. A UML package is a logical construct. You use packages when you are conceptualizing the modules in your system. Later, when it comes to actually assigning physical objects and code to real modules, you will switch to components. In UML terms, a package is a conceptual module, and a component is the physical module of code. You begin design by thinking in terms of packages. Later, when you get down to actually writing code, you will switch from packages to components. If you have done a good job of conceptualizing your packages, there should be a one-to-one relationship between packages (logical groupings) and components (physical groupings). At the moment, we are just beginning our design, so we'll focus on packages.

If your entire application is going to run on a single platform, you don't need to worry about dividing your application into packages and assigning the packages of your application to different platforms. Indeed, if your application is small enough, you can leave all the objects together in a single package and be done with it.

Most Internet applications, however, as well as nearly all midsized or large applications, need to run on multiple platforms. In this case you will usually want to subdivide your code into packages and assign it to different platforms. The simplest Internet application, for example, typically has a Visual Basic application on a server and one or more COM objects that are designed to be downloaded and executed within a client browser environment.

The SalesWeb code that we developed in this book is conceptualized as a three-tiered system. We provide a client, have most of the logic on an Internet server, and assume there are databases on database servers. In fact, the code we include in Appendix A is grouped into two large packages: a client package and a server package. We have included data in flat files that are included on the Internet server. We did this so you wouldn't have to own any specific database software to examine the code, which can be downloaded from the Web site identified in Appendix A.

At a minimum, you should isolate, conceptually, the parts of the application that will be on different tiers. If you are building a simple, two-tiered Internet system, you will need at least two packages: one for the server and another for the client. Of course, the portion of the application that you set up for the client may not be an application package in the traditional sense. It may simply be an ActiveX component that is downloaded along with an HTML Web page, or it may be an OLE object that is incorporated in another application.

By the same token, if you have a three-tiered system, you may not actually have any part of your application that will reside on the mainframe server. You may simply have one or more database objects that sit on the server and manage the communication with the mainframe server. In all but the simplest systems, however, it would be useful to isolate the database interface portion of the application in a separate package.

Each package suggests interfaces to link the packages, and interfaces are always a hassle. On the other hand, each interface isolates a part of the system that can be modified or replaced without changing other parts of the system. In the long run, arranging your system so that you can independently change GUI elements, the business logic, or the databases used in an application will make the system much more robust, and it will significantly reduce the problems of maintaining the system.

13.2.1 Two- and Three-Tiered Class Diagrams

In this book, as we have developed our Visual Modeler and our Rational Rose 98 diagrams, we have avoided the use of three-tiered diagrams and done the diagrams on a blank field. If you have been doing your diagrams by hand, during the analysis phase you have probably also ignored any division into tiers.

As you begin the design phase, it is time to begin considering such issues. If you have drawn diagrams by hand, you will have to redraw them, drawing two vertical lines to divide the classes into tiers. If you are using Visual Modeler or Rose 98, and not using the three-tiered view, you can simply bring up a version of your class diagram, convert that diagram to a three-tiered diagram, and then drag the classes around to indicate how they might be divided.

When we developed our Visual Modeler and Rose 98 diagrams in the earlier chapters of this book, we used a single screen and eliminated the lines. We did that to focus on analysis and to avoid decisions that normally fall in the design phase of a project development effort.

As you begin the design phase, it's an appropriate time to create a new class diagram that is divided into two or three tiers. Using Microsoft's terminology, we'll call the tiers: User Services, Business Services, and Data Services. If you are only doing a two-tiered design, you might prefer to divide your class diagram into two panels, one for User Services and the other for Business and Data Services.

In Figure 13.3, we've placed a three-tiered grid over the initial SalesWeb class diagram we did in Chapter 9 (Figure 9.12).

13.3 UML Implementation Diagrams

The UML notational system provides three diagrams called implementation diagrams:

- Package diagrams allow developers to show how classes could be divided into modules. Package diagrams are logical diagrams and do not necessarily imply a physical division of the classes.
- Component diagrams are used to show the physical modules that a developer might create.
- Deployment diagrams allow developers to model the physical platforms and network connections that will be used in their applications.

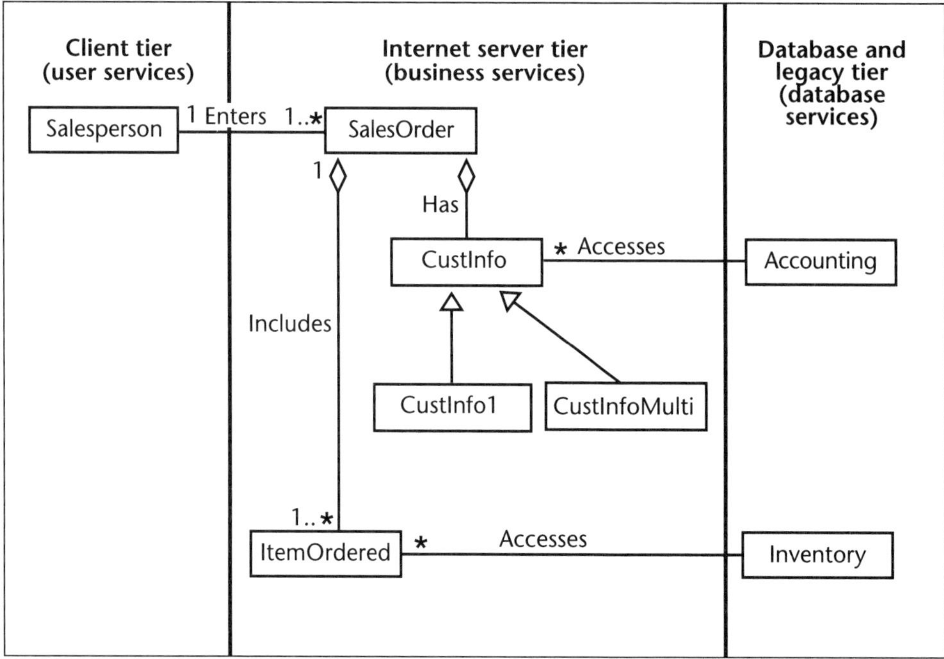

Figure 13.3 *Three-tiered grid laid over the initial class diagram of our SalesWeb application.*

All three diagrams are relatively simple, high-level diagrams compared with the diagrams we have considered earlier. Moreover, in most cases these diagrams are combined to provide more information. Thus, you often create a combined component and deployment diagram to show which components will be placed on which platforms. We'll introduce all three types of implementation diagrams in this chapter and then apply them to our SalesWeb system in this chapter and the next, as appropriate.

13.3.1 *The UML Package Diagram*

UML provides a package diagram that allows the developer to indicate how classes might be divided up. A file folder–shaped icon is used to represent a logical software module, which

UML calls a package. Links between packages are indicated by dashed arrows. The arrows can be labeled to indicate dependency names, if desired. If necessary, you can show packages within packages to any desired depth. The name of the package is usually written inside the package, although if packages are placed within packages, the superpackage name may be written on the tab of the largest folder.

You can show packages to show high-level logical groupings of packages, if the application is large and complex, or you can show the classes inside packages to capture more specific information. As a generalization, an application is a package, and any large application is subdivided into packages to subdivide the code and make it more manageable. In a very detailed diagram, components are usually packages, although you would probably never bother to make each of the ActiveX controls within a form a separate package.

Figure 13.4 illustrates how the SalesWeb application could be subdivided into two packages. The dotted arrow indicates dependencies between the packages. (If, in drawing the classes, there were association lines running between classes that are now in separate packages, you should show that there are dependencies between the two packages.) Package diagrams are often used to show that you intend to modularize your object model. If you do this, you would show the major classes within each package.

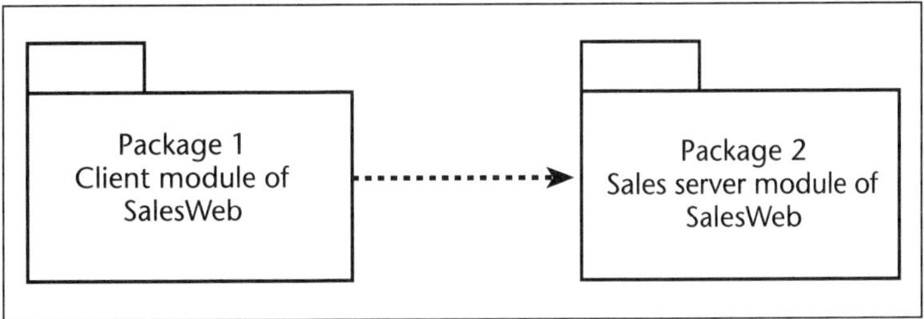

Figure 13.4 *A UML package diagram showing the SalesWeb application divided into two packages.*

13.3.2 The UML Component Diagram

We've already discussed components at several points. Once again, when we get down to specifics, it proves a confusing term. Component diagrams refer to physical components in your design. These high-level physical components may or may not be equivalent to the many smaller components you use in the creation of your application. For example, a single physical user interface component might contain dozens of ActiveX controls that are used to put graphical features on the user interface. A complex interface might be made up of dozens of Visual Basic form objects, each with ActiveX controls.

As far as most developers are concerned, a physical component will usually turn out to be the equivalent of a package. A package is used to show how you might group classes (and smaller scale components). In some cases the package will only be used to indicate a logical grouping to help highlight some particular perspective. In most cases, however, the package will be a first approximation of what will eventually turn into a physical grouping. In that case, the package will become a component.

In some cases a component is composed of classes. In other cases a component may simply be a wrapper for a legacy application. When you plan to compile classes you have developed into components, then you may want to diagram the components, showing the classes inside. When you use ActiveX components from the COM library from an outside vendor, however, you are using a binary object and there really is no point in showing what goes on inside the component. You simply show the component and indicate the interface.

For example, in Figure 13.4, package 1 could be an ActiveX component (an ActiveX EXE Document). In that case, it could just as well be represented as a component. Similarly, package 2 could easily be one or more ActiveX EXEs, or an ActiveX EXE and several ActiveX DLLs, and so forth.

Notice that UML's standard component diagram is different from Microsoft's component diagram that uses a rectangle with lollipops attached to the side. The Microsoft diagram is an alternative UML notation, and we predict that in time it will replace the standard UML component diagram.

The reuse of components will undoubtedly play an ever increasing role in the design and development of component-based applications in the near future as more ActiveX and JavaBeans components become available. We're not sure the UML component diagrams will be useful in representing the components that most developers will use. Keep in mind when you use UML component diagrams that you are describing physical modules of code.

UML also provides a notation for components, and you can create diagrams in which you show several components interacting with each other. A component is represented by the icon shown in Figure 13.5. The names of the components are written on the surface of the icon, and dependencies between components are indicated by dotted arrows.

In most cases you will use component diagrams in conjunction with deployment diagrams to show how physical modules of code are distributed on various hardware platforms. In fact, they might as well be the same diagram: a component/deployment diagram.

13.3.3 The UML Deployment Diagram

In UML deployment diagrams, each node or processing element in the system is represented by a three-dimensional box. Links between the nodes or platforms are shown by solid lines. Figure 13.6 provides the basic UML notation for a deployment diagram.

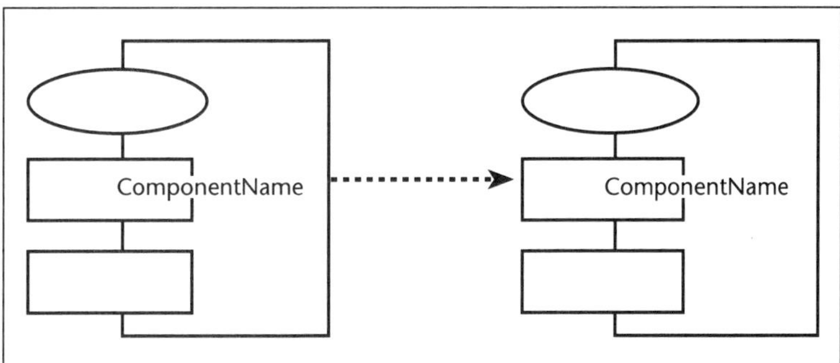

Figure 13.5 *UML component diagram notation.*

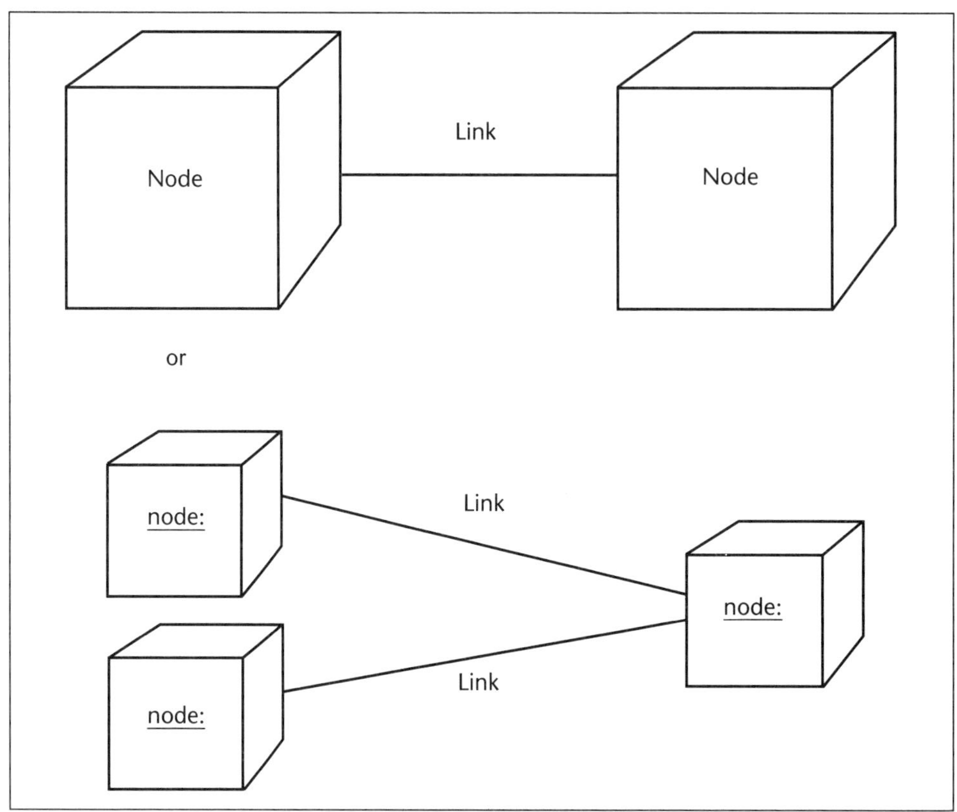

Figure 13.6 *UML deployment diagram notation.*

You can describe a class-level configuration by writing the names of each node as you would the names of the classes, in which case you would only have one node for each type of element in the system. In this case, our SalesWeb application would only show one salesperson's laptop computer. Or, you can label the nodes with names that refer to specific instances of the node and label them as you would objects, underlined with a colon after the "object" portion of the name. If you chose this approach, our SalesWeb application would show several salespeople, each with his or her own laptop, all linked to the common sales department's Internet server.

You can go further and place components inside nodes to show how the actual code will be distributed. You could also show packages or even classes inside the cubes to show which platform specific elements of the system will be placed on, but that can get rather complex. In any case, it involves mixing a physical and logical description of your application and is probably best avoided, except to demonstrate a very specific or narrowly focused aspect of a distributed solution.

13.4 Linking the Tiers

In a distributed system, you might want to do either of two things. First, you might want to pass data from one object to another object or to a database. Or, you might want to have one object ask another object to perform some task. We'll consider how you might deal with data in Chapter 14. At this point, we want to discuss how an object on one platform might send a message to an object on another platform.

If you are running a Visual Basic application on a single platform, you will have no difficulty simply sending a message between two classes. Even on the same machine, however, you could begin to run into problems if you had Visual Basic classes inside different processes (different EXEs). In this case, the easiest thing to do would be to encapsulate the two processes as COM components and let COM handle the message propagation. Similarly, if you were trying to send a message from a Visual Basic object to a C++ object, you would probably want to use COM to encapsulate the Visual Basic and C++ applications and then use COM to handle the message traffic between the two.

It gets more complex as more platforms become involved. If you were building a simple Internet application, you could make the client portion of the system an ActiveX component. In order to use the client ActiveX component, you would then need to create a Web page in HTML. You rely on the client using HTTP to access the server and download the HTML code, which then downloads the client ActiveX component. You could also rely on the ActiveX component to pass the information back to the server.

If you wanted an object on one machine to send and receive messages from one object on another machine, however, you would probably want to turn to DCOM. That's what DCOM is for: to handle messages between objects on different platforms. Unfortunately, DCOM, at the moment, is only supported on Windows 95/98/NT and a very few UNIX platforms. Thus, if you want to create a heterogeneous system, you will probably need to use the OMG's Common Object Request Broker Architecture (CORBA). For example, if you wanted to move messages between a Visual Basic object on a Windows 95/98 platform and a C++ object on an AS400 machine, CORBA would be the easiest way to do it. If you had to develop both the COM object to encapsulate the Visual Basic object, and then write the code to convert that to a CORBA object, it would get rather nasty. Luckily, however, Microsoft has cooperated with IONA, a leading CORBA vendor. IONA offers a tool that will automatically move messages from DCOM systems, via CORBA systems, to CORBA objects, or vice versa.

The bottom line is that when you begin to want to send messages from a Visual Basic object to anything on another machine, you will want to switch from Visual Basic to COM and DCOM, which are designed to handle this type of problem.

13.4.1 COM, DCOM, and CORBA

The minute you encounter more complex problems, you should begin to think about using an object request broker (ORB). An ORB is a communication system that allows one object to send a message to another object without regard to where the other object is located. The objects might be located on the same platform, but ORBs are most valuable when the objects are located on separate platforms. In effect, an ORB keeps track of where objects are (or has a mechanism for finding out where they are) and provides mechanisms for routing a message from the sender to the target without the developer having to worry how it's done. An ORB allows us to locate useful remote objects and make remote procedure calls (RPCs) on those objects.

We've already considered COM and DCOM in Chapter 5. At this point, it might be worth taking a brief look at CORBA, since that would be used if the communication extended to heterogeneous environments. In fact, you could simply say that CORBA is DCOM, redesigned to extend to heterogeneous platforms and to multiple OO languages and components models.

The Object Management Group's CORBA

The Object Management Group's CORBA is implemented on almost all platforms and supports most of the major OO languages. Using CORBA, you can easily send a message from a Visual Basic object or a COM component to a Smalltalk or COBOL object on a different platform. Moreover, Microsoft and IONA, the leading CORBA dealer, are working on tools that will make it possible for ActiveX components to automatically link to CORBA objects and vice versa.

Consider Figure 13.7. Like DCOM, CORBA relies on stubs and skeleton objects. Unlike DCOM, the stubs and skeletons won't always be interfacing with either Visual Basic objects or COM objects. To deal with this, CORBA uses a special language, OMG's Interface Definition Language (IDL), which is different from Microsoft's COM IDL, to represent the operations that objects can interact with. If you are going to create a CORBA system, you need to define all the signatures of all the objects that will be involved in the system. These are placed in an interface repository so that a message from one object can determine which platform the target object might reside on. Thus, messages are changed from the language of the sending object to IDL, are marshalled, sent, unmarshalled, then converted to the language of the target object. In effect, each platform is equipped with a CORBA object that can deal with sending and receiving IDL and marshalling parameters. The CORBA client and server objects can access the interface repository and an implementation repository as needed.

CORBA uses an OO version of TCP/IP, called Internet InterORB Protocol (IIOP), when it transmits IDL. CORBA isn't currently supported by Microsoft's Internet Explorer, but several browser companies, led by Netscape, have proposed IIOP as a standard Internet protocol. Netscape has also incorporated

Figure 13.7 *An implementation of the OMG's CORBA architecture.*

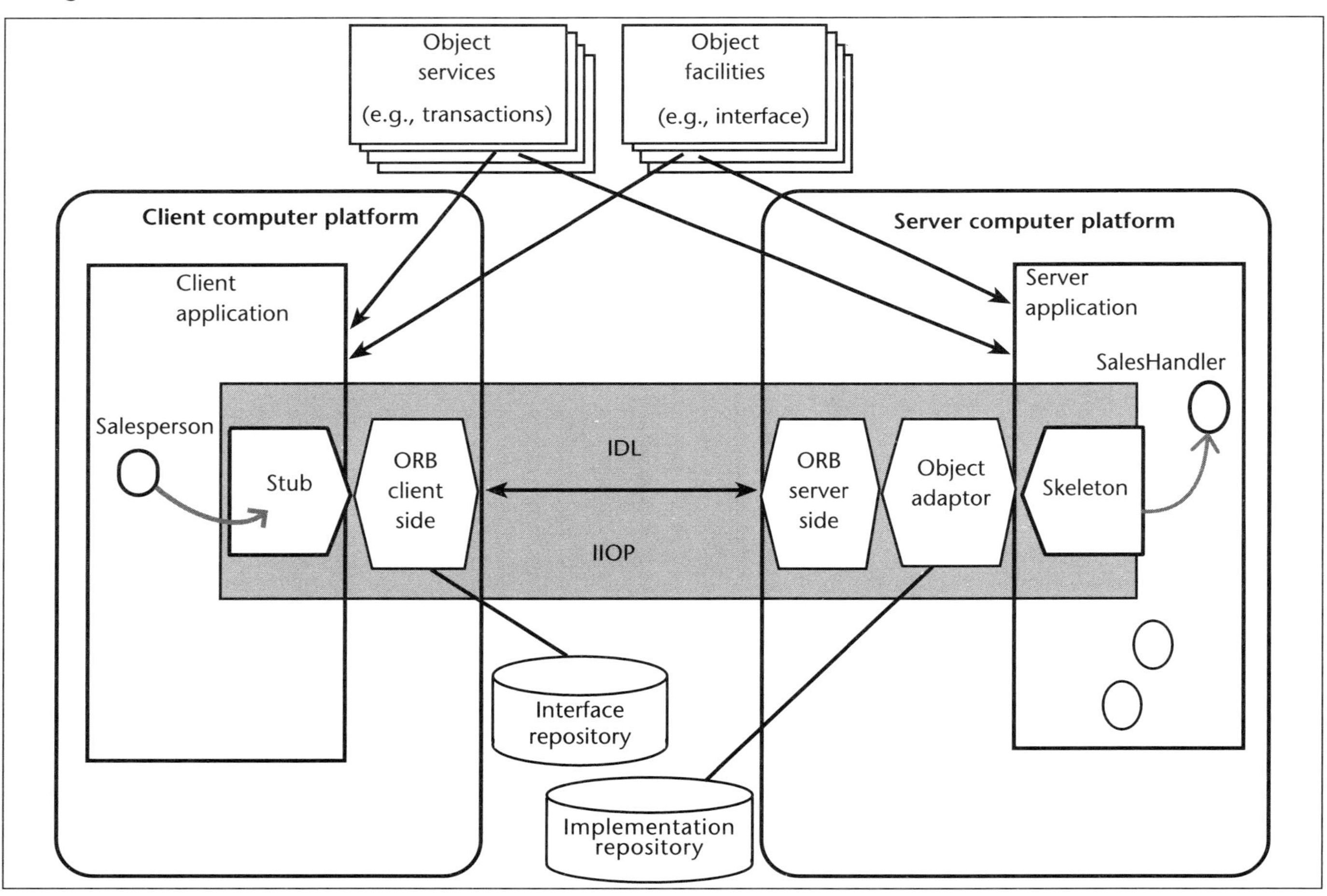

CORBA into their browser and server tools, so any ActiveX component running on a Netscape browser can send a message, via IONA's CORBA, to any object on any server. Netscape simply makes the stubs available in the browser.

Again, this sounds complex, but much of it is transparent. Still, compared with using COM in Visual Basic, there's quite a bit more to CORBA, and it takes more work to set up a CORBA system. This is to be expected, since CORBA can work with multiple servers and can move messages transparently between any of the major OO languages or component models.

CORBA has been around longer than DCOM, and the OMG has standardized a wide variety of classes and frameworks for handling the complex problems involved in dealing with finding objects, handling security, dealing with transaction processing, and so on. The latest CORBA implementations are combining CORBA with transaction processing monitors to handle large-scale asynchronous applications.

Clearly, CORBA isn't appropriate for systems written entirely in Visual Basic, or for systems that run entirely on Windows 95/98 and NT platforms. It is, however, the emerging standard for large systems that have to route messages in a heterogeneous environment. Indeed, Microsoft has recognized this fact when it signed a license agreement with IONA, the leading CORBA vendor, to assure that COM components could use IONA's CORBA implementation with DCOM when developers were faced with applications that needed to run on heterogeneous platforms.

13.5 Summing Up

The three major steps in designing an architecture for an application are (1) identify the platforms, (2) break your application into packages and assign the packages to platforms, and (3) decide how to link your platforms together. You document these decisions with UML's implementation diagrams. In the process you have to modify all of your earlier diagrams to incorporate infrastructure classes and COM components. You also need to define all the attributes (properties) and methods of all your classes.

13.6 The Architecture of the SalesWeb System

Our SalesWeb application could take several forms, but we have assumed from the beginning that we were developing a three-tiered application. Salespeople use laptops and modems. The salespeople could have different types of laptops. Let's assume that some have Intel machines running Microsoft Windows and others have Apple Powerbook laptops running the Macintosh OS (which supports COM). They will contact Moose's sales Internet server via the Internet. Let's assume that the server will be a workstation running Windows NT, version 4.0. We have already assumed that the legacy applications owned by accounting and inventory are mainframe applications supported by DB2 databases. Let's assume they are running on midsized IBM mainframes.

We could diagram the physical layout of our SalesWeb application as shown in Figure 13.8. We have shown the SalesWeb system at the class level and thus only have one generic laptop node.

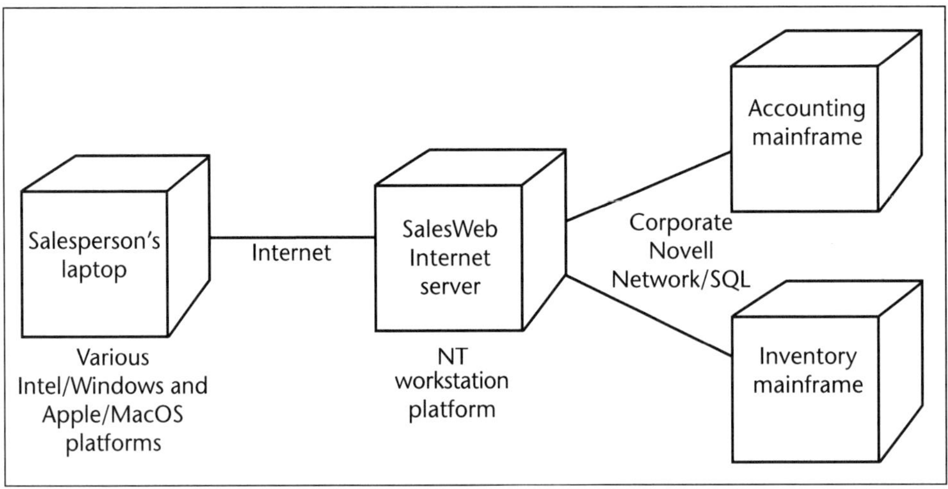

Figure 13.8 *A UML deployment diagram of SalesWeb.*

We developed our SalesWeb application on a single machine. To field it, however, we will need to divide those classes that will go on the salespeople's laptops from those classes that will reside on the sales server. Thus, in effect, we have two SalesWeb packages. Package 1 includes the GUI classes, and Package 2 includes the sales server application. In addition, we would subdivide Package 2 on the Internet server into two subpackages: 2.1, the core business classes, and 2.2, the classes that deal with the database (see Figure 13.9). Obviously, this is simply a logical overview. We might find it convenient to subdivide any of these packages into smaller modules. Similarly, we might want to show the actual classes that we placed in each package.

Figure 13.10 indicates how we plan on modularizing and distributing our final application code. In effect, we will simply change the package on the client into a physical component. In fact, we will turn our two subpackages on the server into a single Visual Basic EXE application in the code we include in Appendix A, but if we were actually doing this for a company, we would probably go through a couple of additional prototypes and then create several modules for the server. Again, we might have subcomponents inside the

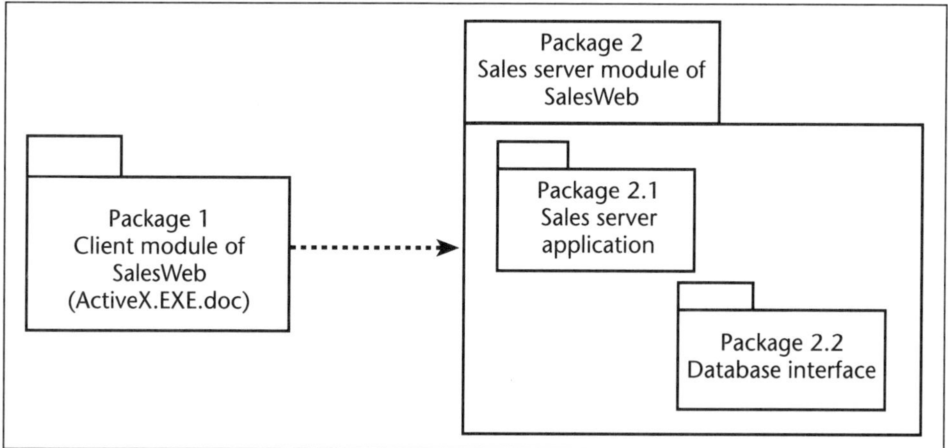

Figure 13.9 *A UML package diagram showing the SalesWeb application broken into four modules.*

Figure 13.10 *UML deployment/component diagram of the SalesWeb application.*

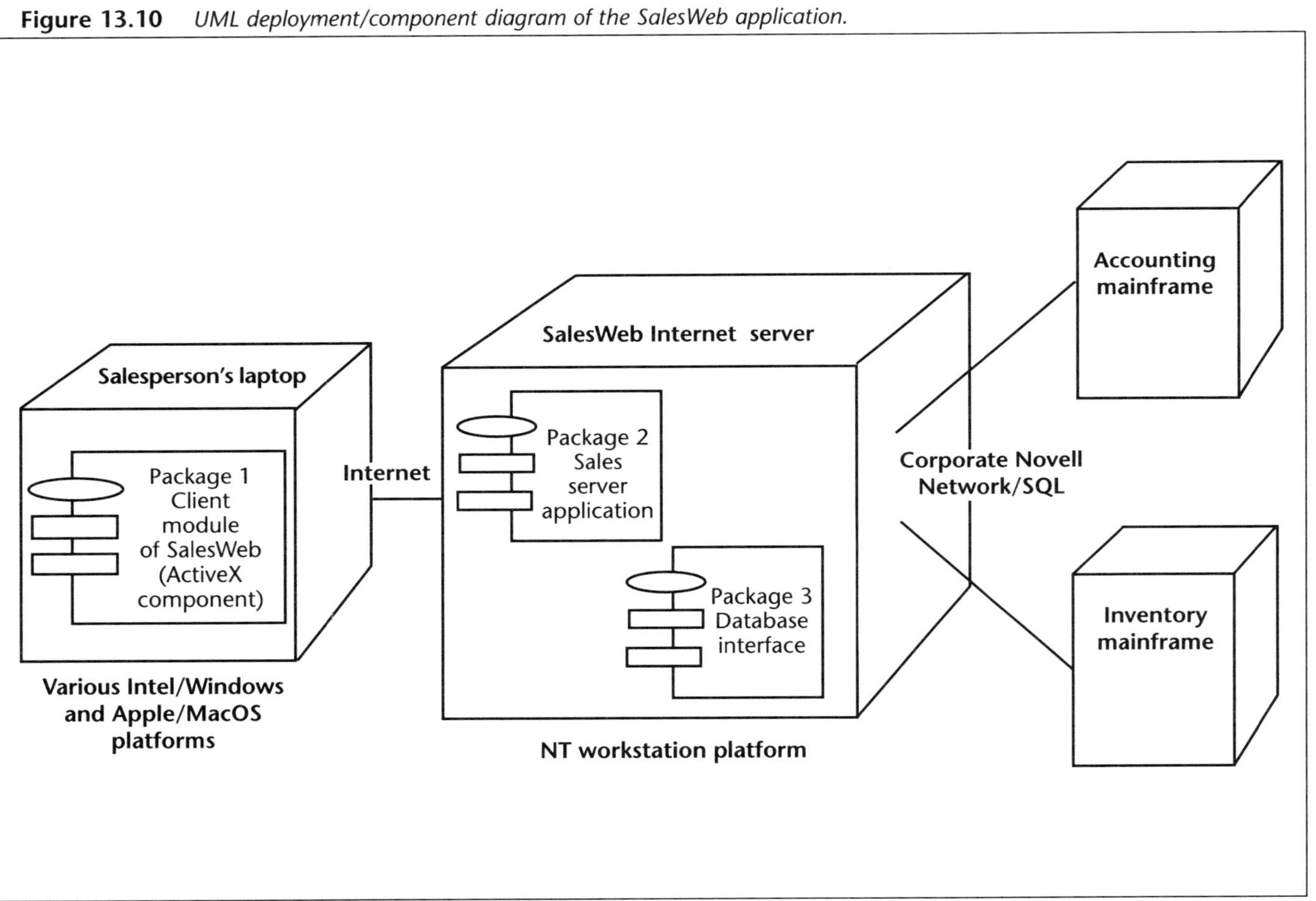

components and could show them if it were useful—but clearly it isn't in the case of our simple SalesWeb application.

In the case of the SalesWeb system, we wanted the linkage to be as simple as possible while still allowing the Visual Basic client applications to pass the appropriate arguments from the client GUI screens to the remote *SalesServer* application. Since both client and server programs support COM/DCOM, we used the Internet and COM to handle the linkage between the client ActiveX components and the server.

13.7 Capturing a Design in a Visual Modeling Tool

Visual Modeler supports UML component and deployment diagrams. Unfortunately, it isn't very easy to mix deployment diagrams with component and package diagrams. Similarly, Rational Rose 98 supports all three diagrams, and it would be easy to create any of these diagrams in Rose 98.

14

Expanding Your Design

Once you have a good idea of the overall architecture of your application, there are still many additional design decisions to be made. We've lumped them under three general headings: (1) expanding your object model, (2) developing user screens or Web pages, and (3) arranging for data access. We've also included a brief note on coding and testing your application.

14.1 Expanding Your Object Model

When you begin the design phase of a cycle, you review each of your earlier UML diagrams and ask more practical questions. For example, you move from specifying that the *Salesperson* object sends a message to the *SalesOrder* object, to trying to pin down exactly how this will occur. The following tasks will help you accomplish this:

- First, you need to extend your existing diagrams to incorporate infrastructure classes.

- Then you need to determine in more detail how the operations you have identified will actually work. This will generally mean thinking harder about specific data to be manipulated and will involve the development of private operations to assist in processing messages. It also means that you will want to study books on patterns to figure out the most efficient ways to handle certain problems.
- You also need to think about using COM library or using other Visual Basic classes or COM components from external sources.

14.1.1 Extending Your Analysis Diagrams

Recall that in Chapter 7, after we had developed our use case diagram of the SalesWeb application, we went on to develop an OOSE ideal class model. In effect, we inserted interface, entity, and control classes into our Report Sales use case. (See Figure 14.1.)

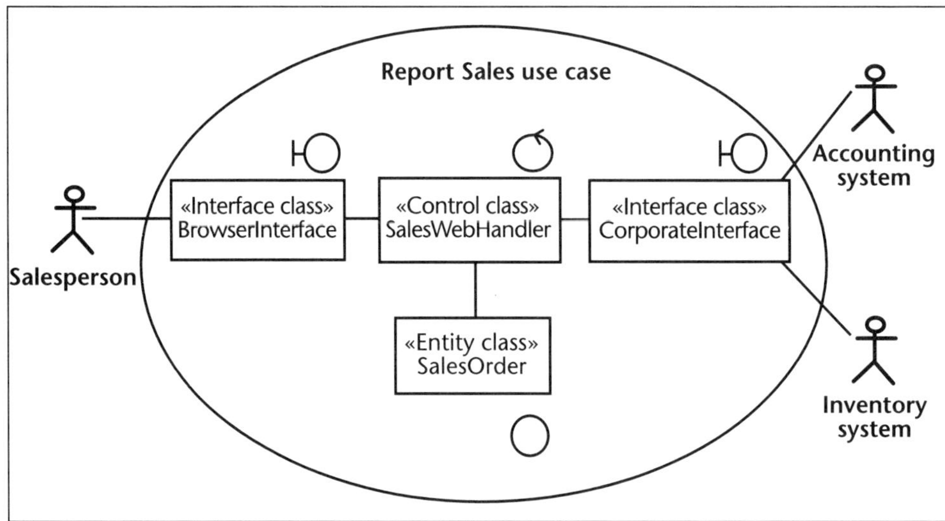

Figure 14.1 *Ideal class model of the Report Sales use case.*

OO developers argue about the value of a control or handler class that manages the overall performance of an application. Some prefer to incorporate any control methods right into business objects. Others prefer to keep the methods that control the overall flow of an application in a single class so they can be easily accessed and modified. In our simple application, we incorporated the control methods directly into the *SalesOrder* class.

After developing the ideal class model, we suggested that during analysis we would only focus on the entity classes, like *SalesOrder,* and the classes outside the use case, like *Salesperson* and *Accounting.* We ignored the infrastructure classes, including the interface classes and the handlers. Now, as we begin the design phase of our development effort, it is time to insert these additional classes. Before we do, however, let's also think about what our tier model suggests. In Figure 14.2 we have

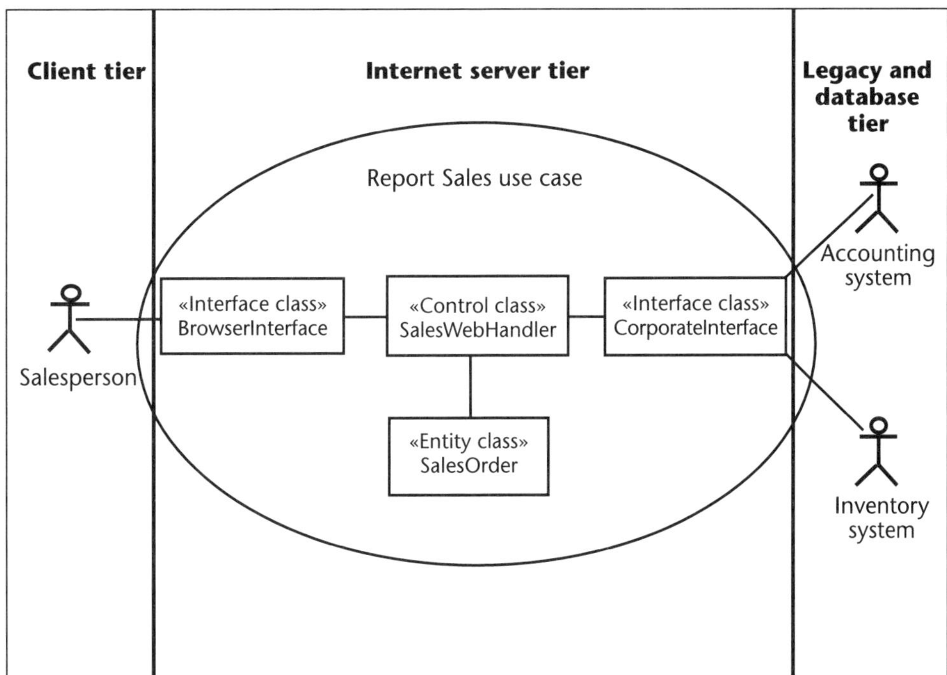

Figure 14.2 *Ideal class model of the Report Sales use case with three-tiered grid overlaid.*

imposed our three-tiered grid over the ideal use case model of the Report Sales use case.

In Chapter 13, when we discussed distributing the different packages on different platforms, we spoke of the need to select a way of linking the different platforms. Linkages do not always imply new classes, but they often do. Thus, looking at Figure 14.2, we can see that if we were to have a Visual Basic class on the client and another on the Internet server, we would probably need a communication interface on both machines. These classes are identified as *ClientMain* and *ServerMain*.

On the database side we will probably need one interface object for each of the two legacy/database systems. On the other hand, we probably won't need to create new interfaces for the database tier. Our database interface classes on the Internet server tier will probably be able to generate SQL and thus deal directly with the existing relational databases. You will need to think through the interfaces your application will need to support and create classes to handle them.

Next, consider the handler we showed in Figures 14.1 and 14.2. In analysis we only focused on the abstract relationship between the *Salesperson* and *SalesOrder* classes. Now, as we consider actually implementing the system, we must think about how many salespeople might want to create orders at any one time. We must also consider what would happen if one salesperson started one order, then, without completing it, started another, and so on. Again, there are lots of different ways to deal with this, but a common approach is to create a control or manager class that is designed to handle the overall operation of the Internet server. In effect, this control class (there's a long tradition in OO of calling them handlers) would allocate the resources of the Internet server, accepting incoming contact requests, sending *Salesperson* applets to browsers, creating *SalesOrder* objects, and controlling the overall flow of data to and from the databases. If you decide to create a handler of this sort, you will need to create new sequence and state diagrams to be sure you understand exactly how the handler will respond to the hundreds of different scenarios it might be faced with.

There's no one right answer about any of these matters, of course. Developers working with different platforms would make different decisions. Similarly, depending on the speed required of the application, there could be very different designs. Our only point here is that design is the time when you must face and address these issues.

Different developers would approach the whole process involved in expanding the analysis diagrams into design diagrams in different ways. Some might start, as we did, with the class diagram and expand the number of classes. Then they might proceed to the sequence diagram, inserting the new interface and control classes and reworking the sequence diagram to see how messages would now flow. Others would probably start with the sequence diagrams, adding new objects to see how things might work, move to the state diagrams to work out the details of the new handler class, and return and expand the class diagram as a kind of summary.

When we last considered the SalesWeb application, we ended up with the class diagram that we last pictured in Figure 13.3. If we add interface classes, we arrive at the class diagram shown in Figure 14.3.

To assure that we understood the SalesWeb class diagram we arrived at in Figure 14.3, we then expanded the sequence diagram we arrived at in Chapter 10 with the new interface objects. This brings us to a new sequence diagram, which is shown in Figure 14.4. To keep things simple, we haven't shown all the events that would occur, but just a sample to suggest how the new classes will interact with the older business classes.

In preparing Figure 14.4, we are forced to consider in some detail things like which objects will continue throughout the entire transaction and which will be terminated as soon as possible. We also need to determine exactly which objects will be communicating with interfaces.

Notice that we have now resolved the problem with the *Salesperson* class. In the new sequence diagram it doesn't represent the salesperson, as such. It is an ActiveX EXE document that is downloaded from the Internet server to the browser on the salesperson's machine. The ActiveX component collects

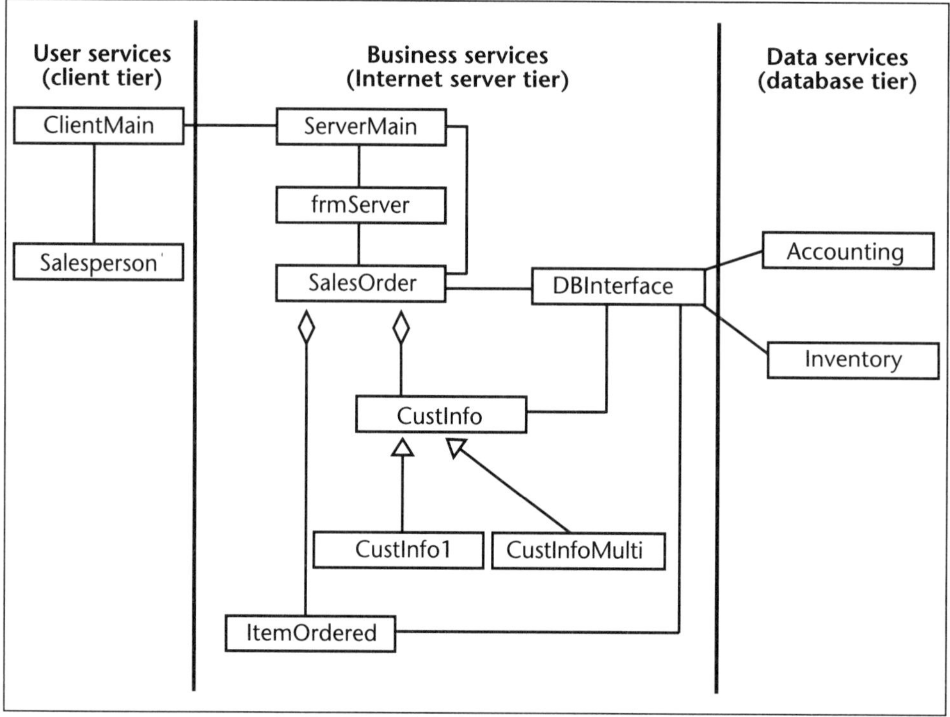

Figure 14.3 *The addition of generic infrastructure classes to the SalesWeb application.*

information about the order and then transmits all the information, in a single blast, to *ServerMain.* There is nothing to keep the salesperson from downloading several different *Salesperson* components, working on each, and then submitting them when they are all complete.

14.1.2 Getting Concrete about Operations

In analysis, we focused on those attributes and operations associated with business objects. We were primarily concerned with a general description of how the business organization functioned. We wanted to know, in the language of CRC, who was responsible for doing what.

During design we need to get much more specific about how things are done. And, as we add infrastructure classes to

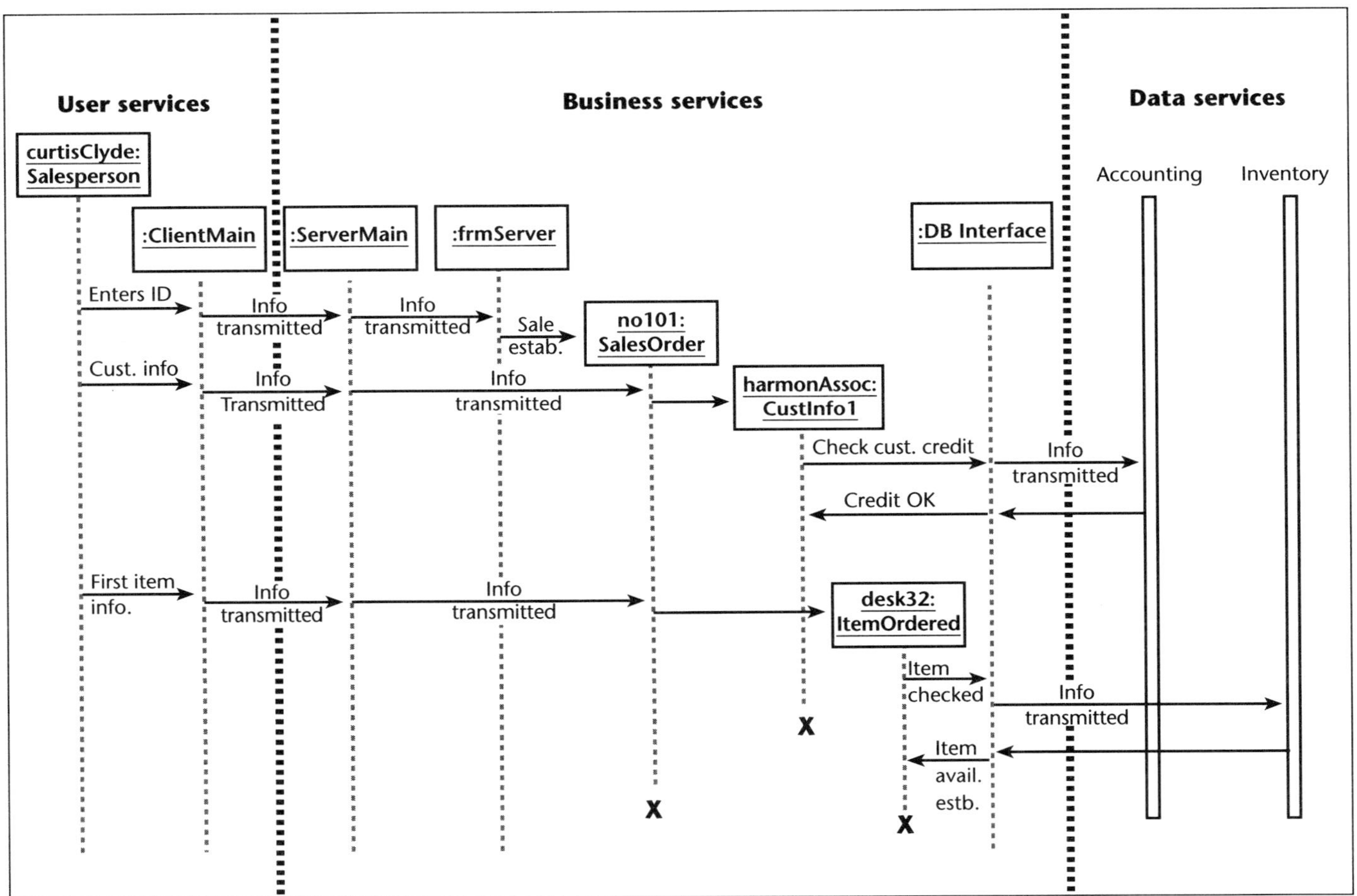

Figure 14.4 *An expanded sequence diagram of Scenario 1 from Figure 8.4.*

our model, we need to add new attributes and operations. Just as infrastructure classes are concerned with programming details, the operations and attributes used by these classes are also very practical.

We also mentioned, when we first introduced operations, that some developers distinguish between public operations that are, in effect, visible and available for other objects to contact, and private operations that simply do things inside the specific object. In the analysis phase, we ignore private operations and focus on the operations that make up an object's interface. When we switch to design and begin preparing written descriptions or pseudocode to define exactly what an operation will do, we often find that we would rather divide an operation into several smaller operations. We leave the public operation in place to accept messages and then create private operations to handle different aspects of processing a message or to handle actions (side effects) that the public operation may initiate.

This isn't a book on programming, and we won't go into any details about how to actually code operations here. We have provided the specific code for the SalesWeb application in Appendix A, and we've annotated the code to suggest why we wrote specific operations in particular ways. More important, however, we can give you very good advice on how to think about operations and the development of interface classes to handle common tasks: Get a book on OO patterns and study it.

14.1.3 Patterns

A *pattern* is a standard way of handling some specific task. You rarely think of patterns during the analysis phase of your development effort. Patterns are something you need when you begin to work on the specific design of your application.

Some patterns are large scale and help to solve major problems. Others are very specific and help with more focused problems. In a sense, a pattern is a design for a module or component. You could let someone else implement the pattern and simply buy the component that provided the functionality you needed. (We fully expect that several vendors will implement common patterns as ActiveX components and offer them for sale during the next year or two.) Or, if you are working in code or with a visual modeling tool, you can study the patterns in one of the books that have been written to describe good OO patterns. In the latter case, you can see exactly how an experienced OO developer recommends you handle a specific problem and decide if it fits your problem. If it does, you simply implement the pattern for your system, incorporating the diagrams provided by the pattern book author and using or converting the code provided by the book into operations in whatever OO language you are working in.

If you are going to be involved in OO development, you should probably buy at least one book on patterns and study it. It will provide you with lots of insights into how developers take advantage of object techniques to solve common programming problems. The best book to start with is *Design Patterns: Elements of Reusable Object-Oriented Software.* It is written by Erich Gamma and three other authors and is listed in the Bibliography at the end of this book. It provides a number of solutions to important and recurring problems that every OO developer will encounter. Each pattern is diagrammed using OMT notation, and both C++ and Smalltalk code solutions are provided. We list other books on patterns in the Bibliography.

Gamma and his coauthors divide common patterns into three groups and define the various patterns appropriate to each group, as follows:

Creational Patterns

Abstract Factory: Provide an interface for creating families of related or dependent objects without specifying their concrete classes.

Builder: Separate the construction of a complex object from its representation so that the same construction process can create different representations.

Factory Method: Define an interface for creating an object, but let subclasses decide which class to instantiate. Factory Method lets a class defer instantiation to subclasses.

Prototype: Specify the kinds of objects to create using a prototypical object, and create new objects by copying this prototype.

Singleton: Ensure a class only has one object, and provide a global point of access to it.

Structural Patterns

Adapter: Convert the interface of a class into another interface clients expect. Adapter lets classes work together that couldn't otherwise because of incompatible interfaces.

Bridge: Decouple an abstraction from its implementation so that the two can vary independently.

Composite: Compose objects into tree structures to represent part-whole hierarchies. Composite lets clients treat individual objects and compositions of objects uniformly.

Decorator: Attach additional responsibilities to an object dynamically. Decorators provide a flexible alternative to subclassing for extending functionality.

Facade: Provide a unified interface to a set of interfaces in a subsystem. Facade defines a higher-level interface that makes the subsystem easier to use.

Flyweight: Use sharing to support large numbers of fine-grained objects efficiently.

Proxy: Provide a surrogate or placeholder for another object to control access to it.

Behavioral Patterns

Chain of Responsibility: Avoid coupling the sender of a request to its receiver by giving more than one object a chance to handle the request. Chain the receiving objects and pass the request along the chain until an object handles it.

Command: Encapsulate a request as an object, thereby letting you parameterize clients with different requests, queue or log requests, and support undoable operations.

Interpreter: Given a language, define a representation for its grammar along with an interpreter that uses the representation to interpret sentences in the language.

Iteration: Provide a way to access the elements of an aggregate object sequentially without exposing its underlying representation.

Mediator: Define an object that encapsulates how a set of objects interact. Mediator promotes loose coupling by keeping objects from referring to each other explicitly, and it lets you vary their interaction independently.

Memento: Without violating encapsulation, capture and externalize an object's internal state so that the object can be restored to this state later.

Observer: Define a one-to-many dependency between objects so that when one object changes state, all its dependents are notified and updated automatically.

State: Allow an object to alter its behavior when its internal state changes. The object will appear to change its class.

Strategy: Define a family of algorithms, encapsulate each one, and make them interchangeable. Strategy lets the algorithm vary independently from clients that use it.

Template Method: Define the skeleton of an algorithm in an operation, deferring some steps to subclasses. Template Method lets subclasses redefine certain steps of an algorithm without changing the algorithm's structure.

Visitor: Represent an operation to be performed on the elements of an object structure. Visitor lets you define a new operation without changing the classes of the elements on which it operates.

Figure 14.5 illustrates one of the patterns described by Gamma et al. They call this pattern the Composite pattern, and here's how they describe it:

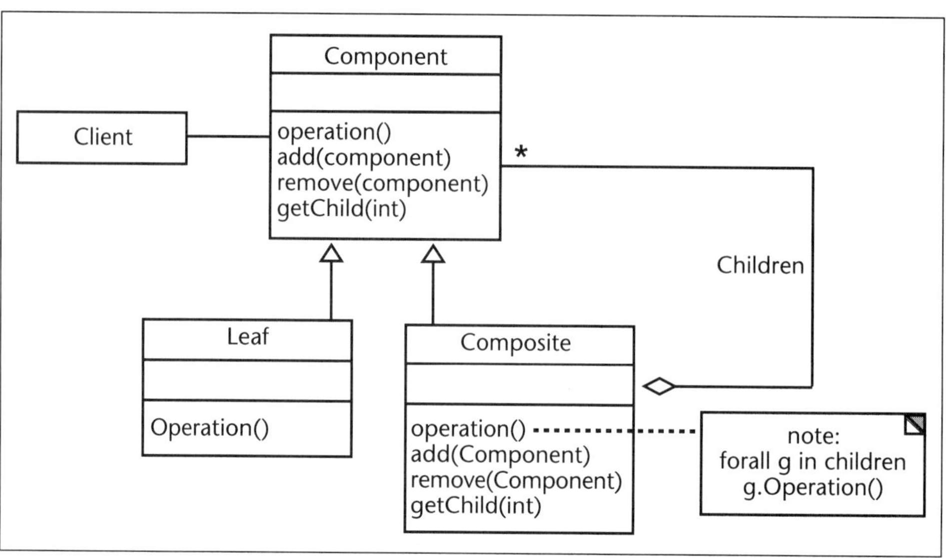

Figure 14.5 *The generic structure of the Composite pattern (modified after Gamma et al.).*

> Graphics applications like drawing editors and schematic capture systems let users build complex diagrams out of simple components. The user can group components to form larger components, which in turn can be grouped to form still larger components. A simple implementation could define classes for graphical primitives such as Text and Lines plus other classes that act as containers for these primitives.
>
> But there's a problem with this approach: Code that uses these classes must treat primitive and container objects differently, even if most of the time the user treats them identically. Having to distinguish these objects makes the application more complex. The Composite pattern describes how to use recursive composition so that clients don't have to make this distinction.

We're not going to describe patterns in the detail Gamma and his coauthors do. They not only discuss the generic pattern and how it functions but provide examples in C++ and Smalltalk code to show how each operation works. (We have modified the diagram, which was in OMT notation, so that it appears in UML notation.)

14.1.4 Using Classes, Interfaces, and Components

At some point in any OO design effort, you should consider what your options for reuse are. If you are using Visual Basic to develop your application, you will undoubtedly be reusing ActiveX controls and Visual Basic forms (objects) to create GUI.

In addition, as you develop your application, you will probably consider using ActiveX components to handle your database interface. In Chapter 5 we showed how ActiveX controls could be used with an Internet application.

Beyond these basics, however, you will want to check to see if there are components or frameworks of business objects you can use to handle more complex aspects of your application. For example, if you are developing an application in the financial area, you will want to check to see if anyone has published a framework of ActiveX components for financial application development. There are probably components to handle converting from one currency to another, for calculating different kinds of interest, and for providing an on-line link to stock market information. There's no reason to worry about the internal design problems of a class if you can borrow or buy a component that provides the functionality you need. Finding the right components or frameworks not only can reduce your design effort, it can really reduce your coding effort as well.

There is no comprehensive source of components or business frameworks at the moment. We've listed a couple of Web sites in the Bibliography that try to keep track of components, but frankly the field is too new and expanding too fast for anyone to stay on top of it at the moment.

The place to begin is to determine whether your company has a library of components or business objects or is part of a consortium that has a library. Also check with Microsoft. They are working with several consortiums of companies to develop frameworks of components or business objects for a number of major industries.

Similarly, some industry groups are working under the auspices of OMG to create business object frameworks for their industries. Getting involved in the OMG and attending some of their technical meetings relative to your industry would be a good way to get up to speed on what's available in your area. If your company isn't part of a consortium, but you discover that there is one in your industry or domain of interest, you should probably correspond or attend a meeting to find out what they offer.

Next, you'll want to talk with people at conferences or via the Web who are developing applications like yours. Similarly, you'll want to look for articles in magazines and newspapers that talk about applications similar to yours and check what components they used. Start keeping track of any mention of component sources that seem likely to provide components you could use.

In addition, a few companies have been set up to sell components. Most of these companies are small, and all are rather narrowly focused, but some exhibit their products at conferences and advertise in magazines. You should certainly check out any company that claims to be selling components in your area of interest.

If you find a class or component that you can use in your core design, you will need to incorporate it into your diagrams. You will need to know what messages (signatures) it responds to and what it returns in response to any messages it receives. Component vendors sometimes provide a detailed description of the source code, and you can treat the component just as you would any other class in your diagram. Most component vendors, however, sell binary components, like ActiveX components, and only describe the interface to the component. In other words, they tell you what messages the component will respond to and what responses it will provide. If the function of the component is clearly specified, an interface specification is usually sufficient.

14.2 Developing User Screens or Web Pages

If your application will have user interfaces, you will need to design the screens. Since we assume that most readers are Visual Basic developers and know how to develop graphical user interfaces in Visual Basic, we won't say much about this. If you are uncertain, there are a number of books available on GUI development in Visual Basic. Most don't describe interface development in object or component terms, but having gotten this far, you know that creating a Visual Basic GUI (form) is essentially a matter of deploying ActiveX controls.

From an overall design perspective, the most important thing you want to do is to isolate any user interface from the objects that make up the core of the application. You do this to keep changes in the core system or the interface screens from affecting each other. For example, if you develop for Windows 95 and then upgrade to Windows 98, you don't want this to affect your core application. The easiest way to conceptualize this is to have an interface object for the user interface. The screens send messages to that object to pass on to the object that actually manipulates the data (in SalesWeb, the *Salesperson* object) and vice versa.

Thus, if you decide to change the screen layout, you can do it without changing how the *Salesperson* object checked the data and organized it for transport across the Internet. While this is good advice, it would be tedious if you only had a simple system with one screen, like the one we developed for SalesWeb. The idea is to begin by conceptualizing the interface and the data objects as separate classes and then, when you actually begin to write methods, decide if it really makes sense to keep them separate. You may want to break up the user interface object and have more specialized versions of it, or even several different interface objects, but the critical thing is to maintain one or more objects as a layer between the user interface and the core of the application.

When it comes time to develop the actual user interface screens, you should use Visual Basic forms and ActiveX controls for buttons, text, and so on. There's no point in writing code for such interface elements, since others have already written and packaged code for most of the common interface environments.

Neither Visual Modeler or Rational Rose 98 provides you with an interface development environment, as such. Each assumes that you will drop down into Visual Basic and create the interfaces in Visual Basic.

14.3 Arranging to Access Data

Broadly, you could either store and access data in a conventional database, or you could store objects. Most objects are transient; they are eliminated as soon as they are used. All of the objects in our SalesWeb application are transient. All of the data created by an interaction between a salesperson and the sales server is transferred to the relational databases associated with the accounting and inventory applications. Objects that are stored between one session and the next are called persistent objects. We'll consider the problems of storing persistent objects in a moment. First, however, we'll consider the problems of storing data in relational databases.

Most corporate data is stored in nonrelational databases that were established in the sixties and seventies. Moreover, early PC databases often used nonrelational techniques. Since the early eighties, however, most new corporate and departmental databases have been built using the relational model. And, since the beginning of the nineties, most PC applications have also relied on relational databases. Relational databases are independent of the specific application that uses them, and thus the data can be used by several different applications. The data in relational databases is stored in tables. The various relational database vendors have standardized on Structured Query Language (SQL) as the language to use to access relational databases.

14.3.1 The Microsoft Database Connectivity Package

OO systems should be designed so that the objects using data are independent of the objects that interface with databases. Visual Basic and COM make this easy, since they provide various packages designed to create and support database objects.

ODBC is a database interface developed by Microsoft. ODBC converts application code to SQL. Each of the popular database vendors has created a driver that interfaces to ODBC. Thus, if there is a database that you can't reach directly, you can reach it indirectly, via ODBC. Visual Studio 6.0 also provides OLE DB for creating links to other databases.

14.3.2 Object-Oriented and Object-Relational Databases

Now let's consider what would happen if you wanted to store a persistent object in a database. You can't store an object directly in a relational database. An object has values, but it also has operations that manipulate those values. Relational databases can store an object's values in a table, but they are forced to store the operations in a file. Thus, you couldn't store an object in a relational database and then send a message to update a value. In order to modify the object, the relational database would have to reassemble the values and the operations. The next generation of relational databases will have OO frontends. In effect, their relational database management systems will be modified so that they can assemble objects in the database management system, use the object's methods to change the values associated with the attributes, and then take the object apart and store it again.

Consider what would happen if you wanted to update an object that was contained within another class. Once the initial object got the message, it would, in turn, send a message to another object to get that object to perform some task and send back the results before it could modify the attributes the original message wanted to change. The object frontend for the relational database would need to get out one object, assemble it, assemble its class and that class's parent to get the operations it needed, assemble the second object to get it to perform the secondary task, and so on. Relational databases aren't very good at storing objects. Relational databases with OO frontends will be better, but they will never be able to support OO systems the way OO databases will. An OO database (OODB) is a database designed to store objects as wholes. OODBs can store and retrieve persistent objects much faster than relational databases.

Most companies rely on relational databases and will continue to use them. Moreover, object-relational databases will extend the life of relational databases for several years. Indeed, relational databases will probably always be preferred for data, independent of objects. As developers create complex OO applications, especially applications with multimedia objects, they will increasingly find they want to store objects in OODBs. The Internet, with its highly graphical emphasis, will push companies to experiment with OODBs.

Imagine how much easier it would be if we could simply create *SalesOrder* objects when each sales order came in and then simply store each *SalesOrder* object directly in an OODB. We wouldn't have to worry about moving the attribute values to the ODBC class and changing them into SQL or vice versa. Everything would be objects. This approach wouldn't be appropriate for our SalesWeb application because Moose's already has massive amounts of data stored in their existing DB2 relational databases. Our SalesWeb application isn't important enough to make anyone consider changing that.

If we were creating a new application and were going to create a new database to support the application, that would be quite different. Many new Web site applications, for example, are using OODBs to improve the speed at which they can access and retrieve complex graphical information. (We've included the names of some of the leading OODB vendors in Appendix D.)

In effect, the Microsoft Repository is a relational database with an object frontend. At the moment, Microsoft Repository is being developed to store the products of application development efforts. Other companies, however, are beginning to use Microsoft Repository for data warehouse applications. As Microsoft Repository becomes more sophisticated, it may evolve into an ideal place to store objects for complex applications.

14.4 The SalesWeb Design

SalesWeb is a simple application. When we finished our analysis, we had nine classes. We decided to make it a three-tiered application and to incorporate the *Salesperson* class into an ActiveX component so that it could be downloaded from the Sales Internet server by any salesperson via any laptop. We wrote a small block of HTML code to accomplish the downloading of the ActiveX component when salespeople contacted the Sales Internet server Web site.

Once the client component is on the salesperson's laptop, it communicates with the Sales Internet server via the Internet, using DCOM. Thus, we needed to add a stub to the client application and a skeleton to the Sales server package to facilitate this communication.

We also needed to communicate with Moose's existing DB2 databases. In theory, we would have used ODBC to create a database class that would then have communicated with a DB2 driver to access the Accounting and Inventory databases.

We incorporated the order entry form that the salesperson has to fill out and submit into the *Salesperson* ActiveX component document. If we were creating a complex system with many forms or user interface screens, we would use a separate class for screens and subclasses for each specific screen. However, for a simple system, it makes the example much more straightforward to simply add a small amount of user interface code to the *Salesperson* class.

The ActiveX controls included in the Salesperson GUI are seven CommandButtons, five TextBoxes, one Slider, two VscrollBars, and one CheckBox.

We have included a detailed description of how we developed the user interface screen in Appendix A with the code, and we also included a picture of the screen.

Our SalesWeb application assumes that values are stored in Moose's legacy relational databases. The example system we have developed does not, in fact, implement that database server portion of the system. In a real system, database access would probably be handled by Moose's legacy Accounting and Inventory systems. In our example, the middle tier uses the ODBC API to directly access local disk files using SQL. We chose this design to meet the following requirements:

- The system must be a simple implementation that can be run on your computer if you have any ODBC-compliant database product. (The example code we provide includes a sample Microsoft Access database that works with the example system.)
- The system should be easily extensible to use a legacy database system.
- The system provides an illustration of a design that could be implemented on a client/server system and could be modified to work with other client/server applications.

No objects in the SalesWeb application are persistent. The database is used to record all sales and other information. As soon as a given session concludes, all of the objects are placed in garbage.

If we did design the SalesWeb application from the ground up and had to create the databases, we would certainly consider a good PC OODB, like Poet. If it was a large application, we would consider one of the larger OODBs that are increasingly tailored to run very efficiently with Internet servers. As it is, for example, we identified furniture items with a number assigned by the developers of the Moose's relational databases. If we had to do it from scratch, we would create a class hierarchy with furniture as our top class and then proceed to work our way down, identifying the categories and then the specific furniture items. (Since Visual Basic doesn't support class inheritance, once we had completed the analysis, we would have to create a number of interface classes and incorporate them to achieve what would be much easier, in this case, in a language like Java or C++.) In any case, ultimately, *Inventory* could have persistent objects to represent real furniture items, and orders could send messages directly to furniture items telling them they were to be shipped to specific customers. If we took this approach, we would have developed a much more comprehensive initial business model. Our class diagram would really have modeled the business process, rather than simply using *Accounting* and *Inventory* to stand for complex processes we don't really understand. It's not an approach that's appropriate for the SalesWeb application, but as you become more familiar with OO development and begin to work on new, strategic applications, it will be an approach that will become increasingly appealing.

You can examine the code for the *Salesperson* class in Appendix A and see exactly how the interface, COM, and ODBC linkages are handled and check the attributes and operations we added to make them all work.

In the early part of this text we described an application that would include three use cases. We then followed only one, Report Sales, through a detailed examination. In the code we developed you can access the complete application, as described in our original use case analysis. Thus, in addition to reporting sales, our salesperson can check on his or her performance. Similarly, sales managers can sign onto the Sales Internet server from their laptops and quickly determine how the salespeople in their regions are doing, either individually or as a group. This additional functionality, which we would have developed during the second prototyping cycle if we had followed the plan laid out in this book, required a new database to keep track of the salespeople in each region and to store information about quota agreements and sales. Thus, the code in Appendix A and the code you can download is slightly more complex than the example we have been discussing up to this point.

14.5 Coding and Testing

There are no UML diagrams that are used for coding or testing. These concerns, in general, lie beyond the concerns of this book. There are numerous books on coding in different OO languages, including Visual Basic.

We do provide all of the Visual Basic code for the SalesWeb application we have been discussing in this book. That code includes some comments on why one approach was used rather than another, and programmers should feel free to look at how we completed the SalesWeb application. Information about how to obtain this code is provided in Appendix A.

We want to make just a few comments on testing OO systems. Testing OO systems isn't easy. There are two ways to approach testing: bottom-up and top-down.

14.5.1 *Bottom-Up Testing Starts with Classes*

Because you are developing classes that are independent of each other, there is a sense in which you can test each class by itself. The easy test is to see if a class does what you expect it to do. You plan on sending it a message and asking it for an account number. You send it the message and you get the account number. In effect, by working your way down the object line in an event trace diagram, you should be able to identify each message that an object should respond to and check that it performs as it should.

Of course, if the class is a subclass, then you are only testing a portion of the hierarchy when you test the specific class. Some messages you send to an object of the class will be handled by the operations and attributes defined in the object's parent class. Others will need to be routed up to superclasses. Assuring that a superclass functions correctly with one of its subclasses doesn't assure that it will work with its other subclasses.

The real problem in testing comes when you try to think of all the errors that could result when someone sends an incorrect message or a value that is wrong—larger than you ever expected anyone to send, for example. How will the object respond to exceptions and minor errors? It's very hard to think of all the exceptions that might occur and test to see that your object will handle them as you would like. This has nothing to do with object technology, as such. It's also a problem with conventional systems design. In theory, you can eliminate most of these problems by generating lots of scenarios and doing event trace diagrams of each of them. Unfortunately, all too often a scenario that no one imagined occurs, resulting in inputs no one ever planned for. There is no solution for this except to work up lots of scenarios and try to think of all the things that could go wrong.

For example, the whole concern about the year 2000 results from the fact that developers coded years with two numbers, assuming that their systems wouldn't be in use when the year 2000 rolled around. Thus, in 1980, no one tested their systems to see what would happen if someone entered a date like Jan. 1, 2001.

Once you are satisfied that a single object works, you need to see how it will work when it has to interact with other objects. In effect, you test one object, then several closely related objects, then a large collection of objects, then each module. Problems tend to emerge as you combine more objects. More complex sets of objects generate those exceptions that you failed to think about when you were only focusing on a single object.

14.5.2 Top-Down Testing Starts with Use Cases

Top-down testing can only occur when you have assembled your prototype. If the prototype provides the functionality of a single use case, then you can test the system by working your way through all of the scenarios that you derived from the use case description. The prototype should respond as suggested in the scenario. If it doesn't, you have a problem.

The best thing about OO development is that you can do it incrementally. If you develop a small prototype to begin with, you'll limit the number of objects you need to test. Moreover, you'll complete your prototype in a reasonably short time and will learn if you have problems before developing lots of additional code. It's easier to test and diagnose a moderately sized prototype than it is to test and debug a large system.

You'll also have fewer testing problems if you use interface objects that keep the core of your system isolated from the user interfaces, databases, and other software applications. The interface objects serve as control points that help you locate any problems. On the other hand, even though it's easier to test a smaller prototype, you will have to test it again whenever you finish another cycle and have an enhanced prototype. Adding new objects can introduce new twists to a set of objects that you have already tested.

We tested our SalesWeb application by running several scenarios that we had originally developed when we created use cases, and we were satisfied that it got the results we expected. We have not tested it with enough scenarios to be sure that it would work as a production system in a real sales environment.

14.6 Expanding Your Design in an Object-Oriented Modeling Tool

If you are familiar with a visual modeling tool, everything we've described in this chapter can be done rather quickly. We have included the final SalesWeb diagrams and code we arrived at with Rose 98 in a file that you can download from the Internet and examine.

Figure 14.6 provides a final summary of the process we went through to develop our SalesWeb application with Rose 98. (We are ignoring Visual Modeler at this point because it doesn't support most of the UML diagrams we used.) We began with use case diagrams.

Instead of moving from use case diagrams to sequence diagrams, we chose instead to begin with a class diagram. Using Rational Rose we created a single class diagram and then continued to expand it throughout the rest of the development effort, adding attributes and operations during analysis and then going back and adding infrastructure-related classes and additional attributes and operations during the design phase. Similarly, once we developed the sequence diagram, we used it to generate the collaboration diagram. We also generated a state diagram of one class to study how it worked in more detail. Then, when we moved into design and enhanced our class diagram, we went back and expanded our sequence diagram at the same time to check how the dynamics of our application would work. Finally, we generated deployment, package, and component diagrams.

We used Visual Basic to generate our user interface screens, incorporating ActiveX controls into a Visual Basic form. And we used an ActiveX component to create a link to our database.

When we were satisfied with our diagrams, we used Rational Rose's ability to generate Visual Basic code to produce most of the Visual Basic code required for our application. We had to write some additional code, the method implementations for example, by hand, and we had a complete application.

Because our example was so simple, we didn't begin to use the capabilities of Rational Rose 98 on the SalesWeb example. For example, Rose 98 could have generated the CORBA IDL code for our application if we had needed to use CORBA rather than DCOM. Or, it could have generated C++ or Java code if we had decided that we would rather have one portion of our application in a language other than Visual Basic.

What a visual modeling tool is especially good at is supporting business object reuse. Since a visual modeling tool saves all the diagrams you create, you can easily access past classes from other applications. Moreover, since visual modeling tools are often used by companies that take efficient software development very seriously, companies with visual modeling tools are likely to have libraries of business objects that you can access. Thus, if we had actually been developing an application like SalesWeb with a visual modeling tool like Rational Rose 98, our company would probably have had libraries of previous work. We might have been able to obtain

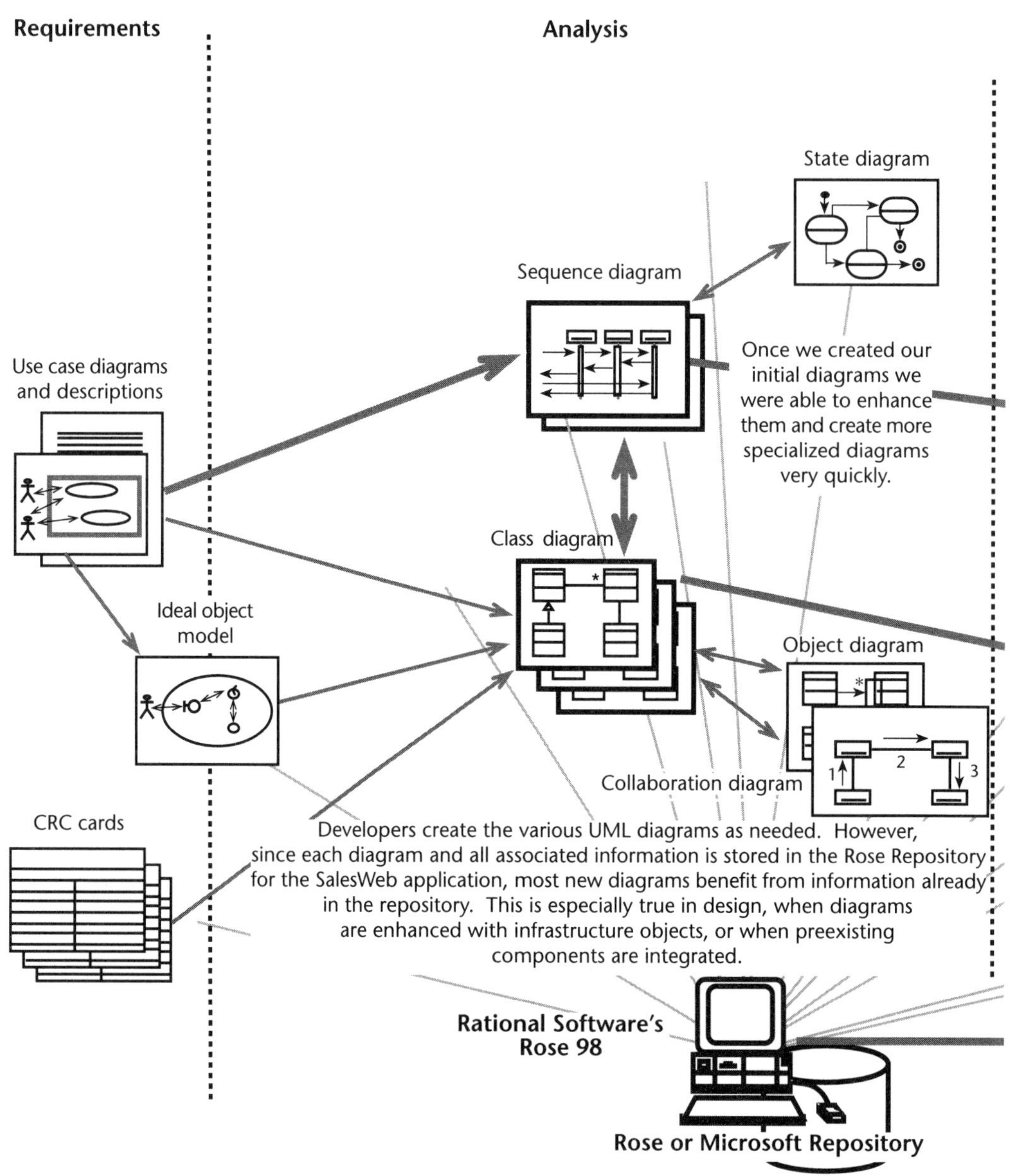

Figure 14.6 *The development of the SalesWeb application using Rational Software's Rose 98.*

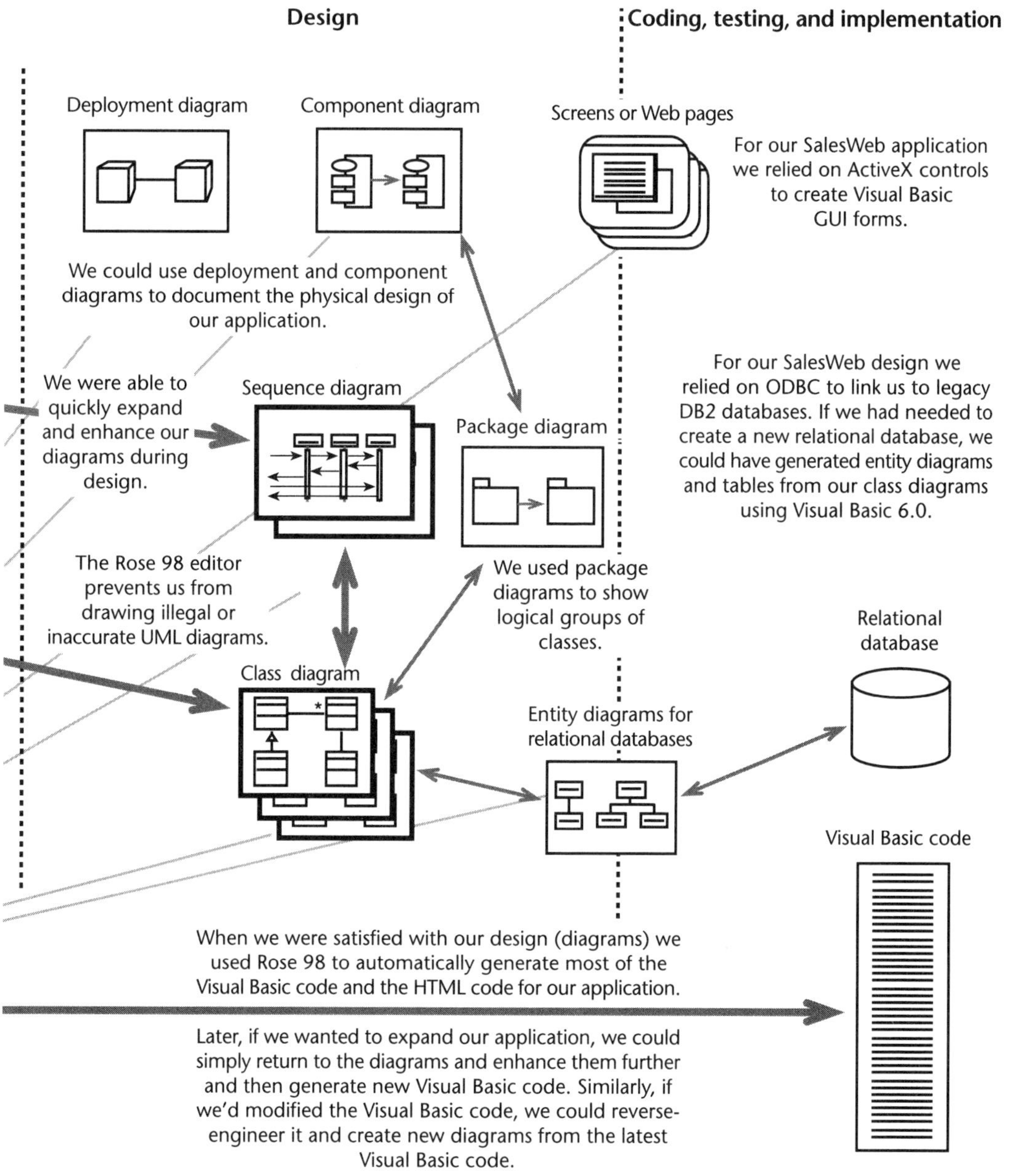

Design

Coding, testing, and implementation

Deployment diagram

Component diagram

Screens or Web pages

For our SalesWeb application we relied on ActiveX controls to create Visual Basic GUI forms.

We could use deployment and component diagrams to document the physical design of our application.

For our SalesWeb design we relied on ODBC to link us to legacy DB2 databases. If we had needed to create a new relational database, we could have generated entity diagrams and tables from our class diagrams using Visual Basic 6.0.

We were able to quickly expand and enhance our diagrams during design.

Sequence diagram

Package diagram

The Rose 98 editor prevents us from drawing illegal or inaccurate UML diagrams.

We used package diagrams to show logical groups of classes.

Relational database

Class diagram

Entity diagrams for relational databases

Visual Basic code

When we were satisfied with our design (diagrams) we used Rose 98 to automatically generate most of the Visual Basic code and the HTML code for our application.

Later, if we wanted to expand our application, we could simply return to the diagrams and enhance them further and then generate new Visual Basic code. Similarly, if we'd modified the Visual Basic code, we could reverse-engineer it and create new diagrams from the latest Visual Basic code.

an existing *SalesOrder* or *ItemOrdered* object and incorporate it into our design without having to re-create it.

As we said at the beginning, using Rose 98 was overkill on an application as simple as SalesWeb. Still, at least one author was able to create and modify UML diagrams in Rose 98 much more quickly than the other. And, using the tool, we were guaranteed that our UML diagrams were consistent and conformed to UML standards. More important, if we were now to decide to expand the SalesWeb application and incorporate it into a more complex corporate enterprise environment, the author with all his diagrams on Rational Rose 98 would have a considerable advantage.

Afterword

We've tried to keep this book simple. Our goal is to popularize UML. In spite of our effort, we're aware that we've introduced a lot of notations and many different concepts in a reasonably short book. We wanted to give you enough information to get you started. Unfortunately, there's a lot to learn even to get started in a new methodology. Suffice it to say that there's a lot more that we didn't introduce. Moreover, we have emphasized getting started and provided you more information on how to think about your first application and how to analyze it than on how to complete it. If this book helps you get a feel for OO development and makes it possible for you to generate diagrams that will help you analyze a system in object terms, we've done what we set out to do.

The greatest temptation for anyone beginning to develop an object-oriented Visual Basic 6.0 application is to think of the problem in procedural terms. It's easy to do, and it will result in bad OO designs. Whenever you find yourself falling back on procedural ways of thinking, recall the CRC card exercise. It's kind of silly, but thinking again of each object as a card and recalling how cards ask other cards for help doing things will remind you of what you are trying to achieve with an OO design.

In the spirit of OO development, we hope you'll start small and work a few simple prototypes through to code. Assuming you have a copy of Visual Basic, you might want to start by downloading the Visual Basic code for the SalesWeb application. Once you have the code, you can also download Visual Modeler from Microsoft's Visual Basic Web site and import the Visual Basic into Visual Modeler so that you can examine and change the class and component diagrams.

Once you're confident how the Sales Web application works, you'll probably begin to wonder how to handle more complex problems. At that point, you should consider reading some more advanced books on UML, Visual Basic 6.0, and COM. We've included a bibliography to help you find some especially good books to read and some Web sites to check when you need more information.

We hope the UML Job Aid we provide in Appendix B will be helpful if you tackle your first projects by hand and have to draw UML diagrams. It summarizes the various notational elements. Photocopy the Job Aid and use the copy to remind yourself of how to notate things for a little while, and you'll have memorized the diagramming techniques with minimal effort.

UML diagrams, especially the use case, class, and sequence diagrams, can help anyone who is trying to create an object- or component-based application. Thus, some knowledge of UML will help anyone who is considering building an application for the Internet.

No matter what size application you tackle, if you develop classes or if you intend to integrate ActiveX components, Visual Modeler will prove a useful extension to your Visual Basic development environment. Even if you only use it to examine an application after you have already written the code and just want to look at a diagram of the object model you have created, you'll find it useful. Similarly, you'll find Visual Modeler useful when you want to look at ActiveX components stored in the Microsoft Repository.

For larger applications, careful analysis and design phases are the best way to assure that the application will do what you agree to do when you first write a requirements statement. If you are undertaking a midsized to large project, the best advice we can give you would be to suggest you use a visual modeling product to help develop your application.

Visual Modeler is ok for an overview of your object model, but once the application effort begins to get complex, you are going to want to have many different views available. You'll want to look at use cases, class diagrams, sequence diagrams, and others. In other words, for complex applications, you'll want a more comprehensive visual modeling tool, one like Rose 98. With a tool, you won't need our job aid. You can generate a diagram just by clicking on notational elements on the various menus. And you can use some diagrams to generate others. More important, you can easily modify and extend your diagrams as you move from one prototype to another. Similarly, a tool can create databases and edit your work for consistency. When you are beginning, there's a lot to learn. A visual modeling tool allows you to focus on the real analysis and design issues while it takes care of most of the details.

Whatever you do, we hope this introduction has helped you decide how you can use UML diagrams and Visual Modeler to make Visual Basic 6.0 development a little easier and a lot more effective.

Visual Basic Example Program

A.1 The SalesWeb Application

This appendix lists the Visual Basic code for an application that implements our SalesWeb example. Though it works for demonstration purposes, our code would need to be extended in a number of ways to make it a "real-world" application. For example, we would need to add more complete error-checking, a more elaborate user interface, and additional business logic.

The code for our SalesWeb application is available for downloading at Morgan Kaufmann's Web site at *www.mkp.com/books_catalog/1-55860-545-2.asp.* If you choose to download the code, you can skip the sections of this appendix that describe how to create the application, and focus on our discussion of how the code actually works.

The code we present in this appendix has been created from scratch. However, had it been created following the traditional "round-trip engineering" process, our first cut at the code would have been generated from Rose 98. We would then have filled in the skeletal definitions with method code, changed variable names, and so on, then imported the code back into Rose, refined our UML diagrams, regenerated code, and continued this cycle until our application was complete.

A.2 Creating the Client Component

To build the SalesWeb application from scratch, we'll start by creating the client component. The client provides a simple data entry screen and sends form data to the server to be processed. As a "thin-client" application, it contains no information concerning business objects (i.e., *SalesOrder, Customer,* and *ItemOrdered*), as these all reside in the server.

To begin creating the client, run Visual Basic 6.0 and select *Standard EXE* as the new project type. (See Figure A.1.) We're going to create a single component called "SalesWebClient" to house all our client information.

Now click on *Project1* in the Project Explorer Window. Then highlight *Project1* beside the *(Name)* property in the Properties Window. Type in *SalesWebClient* and press ENTER to give your new project a name. Your screen should now appear as shown in Figure A.2.

A.2.1 *SalesPersonForm Form*

An empty form titled *Form1* will be created in the Form Window and added to your new project. Following the same steps you used to name the project, click on *Form1* in the Project Window, and fill in *SalesPersonForm* as the new form's name.

We will now go about implementing our *SalesPerson* object as the Visual Basic form *SalesPersonForm.* We have chosen to implement this object as a form (instead of a class) because all the salesperson information—password, PIN number, and so on—exist within our client's user interface form. We could create a separate class for storing all this information and have it interact with a user interface class that would handle user

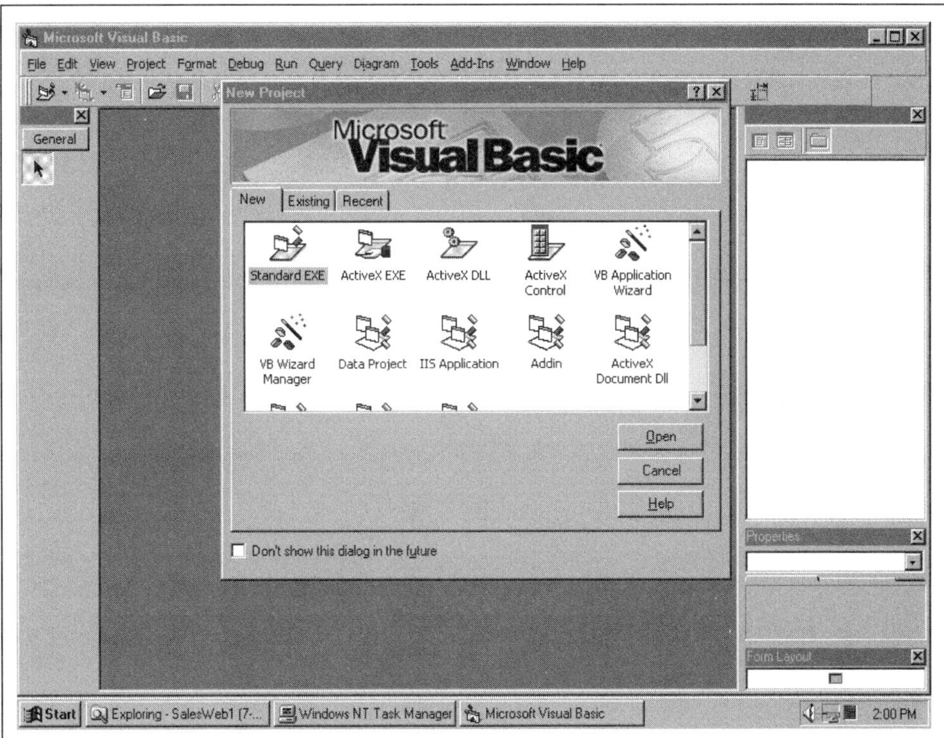

Figure A.1 *Visual Basic screen showing how to create a new project.*

input. But this would really be redundant, as for all practical purposes *SalesPersonForm is* a class. You could think of its "properties" as the ActiveX controls we will add to the form—buttons, text boxes, and so on. And you could think of its "methods" as the event handlers we will add to process events coming from the controls.

Typically a programmer would fill in event handlers as each new control is created. However, for simplicity we will first focus only on creating controls, and later present all their event handlers together as one continuous listing.

Now expand the form to the size shown in Figure A.3 by clicking on the edge of its bottom-right corner, and dragging down and to the right. Next we'll add some ActiveX controls to the form to start building our user interface.

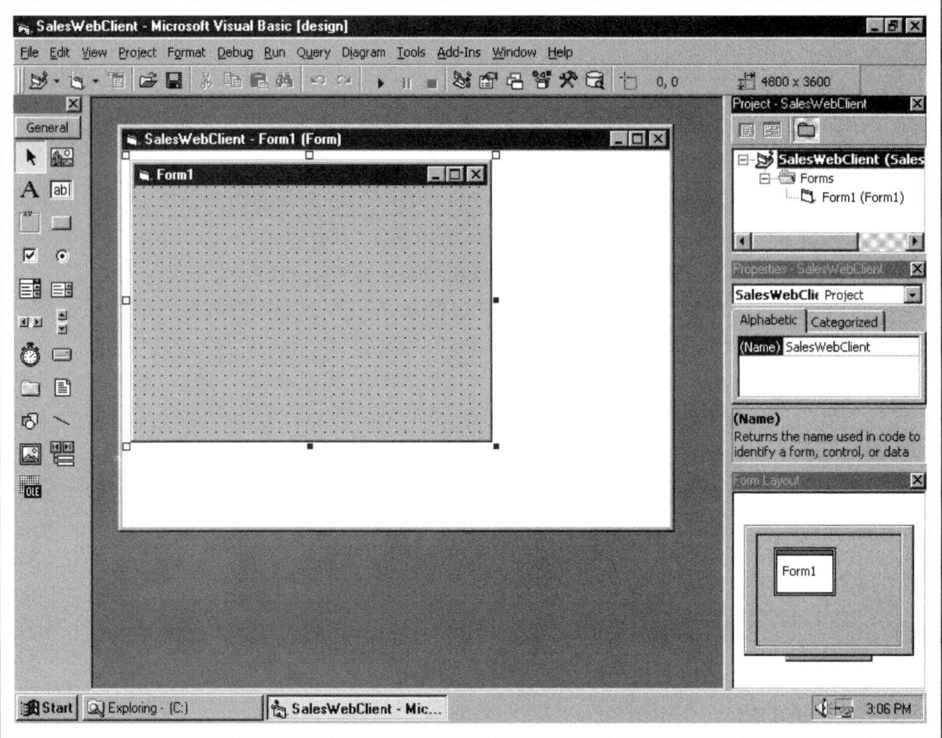

Figure A.2 *Naming the new project.*

We'll start by creating some buttons. Click on the *CommandButton* control in the Toolbox. Now notice, as you drag the mouse pointer into the blank form, the arrow changes to a set of crosshairs. Create a new button on your form by depressing the mouse button and dragging the crosshairs down and to the right, then release the mouse button. Your new button will automatically be named *Command1.* Click on the *(Name)* property in its Properties Window and change the value to *ListParts.* Next, change its *Caption* property to *List Parts.*

Following the same steps, create the buttons on the form shown in Figure A.3, naming them *ListCustomers, ListQuota, SendOrder, ClearOrder, ClearOutput,* and *Quit.* Set their caption text to the captions shown in the figure.

Next, we'll create some text boxes to hold our user input. Click on the *TextBox* control in the Toolbox, then create a new

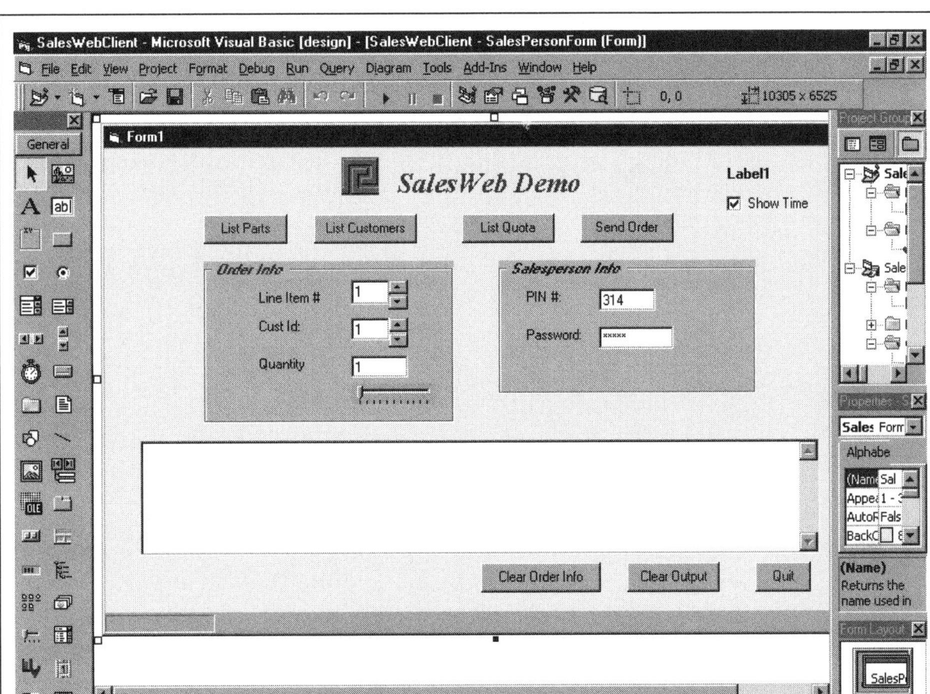

Figure A.3 *Laying out the form elements.*

text box in the upper left of the form and name it *PartNumber.* Repeating the same steps, create the following text boxes shown in Figure A.3 and name them: *CustomerNumber, Quantity, PIN,* and *Password.* Fill in the character "*" in the *PasswordChar* field of the *Password* text box. (This will prevent the user's password from being displayed on the screen.)

Position the new text boxes as shown in Figure A.3, with *CustomerNumber* below *PartNumber* on the left side of the screen, and *Quantity* below that. On the right side of the screen position the *PIN* text box above the *Password* text box.

Now select the *Label* control from the Toolbox, create new text labels beside your five new text boxes, and name them as shown in Figure A.3.

Next, create the label *SalesWeb Demo* and position it at the top center of the screen. Set the label's color and font size in its Properties Window.

Now click on the *Frame* control in the Toolbox, and draw a frame that encloses the three text boxes and labels on the left of the screen. Since this new frame will obscure your controls, right-click on it and select *Send to Back.* Label your new frame *Order Info.* Follow the same steps to create a new frame around the text boxes on the right side of the screen, and label them *Salesperson Info.* You can set the color of the frame by changing the value of its *BackColor* property in the Properties Window.

Next, click on the *TextBox* control in the Toolbox, and create a new textbox for your output area. Position it as shown in Figure A.3, setting its name to *OutputText,* and its *ScrollBars* property to *Vertical.*

To create scrollbars for some of our text boxes, click on *VScrollBar* in the Toolbox. Create a new vertical scrollbar right beside your *PartNumber* text box, name it *Vscroll1,* and set its *Value* property to *9.* Following the same steps, create a scrollbar beside the *CustomerNumber* text box, name it *Vscroll2,* and set its *Value* property to *9.*

To round out our user interface, let's add a few more controls to our form. If the *Slider* control does not exist in your Toolbox, select *Components* from the *Project* menu, and add *Microsoft Windows Common Controls 6.0.* Create a new slider by clicking on the *Slider* in the Toolbox, then clicking inside the left-hand frame towards the bottom. Name the new slider *Slider1.*

Next, create a label to show the time of day by clicking on the *Label* icon in the Toolbox, and placing a new label in the upper-right-hand corner of your form. Name the new label *TimeMessage.* Finally, add a *CheckBox* control below the new label, name it *Check1,* and set its caption to *Time Visible.* Change its *Value* property to *Checked.*

We could continue to embellish our user interface with controls, but for purposes of our demo this interface will be sufficient. We will turn our attention to creating the handlers for the form.

Select *Code* from the *View* menu and type in Listing 1, which defines all of the event handlers for the controls in our form.

The *Form_Load* method, which is called as soon as the form is created, instantiates the remote server component through the line

```
Set SalesWebSvrInst =
    CreateObject("SalesWebServer.SalesOrder")
```

When the *Send Order* button is pressed by the user, the *SendOrder_Click* button handler is automatically called. It uses the *SalesWebSvrInst* object to call the *SubmitOrder* method in the server object *SalesOrder,* passing it the form data as a set of strings:

```
results = SalesWebSvrInst.SubmitOrder(PIN.Text(),
    Password.Text(), PartNumber.Text(),
    Quantity.Text(), CustomerNumber.Text())
```

Other button handlers call methods in the *SalesOrder* object in a similar way. *ListQuota_Click* calls the server object to list salesperson quotas, *ListCustomers_Click* calls the server object to list customers, and *ListParts_Click* calls the server object to list all parts.

The other event handlers in *SalesPersonForm* process events from various user interface elements, updating values when scrollbars are pressed, when sliders are moved, and so on.

Listing 1 **SalesPersonForm**

```
'-------------------------------------------------
' Event handlers for the SalesPersonForm
'
'-------------------------------------------------
' require explicit declaration of all variables
Option Explicit
'-------------------------------------------------
' Handler for clear order form button
'-------------------------------------------------
```

(continued)

```
Private Sub ClearOrder_Click()
  ' initialize all the fields in the order form
  PIN.Text() = ""
  Password.Text() = ""
  PartNumber.Text() = ""
  Quantity.Text() = ""
  CustomerNumber.Text() = ""
End Sub
'-------------------------------------------------
' Handler for clear output button
'-------------------------------------------------
Private Sub ClearOutput_Click()
  OutputText.Text = ""
End Sub
'-------------------------------------------------
' Handler for list customers button
'-------------------------------------------------
Private Sub ListCustomers_Click()
  Dim results As String
  ' call the server object to list customers
  results = SalesWebSvrInst.ListAllCustomers(PIN.Text(),
      Password.Text())
' display the results
  OutputText.Text = results
End Sub
'-------------------------------------------------
' Handler for list parts button
'-------------------------------------------------
Private Sub ListParts_Click()
  Dim results As String
' call the server object to list parts
  results = SalesWebSvrInst.ListLineItems(PIN.Text(), Password.Text())
' display the results
  OutputText.Text = results
End Sub
'-------------------------------------------------
' Handler for list quota button
'-------------------------------------------------
Private Sub ListQuota_Click()
  Dim results As String
```

```
    ' call the server object to fetch quota data
  results = SalesWebSvrInst.FetchQuotaInfo(PIN.Text(), Password.Text())
  OutputText.Text = results
End Sub
'-------------------------------------------------
' Handler for send button
'-------------------------------------------------
Private Sub SendOrder_Click()
  Dim results As String
  ' call the server object to process as sales order
  results = SalesWebSvrInst.SubmitOrder(PIN.Text(), Password.Text(),
      PartNumber.Text(), Quantity.Text(), CustomerNumber.Text())
  ' display the results
  OutputText.Text = results
End Sub
'-------------------------------------------------
' Handler for Slider Object 1
'
'-------------------------------------------------
Private Sub Slider1_Click()
    Dim curr As Integer
    curr = CInt(Quantity.Text())
    curr = Slider1.Value()
    Quantity.Text() = CStr(curr)
End Sub
'-------------------------------------------------
' Handler for Scroller Object 1
'-------------------------------------------------
Private Sub VScroll1_Change()
    Dim curr As Integer
    curr = CInt(PartNumber.Text())
    curr = 10 - VScroll1.Value()
    If (curr < 1) Then curr = 1
    If (curr > 10) Then curr = 10
    PartNumber.Text() = CStr(curr)
End Sub
'-------------------------------------------------
' Handler for Scroller Object 2
'-------------------------------------------------
```

(continued)

```
Private Sub VScroll2_Change()
    Dim curr As Integer
    curr = CInt(CustomerNumber.Text())
    curr = 10 - VScroll2.Value()
    If (curr < 1) Then curr = 1
    If (curr > 10) Then curr = 10
    CustomerNumber.Text() = CStr(curr)
End Sub
'-----------------------------------------------
' Handler for Checkbox Object
'-----------------------------------------------
Private Sub Check1_Click()
    If (TimeMessage.Visible) Then
        TimeMessage.Visible = False
    Else
        TimeMessage.Visible = True
    End If
End Sub
'-----------------------------------------------
' Handle the Quit button
'-----------------------------------------------
Private Sub Quit_Click()
    End
End Sub
'-----------------------------------------------
' Initialize the sales order form
'-----------------------------------------------
Private Sub Form_Load()
  Me.Show
  TimeMessage.Caption = Format((Now), "h:mm AM/PM")
  OutputText.Text = "Instantiating the Server"
  Set SalesWebSvrInst = CreateObject("SalesWebServer.SalesOrder")
End Sub
```

A.2.2 ClientMain Module

We also need a short program module to get our client started and instantiate its data entry form. To create this module, select *Add Module* from the *Project* menu and name the new module *ClientMain*. Fill it in with the code shown in Listing 2.

Listing 2 ClientMain

```
Option Explicit
Global SalesWebSvrInst As Object
'-----------------------------------------------
' this method instantiates the salesperson
' form.
'-----------------------------------------------
Sub Main()
On Error GoTo MainError
  Load SalesPersonForm
Exit Sub
MainError:
  MsgBox Error$ & " - " & Str$(Err), vbCritical, "SalesWeb Client
      Startup Error"
  Exit Sub
End Sub
```

We have now finished creating our client component for SalesWeb. It's time to move on to the server component.

A.3 Creating the Server Component

We're now going to create a single component called "Sales-WebServer" to house all our server objects. Our SalesWeb server has no UI to speak of, except for a small dialog box that pops up to show the server has been activated. The dialog box also lists the number of client instances that are currently active.

To create the new server project, select *Add Project* from the *File* menu, select *Standard EXE,* and name the new project *SalesWebServer.*

A.3.1 frmServer Form

Now create a new form called *frmServer* with a label reading *Number of Instances* and a text box named *InstanceCounter* (see Figure A.4). Next create a *CommonDialog* control from the

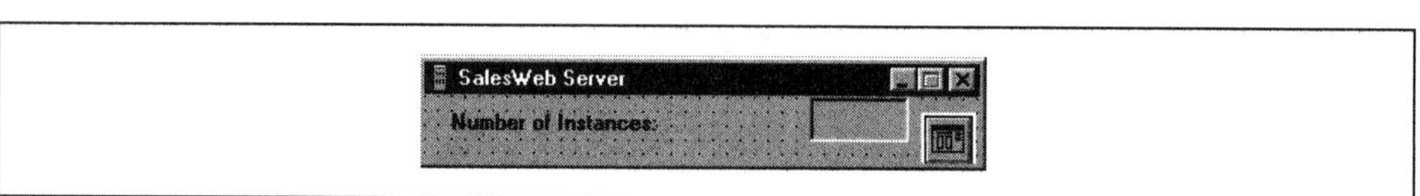

Figure A.2 *The* frmServer *form.*

ToolBox, position it in the bottom-right corner of the form, and name it *CommonDialog1*. (If the *CommonDialog* control does not appear in your Toolbox, select *Components* from the *Project* menu, and add *Microsoft Common Dialog Control 6.0.*)

A.3.2 ServerMain Module

Next, we need to create a short program module to house global variables used by the server. Select *Add Module* from the *Project* menu and name the new module *ServerMain*. Fill it in with the following code:

Listing 3 ServerMain

```
Option Explicit
'---------------------------------------------------
' global definitions for the salesweb server
'---------------------------------------------------
Global gintInstanceCount As Integer
Global globDatabase As Database
Global globWorkspace As Workspace
Global globDatabaseName As String
Sub Main()
End Sub
Sub ServerMsg(rstrMessage As String, rintButtons As Integer, rstrTitle
    As String)
  #If gbDEBUG Then
    MsgBox rstrMessage, rintButtons, rstrTitle
  #End If
End Sub
```

A.3.3 CustInfo Class

Next, we will create a class to store customer information. Select *Add Class Module* from the *Project* menu, and name the new class *CustInfo*. Fill it in with the code shown in Listing 4.

CustInfo is a base class that contains the methods and properties associated with a particular customer. Notice that all the properties of the class begin with "m_". This convention indicates that they are private members of the class and should not be referenced directly, as this would violate encapsulation. Instead, each property can be accessed through its "access methods"—for each property there is a *Get* method to get the property's value, and a *Let* method to sets its value.

CustInfo's interface is implemented by its two children: *CustInfo1* and *CustInfoMulti*. *CustInfo* defines all of the properties and methods common to both children, and the children add their own unique properties and methods.

The *Class_Initialize* method in *CustInfo* initializes all its properties and is called as soon as the class is created. The *Class_Terminate* method (not defined for this class) is called when the class is destroyed.

Listing 4 CustInfo

```
'-----------------------------------------------------
'
' A Simple base class that represents customers
'
'-----------------------------------------------------
Option Explicit
Private m_ID As String
Private m_custName As String
Private m_custBillingAddress As String
Private m_custCreditLtd As Integer
'-----------------------------------------------------
' get the value of the custCreditLtd member
'-----------------------------------------------------
```

(continued)

```
Public Property Get custCreditLtd() As Integer
    custCreditLtd = m_custCreditLtd
End Property
'-------------------------------------------------
' set the value of the custCreditLtd member
'-------------------------------------------------
Public Property Let custCreditLtd(valNew As Integer)
    m_custCreditLtd = valNew
End Property
'-------------------------------------------------
' get the value of the ID member
'-------------------------------------------------
Public Property Get ID() As String
    ID = m_ID
End Property
'-------------------------------------------------
' set the value of the ID member
'-------------------------------------------------
Public Property Let ID(valNew As String)
    m_ID = valNew
End Property
'-------------------------------------------------
' get the value of the custBillingAddress member
'-------------------------------------------------
Public Property Get custBillingAddress() As String
    custBillingAddress = m_custBillingAddress
End Property
'-------------------------------------------------
' set the value of the custBillingAddress member
'-------------------------------------------------
Public Property Let custBillingAddress(valNew As String)
    m_custBillingAddress = valNew
End Property
'-------------------------------------------------
' get the value of the name member
'-------------------------------------------------
Public Property Get custName() As String
    custName = m_custName
End Property
'-------------------------------------------------
```

```
' set the value of the custName member
'-------------------------------------------------
Public Property Let custName(valNew As String)
    m_custName = valNew
End Property
'-------------------------------------------------
' initialize the class
'-------------------------------------------------
Private Sub Class_Initialize()
    m_custCreditLtd = 0
    m_ID = ""
    m_custName = ""
    m_custBillingAddress = ""
End Sub
```

A.3.4 CustInfo1 Class

Next we will create the *CustInfo1* class, which represents customers whose billing address is the same as their shipping address. Select *Add Class Module* from the *Project* menu, and name the new class *CustInfo1*. Fill it in with the code shown in Listing 5.

The *CustInfo1* class is a child of *CustInfo* and inherits its interface. This is accomplished by the line at the start of the file:

```
Implements CustInfo
```

Since Visual Basic 6.0 does not support class inheritance is the true sense, we use the technique of "delegation" to achieve some of the same benefits. Delegation spares us from having to copy all the code from the base class's methods into its child's methods. Instead, we add a new property to the child that contains an instance of the parent class. Then we use this property to pass calls made to methods in the child to the corresponding methods of the parent.

CustInfo1 uses the property *m_CustInfo* to delegate to the base class. A new instance of the base class is created in the *Class_Initialize* routine, in the line

```
Set m_CustInfo = New CustInfo
```

m_CustInfo then is used to delegate the *Get* and *Let* methods to the base class. This is done in the following method in *CustInfo1*:

```
Private Property Let CustInfo_custName(valNew As
    String)
  m_CustInfo.custName = valNew
End Property
```

This method is passed a value to assign to the *custName* property. But rather than assigning the value directly, the method uses *m_CustInfo* to delegate the call to the *Let custName* method in the base *CustInfo* class.

Since this method only contains a simple assignment, not much work is saved by delegation. However, if our method contained a couple pages of code, delegation would spare us from having to copy all that code into the child class. Delegation also makes maintenance easier, as only one copy of a method needs to be altered when changes arise.

Notice *CustInfo1* also contains a method called *CheckCredit*. (In a real-world application, *CheckCredit* would be implemented in the *CustInfoMulti* class as well, but for simplicity we have left it out.) The *CheckCredit* method is passed an integer value, which signifies the price of the order. Then the method queries the Customer table, searching for the current customer based on their ID (which is retrieved by means of the delegated property *m_CustInfo.ID*).

The total order price is compared with the customer's credit limit, and a boolean value is returned to signify whether the order should be fulfilled. In a real-world application this is where we would put business rules to determine if the customer's credit limit needs to be increased.

Listing 5 **CustInfo1**

```
'-----------------------------------------------
'
' A derived class that represents customers
'
'-----------------------------------------------
Option Explicit
Implements CustInfo ' Inherits from CustInfo
```

```
' Declare an instance for delegation
Private m_CustInfo As CustInfo
' member variables relating to database access
Private m_Recordset As Recordset
Private m_dbinst As DBInterface
'--------------------------------------------------
' get the value of the custCreditLtd member
'--------------------------------------------------
Private Property Get CustInfo_custCreditLtd() As Integer
  CustInfo_custCreditLtd = m_CustInfo.custCreditLtd
End Property
'--------------------------------------------------
' set the value of the custCreditLtd member
'--------------------------------------------------
Private Property Let CustInfo_custCreditLtd(valNew As Integer)
    m_CustInfo.custCreditLtd = valNew
End Property
'--------------------------------------------------
' get the value of the id member
'--------------------------------------------------
Private Property Get CustInfo_ID() As String
  CustInfo_ID = m_CustInfo.ID
  End Property
'--------------------------------------------------
' set the value of the id member
'--------------------------------------------------
Private Property Let CustInfo_ID(valNew As String)
   m_CustInfo.ID = valNew
 End Property
'--------------------------------------------------
' get the value of the custName member
'--------------------------------------------------
Private Property Get CustInfo_custName() As String
  CustInfo_custName = m_CustInfo.custName
End Property
'--------------------------------------------------
' set the value of the custName member
'--------------------------------------------------
```

(continued)

```
Private Property Let CustInfo_custName(valNew As String)
  m_CustInfo.custName = valNew
End Property
'-----------------------------------------------------
' get the value of the custBillingAddress member
'-----------------------------------------------------
Private Property Get CustInfo_custBillingAddress() As String
  CustInfo_custBillingAddress = m_CustInfo.custBillingAddress
End Property
'-----------------------------------------------------
' set the value of the custBillingAddress member
'-----------------------------------------------------
Private Property Let CustInfo_custBillingAddress(valNew As String)
  m_CustInfo.custBillingAddress = valNew
End Property
'-----------------------------------------------------
' access the database and fill in the custCreditLtd member
'-----------------------------------------------------
Public Function CheckCredit(limit As Integer) As Boolean
  Dim QuerySQL As String
  Dim objField1 As Object
  Dim objField2 As Object
  CheckCredit = False
  QuerySQL = "SELECT balance FROM Customer where ID = " +
      m_CustInfo.ID
  Set m_Recordset = m_dbinst.DBGet(QuerySQL)
  Set objField1 = m_Recordset.Fields("balance")
  m_CustInfo.custCreditLtd = objField1
  QuerySQL = "SELECT name FROM Customer where ID = " + m_CustInfo.ID
  Set m_Recordset = m_dbinst.DBGet(QuerySQL)
  Set objField2 = m_Recordset.Fields("name")
  m_CustInfo.custName = objField2
  If (m_CustInfo.custCreditLtd < limit) Then CheckCredit = True
End Function
'-----------------------------------------------------
' sets the customer credit
'-----------------------------------------------------
Public Sub setCustCredit(iparam As Integer)
  m_CustInfo.custCreditLtd = iparam
End Sub
'-----------------------------------------------------
' initialize the class
'-----------------------------------------------------
```

```
Private Sub Class_Initialize()
    Set m_dbinst = New DBInterface
    Set m_CustInfo = New CustInfo
End Sub
'--------------------------------------------------
' terminate the class
'--------------------------------------------------
Private Sub Class_Terminate()
    Set m_CustInfo = Nothing
End Sub
```

A.3.5 CustInfoMulti Class

Next, following the same steps you used to create the *CustInfo1* class, create a new class called *CustInfoMulti,* and fill it in with the code in Listing 6.

The *CustInfoMulti* class represents customers whose billing address differs from their shipping address. It adds an additional property, *m_custShippingAddress,* to store this additional information. (In our application, the customer's address is saved as a simple string, but in a "real-world" application it would be implemented as an object, with properties for state, country, zip code, etc.)

Like *CustInfo1, CustInfoMulti* inherits its interface from the *CustInfo* class, and uses *m_CustInfo* to delegate its methods to the base class.

Listing 6 CustInfo Multi

```
'--------------------------------------------------

'
' A derived class that represents customers
' with multiple address fields
'
'--------------------------------------------------
Option Explicit
Implements CustInfo ' Inherits from CustInfo
' Declare an instance for delegation
Private m_CustInfo As CustInfo
Private m_address1 As String
Private m_custShippingAddress As String
```

(continued)

```
'---------------------------------------------------
' get the value of the custCreditLtd member
'---------------------------------------------------
Private Property Get CustInfo_custCreditLtd() As
     Integer
  CustInfo_custCreditLtd = m_CustInfo.custCreditLtd
End Property
'---------------------------------------------------
' set the value of the custCreditLtd member
'---------------------------------------------------
Private Property Let CustInfo_custCreditLtd(valNew As
     Integer)
     m_CustInfo.custCreditLtd = valNew
End Property
'---------------------------------------------------
' get the value of the id member
'---------------------------------------------------
Private Property Get CustInfo_ID() As String
  CustInfo_ID = m_CustInfo.ID
  End Property
'---------------------------------------------------
' set the value of the id member
'---------------------------------------------------
Private Property Let CustInfo_ID(valNew As String)
   m_CustInfo.ID = valNew
 End Property
'---------------------------------------------------
' get the value of the custName member
'---------------------------------------------------
Private Property Get CustInfo_custName() As String
  CustInfo_custName = m_CustInfo.custName
End Property
'---------------------------------------------------
' set the value of the custName member
'---------------------------------------------------
Private Property Let CustInfo_custName(valNew As
     String)
  m_CustInfo.custName = valNew
End Property
'---------------------------------------------------
' get the value of the custBillingAddress member
'---------------------------------------------------
```

```
Private Property Get CustInfo_custBillingAddress() As
    String
  CustInfo_custBillingAddress =
      m_CustInfo.custBillingAddress
End Property
'--------------------------------------------------
' set the value of the custBillingAddress member
'--------------------------------------------------
Private Property Let
CustInfo_custBillingAddress(valNew As String)
  m_CustInfo.custBillingAddress = valNew
End Property
'--------------------------------------------------
' get the value of the custShippingAddress member
'--------------------------------------------------
Property Get custShippingAddress() As String
     custShippingAddress = m_custShippingAddress
End Property
'--------------------------------------------------
' get the value of the custShippingAddress member
'--------------------------------------------------
Property Let custShippingAddress(valNew As String)
    m_custShippingAddress = valNew
End Property
'--------------------------------------------------
' initialize the class
'--------------------------------------------------
Private Sub Class_Initialize()
    Set m_CustInfo = New CustInfo
End Sub
'--------------------------------------------------
' terminate the class
'--------------------------------------------------
Private Sub Class_Terminate()
    Set m_CustInfo = Nothing
End Sub
```

A.3.6 DBInterface Class

Next, create a new class in the server project and name it *DBInterface,* and fill it in with the code provided in Listing 7.

In order to access the database, we use the predefined database class *Database,* which is part of the DAO library (Direct Access Objects), included in Visual Basic 6.0. DAO enables you to use Visual Basic code to access and manipulate data in local or remote databases, and to process SQL queries. To enable DAO in our SalesWeb application, select *References* from the *Project* menu, and make sure *Microsoft DAO 3.5 Object Library* is checked.

Our example makes use of a local Microsoft Access database, *UMLdb.mdb,* that contains the tables *Customer, Inventory, Order,* and *SalesPerson.* (If you haven't downloaded the SalesWeb example from our Website, you'll need to create the Microsoft Access database manually at this point.)

The *Customer* table contains the following columns:

name (Text)
balance (Currency)

The *Inventory* table contains the following columns:

part_name (Text)
cost (Currency)
number_on_hand (Number)
number_on_order (Number)

The *Order* table contains the following columns:

sales_person (Text)
customer (Text)
part_name (Text)
number_ordered (Number)

The *SalesPerson* table contains the following columns:

PIN (Number)
name (Text)
password (Text)
region (Text)

quota (Currency)

sales_total (Currency)

The DBInterface class handles access to our database. It contains a single method, *DBGet,* that is passed an SQL query in the form of a string. *DBInterface* then calls the *OpenDatabase* method in the DAO class *Workspaces* to establish a database connection.

Next, the method instantiates *m_Database* as an instance of the DAO class *Database,* and calls *OpenRecordset* to process the SQL query. The results of the query are returned back as a String.

Listing 7 DBInterface

```
'-------------------------------------------------
'
' A Simple class that represents database queries
'
'-------------------------------------------------
Private m_Database As Database ' from DAO library
Public Function DBGet(QuerySQL As String) As Recordset
 Set m_Database = Workspaces(0).OpenDatabase("UMLdb.mdb", False, True)
 Set DBGet = m_Database.OpenRecordset(QuerySQL, dbOpenSnapshot,
     dbForwardOnly)
End Function
```

A.3.7 *ItemOrdered Class*

Next, create a class called *ItemOrdered,* and fill it in with the code shown in Listing 8.

This class stores the properties and methods associated with an item that a customer has ordered. *Get* and *Let* methods are provided to access the properties of the class. The *CheckItem* method, given a part's ID, will access the database to find out if the part exists in the inventory. If so, it retrieves the number of items on hand, the item's part name, and its cost. These values are assigned to the appropriate properties of the *ItemOrdered* class.

As in most of our classes, the *Class_Initialize* method in *ItemOrdered* initializes all the properties of the class and is called as soon as the class is created. The *Class_Terminate* method is called when the class is destroyed.

Listing 8 ItemOrdered

```
'-----------------------------------------------------
'
' Simple class that represents parts in the inventory
'
'-----------------------------------------------------
Option Explicit
Private m_itemName As String
Private m_itemNumber As String
Private m_itemPrice As String
Private m_numOfItems As Integer
Private m_description As String
Private m_salesTax As Integer
Private m_shippingCost As Integer
Private m_dbinst As DBInterface
Private m_Recordset As Recordset
'-----------------------------------------------------
' get the value of the itemNumber member
'-----------------------------------------------------
Property Get itemNumber() As String
    itemNumber = m_itemNumber
End Property
'-----------------------------------------------------
' set the value of the itemNumber member
'-----------------------------------------------------
Property Let itemNumber(valNew As String)
    m_itemNumber = valNew
End Property
'-----------------------------------------------------
' get the value of the itemPrice member
'-----------------------------------------------------
Property Get itemPrice() As String
    itemPrice = m_itemPrice
End Property
'-----------------------------------------------------
' set the value of the itemPrice member
'-----------------------------------------------------
Property Let itemPrice(valNew As String)
    m_itemPrice = valNew
```

```
End Property
'-------------------------------------------------
' get the value of the numOfItems member
'-------------------------------------------------
Property Get numOfItems() As Integer
    numOfItems = m_numOfItems
End Property
'-------------------------------------------------
' set the value of the numOfItems member
'-------------------------------------------------
Property Let numOfItems(valNew As Integer)
    m_numOfItems = valNew
End Property
'-------------------------------------------------
' get the value of the itemName member
'-------------------------------------------------
Property Get itemName() As String
    numOfItems = m_itemName
End Property
'-------------------------------------------------
' set the value of the itemName member
'-------------------------------------------------
Property Let itemName(valNew As String)
    m_itemName = valNew
End Property
'-------------------------------------------------
' get the value of the description member
'-------------------------------------------------
Property Get description() As String
    description = m_description
End Property
'-------------------------------------------------
' set the value of the description member
'-------------------------------------------------
Property Let description(valNew As String)
    m_description = valNew
End Property
'-------------------------------------------------
' get the value of the salesTax member
'-------------------------------------------------
```

(continued)

```
Property Get salesTax() As Integer
    salesTax = m_salesTax
End Property
'-------------------------------------------------
' set the value of the salesTax member
'-------------------------------------------------
Property Let salesTax(valNew As Integer)
    m_salesTax = valNew
End Property
'-------------------------------------------------
' get the value of the shippingCost member
'-------------------------------------------------
Property Get shippingCost() As Integer
    shippingCost = m_shippingCost
End Property
'-------------------------------------------------
' set the value of the shippingCost member
'-------------------------------------------------
Property Let shippingCost(valNew As Integer)
    m_shippingCost = valNew
End Property
'-------------------------------------------------
' access the Inventory table in the database
' and fill in the itemNumber, description, and
' itemPrice members, check if item is avail
'-------------------------------------------------
Function CheckItem() As Boolean
  Dim QuerySQL As String
  Dim objField1 As Object
  Dim objField2 As Object
  Dim objField3 As Object
  CheckItem = False
  QuerySQL = "SELECT number_on_hand,part_name,cost FROM Inventory where
      ID = " + m_itemNumber
  Set m_Recordset = m_dbinst.DBGet(QuerySQL)
  Set objField1 = m_Recordset.Fields("number_on_hand")
  m_itemNumber = objField1
  Set objField2 = m_Recordset.Fields("part_name")
  m_description = objField2
  Set objField3 = m_Recordset.Fields("cost")
  m_itemPrice = objField3
  If (m_itemNumber > 0) Then CheckItem = True
End Function
```

```
'-------------------------------------------------
' totals up the order
'-------------------------------------------------
Function TotalOrder() As Integer
  TotalOrder = m_itemPrice 'since only one part is ordered
End Function
'-------------------------------------------------
' initialize the class
'-------------------------------------------------
Private Sub Class_Initialize()
    ' initialize the members
    Set m_dbinst = New DBInterface
    m_itemName = ""
    m_itemNumber = 0
    m_itemPrice = 0
    m_numOfItems = 0
    m_description = ""
    m_salesTax = 0
    m_shippingCost = 0
End Sub
Private Sub Class_Terminate()
End Sub
```

A.3.8 SalesOrder Class

Finally, create a new class in the server project called *SalesOrder,* and fill it in with the code shown in Listing 9.

The *SalesOrder* class implements all the functionality for sales order processing, as well as handling other database queries. The *SubmitOrder* method handles the actual order processing. Called from the client, this method is passed a PIN number and password in the form of two string parameters.

First it calls a private method, *ConfirmPassword,* to query the *SalesPerson* table to make sure the employee's password is correct. This is done by finding the password of the employee (based on their PIN number) and then comparing it with the password given by the user. If the passwords match, the method returns a value of *True.*

Once the password is verified, the *SubmitOrder* method creates a new instance of *CustInfo1,* which stores information for customers with a single address field. In a real-world application, our method would instantiate *CustInfoMulti* if the customer had multiple addresses. For purposes of this example, we will assume the customer's billing address and shipping address are the same. However, we have included the class definition for *CustInfoMulti* to show how inheritance can be achieved in Visual Basic 6.0.

Once we have created a new instance of *CustInfo1*, we need a way to access the interface that it inherits from *CustInfo*. This is done through the line

```
Set m_ICustInfo = m_CustInfo1
```

Now whenever we want to call methods in *CustInfo1* that are defined in the base interface class *CustInfo*, we can make these calls using *m_IcustInfo*. We can see this done in the following code, where the customer's ID, credit limit, and billing address are all assigned values through the interface defined in *CustInfo*.

```
    m_ICustInfo.ID = customerID
    m_ICustInfo.custCreditLtd = 0
    m_ICustInfo.custBillingAddress = "address of
        customer"
```

The preceeding three assignments are examples of "late binding"—at compile time Visual Basic has no idea what properties and methods *m_IcustInfo* supports. Visual Basic only checks to see if the methods are supported when the actual method calls are made.

Once an instance of *CustInfo1* is created, our method creates a new instance of the *ItemOrdered* class. This class serves as a container to store information about an inventory item—its part number, description, and so on. In a real-world application this class would have methods that contained detailed business rules, but in our example our rules are very simple. A call to the *CheckItem* method in the *ItemOrdered* class checks the database to see if the part exists in the inventory, returning a value of *True* or *False*.

If the part exists, a method is called in *ItemOrdered* to total up the cost for the order. The total cost is then passed the *CheckCredit* method to the *CustInfo1* object. This method retrieves credit information from the Customer database and determines if the order can proceed. If so, the method returns a value of *True*. Again, in a real-world application this method would contain detailed business rules to see if a customer's credit limit could be increased in the event they had surpassed their limit.

Finally, assuming credit has been approved, the order is entered into the *Order* database table. A query is made to the *Salesperson* table to get the salesperson's name, and then a new record is added into the *Orders* table with information about the new order. This includes the salesperson's name, the name of the customer, the name of the part being ordered, and the number of units ordered. Lastly, the private *ListAllOrders* method is called to return a list of all the pending orders back to the client.

The *SalesOrder* class contains three additional methods for querying the database: *ListLineItems,* which lists items in the *Parts* table, *FetchQuotaInfo,* which retrieves quota information for a given salesperson, and *ListAllCustomers,* which lists the contents of the *Customers* table. Each of these three methods is called by pressing its corresponding button on the client entry form.

Listing 9 SalesOrder

```
'-----------------------------------------------
'
' Class that represents SalesOrders
'
'-----------------------------------------------
Option Explicit
Private m_CustInfoMulti As CustInfoMulti
Private m_CustInfo1 As CustInfo1
Private m_ICustInfo As CustInfo
Private m_dbinst As DBInterface
Private m_Recordset As Recordset
Private m_totalCost As Integer
Private m_part As ItemOrdered
Private Sub Class_Initialize()
```

(continued)

```
On Error GoTo InitErr
' instantiate the database interface
  Set m_dbinst = New DBInterface
  If gintInstanceCount = 0 Then
    frmServer.Show
    gintInstanceCount = 0
    globDatabaseName = App.Path & "\UMLdb.mdb"
    DoEvents
    Set globWorkspace = Workspaces(0)
   Set globDatabase = globWorkspace.OpenDatabase(globDatabaseName,
       False)
  End If
  gintInstanceCount = gintInstanceCount + 1
  frmServer.InstanceCounter.Caption = Format$(gintInstanceCount)
  Exit Sub
InitExit:
Screen.MousePointer = vbDefault
Exit Sub
InitErr:
   If Err = 3024 Then
      ' set up dialog for file name entry
      With frmServer.CommonDialog1
        .DialogTitle = "Unable to find the UMLdb.mdb file location"
        .Filter = "(*.mdb)|*.mdb"
        .InitDir = CurDir
        .filename = ""
        .Flags = cdlOFNExplorer Or cdlOFNFileMustExist Or
            cdlOFNPathMustExist
        .ShowOpen
         If .filename  "" Then
           If Right(UCase(.filename), Len("UMLdb.mdb")) = "UMLDB.MDB"
               Then
            globDatabaseName = .filename
            Set globWorkspace = Workspaces(0)
          End If
          Resume
        End If
      End With
  ElseIf Err  0 Then
      ServerMsg Error$ & " - " & Str$(Err), vbCritical, "Server Error"
      End
  End If
```

```
  Resume InitExit
End Sub
Private Sub Class_Terminate()
  gintInstanceCount = gintInstanceCount - 1
  frmServer.InstanceCounter.Caption = Format$(gintInstanceCount)
  If gintInstanceCount = 0 Then
    Unload frmServer
  End If
End Sub
'-----------------------------------------------
' This method is called from the remote client application
' with all the screen information for a query or a new sales
' order
'-----------------------------------------------
Public Function SubmitOrder(pin As String, password As String, part_ID
    As String, quantity As String, customerID As String) As String
 SubmitOrder = ""
 Dim quan As Integer
 Dim QuerySQL As String
 Dim objField As Object
 Dim salespersonName As String
 If (ConfirmPassword(pin, password) = False) Then
    SubmitOrder = "Password does not match"
 Else
 ' Instantiate a new class to hold customer info
   Set m_CustInfo1 = New CustInfo1
   Set m_ICustInfo = m_CustInfo1
m_ICustInfo.ID = customerID
   m_ICustInfo.custCreditLtd = 0
   m_ICustInfo.custBillingAddress = "address of customer"
quan = CInt(quantity)
  ' Instantiate a new class to hold info about the item that
  ' that has been ordered
   Set m_part = New ItemOrdered
   m_part.itemNumber = part_ID
   m_part.numOfItems = quan
   ' Determine availability of Item
   If (m_part.CheckItem() = True) Then
     ' total up the order
      totalCost = m_part.TotalOrder
     ' check it against credit limit
```

(continued)

```
     If (m_CustInfo1.CheckCredit(totalCost) = True) Then
' query SalesPerson table to get the Salesperson's name
QuerySQL = "SELECT name FROM SalesPerson where PIN = " + pin
Set m_Recordset = m_dbinst.DBGet(QuerySQL)
Set objField = m_Recordset.Fields("name")
      salespersonName = objField
      If IsObject(m_Recordset) Then m_Recordset.Close
' add an order to the Orders table of out test database
QuerySQL = "INSERT INTO ORDERS (salesperson, customer, partname,
    numberordered) VALUES ('" + salespersonName + "' , '"
      QuerySQL = QuerySQL + m_ICustInfo.custName + "' , '"
      QuerySQL = QuerySQL + m_part.description + "' , "
      QuerySQL = QuerySQL + CStr(quan) + ")"
globDatabase.Execute (QuerySQL)
      SubmitOrder = "You order has been submitted, current orders:" +
          Chr(13) + Chr(10) + Chr(13) + Chr(10)
      SubmitOrder = SubmitOrder + ListAllOrders(pin, password)
    End If
  End If
End If
End Function
'----------------------------------------------
' This method is called from the remote client application
' with a pin number and the password, and will list
' all the line items in the Inventory table of the database
'----------------------------------------------
Public Function ListLineItems(pin As String, password As String) As
    String
 ListLineItems = ""
Dim QuerySQL As String
If (ConfirmPassword(pin, password) = False) Then
    ListLineItems = "Password does not match"
 Else
QuerySQL = "SELECT * FROM Inventory"
Set m_Recordset = m_dbinst.DBGet(QuerySQL)
ListLineItems = "part/line #, part name, cost, # inventory, # ordered"
    + Chr(13) + Chr(10)
  ListLineItems = ListLineItems + "-------------------------------
      -------------" + Chr(13) + Chr(10)
Do While Not m_Recordset.EOF
```

```
    ListLineItems = ListLineItems + CStr(m_Recordset.Fields(0)) + "," +
        m_Recordset.Fields(1) + "," + CStr(m_Recordset.Fields(2)) +
        "," + CStr(m_Recordset.Fields(3)) + ", +
        CStr(m_Recordset.Fields(4)) + Chr(13) + Chr(10)
    m_Recordset.MoveNext
  Loop
 End If
End Function
'---------------------------------------------------
' This method is called from the remote client application
' with a pin number and the password, and will list
' quota info for a given salesperson
'---------------------------------------------------
Public Function FetchQuotaInfo(pin As String, password As String) As
    String
 FetchQuotaInfo = ""
 Dim QuerySQL As String
 Dim objField As Object
If (ConfirmPassword(pin, password) = False) Then
    FetchQuotaInfo = "Password does not match"
 Else
QuerySQL = "SELECT * FROM SalesPerson where PIN  1223"
  Set m_Recordset = m_dbinst.DBGet(QuerySQL)
  FetchQuotaInfo = "ID, PIN, name, password, region" + Chr(13) +
      Chr(10)
  FetchQuotaInfo = FetchQuotaInfo + "---------------------------------
---------------" + Chr(13) + Chr(10)
  Do While Not m_Recordset.EOF
   FetchQuotaInfo = FetchQuotaInfo + CStr(m_Recordset.Fields(0)) + ", +
       CStr(m_Recordset.Fields(1)) + "," + CStr(m_Recordset.Fields(2))
       + "," + CStr(m_Recordset.Fields(3)) + "," +
       CStr(m_Recordset.Fields(4)) + "," + CStr(m_Recordset.Fields(5))
       + "," + CStr(m_Recordset.Fields(6)) + Chr(13) + Chr(10)
    m_Recordset.MoveNext
  Loop
End If
End Function
'---------------------------------------------------
' This method is called from SubmitOrder method,
' and will list all the orders in the Order table
' of our database
```

(continued)

```
'----------------------------------------------------
Private Function ListAllOrders(pin As String, password As String) As
    String
 ListAllOrders = ""
 Dim QuerySQL As String
 Dim objField As Object
 If (ConfirmPassword(pin, password) = False) Then
    ListAllOrders = "Password does not match"
 Else
QuerySQL = "SELECT * FROM ORDERS"
Set m_Recordset = m_dbinst.DBGet(QuerySQL)
Do While Not m_Recordset.EOF
   ListAllOrders = ListAllOrders + CStr(m_Recordset.Fields(0)) + "," +
       CStr(m_Recordset.Fields(1)) + "," + CStr(m_Recordset.Fields(2))
       + Chr(13) + Chr(10)
    m_Recordset.MoveNext
  Loop
  'If IsObject(m_Recordset) Then m_Recordset.Close
End If
End Function
'----------------------------------------------------
' This method is called from the remote client application
' with a pin number and the password, and will list
' all the customers in the Customer table of the database
'----------------------------------------------------
Public Function ListAllCustomers(pin As String, password As String) As
    String
 ListAllCustomers = ""
 Dim QuerySQL As String
 Dim objField As Object
If (ConfirmPassword(pin, password) = False) Then
    ListAllCustomers = "Password does not match"
 Else
QuerySQL = "SELECT * FROM CUSTOMER"
  Set m_Recordset = m_dbinst.DBGet(QuerySQL)
ListAllCustomers = "ID, Customer name, balance" + Chr(13) + Chr(10)
  ListAllCustomers = ListAllCustomers + "------------------------------
      ------------------" + Chr(13) + Chr(10)
Do While Not m_Recordset.EOF
   ListAllCustomers = ListAllCustomers + CStr(m_Recordset.Fields(0)) +
       "," + CStr(m_Recordset.Fields(1)) + "," +
       CStr(m_Recordset.Fields(2)) + Chr(13) + Chr(10)
    m_Recordset.MoveNext
```

```
  Loop
If IsObject(m_Recordset) Then m_Recordset.Close
End If
End Function
'----------------------------------------------------
' This method is called from the remote client application
' with a pin number and the password, and will check to see
' if the password is correct.
'----------------------------------------------------
' ( In our sample database, our PIN # is 314,
'   password is sammy, ID is 1)
Private Function ConfirmPassword(pin As String, password As String) As
    Boolean
 Dim objField As Object
 Dim QuerySQL As String
 ConfirmPassword = False
 QuerySQL = "SELECT password FROM SalesPerson where PIN = " + pin
 Set m_Recordset = m_dbinst.DBGet(QuerySQL)
If (m_Recordset.EOF = False) Then
    Set objField = m_Recordset.Fields("password")
If (objField = password) Then
         ConfirmPassword = True
    End If
 End If
If IsObject(m_Recordset) Then m_Recordset.Close
End Function
'----------------------------------------------------
' get the value of the customer member
'----------------------------------------------------
Property Get customer() As CustInfo1
    customer = m_CustInfo1
End Property
'----------------------------------------------------
' set the value of the customer member
'----------------------------------------------------
Property Let customer(valNew As CustInfo1)
    m_CustInfo1 = valNew
End Property
'----------------------------------------------------
' get the value of the part member
'----------------------------------------------------
```

(continued)

```
Property Get part() As ItemOrdered
    part = m_part
End Property
'-----------------------------------------------------
' set the value of the part member
'-----------------------------------------------------
Property Let part(valNew As ItemOrdered)
    m_part = valNew
End Property
'-----------------------------------------------------
' get the value of the totalCost member
'-----------------------------------------------------
Property Get totalCost() As Integer
    totalCost = m_totalCost
End Property
'-----------------------------------------------------
' set the value of the totalCost member
'-----------------------------------------------------
Property Let totalCost(valNew As Integer)
    m_totalCost = valNew
End Property
```

A.4 Running SalesWeb in Stand-Alone Mode

To run the SalesWeb application, load the SalesWeb project into Visual Basic 6.0 and select *Make Project Group* from the *File* menu. This will build both the client and the server components. Next, choose *Start* from the *Run* menu. This will execute both the client and server. (For our example, both client and server are running on the same machine, but the server component could just as well exist on a remote machine.)

Once the application is running, a dialog will come up asking you to locate the file *UMLdb.mdb*. Browse to find the file and double-click on it.

Now fill in the form with data, entering *314* as the PIN number and *sammy* as the password. Click on *Send Order* and a new order will be processed and added to the database. A list of all pending orders in the *Order* table will be displayed once order processing is complete. You can click on the other buttons in the client form to list parts in the database, customers, or quota information.

A.5 Running the SalesWeb Client Component in a Web Page

Now that our client is running as a stand-alone application, let's convert it to an "active document" so that it can run as a Web page within Internet Explorer. That way our salespeople in the field could simply point their browser to the URL where the active document is stored, and the client application would immediately be downloaded and would run within their browser.

Visual Basic 6.0 contains an add-in application called the Active Document Migration Wizard. If it does not already exist in your *Add-Ins* menu, select the *Add-in Manager* option from the *Add-Ins* menu, and select "Loaded" for the *VB 6 ActiveX Doc Migration Wizard.*

Select *SalesWebClient* in the *ProjectGroup* window, then choose *VB 6 ActiveX Doc Migration Wizard* from the *Add-Ins* menu, and click *Next.* Check *SalesPersonForm,* and click *Next.*

If *Comment out invalid code* or *Remove original forms after conversion* are checked, uncheck them. For project type, choose *Convert to an ActiveX EXE,* and then choose *Finish.*

Click *OK* and *Close.* The wizard will automatically create a "UserDocument" that corresponds to *SalesPersonForm.* A UserDocument is very similar to a form, but can be used within an ActiveX document. All the original SalesWeb code will work fine, but one small change is required in the code for *SalesPersonForm.* At the start of the *Form_Load* method, comment out the line that reads *"Me.Show"*. (The display of Active Documents are handled by the "container application," in this case the Web browser, so this line is no longer necessary.)

Now you can run the SalesWeb client from within Internet Explorer. To do this, from Visual Basic run the application by pressing *F5*. Click on *OK* in the *Project Properties*.

The SalesWeb client application should now be running inside the browser window, just like any other Web page (see Figure A.5).

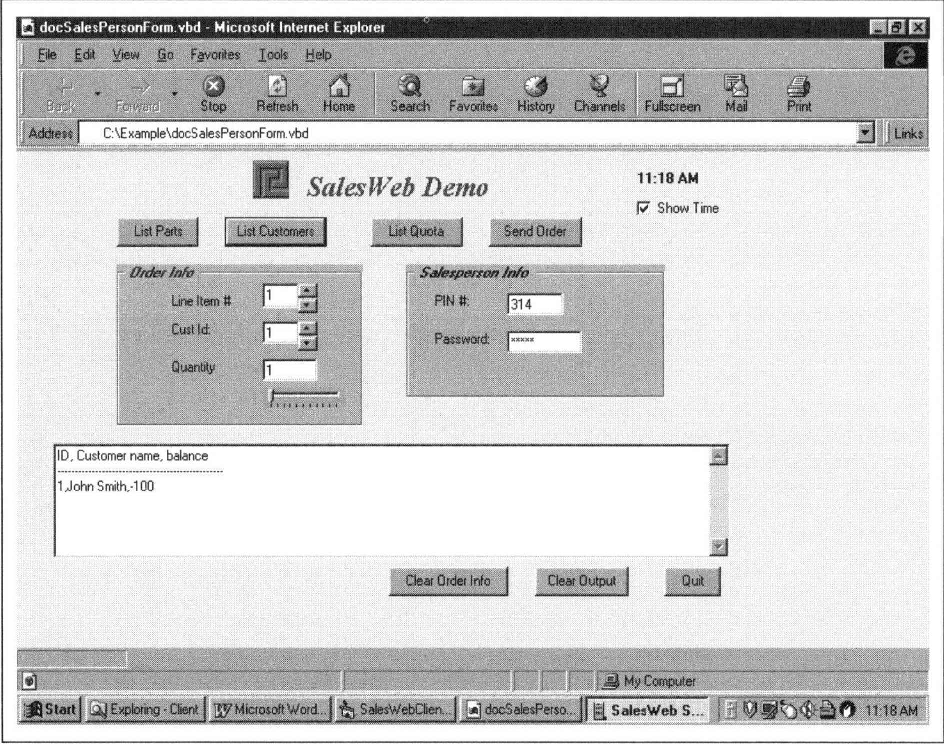

Figure A.5 *Screenshot of SalesWeb running in the Web browser.*

Appendix B

UML Job Aid

In the following pages we've summarized the key notational symbols used when developing UML diagrams. You can copy these pages and keep them on your desk when you undertake your first UML analysis effort. They will remind you of any diagramming details you may have forgotten.

Figure B.1 *UML Job Aid.*

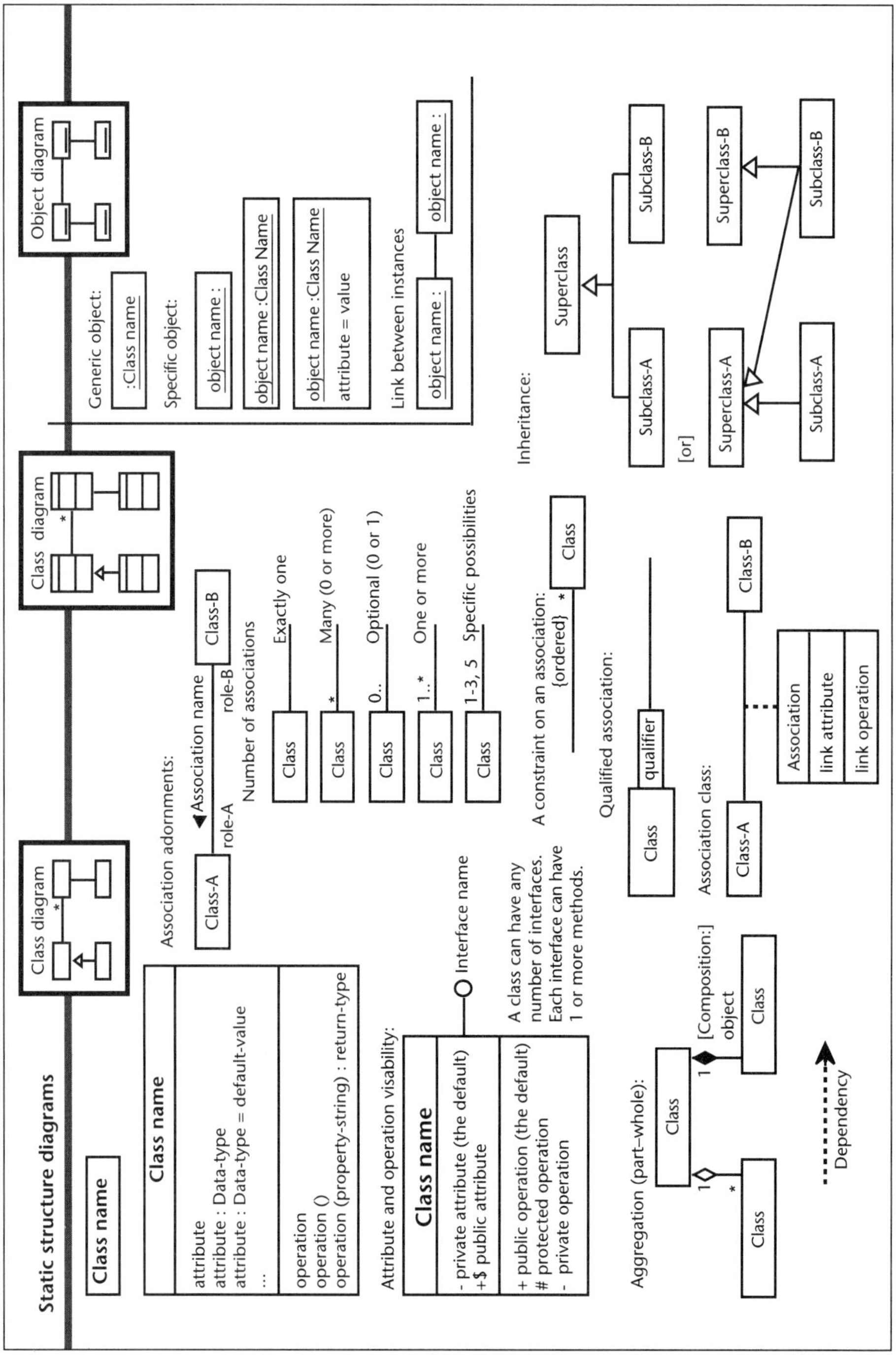

Static structure diagrams

Class diagram

Class diagram

Object diagram

Class name

Class name

attribute
attribute : Data-type
attribute : Data-type = default-value
...

operation
operation ()
operation (property-string) : return-type

Attribute and operation visability:

Class name

- private attribute (the default)
+$ public attribute

+ public operation (the default)
# protected operation
- private operation

Interface name

A class can have any number of interfaces. Each interface can have 1 or more methods.

Aggregation (part–whole):

Class
1 *
Class

1 [Composition:] object
Class

Dependency

Association adornments:

Class-A ◀Association name Class-B
role-A role-B

Number of associations

Class — Exactly one

Class * Many (0 or more)

Class 0.. Optional (0 or 1)

Class 1..* One or more

Class 1-3, 5 Specific possibilities

A constraint on an association:
{ordered} * Class

Qualified association:

Class qualifier

Association class:

Class-A Class-B

Association
link attribute
link operation

Generic object:

:Class name

Specific object:

object name :

object name :Class Name

object name :Class Name
attribute = value

Link between instances

object name : object name :

Inheritance:

Superclass
Subclass-A Subclass-B

[or]

Superclass-A Superclass-B
Subclass-A Subclass-B

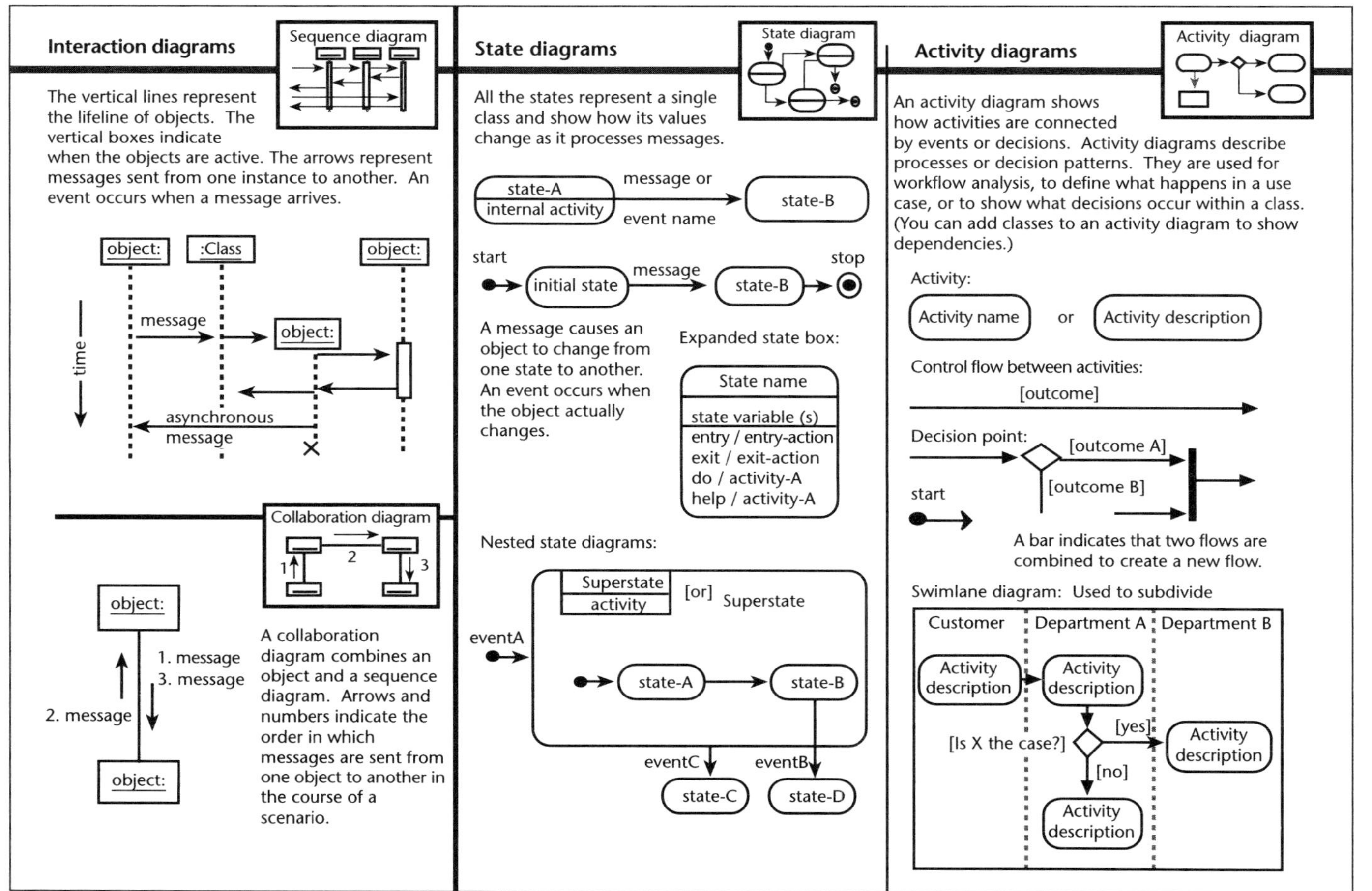

Figure B.1 *Continued.*

Figure B.1 *Continued.*

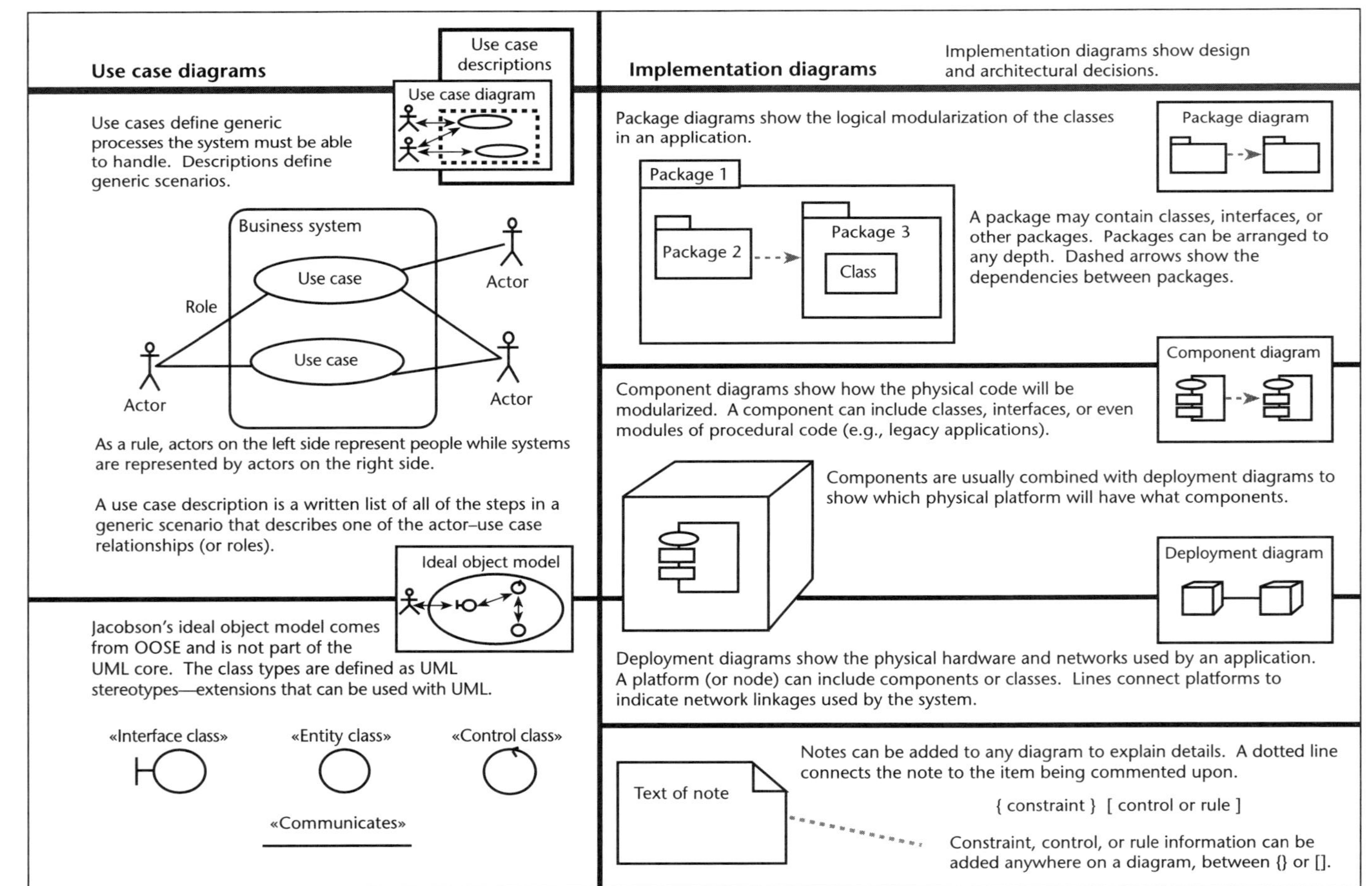

Comparison of UML, OMT, and Booch Notations

Over 60% of the developers currently using OO notations use either OMT (developed by Rumbaugh and others) or Booch notations. The rest of the developers use a wide variety of notations, including Responsibility Driven Design (CRC cards) and Jacobson's Objectory Methodology (use cases, ideal object diagrams). To make it easy for readers who are familiar with Booch or Rumbaugh notations to determine the equivalent notation in UML, we've included Table C.1, which compares the notations. As in the body of this book, we have not included all of the details of each notation, but only the important features that readers will need to handle most applications.

Notational item	***UML***	***OMT***	***Booch***
Class and object diagrams			
Class	Solid rectangle	Solid rectangle	Dashed cloud
Sections of class rectangle	Top: name Middle: attributes Bottom: operations	Name Attributes Operations	Name All members
Attribute characteristics	Name : type = initial value	Name, type, initial value	Name, type, initial value
Operation characteristics	Name (argument list) : result_type	Full signature	Full signature
Visibility	+ public # protected - private null unspecified	+ public # protected - private	null public I protected II private III implementation
Parameterized class	Class rectangle with a smaller dashed rectangle overlying the right corner with the list of template arguments in attribute format	C++-like syntax with a list of parameters and their types	Class cloud with a smaller dashed rectangle
Object	Solid rectangle (same as class) but with object or class name underlined	Solid rectangle with object name: class	Solid cloud
Object attributes	Name = value	Name = value	Name = value
Instantiation	Dashed line from object to class	Dashed arrow from object to class	Dashed arrow from object to class
Inheritance	Line from subclass to superclass with open triangle pointing to superclass	Tree from triangle fanning out to subclasses	Solid arrow from subclass to superclass

Table C.1 *A comparison of UML, OMT, and Booch.*

Notational item	***UML***	***OMT***	***Booch***
Nested class or object diagram	Nested class rectangle within superclass box	None; discouraged	Nested cloud within superclass cloud
Sequence diagram	Sequence diagrams are like message trace diagrams in both OMT and Booch.		
Collaboration diagram	Shows object diagrams with arrows and numbered messages superimposed to show message flow and sequence. New in UML. Not previously used in either OMT or Booch.		
State diagram	Basic Harel diagrams are used in all three.		
Activity diagram	A special variation of the state diagram that shows activity flows internal to a class. New in UML. Not previously used in either OMT or Booch.		
Package diagram and component diagram	File folders represent logical modules of code called packages. Rectangle with oval and two small rectangles crossing left side used to represent a component.	No equivalents	Rectangle with oval and two small rectangles crossing left side used to represent a module. No distinction between package and component.
Deployment diagram	Cubes used to represent processors or other hardware devices	No equivalents	Cubes used to represent processors or other hardware devices. Called a process diagram.
Use case diagram	Use cases and use case descriptions incorporated into UML from OOSE. OOSE also supports ideal and actual object (class) diagrams and many other conventions not directly incorporated into UML. UML allows "stereotypes" or extensions of the notation. In effect, ideal object diagrams are a stereotype of UML class diagrams.		
Misc. notations	Notes: dog-eared rectangle attached to element by dashed line	Text in braces near the target	Dog-eared rectangle attached to target by a dashed line

Table C.1 *Continued.*

Products Mentioned in This Book

At various points in the book we've mentioned specific organizations or products, or referred to groups of products. Here we've listed contact information for many products or organizations we've mentioned.

Chapter 3: A Simple Object-Oriented Methodology

More information about IBM's San Francisco Project Java components can be obtained from IBM's Web site: *www.ibm.com/java/sanfrancisco.*

Chapter 5: Developing Applications in Visual Basic 6.0

The key product here is Microsoft's Visual Basic 6.0, which comes alone (in three versions) and as part of Visual Studio 6.0. Information about specific versions of the Visual Basic product can be found at Microsoft's Web site: *www.microsoft.com/product.* Go there and then select the specific version you want more information on. Technical information on Visual Basic and associated products is available at *www.eu.microosft.com/vbasic/techmat.* At this location you will find white papers on a wide variety of Visual Basic topics.

Chapter 6: Development with a Visual Modeling Tool

The two visual modeling tools that we feature in this book are

Microsoft's Visual Modeler

This comes with the Enterprise Editions of Visual Basic 6.0 and Visual Studio 6.0. If you have a copy of Visual Basic that didn't include Visual Modeler, you can go to the Visual Basic *www.microsoft.com /vbasic/owner* site and download a free copy.

Rational Rose 98

Rational Software
Phone: 408-496-3600, Fax: 408-496-3636
Internet: product_info@ rational.com
Web site: *www.rational.com*

Rational put out an earlier version of Rose, Rose for Visual Basic, that only generated Visual Basic code. Rose 98 generates Visual Basic, Java, or C++ code. Either of these products would work for Visual Basic development.

There are various other visual modeling tool vendors who offer good products. Most don't support Visual Basic, however.

Chapter 7: Use Case Diagrams and Ideal Object Models

The most systematic approach to developing OO applications via use cases was Objectory's Objectory OO CASE tool. Objectory was acquired by Rational Software when they hired Jacobson and may still be available from Rational, although Rational has indicated that it will not be pushing it. Instead, they are promoting the Rational Rose OO CASE line. (Rational is listed with the OO CASE vendors under products mentioned in Chapter 6.)

Most OO modeling tools support a use case utility of some kind. Check the list under Chapter 6 for OO CASE vendors.

Chapter 8: CRC Cards

Popkin Software has a product available, SA/CRC Cards Modeling Tool, which makes it easy to develop CRC cards automatically. For more information, check with

Popkin Software

11 Park Place, New York, NY 10007
Phone: 212-571-3434
Web site: *www.popkin.com*

Chapter 13: Choosing an Object-Oriented Architecture

Microsoft's DCOM is included in Windows 95/98 and Windows NT operating systems. For more information, check *www.microsoft.com.*

For information about the OMG's CORBA, check the OMG Web site: *www.omg.org.*

If you are interested in a specific product, we suggest you check with IONA. IONA is not only the most popular CORBA vendor, but they are the vendor that has worked most closely with Microsoft to assure that DCOM and CORBA can be easily linked.

IONA Technologies

Product: Orbix
Phone: 617-949-9000
Web site: *www.iona.com*

Chapter 14: Expanding Your Design

ActiveX Components

Here are some of the best Web sites for locating information about available ActiveX or other COM components available for use or resale.

- Microsoft's ActiveX Web site: *www.microsoft.com /activeX/*—site to check for all official new announcements about ActiveX.
- CMP Media Inc. Web site: *www.activextra.com*—A comprehensive source on all aspects of ActiveX, including news, references, and products.
- Fawcette Publications Web site: *www.windx.com*—A developers' exchange and ActiveX controls directory.
- NCompass Web site: *www.ncompass.com*—A Canadian company that builds various forms of ActiveX plug-ins for Java.
- CNET Web site: *www.cnet.com/activex*—Another comprehensive Web site with lots of information on ActiveX.
- AtOnce Software Web site: *www.webtools.atonce software.com*—Provider of Microsoft Store. They will be selling ActiveX controls and products in the future.
- Innovision Web site: *www.active-x.com*—Seller of ActiveX controls, provides samples and information.

- Micro Modeling Associates Web site: *www.netcompany.com/activex*—Another comprehensive Web site that hopes to be a major resource for the international ActiveX development community.
- Part Bank Web site: *www.partbank.com/activex*—Magazine and repository of ActiveX components.
- Programmers' Paradise Web site: *www.pparadise.com/*—Onsite catalog with ActiveX section.
- ActiveXtras Web site: *www.xrta.com/activex*—A reseller site dedicated to ActiveX Web solutions.
- Other: *components.software.net/activex.htm*—An ActiveX marketplace where components can be purchased and downloaded in real time.

Object-Oriented Database Vendors

There are several OODB vendors, and we can't list them all. Probably the best-known small, inexpensive OODB for PCs is Poet.

Objectivity Inc.

Product: Objectivity/DB
Phone: 415-254-7100
Email: info@objy.com
Web site: *www.objy.com*

Object Design, Inc. (ODI)

Product: ObjectStore
Phone: 800-962-9620
Email: info@odi.com
Web site: *www.odi.com*

Poet Software

Product: Poet (most popular inexpensive OODB product for Windows)
Phone: 800-950-8845
Email: info@poet.com
Web site: *www.poet.com*

Versant Object Technology

Product: Versant
Phone: 800-837-7268
Email: info@versant.com
Web site: *www.versant.com*

In effect, Microsoft Repository is an OO frontend for Microsoft's relational database.

Bibliography, Notes, and Web Sites

The Object Management Group published its official UML standard at the end of 1997. At the moment, the best way to get a detailed technical description of the new UML standard is to go to the OMG Web site and download their official version of the new notational standard (*www.omg.org*).

In the next few months there will probably be several books published on the new UML standard. Among the most comprehensive and authoritative will be books by Booch, Rumbaugh, and Jacobson. In addition, other methodologists, such as James Odell, who cochaired the OMG standardization task force, are likely to write authoritative books. Most books will probably mix a presentation of the UML notation with an OO development methodology.

It's hard to keep up with the rapid, ongoing changes in the object and component technology market. The senior author of this book edits a monthly newsletter that is designed to help managers stay on top of new development in all areas of object technology. For more information, check out the Cutter Web site and download a copy of the "Component Development Strategies" newsletter *(www.cutter.com/cds)*.

In the meantime, we have listed books here that discuss older methodologies and notations that led to UML, including books on Booch, OMT, and OOSE methodologies. These books will soon be out of date as far as their notation goes, but they will continue to be a source of good advice on the OO development process. Unfortunately, all of these earlier methodology books were written before the Internet and most illustrate their points with C++ examples rather than Visual Basic code.

This is not a scholarly book, so we have avoided footnotes and are not including an extensive bibliography. We have included references to the books we would recommend that you look at next if you want more information on any specific chapter. The books we list provide a lot more detail than we do and provide bibliographies that will allow you to pursue specific ideas much further. We have also provided a few Web site (URL) listings that will provide you with more information about indicated topics. The books and notes are organized by chapter.

Chapter 2: The Vocabulary of Object Technology

The best book we know that provides a high-level overview of object technology for managers is

Taylor, David. *Object-Oriented Technology: A Manager's Guide*. Reading, MA: Addison-Wesley, 1992. ISBN 0-201-56358-4.

A good but rather technical overview of component technology is provided by

Szyperski, Clemens. *Component Software: Beyond Object-Oriented Programming.* Reading, MA: Addison-Wesley, 1998. ISBN 0-201-17888-5.

Beyond a high-level overview, because Visual Basic is really a component development language rather than an OO language, we suggest you stick primarily to books that introduce objects in the context of Visual Basic.

If you are new to OO development and would like some examples of the kinds of applications that were developed by companies who won recognition in the OMG's annual contest for the best OO applications, consider this book:

Harmon, Paul, and William Morrissey. *The Object Technology Casebook: Lessons from Award-Winning Business Applications.* New York: John Wiley & Sons, 1996. ISBN 0471-14717-6.

In addition, most of the books about OO methodologies will provide a more or less general introduction to object technology.

Chapter 3: A Simple Object-Oriented Methodology

As we finish this book there are no good books on methodologies specifically for UML, but there soon will be.

Jacobson, Ivar, Grady Booch, and James Rumbaugh. *The Objectory Software Development Process.* Reading, MA: Addison-Wesley, 1997. ISBN 0-201-57169-2.

This book will be part of the three-volume description of UML from the gurus at Rational Software. As the title suggests, this will be Jacobson's version of a methodology. Jacobson usually isn't very concise, but he always has lots of good, pragmatic suggestions.

Meanwhile, the reader should consult one of the books listed below to get an in-depth discussion of either analysis, design, or an overall approach to OO development.

Booch, Grady. *Object-Oriented Analysis and Design with Applications.* 2nd ed. Reading, MA: Addison-Wesley, 1994. ISBN 0-8053-5340-2.

This describes Booch's methodology, which is slightly different from OMT, but it also provides lots of practical advice about designing OO applications and getting them to work.

Martin, James, and James Odell. *Object-Oriented Analysis and Design.* Englewood Cliffs, NJ: Prentice Hall, 1993. ISBN 0-13-630245-9.

Rumbaugh, James, Michael Blaha, Williama Premerlani, Frederick Eddy, and William Lorenzen. *Object-Oriented Modeling and Design.* Englewood Cliffs, NJ: Prentice Hall, 1991. ISBN 0-13-629841-9.

This is the source of information on the OMT methodology. Since this book has been published, James Rumbaugh has published a number of articles suggesting modifications to this book. Some people refer to these articles, collectively, as OMT-2.

Shlaer, Sally, and Stephen J. Mellor. *Object Lifecycles: Modeling the World in States.* New York: Simon and Schuster, Yourdon Press, 1992. ISBN 0-13-629940-7.

Yourdon, Edward. *Object-Oriented Systems Design: An Integrated Approach.* New York: Simon and Schuster, Yourdon Press, 1994. ISBN 0-13-636325-3.

We haven't said much in this book on managing OO projects or on strategies for software reuse. If you are going to use a modeling tool, you will probably face management and coordination problems. The best book on how to plan and manage OO projects is

Goldberg, Adele, and Kenneth Rubin. *Succeeding with Objects*. Reading, MA: Addison-Wesley, 1995. ISBN 0-201-62878-3.

Booch, Grady. *Object Solutions: Managing the Object-Oriented Project*. Reading, MA: Addison-Wesley, 1996. ISBN 0-8053-0594-7.

This book isn't very systematic, but it provides lots of good advice.

The best book on how to reorganize your IS group to support large-scale software reuse is

Jacobson, Ivar, Martin Griss, and Patrik Johsson. *Software Reuse: Architecture, Process and Organization for Business Success*. Reading, MA: Addison-Wesley, 1997. ISBN 0-201-92476-5.

Chapter 4: The Unified Modeling Language

There are several books on UML although the methodologists who created UML have yet to release their books on the subject. As we've already mentioned, the best source of detailed information on UML is the documentation on the work of the OMG A&D task force, which can be found on the OMG Web site.

Both Microsoft and Rational provide descriptions of UML with their product documentation.

Rational Software has announced books in a series on UML. The OMG board has finally approved the OMG analysis and design standards. The easy way to get it is to go to the OMG Web site and download the official specification. The books by Booch, Rumbaugh, and Jacobson constitute an informal but comprehensive description of UML. The specification by the OMG constitutes the official specification that OO modeling tool and repository vendors will want to use.

Booch, Grady, James Rumbaugh, and Ivar Jacobson. *Unified Modeling Language User Guide*. Reading, MA: Addison-Wesley, 1997. ISBN 0-201-57168-4.

Rumbaugh, James, Ivar Jacobson, and Grady Booch. *Unified Modeling Language Reference Manual*. Reading, MA: Addison-Wesley, 1997. ISBN 0-201-30998-X.

These two books constitute Rational Software's official description of UML. Anyone serious about using UML for large projects will want to obtain and study these books.

Booch, Grady, James Rumbaugh, and Ivar Jacobson. *The Unified Modeling Language for Object-Oriented Development*. Documentation Set, Version 1.0. Available from Rational Software, Santa Clara, CA, 1996 (Web site: *www.rational.com*).

Other books you might want to check, include

Fowler, Martin, and Kendall Scott. *UML Distilled: Applying the Standard Object Modeling Language*. Reading, MA: Addison-Wesley, 1997. ISBN 0-201-32563-2.

An introductory overview of UML with an example similar to the one in this book. Interesting to compare and contrast details of the example.

Quatrani, Terry. *Visual Modeling with Rational Rose and UML*. Reading, MA: Addison-Wesley, 1998. ISBN 0-201-31016-3.

A good book on the ins and outs of using the Rational Rose visual modeling tool. (Rational includes this in the Rose 98 package.)

Chapter 5: Developing Applications in Visual Basic 6.0

The release of Visual Basic 5.0 served as the watershed in OO development as it finally allowed for true OO development. Visual Basic 6.0 includes only minor improvements over

Visual Basic 5.0. Thus, we have included a few of the many books on Visual Basic 5.0 and COM that are especially outstanding.

Rinehart, Martin L. *Visual Basic 5 Power OOP.* Foster City, CA: IDG Books Worldwide, 1997. ISBN 0-7645-3029-1.

There are three really good books on developing object-oriented Visual Basic programs, and this is the one that is best on the coding details.

Kurata, Deborah. *Doing Objects in Microsoft Visual Basic 5.0*. Emeryville, CA: Ziff-Davis Press, 1997.

This book is really good on conceptualizing the development of an OO Visual Basic application.

Lhotka, Rockford. *Professional Visual Basic 5.0 Business Objects*. Chicago, IL: Wrox Press, 1997.

This book is a must-have handbook if you are going to code large Visual Basic 5.0 applications. This book provides the best balance of overview and coding details.

COM and ActiveX

Chappell, David. *Understanding ActiveX and OLE: A Guide for Developers and Managers.* Redmond, WA: Microsoft Press, 1997. ISBN 1-57231-216-5.

A great introduction to a very complex subject.

Box, Don. *Essential COM.* Reading, MA: Addison-Wesley, 1998. ISBN 0-201-63446-5.

The best technical book on COM with lots of help for those trying to figure out the code.

Chapter 6: Development with a Visual Modeling Tool

There are no books that survey the range of visual modeling tools, or those especially tailored for Visual Basic. Nor is there a good book that combines using a Visual Modeling tool with UML and component-based development.

The book by Quatrani, *Visual Modeling with Rational Rose and UML,* is good on the details of using Rose.

Probably the best book at the moment that tries to pull everything together is

Allen, Paul, and Stuart Frost. *Component-Based Development for Enterprise Systems: Applying The SELECT Perspective.* New York: SIGS Books, 1998. ISBN 0-521-64999-4.

This book describes how to do component-based development with SELECT's visual modeling tool. It's good on the use of UML and visual modeling and discusses an approach to using components, but doesn't deal specifically with ActiveX or COM.

Chapter 7: Use Case Diagrams and Ideal Object Models

The best book on use cases and the only good book on ideal object models is Jacobson's:

Jacobson, Ivar, Magnus Christerson, Patrik Jonsson, and Gunnar Overgaard. *Object-Oriented Software Engineering: A Use Case Driven Approach,* 4th Revision. Reading, MA: Addison-Wesley, 1992. ISBN 0-201-54435-0.

The best explanation of use cases and ideal object models and a very good introduction to object development.

Chapter 8: CRC Cards

There are two good books on CRC cards. One, by Wirfs-Brock, is more oriented to methodology and theory. The other, by Wilkinson, is very pragmatic and a must-read book for anyone serious about CRC cards.

Wilkinson, Nancy M. *Using CRC Cards: An Informal Approach to Object-Oriented Development.* New York: SIGS Books, 1995. ISBN: 1-884842-07-0.

The best practical introduction to using CRC cards.

Wirfs-Brock, Rebecca, Brian Wilkerson, and Laura Wiener. *Designing Object-Oriented Software.* Englewood Cliffs, NJ: Prentice Hall, 1990. ISBN 0-13-629825-7.

A good description of the RDD methodology with lots of information on CRC cards.

Chapters 9, 10, and 11: UML Diagrams

When it comes to the UML diagrams, the source is the Rational UML documentation, version 1.0, cited earlier, under Chapter 4.

Chapter 12: Designing an Object-Oriented System

The place to start looking for information on OO design is with the same methodology books we cited under Chapter 3. They are increasingly dated, however, because the Internet and the use of components were not available and hence not adequately considered when they were developed.

Chapter 13: Choosing an Object-Oriented Architecture

Once again, the place to start is with the basic OO methodology books. There is also a lot of good advice in the three Visual

Basic 5.0 programming books we cited under Chapter 5. Then for the more specialized aspects discussed, consider the following:

CORBA and Object Distribution Systems

Siegel, Jon, ed. *CORBA: Fundamentals and Programming.* New York: John Wiley & Sons, 1996. ISBN 0-471-12148-7.

DCOM and ActiveX

Chapman, David. *Understanding ActiveX and OLE: A Guide for Developers & Managers.* Redmond, WA: Microsoft Press, 1996. ISBN 1-57231-216-5.

The best introduction to ActiveX.

If you're working on a large system that will include legacy applications and databases, you should certainly check out this title:

Brodie, Michael L., and Michael Stonebraker. *Migrating Legacy Systems: Gateways, Interfaces & the Incremental Approach.* San Francisco: Morgan Kaufmann, 1995. ISBN 1-55860-330-1.

Chapter 14: Expanding Your Design

Once again, for advanced discussions, consider the following:

Patterns

The best general source on what's happening in patterns is the Patterns Home Page: *st-www.cs.uiuc.edu/users/patterns/patterns.html.*

Beck, Kent. *Smalltalk Best Practice Patterns.* Englewood Cliffs, NJ: Prentice Hall, 1996. ISBN 0-13476-904-x.

Coad, Peter, David North, and Mark Mayfield. *Object Models: Strategies, Patterns, and Applications.* Englewood Cliffs, NJ: Prentice Hall, 1995. ISBN 0-13-108614-6.

Gamma, Eric, Richard Helm, Ralph Johnson, and John Vlissides. *Design Patterns: Elements of Reusable Object-Oriented Software.* Reading, MA: Addison-Wesley, 1995. ISBN 0-201-63361-2.

The best source of descriptions of patterns.

Mowbray, Thomas J., and Raphael C. Malveau. *CORBA Design Patterns.* New York: John Wiley & Sons, 1997. ISBN 0-471-15882-8.

Pree, W. *Design Patterns for Object-Oriented Software Development.* Reading, MA: Addison-Wesley, 1995. ISBN 0-201-42294-8.

Components

Jacobson, Ivar, Martin Griss, and Patrik Jonsson. *Software Reuse: Architecture, Process, and Organization for Business Success.* New York: ACM Press/Addison-Wesley Longman, 1997. ISBN 0-201-92476-5.

Object Databases

There are lots of good books on relational databases, and any OO design book will discuss how to link to a relational database. As Oracle begins to promote Oracle8, there will probably be lots of new books on object-relational databases. The best book on the advantages and disadvantages of OO vs. object-relational and relational databases is

Barry, Doug. *The Object Database Handbook: How to Select, Implement and Use Object-Oriented Databases*. New York: John Wiley & Sons, 1996. ISBN 0-471-14718-4.

More information is available from the Object Database Management Group's Web site: *www.odmg.org,* and Barry publishes an expensive but very authoritative report comparing OODBs. For more information on that, send email to DougBarry@aol.com.

Index

C

D

E

F

G

H

I

J

L

M

N

O

P

Q

R

S

T

U

V

W

About the Authors

Paul Harmon is the editor of "Object-Oriented Strategies," a monthly newsletter that he writes for corporate managers and developers who want to keep abreast of the latest developments in OO technology. He is the past editor of "CASE Strategies" newsletter. He is on the program committee of the OMG's ObjectWorld Conference, and he is chairman of DCI's OO CASE Conference. Mr. Harmon consults with large companies about using new software technologies. He has written several books, including *The Object Technology Casebook* (with Bill Morrissey) and *Objects in Action* (with David Taylor).

Brian Sawyer is a software designer and developer who has created several popular products, including VP Expert, the bestselling expert system-building tool, and ObjectCraft, a visual modeling tool for OO system development. He is also the author of several computer books, including *Creating Expert Systems for Business and Industry,* which he coauthored with Paul Harmon. He holds a B.A. in computer science from the University of California, Berkeley.